B2B Integration Using SAP NetWeaver® PI

 PRESS

SAP PRESS is a joint initiative of SAP and Galileo Press. The know-how offered by SAP specialists combined with the expertise of the publishing house Galileo Press offers the reader expert books in the field. SAP PRESS features first-hand information and expert advice, and provides useful skills for professional decision-making.

SAP PRESS offers a variety of books on technical and business related topics for the SAP user. For further information, please visit our website: *www.sap-press.com*.

Alexander Davidenkoff, Detlef Werner
Global SAP Systems – Design and Architecture
320 pp., 2008, hardcover
ISBN 978-1-59229-183-0

Valentin Nicolescu et al.
SAP Exchange Infrastructure for Developers
341 pp., 2007, hardcover
ISBN 978-1-59229-118-2

Martin Raepple
The Developer's Guide to SAP NetWeaver Security
548 pp., 2008, hardcover, with CD
ISBN 978-1-59229-180-9

Nils Bürckel, Alexander Davidenkoff, Detlef Werner
Unicode in SAP Systems
320 pp., 2007, hardcover
ISBN 978-1-59229-135-9

Sam Raju, Claus Wallacher

B2B Integration Using
SAP NetWeaver® PI

Galileo Press

Bonn • Boston

ISBN   978-1-59229-163-2

© 2009 by Galileo Press Inc., Boston (MA)
1st Edition 2009

Galileo Press is named after the Italian physicist, mathematician and philosopher Galileo Galilei (1564–1642). He is known as one of the founders of modern science and an advocate of our contemporary, heliocentric worldview. His words Eppur si muove (And yet it moves) have become legendary. The Galileo Press logo depicts Jupiter orbited by the four Galilean moons, which were discovered by Galileo in 1610.

Editor Stefan Proksch
Copy Editor Ruth Saavedra, Saratoga (CA)
Cover Design Nadine Kohl
Photo Credit Getty Images/Cheryl Conlon
Layout Design Vera Brauner
Production Katrin Müller
Typesetting SatzPro, Krefeld (Germany)
Printed and bound in Canada

Contents at a Glance

Contents

3   Adapter Concepts 107

4   B2B and Industry Standard Support 137

5   Central Monitoring 167

Part II: Process Integration Implementation Aspects

10   Security Considerations 427

11   Testing Considerations 461

12 Real-Life Test Scenarios 475

Appendix

Introduction

In recent years, globalization and extreme competition have forced organizations to rely on electronic means to extend their business processes to their business partners. Business-to-business (B2B) integration has emerged as one of the key drivers in sustaining the organization's competitive advantage. Many companies are investing in the latest B2B technologies to be more efficient and cost-effective in integrating their applications with their trading partners.

However, exchanging business documents representing a high monetary value over the Internet has an effect on the dynamics and traditional processes in B2B, forcing organizations to address more stringent requirements for communicating with their business partners. For a successful B2B implementation, the organization should maintain a comprehensive business integration strategy that should clearly state the different business processes that can be integrated with business partners in a secure and reliable manner, and should have the ability to adapt to the changes in the technology quickly and easily. This ability along with the robust integration functionality has become a prerequisite for the future success of organizations in many sectors.

SAP NetWeaver Process Integration (PI) reduces the complexities of B2B integration by providing an open integration platform and by providing message-based and standards-based methods to connect an enterprise's business processes with those of its business partners. This book provides a comprehensive guide to the B2B integration capabilities of SAP NetWeaver PI.

The book is based on SAP NetWeaver Process Integration 7.1, but most of the features discussed in this book also work for earlier releases of SAP NetWeaver PI. It is noted explicitly if a feature discussed in the book is only available as of release 7.1 of SAP NetWeaver PI.

Contents

This book is divided into two parts. The first part focuses on the basic concepts of SAP NetWeaver PI and its B2B capabilities. The following overview highlights the content of each chapter:

▶ **Chapter 1** gives a high-level overview of B2B, its nature, and its evolution over time. It also includes discussion of service-oriented architecture and SAP NetWeaver's role in B2B integration.

▶ **Chapter 2** provides an overview of the architecture of SAP NetWeaver PI and discusses its features and functions on a conceptual level. This chapter discusses the general capabilities of SAP NetWeaver PI and is not limited to B2B-related topics.

▶ **Chapter 3** discusses the concepts of adapters and the Adapter Framework within SAP NetWeaver PI and provides a brief introduction to the adapters delivered as part of SAP NetWeaver PI.

▶ **Chapter 4** gives an overview of some of the most common cross-industry standards and industry-specific standards used for B2B communication, and it discusses the support available within SAP NetWeaver PI for some of these standards.

▶ **Chapter 5** discusses the various monitoring capabilities available within SAP NetWeaver PI. It also discusses the alerting capabilities that are built into SAP NetWeaver PI.

▶ **Chapter 6** discusses the general concepts of business process management and provides an overview of the cross-component BPM capabilities of SAP Net-Weaver PI. Some concrete examples of its use are discussed in the Appendix of this book.

The second part of the book focuses on the implementation aspects of B2B integration scenarios within SAP NetWeaver PI. The following overview highlights the content of each chapter.

▶ **Chapter 7** gives an overview of the tasks that need to be done when setting up a B2B integration scenario. Here we also take a closer look at the options for how to enhance the backend functionality in case we need to bridge some functional gaps within the backend.

▶ **Chapter 8** provides a comprehensive overview of the objects relevant for B2B integration scenarios in the System Landscape Directory and in the Enterprise

Services Repository. We provide step-by-step instructions for the creation and maintenance of all of the objects you need to have in place to run a successful B2B integration scenario.

▶ **Chapter 9** provides a comprehensive overview of the configuration objects relevant for B2B integration scenarios in the Integration Directory. We provide step-by-step instructions for the creation of all of the configuration objects you need to have in place to run a successful B2B integration scenario. In addition, we show a number of wizards that guide you through the process of creating these configuration objects.

▶ **Chapter 10** discusses the various security aspects that play an important role in B2B communication. We explain the concepts of authentication and authorization and transport-level and message-level security, as well as the principles of different encryption algorithms and show how these features are supported within SAP NetWeaver PI.

▶ **Chapter 11** discusses how to test B2B integration scenarios and shows which tools SAP NetWeaver PI provides to support different test requirements.

▶ **Chapter 12** provides you with step-by-step instructions on how to implement a real-life B2B integration scenario in SAP NetWeaver PI using various industry standards.

Who Should Read this Book

This book covers the concepts of SAP NetWeaver PI and its role in building the enterprise service-oriented architecture for business applications in general, and provides a comprehensive overview of B2B processes and reveals the key elements required for a successful B2B implementation within your organization using the SAP NetWeaver PI technology platform, in particular.

So, this book is intended for all readers including new and experienced users of SAP NetWeaver PI and should provide value to administrators, solution and business consultants, project managers, and business analysts.

Acknowledgements

This book would not have been possible without the encouragement, support, and input received from many of our friends and colleagues. First, we would like to thank Lucy Chernobrod, Sindhu Gangadharan, James Guanzon, Ralf Hübel,

Prasad Illapani, Peter McNulty, and Udo Paltzer for their valuable feedback. We also would like to thank Nadja Dausch and Thomas Kamper from SEEBURGER for their critical review of and feedback on the EDI scenario in Chapter 12. Special thanks go to Venkitesh Subramanian, who provided us with deep insights on many different topics, and to Yukai (Steven) Shi for providing us with the Java mapping examples. Finally, we want to thank our editor, Stefan Proksch, for his support and his patience during the creation of this book.

Sam Raju would like to thank all of the colleagues of the SAP NetWeaver Regional Implementation Group and, in particular, Margaret Anderson and Bryan Katis for their encouragement and support in creating this book. Sam Raju would like to say a very special thanks to his wife, Madhavi Raju, and kids, Avinash and Akhila Raju, for their patience, encouragement, and support in writing this book. Sam Raju would like to dedicate this book to his mom, Samanthapudi Padmavathi Raju, who passed away while he was writing this book and his dad, Samanthapudi S. Raju.

Claus Wallacher would like to thank his coworkers in his development team for their support while writing this book, in particular, Michael Fiechtner for providing him with the opportunity to work on collaboration topics from many different angles. Special thanks go to his family, who sacrificed many evenings and weekends while he was working on the book and having many phone conversations with Sam.

PART I
Process Integration Concepts

As a high-level overview of business-to-business integration, this chapter explains the importance of B2B integration and discusses the B2B integration in general, emergence of industry standards, and service-oriented architecture.

1　B2B Integration and SAP NetWeaver

Over the past two decades, the Internet has changed the way in which organizations engage in business. Although changes in this area have been touted as a boon for modern businesses, the reality is that the changes have increased the pace of business and have forced organizations to reexamine many of the basic business relationships that have been established for normal organizational discourse.

One of the most notable organizational areas to be impacted by the Internet is business-to-business (B2B) integration. In simple terms, business-to-business integration is an automated exchange of business data and sharing of business processes across multiple organizations. It requires the ability to maintain the trading partner information and communicate with the trading partners through an agreed protocol.

Globalization, extreme competition, distributed supply chain networks, and other powerful market forces are driving companies to enable full B2B process communication up and down the supply chain. Companies operating in a global economic environment require greater speed and productivity. The ability to plan and execute as well as respond to continuous business changes such as rising transportation costs and customer demands are becoming the factors of competitive advantage. Because of the changes that have occurred in B2B integration, companies are seeking ways to meet these demands and are forced to find new and innovative methods for interacting with their trading partners.

Integrating trading partners into business processes has become a primary requirement for leading organizations. These organizations relied on electronic means to transfer order-to-cash and other business processes to their trading partners. These business processes involved the transfer of legally binding documents representing a high monetary value, forcing the organizations to address more stringent requirements for partner communication processes.

1.1 What Is B2B Integration?

The basic definition of B2B integration indicates that "B2B integration is an automated exchange of business information between an enterprise and its trading partners such as customers, suppliers, and partners." One of the challenges of B2B integration is to be able to share data and processes without having to make too many changes to the existing application infrastructure.

Business-to-business integration has been around for a number of years; however, it has only recently received a considerable amount of attention. This is because the Internet changed B2B integration so substantially that traditional methods of B2B integration have become, in many cases, obsolete. The change created in this area has promoted new interest in B2B integration and the methods that are used to achieve it. As shown in Figure 1.1, B2B integration is the message-based and standards-based integration of intercompany processes between an enterprise and its trading partners.

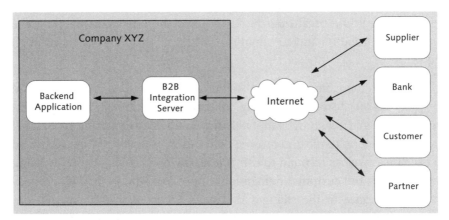

Figure 1.1 B2B Integration

Traditionally, companies have relied on batch process and aging technologies such as electronic data interchange (EDI) to share information with their trading partners. This process is complex, costly to implement, and makes heavy use of value added networks (VAN), limiting it only to largest buyers and suppliers. The emergence of the Internet and standards-based technologies such as Extensible Markup Language (XML) and Secure Socket Layer (SSL) created a new dimension of electronic B2B. XML has emerged as a new standard for exchanging structured information over the Internet, and SSL has emerged as the de facto standard protocol for establishing secure connections between an enterprise and its remote trading partners.

B2B integration has become a critical component to automate the exchange of information. The fundamental benefits of B2B integration include reducing the total cost of ownership (TCO), reducing transaction costs, establishing communication over the Internet, and conducting business with a broader network of supply chain partners. Because of these benefits, companies started exploring open, XML-based standards to develop a common business language and process methodology for Internet-based collaboration, communication, and commerce. As a result, a number of potential standards began to proliferate. These standards were formed as a consortium with members from within specific industries. Some of these standards include RosettaNet for the high tech industry, CIDX for the chemical industry, SWIFT for the banking industry, and so on. Their main goal is to form a common e-business language, aligning processes between supply chain partners on a global basis.

1.2 Intra-Company and Cross-Company Application Integration

The communication between B2B applications is generally based on manually declared interfaces, message formats, and arrangements between business partners. Whereas internal integration is clearly an important issue for moving B2B operations forward, cross-company integration is also an important tool to facilitate greater B2B integration.

Global competition continues to drive organizations to find new ways of driving cost out of their supply chain. Organizations began to realize that a major portion of their operating costs resulted from issues occurring with their customers and suppliers. The early efforts focused on the EDI technology to resolve these issues. The rise of Internet, EDI and XML enabled minor cross-company achievements in supply chains, but major improvements remained elusive. Later on, some organizations began to focus on the problem from a business perspective rather than a technical one. The answer seemed to lie in standards for business processes across companies. As a result, RosettaNet and similar business process standards began to proliferate, and their main goal is to combine the open standards of XML with an open business language that would facilitate cross-company application integration.

Creating cross-company application integration with suppliers has numerous benefits for all parties involved. The benefits include operational cost savings, supply chain efficiency improvements, efficiencies gained from information technology, and the differentiators that provide companies with a competitive advantage. Cross-company integration may lead suppliers to operate as strategic collaborators. A partnership of this nature is characterized by a long-term commitment between the collaborators, openness of communication, and mutual trust. Partners work together to ensure high product quality and low costs, with both companies sharing in the benefits. Further cross-company integration can bring suppliers into business operations before product development takes place. In doing so, suppliers can provide valuable information to the organization that can reduce product development and production costs.

When examined overall, it becomes evident that although internal and cross-company application integration have been widely utilized components of business-to-business integration practices throughout history, the advent and proliferation of the Internet has spurred notable change in this area. In particular, organizations have had to push for more integration such that activities taking place in the organization can keep pace with activities that are occurring outside the organization. Overall, the pace of business has accelerated as a result of changes in the B2B environment. To successfully keep pace, intra-company and cross-company integration are essential.

1.3 Making the Business Case for B2B Integration

Business-to-business integration is a notably complex process that can require the organization to effectively operate outside of its comfort zone. To effectively engage in B2B transactions, organizations must create open business plans that allow for other organizations to understand the inner workings of their operations. Although this information is almost always utilized for creating and establishing positive business-to-business partnerships, security and manipulation issues may result as a consequence of so much transparency.

Despite the potential pitfalls that may result from the development of business-to-business enterprises, it is evident that a host of benefits can be garnered from business-to-business integration:

▶ On an organizational level, B2B integration can streamline internal operations and create greater efficiency for the organization.

▶ Externally, business-to-business integration can provide the organization with a more integral understanding of the challenges that can occur in the development or distribution of a new product.

In short, B2B integration can allow the organization to effectively mitigate risk and eliminate pertinent problems before they become detrimental to the organization. When placed in this context, it becomes evident that business-to-business integration holds a number of potential benefits for the organization. As more companies begin to expand operations to meet global demands, business-to-business integration will become the rule rather than the exception. As such, even though organizations may be able to use this tool as a means to create a competitive advantage, many organizations will soon find that they have to engage in B2B integration in an effort to remain viable in their industry.

1.4 Evolution of Business-to-Business Integration

B2B integration has evolved over a period of time in several stages. It has been spurred by the development and proliferation of the Internet. The internet has changed the way in which organizations operate and structure their business activities. This change prompted a number of new issues for businesses as efforts to adopt new practices were implemented to accelerate the pace of business.

These changes further fueled the "electronization" of B2B integration, creating an arena in which e-commerce B2B practices evolved. Business transactions were conducted over public or private networks, including public and private transactions, and used the Internet as a delivery vehicle. These transactions include financial transfers, on-line exchanges, auctions, delivery of products and services, supply-chain activities, and integrated business networks. Thus, while the Internet served as the impetus to open up new channels for B2B integration, it has also made it possible for organizations to facilitate the development of new B2B models.

As shown in Figure 1.2, whereas the application of the Internet to external business-to-business partnerships appears to be quite evident given the number of organizations engaged in e-commerce, the Internet has also spurred internal application integration in the organization. In particular, the evolution of intranets has had a substantial impact on the ability of organizations to share internal information. Intranets provide the organization with a vehicle for connecting all departments of the organization, even though different departments may be located in different geographical regions. This connection facilitates knowledge sharing, which in turn, serves as the basis for improving organizational effectiveness and efficiency.

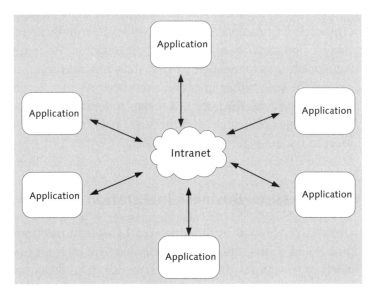

Figure 1.2 Internal Application Integration

As shown in the Figure 1.3, in addition to the evolution of intranets, external, cross-company application integration has been achieved through the development of extranets. Extranets are the controlled sections of intranets to securely share part of the organization's information or operations with business partners. Thus, the extrapolation of Internet technology in these specific domains has further promoted the electronization of business-to-business practices. In this context, it becomes clear that B2B practices, fueled by the development of the Internet, have utilized Internet technology as a principle means to expand their limits and functionality.

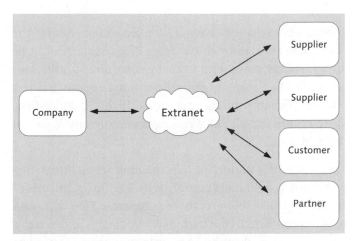

Figure 1.3 Cross-Company Application Integration

1.5 Electronic Trading and Interchange

The evolution of B2B integration has clearly been facilitated by the Internet. One of the principle areas in which B2B transactions have expanded in recent years has been the digital marketplace. Business-to-business exchanges and interchanges have been created in an effort to provide businesses looking for partners with critical information needed for decision making. In these exchanges, individual businesses provide information on their backend operations such that other businesses can determine if a business will meet an organizational need. B2B exchanges create some degree of vulnerability for the organization; however, these exchanges are viewed as essential for the success of electronic B2B operations.

In addition to providing the organization with new opportunities, B2B exchanges also reduce the inefficiency that can be created in the buying and selling process. Whereas supply chains are not completely eliminated, they can be streamlined by placing the organization into direct contact with suppliers. This increases the efficiency of the supply chain and reduces the costs and inefficiency typically associated with the supply chain process. Furthermore, B2B exchanges have clearly defined rules for participation; the existence of these structures ensures that transparency is increased for all organizations. This holds all participants to a higher standard of business practices, which can ensure the integrity of business partnerships.

Even though business-to business exchanges have a number of benefits for the organization, there are also some substantial drawbacks. B2B exchanges can be costly to implement, and in most instances, B2B exchanges require specific software that must be purchased. Further, many organizations must engage in a host of B2B exchanges to optimize efficiency in all operations. If this is indeed the case, efforts must be made to ensure that all B2B exchanges are compatible so that internal integration can be achieved.

The multidimensional quality of B2B is important to remember when integrating B2B into your organization. Each system must comply with existing standards of doing business and the technology that supports those standards. Thus, the business rules are programmable to conform to the various technologies and systems in use in the marketplace today. Each of these business rules will then encapsulate the way a particular function should be implemented, taking into account security, business processes, payment, quality, and sign-off processes.

In addition to the costs that can be incurred in the development of B2B exchanges, these tools can be unscrupulously utilized by some organizations. Efforts to avoid this problem are often addressed in the security protocols implemented in the exchange software. However, access to information from individual organizations can prompt abuse of information use for greater manipulation of the market. As such, organizations must utilize caution when developing back-end data profiles.

1.6   EDI versus XML

While various electronic exchanges have been developed to facilitate B2B integration and aggregation, basic platforms for B2B exchanges have been established that provide internal controls for ensuring the integrity of B2B transactions. Electronic data interchange (EDI) has been the primary method for facilitating transactions between businesses.

EDI systems provide the mechanism for input, authentication, validation, agreement, and payment transactions to occur over a secure network. EDI systems were utilized before the advent of the Internet; however, costs to implement these systems were often quite extensive because they required considerable customization. They also make heavy use of value added networks (VANs) limiting them to only the largest buyers and suppliers.

Although EDI has been the industry standard for B2B transactions, emergence of the Internet and other standard-based technologies such as Extensible Markup Language (XML) created a new dimension for electronic B2B operations. XML has become the preferred choice for organizations looking to enter e-commerce. It has become the standard protocol for Internet transactions and provides users with an efficient means to tap the potential of the electronic marketplace. For organizations utilizing EDI, XML provides a viable choice for overcoming many of the limitations created by EDI. EDI is primarily a one-to-one technology, whereas Web-based marketplaces allow many-to-one connectivity. XML, which provides many-to-one connectivity, has become the alternative choice for many organizations seeking B2B transactions.

As shown in Figure 1.4, both EDI and XML documents use groups of elements to assign business meaning to a message. EDI builds messages using highly structured predefined segments. Each element in the segment is identified by its position in the segment. XML elements, on the other hand, build messages with a combination of tags and metadata. XML files are easy to read compared to EDI files, which are rather cryptic. This provides a notable advantage of XML over EDI.

```xml
<?xml version = "1.0"?>
<PurchaseOrder>
  <Header>
    <ponumber>1234</ponumber>
  </Header>
  <ShipTo>
    <company>Company XYZ</company>
    <address>
      <street>Shipping Address</street>
      <city>City</city>
      <st>TX</st><postcode>77122</postcode>
    </address>
  </ShipTo>
  <Items>
    <item>
      <productNumber>12345</productnumber>
      <productName>monitors</productname>
      <quantity>4</quantity>
      <unitprice>150.00</unitprice>
      <price>600.00</price>
    </item>
  </Items>
</PurchaseOrder>
```

```
ISA*00* *00* *01*012345678 *01*012341234
*123456*2008*U*00401*000000123*0*P*A~
GS*PO*TEST*1234*20020222*2008*214*X*004010~
ST*850*000001234~
BEG*00*SA*2619003**20020222~
PER*OD*John Smith*123-123-1234~
REF*DP*123~
DTM*002*20080102~
N1*VN*Company ABC*92*1276~
N1*ST*92*01234567890~
PO1*1*1*EA*10.22**VP*123456781234*SK*123*UP*0314281~
CTT*1~
SE*32*000001234~
GE*1*214~
IEA*1*000000123~|
```

Sample XML PO document	Sample EDI 850 PO document

Figure 1.4 EDI vs XML

XML provides the user with a high degree of efficiency that simply cannot be achieved through the application of EDI. Furthermore, XML is vendor independent, which increases its overall utility for businesses just entering e-commerce. Finally, because XML can be effectively shaped and controlled by the organization, it provides the ability for users create considerable customization.

Although XML provides notable advantages over EDI, many organizations still utilize both technologies. This is because EDI offers a number of notable advantages when it comes to one-to-one transactions. The benefits of EDI make it difficult for those who rely on the system to relinquish it completely. For this reason, most industry experts believe EDI and XML will coexist over the long term, offering organizations a wide range of options for developing business-to-business transactions and partnerships.

1.7 Emergence of Industry Standards

It has become evident that the evolution of business-to-business enterprises has expedited business processes, creating more efficiency for most organizations. Whereas increased efficiency is one notable asset of implementing e-commerce B2B integration, this process can have marked ramifications for the organization's bottom line. The return on investment for B2B integration is extremely high, and it has been estimated to have a 5 to 15 times payback over a period measured typically in months. This coupled with the need to create uniformity in B2B exchanges has served as the impetus for the evolution of industry standards.

Considering some of the specific goals that can be achieved through the imposition of standards, supply chain improvements will be possible for all companies participating in the exchange. The standards can provide organizations with clear advantages for improving the bottom line and becoming more competitive in the global marketplace. Organizations taking advantage of these standards will benefit, increasing competition in the marketplace and encouraging other organizations to follow the same standards.

Standards have also emerged as a principle means to ensure that organizations are able to protect the integrity of their relationships with B2B partners and customers. As the number of transactions over the Internet increases, companies will face greater security threats. To create more security, standards are being developed that must be employed by all organizations.

1.8   Service-Oriented Architecture

Further complimenting the development of electronic business-to-business integration is the evolution of service-oriented architectures (SOA). These platforms are flexible and dynamic, enabling greater B2B integration for the organization.

As shown in the Figure 1.5, service-oriented architectures consist of three functional building blocks accessible over the standard Internet protocols:

▸ The *Service Provider* building block creates a Web service and publishes its interface and access information to the Service Registry.

▸ The *Service Registry* block makes this information available to any potential service consumers.

▸ The *Service Consumer* block explores the services in the Service Registry and makes a request to the service provider to invoke one of the services.

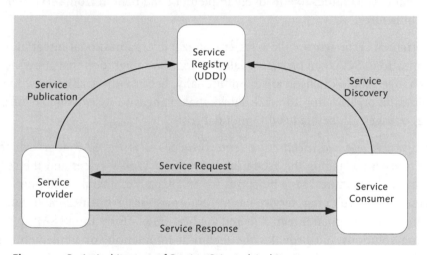

Figure 1.5 Basic Architecture of Service-Oriented Architecture

Service-oriented architectures are one import kind of dynamic architectures. They allow for automated service publication and discovery at runtime. For instance, whenever a service cannot be provided with the required quality of service any longer, the service requester could dynamically search for and change to a new service.

Service oriented architectures were developed to improve IT integration for the organization. In the past a "one-size-fits-all" approach to business transactions was typically utilized. This process undermined the efficiency of the organization. To facilitate improvements in this area, SOAs were invented.

Although the evolution of service-oriented architecture was clearly motivated by collective desire to improve business interactions, SOA has a number of notable advantages for the organization. Service-oriented architectures enable companies to introduce new business practices and processes more rapidly and at a lower cost. Such innovations accumulate by increments into a strategic advantage. As such, these platforms provide the organization with the ability to tailor its transactions with other businesses and suppliers. In doing so, organizations can create competitive advantages that can be otherwise acquired.

In addition to the fact that service-oriented architectures provide organizations with a means to optimize their strategic advantage, implementation of these platforms requires little organizational change. Organizations do not have to develop new internal IT capabilities to effectively implement and benefit from service-oriented architectures.

Service-oriented architectures allow for customizable organizational integration. For organizations, SOAs can provide a valuable tool for integration that allows for flexible change should the need arise. Additionally, because the architecture does not require the organization to make substantial changes to its existing IT infrastructure, changes can be made with minimal cost.

Enterprise service-oriented architecture (enterprise SOA) is the SAP approach to SOA and aims at leveraging the established aspects of Web services and the service-oriented architecture. It is a blueprint for an adaptable, flexible, and open IT architecture for developing service-based, enterprise-scale business solutions. SAP NetWeaver is an open integration and application platform for all SAP applications and solutions and provides the technical foundation for implementing enterprise SOA. Enterprise SOA is based on SAP NetWeaver's SOA platform and aims at connecting the business domain with the technology domain in a holistic and consistent manner.

At the heart of enterprise SOA is the concept of *enterprise services*. These enterprise services are highly integrated Web services combined with a business logic and semantics that can be accessed and used repeatedly to support a particular business process. They are based on open standards such as WSDL and are created by using UN/CEFACT Core Component Technical Specifications (CCTS)-

based Global Data Types. B2B enterprise services are defined in compliance with e-business standards, where applicable.

To simplify the process of adopting enterprise SOA and make it as easy as possible, SAP has enabled its SAP Business Suite by exposing its business functionality in the form of enterprise services as ready-to-consume process steps with built-in business semantics. The *Enterprise Services Bundles* provided by SAP are grouped along business scenarios and are based on a sophisticated governance model, together with lifecycle management capabilities and an enhancement concept.

1.9 SAP NetWeaver's Role in B2B Integration

SAP NetWeaver plays a major role in end-to-end process integration and reduces the B2B integration complexity by providing an open integration platform that integrates collaborative business processes across multiple applications both within and beyond enterprise boundaries. It provides message-based and standards-based methods to connect an enterprise's business processes with those of its business partners.

SAP NetWeaver Process Integration (PI)—formerly known as SAP NetWeaver Exchange Infrastructure (XI)—offers a comprehensive solution that addresses the problems with business-to-business integration using the hub-and-spoke model. SAP NetWeaver incorporates industry standards and approaches such as XML, Java, Web services, and the enterprise SOA concept as well as vertical industry standards.

In the hub-and-spoke model, the central processing hub handles all of the B2B integration activities such as document formats, routing rules, and security requirements and is connected to all of the relevant internal and partner applications through the spokes. The spoke adapters for partner communication support a variety of processes and connectivity requirements such as data and process security, reliability, and validity. In addition to the standard application-to-application exchange mechanisms, SAP NetWeaver PI also supports industry-standard partner exchange mechanisms such as EDIINT, RNIF, UCCNet, SWIFT, and many others through its spoke adapters.

SAP NetWeaver provides out-of-the-box support for these industry standard verticals by providing them with predefined integration content in the form of business packages. Customers can take advantage of these business packages to quickly get connected to their different business partners, vendors, and suppliers.

As shown in Figure 1.6, integration knowledge ranging from design time to configuration time is stored and managed in a central Enterprise Services Repository and Integration Directory. Whereas the Enterprise Services Repository contains integration information such as interface schema, required mappings, integration scenarios, and integration processes, the collaboration partner profiles and agreements are stored in the Integration Directory. SAP NetWeaver PI serves as a service bus mediating between service consumers and service providers.

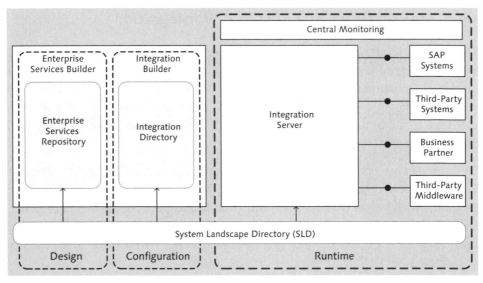

Figure 1.6 B2B Integration in SAP NetWeaver PI

The support for industry standard-protocols such as RosettaNet, AS2, and CIDX is provided through specialized adapters and corresponding mappings. SAP NetWeaver PI provides a robust and high-performance integration server to run the collaborative business processes using various adapters to connect to other applications, files, and databases and to connect using various protocols and industry standards. The business partner agreements regarding connectivity, security, and other essential operations between an enterprise and its business partners are maintained in the Integration Directory.

SAP NetWeaver drives and controls complex business processes across business applications and enterprise boundaries using cross-component Business Process Management (ccBPM). It orchestrates messaging between systems and business partners by using stateful interactions. The central monitoring infrastructure provides different interfaces for monitoring and tracking the B2B messages.

1.10 Summary

After reading this chapter you should understand the concepts, techniques, and technologies that enable business-to-business application integration between trading partners. You should also understand the emergence of industry standards and their role in B2B integration and the concepts of service-oriented architecture and SAP NetWeaver's role in the B2B integration processes.

This chapter provides you with an overview of the architecture of SAP NetWeaver PI and its concepts and key capabilities. The chapter explains each of the PI components such as System Landscape Directory, Enterprise Services Repository (design time), Integration Directory (configuration time), and the Process Integration Runtime in detail.

2 General Concepts

SAP NetWeaver Process Integration provides one integration platform to centrally manage the design, configuration, and execution of business processes and integration scenarios. It supports process-centric collaboration among SAP and non-SAP application components both within and beyond enterprise boundaries. Furthermore, it plays a major role in the SAP strategy to support the adoption of an enterprise service-oriented architecture (enterprise SOA). It enables an easy integration of applications and business partners and ensures openness and interoperability by using open standards for integration, thereby leveraging existing investments.

2.1 Overview

SAP NetWeaver PI incorporates industry standards and approaches such as XML, Java, Web services, and service-oriented architecture and provides support for vertical industry standards such as RosettaNet for the high tech industry. It provides predelivered integration content that allows an out-of-the-box integration of SAP solutions with other third-party products.

A lot of new functionality is provided with release 7.1 of SAP NetWeaver PI. In addition to leveraging the power and capability of ABAP, its robust architecture is based on Java EE 5, which promotes less memory consumption and easier installation. SAP NetWeaver PI uses XML-based communication to exchange messages in application-to-application (A2A) and business-to-business (B2B) scenarios both within and beyond company boundaries and provides a large selection of connectivity options for these scenarios. Among these options are connections to external business partners as well as SAP and third-party applications using various protocols and industry standards. In addition, it provides support for third-party middleware from third-party providers for the integration of applications using standards such as EDI or SWIFT.

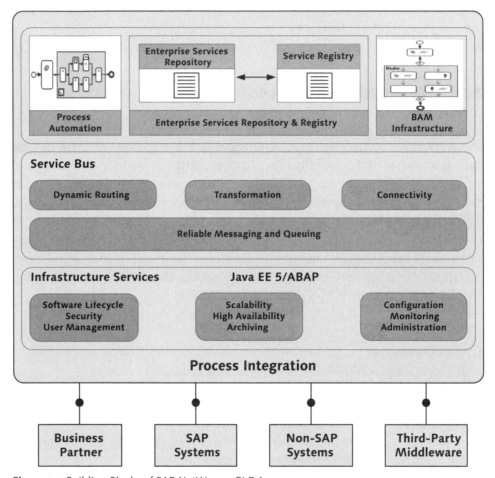

Figure 2.1 Building Blocks of SAP NetWeaver PI 7.1

As shown in Figure 2.1, the architecture of SAP NetWeaver PI provides the following key capabilities:

▶ The *Enterprise Services Repository* acts as the master data repository of service objects for enterprise SOA and is used to store and model the enterprise services. Furthermore, it serves as the central location for storing all the design-time objects that are necessary for A2A and B2B integration.

▶ The *Services Registry* is based on UDDI version 3.0 and acts as a catalog for the services within an enterprise SOA. It is used for publishing, classifying, and discovering the enterprise services.

▶ The *Process Automation* capabilities of SAP NetWeaver PI include the design, configuration, and execution of integration processes for the stateful exchange of messages on the Integration Server.

▶ The *Business Activity Monitoring* (BAM) infrastructure within the SAP NetWeaver platform provides real-time information about the status and results of various operations, processes, and transactions. It supports BAM in three primary ways:

  ▶ Process integration functionality provides a process-centric structure for monitoring business activities of SAP and non-SAP resources.

  ▶ Business intelligence functionality provides analytical services.

  ▶ Portal functionality provides alerting and resolution dashboards that act as a central point of access to collect and coordinate user interactions.

▶ The *Service Bus* infrastructure within SAP NetWeaver PI enables integration between disparate applications. It essentially covers all the functions that are necessary for exchanging messages in a heterogeneous system landscape such as transformation and mapping, service orchestration, communication infrastructure, security, quality of service, support for standards, and others. It provides dynamic routing and enables the receiver to be determined dynamically at runtime by using information from the message payload. The *Integration Server* together with the *Advanced Adapter Engine* (AAE) provides various connectivity functions for connecting to various SAP and third-party systems both within and beyond enterprise boundaries.

The service bus infrastructure also provides functions for the reliable processing of messages and for the support of different qualities of services by means of queues. It provides support for synchronous and asynchronous delivery of messages and uses the quality of services such as *exactly once* (EO), *exactly once in order* (EOIO), and *best effort* (BE) to guarantee the consistency of data. It also provides support for XML schema validation for validating the structure of a message payload against an XML schema.

▶ Information flow is critical to enterprises involved in cross-company and cross-system processes. High availability of the integration tool should be guaranteed for this purpose. Any integration tool should be scalable so that it can easily adapt to changes in enterprise infrastructure. The *Infrastructure Services* as part of SAP NetWeaver PI cover these requirements of high availability and scalability. In addition, the infrastructure services cover other requirements such as software lifecycle management, security, user administration, archiving, configuration, monitoring, and administration.

Performance is the key factor for any integration tool, and SAP NetWeaver PI provides several features to boost performance. In particular, high-volume message processing is supported by the following techniques:

▶ Direct connections, to skip SAP NetWeaver PI traffic

▶ Packaging, to group small messages

▶ Local processing in the Advanced Adapter Engine (AAE) to boost performance in the supported scenarios

In addition, the cross-component BPM (Business Process Management) of SAP NetWeaver PI provides several features to improve performance including parallel processing, packaging, and enhanced transaction handling.

With the architecture of SAP NetWeaver PI and its key capabilities discussed in detail, for the purpose of this book it is sufficient to split the PI architecture into a three-stage process as shown in Figure 2.2:

▶ At *design time*, you define the collaborative processes that are necessary for the message exchange between the application components.

▶ At *configuration time*, you configure these collaborative processes for a specific system landscape.

▶ The configuration data is evaluated at *runtime* and controls the communication. You can monitor the message flow at runtime by using the central message monitoring.

As discussed before, SAP NetWeaver PI consists of Java- and ABAP-based applications that run on SAP NetWeaver Application Server (release 6.40 and higher). To start the Java-based applications, you need to have access to the ABAP system in which the integration engine is configured. Once you log on to the system, you use the transaction Start Integration Builder to start the SAP NetWeaver PI start page.

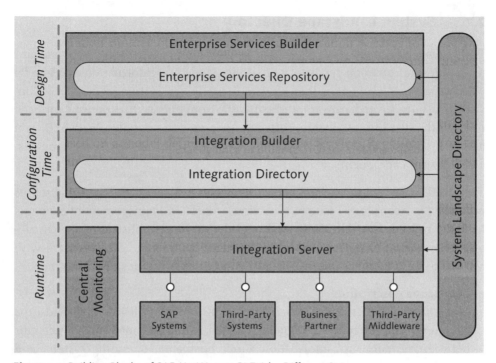

Figure 2.2 Building Blocks of SAP NetWeaver PI 7.1 by Different Stages

Figure 2.3 shows the start page of SAP NetWeaver PI. From this start page, you should be able to launch the design time, configuration time, and runtime components such as Enterprise Services Repository, Service Registry, Integration Directory, System Landscape Directory, SAP NetWeaver Administrator, and Runtime Workbench.

Figure 2.3 Start Page of SAP NetWeaver Process Integration

2.2   System Landscape Directory

The *System Landscape Directory* (SLD) is a component of SAP NetWeaver and acts as a central information repository of system landscape information that is relevant for the management of the software lifecycle in a system landscape. It consists of a number of hardware and software components that depend on each other with regard to installation, software updates, and upgrades. With SLD, you can view and manage technical systems, landscapes, business systems, products, and software components.

The SLD is based on the open *Common Information Model* (CIM) standard that is expressed in a conceptual schema that allows consistent management of elements in a system landscape. The CIM standard is defined and published by the *Distributed Management Task Force* (DMTF). SAP has enhanced the CIM standard with classes for SAP-specific content. The SLD consists of two types of information:

▶ **Landscape description**
The landscape description contains information about all installed landscape elements. This includes version and patch level information, connections between systems, and information about hostname, operating system, and database.

▶ **Component information**
The component information describes the building blocks of solutions and their possible combinations and dependencies. It contains information about all available SAP products and software components including their versions, patch levels, and dependencies information. Customers can add their own component information by defining their third-party products and software components.

The information in the SLD is used by various applications and tools, such as SAP NetWeaver PI, SAP Solution Manager, and SAP NetWeaver Administrator. This chapter mainly focuses on the SLD in regard to SAP NetWeaver PI.

SAP NetWeaver provides a web-based user interface for the SLD to define and manage the landscape elements as shown in Figure 2.4. In the next sections, we discuss the relevant features of the SLD in more detail.

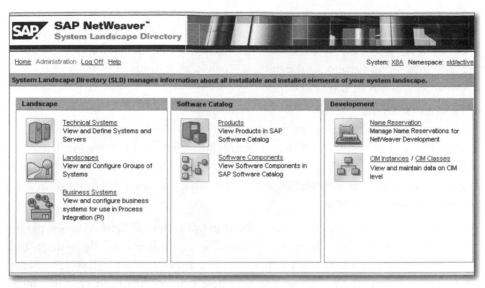

Figure 2.4 Entry Screen to the System Landscape Directory (SLD)

2.2.1 Landscape Description

The *landscape description* contains information about technical systems, the landscape, and business systems installed in a particular system landscape at a customer site. This includes information about SAP and non-SAP systems:

▶ **Technical systems**

Technical systems are SAP or non-SAP application systems installed in a system landscape. In the SLD, these systems can be defined as one of the following types:

▶ SAP NetWeaver Application Server ABAP (AS ABAP), which are SAP systems such as SAP ERP or SAP CRM

▶ SAP NetWeaver Application Server Java (AS Java), which are SAP systems consisting of one or more instances of an AS Java System, each one installed on a separate host

▶ A standalone Java system, which is used for standalone Java applications.

▶ A third-party technical system, which are third-party systems and contain information about business third-party software components and products.

For the SLD, applications that do not run on AS ABAP or AS Java are considered to be third-party systems. These technical systems contain information about version and patch levels, business systems, installed software, the hostname, operating system, and database. Technical systems are the basis for the business systems in the landscape.

▶ **Business systems**
Business systems are logical systems, where each business system is associated with a technical system within a system landscape. The information from the business systems and their corresponding technical systems is used in the Integration Directory of SAP NetWeaver PI to drive the specific configuration of the integration scenarios.

In a system based on AS ABAP, each client in the system is defined as a separate business system. These business systems are addressed as the sender and receiver of messages in the Integration Directory. The logical system name must be defined for the business system based on AS ABAP, in case this business system should act as a sender and receiver of IDocs. The IDoc adapter in SAP NetWeaver PI will make use of this entry to resolve the business system name into an ALE logical system name[1] and vice versa.

▶ **Landscape**
The *landscape* represents a logical, complex unit that consists of multiple distributed components such as systems, services, installed products, or managed elements. In the SLD you can maintain the following types of landscapes:

  ▶ An *administration landscape* that is created for administration purposes

  ▶ A *general landscape* that contains all types of application systems

  ▶ *Scenario landscapes* that are created for specific business scenarios

  ▶ *Transport landscapes* that are created for transport purposes

  ▶ *Web service landscapes* that are created to collect systems offering Web service and their clients

2.2.2   Software Catalog

The *software catalog* in the SLD contains the information about the SAP and third-party registered products, software components, and their versions. The informa-

---

1 The ALE logical system is the representation of an SAP or non-SAP system in SAP applications for the distribution of data to and from the SAP system.

tion about SAP products and software components is provided by SAP and includes the component information of SAP-supported B2B standards such as RosettaNet and CIDX. Customers can register their own products and software components as third-party products.

Figure 2.5 shows the relationship of the different objects maintained in the software catalog:

▶ A *product* is an installable unit that can be delivered to the customer. Each product consists of one or more *product versions*.

▶ The *software component version* (SWCV) is the smallest shipment unit for design objects in the Enterprise Services Repository and for development objects in the relevant application system. You use software component versions to group together objects in the Enterprise Services Repository of SAP NetWeaver PI. To avoid conflicts with the SAP software updates, customer developments must be executed in the customer-specific software component versions.

▶ The *software unit* acts as a logical link between a product version and a software component version. Each product version consists of one or more software units, and each of the software units is implemented by various software component versions.

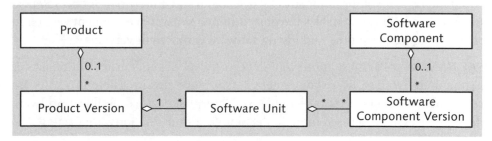

Figure 2.5 Products and Software Components in the SLD

Table 2.1 shows an example of the SAP product SAP R/3 for version 4.6C with its associated software units and software component versions.

When you define a technical system or a business system in the SLD, you can specify the products and software components available on this system. This helps the Integration Builder at configuration time to determine which interfaces a business system supports. Each business system can have multiple products and software components installed on it.

Product Version	Software Unit	Software Component Version
SAP R/3 4.6C	SAP R/3: R/3 Server	SAP_BASIS_46C
		SAP_HR_46C
		SAP_ABA_46C
		...
	SAP R/3: XI Content	XICNT_SAP_ABA_46C
		XICNT_SAP_HR_46C
		...
	...	...
SAP R/3 4.6B	...	...

Table 2.1 Content of Product Version SAP R/3 4.6C

An existing software component version is often a prerequisite for another software component version. For example, the customer development can be based on a particular SAP component from which objects are to be reused. SAP NetWeaver PI allows you to create dependencies between one or more software components that will be automatically detected in the Enterprise Services Repository. This relationship enables the objects in one software component version to reference objects from the underlying software component versions.

SAP NetWeaver PI also supports multilevel software dependencies. The objects of all the underlying software component versions are always visible in a software component version (see also Section 2.3.1 Enterprise Services Builder). Software dependencies are discussed more in detail in Section 8.2.2 Software Catalog.

2.3 Overview of Enterprise Services Repository

As shown in Figure 2.2, the *Enterprise Services Repository* is one of the key building blocks within SAP NetWeaver PI and contains the metadata to model and specify objects that are used in the following scenarios:

► **Enabling enterprise services**

As the name implies, the Enterprise Services Repository serves as the central repository for the definition of enterprise services. Each enterprise service that is used in one of SAP's backend application systems is modeled using the Enterprise Services Repository. The implementation of the enterprise service is then carried out in the respective SAP backend application system. In addition, it is possible to create Web services in SAP NetWeaver PI itself. Enterprise services can be used for consumption in A2A and B2B scenarios.

► **Enabling application-to-application (A2A) processes**

The Enterprise Services Repository contains all interface definitions that are required for consumption in A2A scenarios. The interface definition can be part of an enterprise service, but other message types are also supported. In addition, some other objects relevant for the enablement of A2A processes are maintained in the Enterprise Services Repository.

► **Enabling business-to-business (B2B) processes**

The Enterprise Services Repository contains all interface definitions that are required for consumption in B2B scenarios. The interface definition can be part of an enterprise service, but other message types are also supported, especially interface definitions provided by various standards organizations. In addition, some other objects relevant for the enablement of B2B processes are maintained in the Enterprise Services Repository.

In this book we only focus on the enablement of B2B processes and all relevant objects for such enablement. However, because enterprise services are starting to play a more important role in any type of collaboration scenario (including B2B), we will also discuss how the Enterprise Services Repository is used to model enterprise services.

Figure 2.6 gives you an overview of the objects available in the Enterprise Services Repository. You can also see how the Enterprise Services Repository can be accessed using various visual editors provided by the Enterprise Services Builder for the design and modeling of service objects and enterprise services.

After the following introduction to the Enterprise Services Builder in Section 2.3.1 Enterprise Services Builder, we discuss the building blocks of the Enterprise Services Repository as outlined in Figure 2.6 in more detail. We conclude this section with a discussion of the modeling of enterprise services and the registration of services.

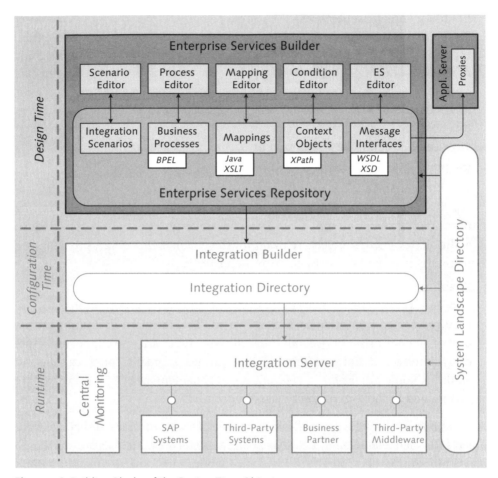

Figure 2.6 Building Blocks of the Design-Time Objects

2.3.1 Enterprise Services Builder

As shown in Figure 2.6, the *Enterprise Services Builder* provides various graphical editors to define and manage the design-time objects in the Enterprise Services Repository. These objects are created using various web standard languages and protocols such as:

▶ WSDL (Web Services Description Language)

▶ XSD (XML Schema Definition)

▶ XPath

- ▸ XSLT (XSL Transformations)
- ▸ Java
- ▸ BPEL (Business Process Execution Language)

Figure 2.7 shows the overall layout of the Enterprise Services Builder with the following main areas:

- ▸ The *main menu bar and standard toolbar* are located on the top of the screen and offer the standard navigation features as well as some other generic features.

- ▸ The *navigation bar* is located on the left-hand side and consists of a number of tabs that serve different purposes.

  - ▸ Under the **Design Objects** tab all objects of the Enterprise Services Repository are displayed in a tree structure. The grouping within the tree structure is based on a number of elements (e.g., *software components*, *software component versions*, *namespaces*, and *folders*) that are discussed in more detail below.

  - ▸ Under the **Change Lists** tab you find all objects that you have been changed and that still need to be activated. These change lists are grouped into three different branches, namely *open*, *transportable*, and *closed*. Open change lists contain objects that need to be activated. Transportable change lists contain active objects that can be released for transport. Closed change lists contain objects that have been released for transport. In addition, you can view objects that have been changed by other users, provided you have the right user authorization in place. We discuss the use of change lists in more detail below.

  - ▸ Under the **Conflicts** tab you find all objects that have any version conflicts due to the import of new object versions. Such conflicts can only occur if an object has been enhanced by a customer and the original object has been updated after the enhancement took place.

- ▸ The *object editor* on the right-hand side serves as the work and display area for all Enterprise Services Repository objects. The object editor itself can be split into different areas depending on the type of object you work with. Figure 2.7 shows an example of a data type that is displayed in the object editor. You can detach the object editor from the main window to maximize your available work space.

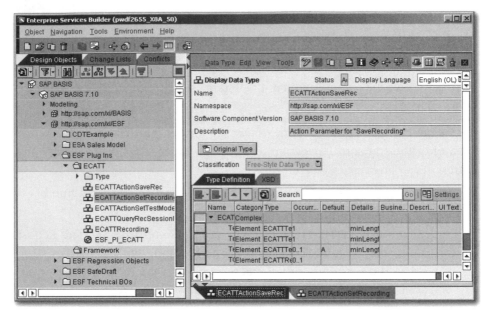

Figure 2.7 Layout of the Enterprise Services Builder

Let's take a closer look at some of the main objects and features you utilize when working in the Enterprise Services Builder.

Tree Structure for Display of Enterprise Services Repository Objects

Within the Enterprise Services Builder all Enterprise Services Repository objects are listed in a tree structure under the **Design Objects** tab. Therefore, it is important to understand how the tree structure is organized so you can find your objects quickly. With SAP NetWeaver PI 7.1 a number of new tree structure elements have been added that are not available in previous releases.

Table 2.2 shows the first two levels of the tree hierarchy, which are both based on the software components and its versions (see also Figure 2.7). As discussed in Section 2.2.2 Software Catalog, the *software component version* (SWCV) is the smallest shipment unit and the primary container for all the design objects in the Enterprise Services Repository. There are two types of software component versions:

▸ **Local software component version**
The local software component version allows you to create temporary design objects locally that can be used for testing purposes only. These objects are not

visible within the Integration Directory and are not available for proxy generation.

▶ **SLD-based software component version**
The SLD-based software component versions must exist in the SLD before they can be imported into the Enterprise Services Repository. Once it is imported, the SWCV can be edited to add namespaces, imported interfaces, and modeling objects.

Level 1	Level 2
A fixed node Local Software Component Versions	All local software component versions
All software components (SWC) that are imported from the SLD	All SLD-based software component versions that exist under the SWC

Table 2.2 Tree Hierarchy for Display of Enterprise Services Repository Objects (Part 1)

As shown in Table 2.2, the tree structure for displaying the Enterprise Services Repository objects starts with one entry holding all local software component versions followed by all software components and their versions that are imported from the SLD.

The next level in the tree structure is common for both local and SLD-based software component versions and is shown in Table 2.3 (see also Figure 2.7). As we can see in Table 2.3, the next levels in the tree structure utilize some different objects:

▶ **Namespaces**
All objects in the Enterprise Services Repository are organized by namespaces. These namespaces are used to identify objects within a software component version. You can define several namespaces within a software component version to differentiate between subprojects. A namespace should be a globally unique identifier, so it must be defined as uniquely as possible worldwide. These namespaces are expressed as either a uniform resource indicator (URI), for example, *http://sap.com/xi/<name>*, or a uniform resource name (URN), for example, *urn:sap-com:<name>*, according to the W3C's XML namespace specifications.

▶ **Folders**
Folders and subfolders can be defined to organize the design objects within a namespace. The folder concept is new with SAP NetWeaver PI 7.1 and does

not exist in any of the previous releases. You can simply create a folder by right-clicking on the object you want to create the folder under (a namespace or another folder) and then selecting **New Folder**.

Level 3	Level 4
A fixed node Modeling.	A fixed folder Model and optional additional subfolders underneath.
All namespaces that have been defined under the software component version.	Folders and subfolders. These entries only exist if folders have been created under the respective namespace.
	Object types. These entries only exist if objects are created without an assignment to a folder.
A fixed node Basis Objects. This node only exists if the SWCV contains underlying SWCVs.	The list of the underlying SWCVs followed by the level 3 structure.
A fixed node Imported Objects.	A fixed node with the name RFCs. This node only exists if any RFCs have been imported to this SWCV.
	A fixed node with the name IDocs. This node only exists if any IDocs have been imported to this SWCV.

Table 2.3 Tree Hierarchy for Display of Enterprise Services Repository Objects (Part 2)

After the fourth level you find the actual design objects in the tree structure. Depending on the path, the type of allowed design objects can be limited:

► Underneath the level 3 node **Modeling** you can only define the design objects **Model** and **Object Definition**. Both objects are used as part of the ARIS modeling tool, which we discuss in more detail in Appendix D.

► Underneath the level 3 node **Imported Objects** you can only import intermediate documents (IDocs) and remote function calls (RFCs) from an SAP backend system. The import of objects is discussed in detail in section 8.3.6 Imported Objects.

► All other design objects require an assignment to a namespace and can be found under the respective namespace of the tree structure.

Working with Change Lists

The Enterprise Services Builder also offers a convenient platform for development in a multiuser environment. Any user (with the appropriate authorizations) is allowed to create or change design objects in the Enterprise Services Repository. When you decide to change an object, the following happens:

► Any other user is blocked from changing the same object or from creating an object with the same name.

► A new version of this object is stored (after the first save) in the Enterprise Services Repository with the status **In Process**. This new object version is only visible to you as the creator of this version. Any other user can only see the last active version of this object.

You can now continue to adjust all objects that you have in status **In Process** until you have reached a state where you want to *activate* these object versions and make them available for everybody to use. With the activation of an object version, the following happens:

► The status of the object version is set to **Active**. With the activation, the object is first checked automatically for consistency.

► The new version of the object becomes visible to every user (with the appropriate authorizations).

In the *navigation bar* under the **Change Lists** tab are listed all design objects that you have changed but not yet activated. From here you can activate them easily by right-clicking on an object or the folder above and then by selecting the option **Activate**. You can also view the change lists of other users if you have the appropriate authorizations.

User Roles and Authorizations

We just talked about required authorizations for viewing or changing objects. Therefore, it is time to look at the authorization concept offered by SAP NetWeaver PI. SAP delivers a set of predefined user roles that carry all required authorizations to perform the tasks of a specific role. Table 2.4 shows a list of the most important user roles delivered by SAP.

User Role	Description
SAP_XI_DISPLAY_USER	Read-only access to the Integration Directory and the Enterprise Services Repository
SAP_XI_DEVELOPER	Design and development of integration processes
SAP_XI_CONFIGURATOR	Configuration of business integration content
SAP_XI_CONTENT_ORGANIZER	Maintenance of SLD content
SAP_XI_MONITOR	Monitoring of SAP NetWeaver PI components and messages
SAP_XI_MONITOR_ENHANCED	Monitoring of SAP NetWeaver PI components and messages including message editing
SAP_XI_ADMINISTRATOR	Technical configuration and administration of SAP NetWeaver PI

Table 2.4 User Roles Delivered by SAP

In the Enterprise Services Repository, you can restrict authorizations for accessing the objects in the Enterprise Services Repository. The Enterprise Services Builder provides a wizard to define and edit authorizations. The roles, users, and groups must be defined in the central user management before you can define authorizations for the selected objects. These authorizations can be set for the directory, the software component version, and the namespace. If no authorizations are defined, the default setting takes effect. These authorizations can be inherited from a higher level and can be propagated to all the substructures.

2.3.2 Message Interface Objects

Among the most important objects to be maintained in the Enterprise Services Repository are the design objects related to message interfaces. Figure 2.8 gives an overview of all of the objects that are part of the message interface definitions and the business object interface definitions, as well as the relationships between these objects.

In the following we discuss the design objects listed in Figure 2.8 in more detail, and in Section 2.3.7 Enterprise Services Definition we show how these objects work together in the definition of enterprise service scenarios.

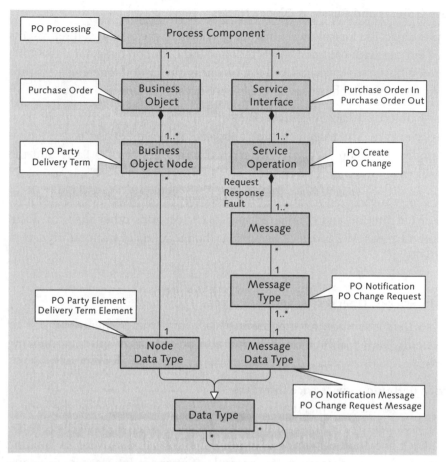

Figure 2.8 Overview of Message Interface Objects

Process Components

The process component is a central modeling object that describes a part of a value chain that is normally performed in a company's department through the associated *business objects*, *service interfaces*, and *operations*. An example of a process component is the **Purchase Order Processing**. Each process component must contain at least one business object.

The process component is not relevant for the definition and configuration of B2B scenarios in SAP NetWeaver PI other than for documentation purposes. We take a closer look at the modeling of process components in Appendix D.

Business Objects and Business Object Nodes

A business object is a logical object that is significant to the business. It represents a class of entities with common characteristics and common behavior describing well-defined business semantics. You use business objects to model business processes. An example of a business object is the Purchase Order.

A business object is typically composed of multiple segments, each with its own business relevance. These segments are modeled as *business object nodes*. Examples of nodes of the business object Purchase Order are the PO Party and the Delivery Terms.

Just like the process component, the business objects and its nodes are not relevant for the definition and configuration of B2B scenarios other than for documentation purposes. We take a closer look at the modeling of business objects in Appendix D.

Service Interfaces, Operations, and Messages

A service offers a solution for a predefined task and is implemented in one or more systems. Each realization of a service can be separated into the following two parts:

▶ **Service definition via service interface**
This is the abstract (implementation-independent) description of the service that is provided by the service interface along with a set of associated operations. Each operation contains one or more messages that provide the binding to the actual message structure. An example of a service interface is an Incoming Sales Order with the operations Create, Change, and Cancel.

▶ **Service implementation**
This is the concrete implementation of the service in the system based on the description provided by the service interface. Multiple implementations can be in place for different backend systems, for example, one implementation for the incoming sales order in SAP ERP and one in SAP CRM.

In a B2B environment, the service interface definitions are of particular interest because the message structures for communication with your trading partner are often required to be an external (industry) standard, whereas the communication with your own backend system requires a different format. In this case we need to have both service interface descriptions in place and provide a mapping (*see* Section 2.3.4 Mappings) between the two message structures.

As mentioned above, the definition of the service interface is independent of any implementation. The *Web Services Description Language* (WSDL) has been introduced as an open standard by the W3C organization to describe service interfaces with their operations and assigned messages. SAP NetWeaver PI follows this recommendation and defines service interfaces using WSDL. Because the Enterprise Services Builder offers a graphical editor for the definition of service interfaces and operations, you don't need to be familiar with WSDL to create these objects. However, an understanding of the concepts of the WSDL description language is useful for a better understanding of the architecture chosen in SAP NetWeaver PI for the definition of message interfaces. Table 2.5 lists the main WSDL objects used for the definition of a service.

WSDL Object	Description
Port Type	A port type is a set of abstract operations.
Operation	An operation is an abstract description of an action. Each operation can be assigned to an `input` message, an `output` message, and several `fault` messages.
Message	The message is an abstract definition of the data being transmitted. A message can consist of multiple logical parts.
Part	A part provides the link to the actual data type used for a message.

Table 2.5 WSDL Objects Used for the Definition of a Service

The translation of a WSDL description to the SAP NetWeaver PI objects is shown in Figure 2.9. Here you can also see how the terms used in SAP NetWeaver PI correlate to the terms used in WSDL. Note that the terminology is different in a few cases. For example, the WSDL object `operation` contains messages of the type `input`, `output`, and `fault`, whereas the SAP NetWeaver PI object **Operation** contains messages of the type `Request`, `Response`, and `Fault`. Table 2.10 shows how the different message types are mapped to each other.

Now let us take a look at the graphical editor provided by the Enterprise Services Builder for the definition of service interfaces, operations, and messages. As you can see in Figure 2.10, you define the set of operations assigned to a service interface on the left-hand side of the editor.

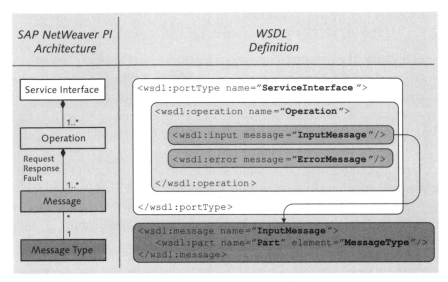

Figure 2.9 Service Interfaces and Their Related WSDL Definitions

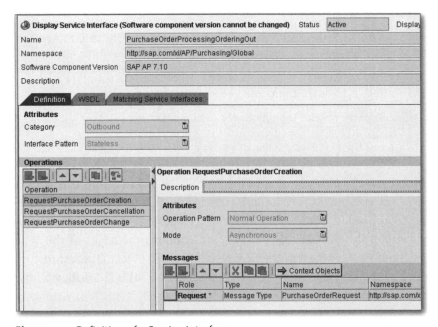

Figure 2.10 Definition of a Service Interface

For each operation you can define the associated messages on the right-hand side of the editor after you have highlighted the corresponding operation.

Figure 2.10 also shows that a number of attributes need to be maintained on the service interface level and on the operation level to categorize the services for the use in different environments. On the service interface level you need to maintain the following attributes:

▶ **Category**
The category describes if a service interface is used in an inbound scenario or in an outbound scenario. In addition, the service interface can be defined as an abstract scenario where the direction is not specified. The complete list of possible categories can be found in Table 2.6. All options are relevant in a B2B environment.

▶ **Interface pattern**
The interface pattern describes the type of communication that is to be executed on the message. The complete list of possible interface patterns can be found in Table 2.7. In a B2B environment only the stateless patterns are used.

Category	Description
Inbound	The category **Inbound** is used for service interfaces of a service provider that can be called by a consumer application.
Outbound	The category **Outbound** is used for service interfaces of a service consumer that calls the service interface of a service provider.
Abstract	The category **Abstract** is used for service interfaces that can be sent and received. This type of service interfaces must be used within integration processes.

Table 2.6 Possible Values for the Service Interface Category

Interface Pattern	Description
Stateful	In a stateful communication pattern the status of the provider can be saved. This pattern can be used in synchronous scenarios only.
Stateless	In a stateless communication pattern the status of the provider cannot be saved. This status is only used in point-to-point communication using Web services.

Table 2.7 Possible Values for the Service Interface Pattern

Interface Pattern	Description
Stateless (XI30-Compatible)	In this version of a stateless communication pattern the status of the provider cannot be saved either. This pattern limits the options on how to set up operations within the service interface to make it compatible with previous SAP NetWeaver PI releases.
TU&C/C	The *Tentative Update & Confirm/Compensate* (TU&C/C) pattern supports cross-system rollbacks in case one out of a series of operations has failed. This pattern is not used in B2B environments.

Table 2.7 Possible Values for the Service Interface Pattern (cont.)

The interface pattern can describe the communication via a service interface as stateful or as stateless. It is important to emphasize the meaning of these terms within this context. The terms *stateful* and *stateless* refer to the state of the service provider in the backend system and not of the integration server. Therefore, in the case of a stateless communication, once a message has passed the integration server layer successfully and has reached the backend system, the state at the backend cannot be utilized. That means that you still can create stateful integration processes within the integration server using service interfaces with a stateless interface pattern.

On the operation level you need to maintain the following attributes. The possible values for each of these attributes depend on the settings of the attributes on the service interface level.

▶ **Operation pattern**
The stateful interface pattern and the TU&CC interface pattern allow a special sequence of operations to take place. The operation pattern allows you to assign an operation to a specific part within this sequence. The complete list of possible operation patterns can be found in Table 2.8. In a B2B environment only stateless interface patterns are used, so only the operation pattern **Normal Operation** is utilized.

▶ **Mode**
Each operation can run in a synchronous mode or in an asynchronous mode. The complete list of possible modes can be found in Table 2.9. Usually, in a B2B environment only the **Asynchronous** mode is used.

Operation Pattern	Description
Commit Operation	This operation is used only in the stateful interface pattern for the commit operation.
Compensate Operation	This operation is used only in the TU&CC pattern for a compensate operation.
Confirm Operation	This operation is used only in the TU&CC pattern for a confirm operation.
Normal Operation	This operation is available for all interface patterns. In patterns with a sequence of operations this is the starting operation.
Rollback Operation	This operation is used only in the stateful interface pattern for a rollback operation.
Tentative Update Operation	This operation is used only in the TU&C/C pattern for the tentative update operation.

Table 2.8 Possible Values for the Operation Pattern

Mode	Description
Asynchronous	In an asynchronous mode the session initiating the communication does not wait for a response message.
Synchronous	In a synchronous mode the session initiating the communication waits until a response message is received.

Table 2.9 Possible Values for the Operation Mode

Based on the settings of the service interface category (see Table 2.6) and the operation mode (see Table 2.9), each operation can be assigned to a combination of request, response, and fault messages. Table 2.10 shows the possible combinations of message assignments. It also provides you with the translation from the SAP NetWeaver PI definition of a message (request, response, fault) to the WSDL definition of a message (input, output, fault).

Category	Mode	Request	Response	Fault
Inbound	Synchronous	input	output	fault
Outbound	Synchronous	input	output	fault
Abstract	Synchronous	input	output	fault
Inbound	Asynchronous	input		fault
Outbound	Asynchronous	input		
Abstract	Asynchronous	input		

Table 2.10 Available Message Types for Different Categories and Modes

The final step in the transaction for the creation of service interfaces is the assignment of an object carrying the message structure information to each message. Analogous to the WSDL specifications, SAP NetWeaver PI allows a number of different formats for the definition of the message structure. In particular, the following types are supported:

▶ **Message type**
The message type is used for message structures defined within SAP NetWeaver PI. For example, enterprise services are defined via message types.

▶ **External definition**
The external definition is used to import message structures defined externally (e.g., by a standard organization) in form of a DTD, an XML schema definition, or a WSDL.

▶ **IDoc definition**
The IDoc definition can be imported from an SAP application system for the definition of an IDoc structure.

▶ **RFC definition**
The RFC definition can be imported from an SAP application system for the definition of an RFC interface.

We discuss the definition of message types in detail in the next section, because they are essential for the definition of enterprise services in the Enterprise Services Repository. We also briefly touch on the external definitions and import of IDocs and RFCs, but defer the detailed discussion to Chapter 8 Development, because they are not relevant for the understanding of the concepts of the Enterprise Services Repository.

Message Types and Data Types

We just learned in the previous section that each message of a service interface must be assigned to an object that defines the actual message structure. One of the possible object types is the message type, which we discuss now in detail. Figure 2.11 shows the relationship between message types and data types.

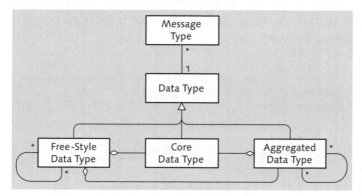

Figure 2.11 Message Types and Data Types

With *data types* you define single elements and attributes that are utilized in your message structure. You can reference other data types within a data type, but recursive references are not permitted. Even though data types are defined in form of an XSD schema, you don't need to be familiar with XSD schemas to build them because SAP NetWeaver PI offers a graphical editor for building these data types.

As shown in Figure 2.11, data types are categorized into three different types:

▶ **Data Types based on the UN/CEFACT Core Component Technical Specification (CCTS)**
The *UN/CEFACT Core Component Technical Specification* (CCTS) specifies a standardized way of modeling data types that SAP adheres to for its definition of enterprise services. All data types following the CCTS specification are based on *core component types* (which are defined in CCTS) or on aggregations of data types that are based on the CCTS specifications. To provide tool-based support for the definition of data types based on the CCTS specification, you must classify each data type as one of the following types:

> ▶ Data types defined with a **Classification** of **Core Data Type** do not carry any syntactical information and are based on the list of core component

types as defined by CCTS. As you can see in Figure 2.12, you need to specify a **Representation Term** that relates to a core component type. Then the template for the selected core component type is presented, where you can maintain the data type specific information.

▶ Data types defined with a **Classification** of **Aggregated Data Type** are composed of core data types and other aggregated data types. The editor for maintaining aggregated data types is similar to the editor for free-style data types that is shown in Figure 2.13.

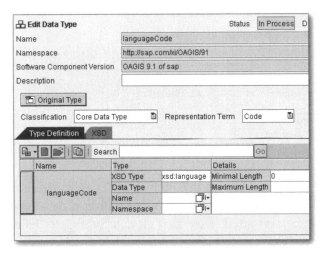

Figure 2.12 Definition of a Core Data Type

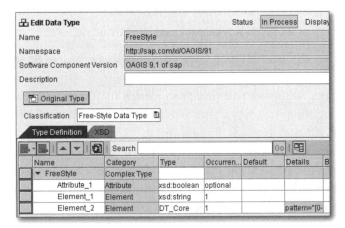

Figure 2.13 Definition of a Free-Style Data Type

▶ **Freely Modeled Data Types**

Freely modeled data types are modeled based on language elements provided by an XML schema definition, but they do not need to follow the CCTS recommendations. You need to use **Free-Style Data Type** as **Classification** when you define such a data type (see Figure 2.13). You can reference any other data type (free-style, core, aggregated) within such a data type. Data types modeled in a prior release of SAP NetWeaver PI are always classified as free-style data types.

Note

Customers can define *data type enhancements* for free-style or aggregate data types in the Enterprise Services Repository to meet their specific requirements. We take a closer look at data type enhancements in Appendix C.

As we saw in Figure 2.8, the link between the definition of the message structure (via data types or other means) and the message definition within the service interface is provided by the *message type*. In Figure 2.9 we also saw how the message type relates to the WSDL description of a message. The message type determines the name of an actual message and references to exactly one data type. As we will see in Section 2.3.4 Mappings, message types are further used within message mappings. Figure 2.14 shows an example of the definition of a message type. You only need to enter the link to the data type, and then the structure information is pulled in automatically.

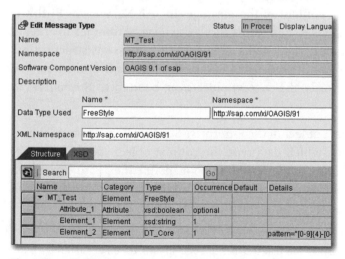

Figure 2.14 Definition of a Message Type

From Table 2.10 we know that within a service interface we can have messages of the type Request, Response, and Fault. Because fault messages must be linked to a message structure with a specific format, a separate fault message type has been introduced in the Enterprise Services Repository, enforcing the use of the appropriate message structure. Fault message types are only intended for use in synchronous communication. When an application-specific error occurs in communication, the application can send a fault message to handle the error.

External Definitions and Imported Objects

SAP NetWeaver PI allows you to reuse message definitions from other sources, such as message definitions from external standard organizations or IDoc and RFC definitions from previous SAP releases. You can import these definitions as **External Definitions** or as **Imported Objects** and utilize them in place of the message type. They play an important role in B2B environments because message structures used in B2B communication are often defined externally by different standards organizations. Therefore, we discuss external definitions and the import of IDocs and RFCs in detail in Sections 8.3.2 through 8.3.6.

2.3.3   Context Objects

Sometimes it is necessary to access the content of a field or an element of a particular message at runtime. For example, you need to identify a receiver based on a condition defined in the content of the message. In SAP NetWeaver PI this is done using *XPath* expressions.[2] These expressions can be very complex to enter at design time or configuration time if the elements in a message structure are deeply nested. In those cases, it is easier to encapsulate the path to the data in a context object. In other words, the context objects can be used as alternatives to XPath expressions.

You simply define a context object in the Enterprise Services Repository as shown in Figure 2.15. You define which data type the context object should reference (string, integer, date, or time). In the second step you define the XPath expression that the context object should represent by simply adding it to the representation of the corresponding message structure as shown in Figure 2.16.

---

2 The XPath expression is an expression that searches through an XML document and finds information in the nodes.

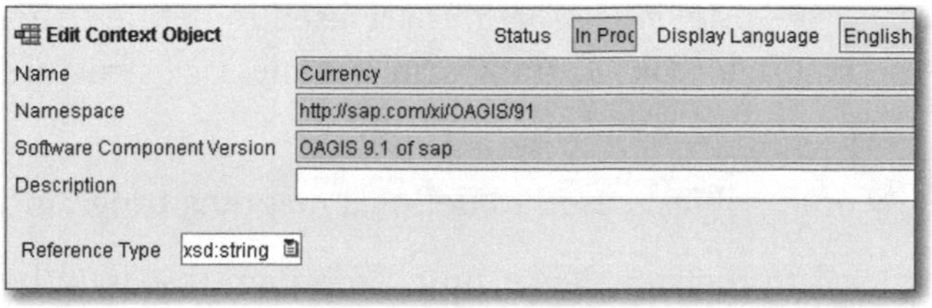

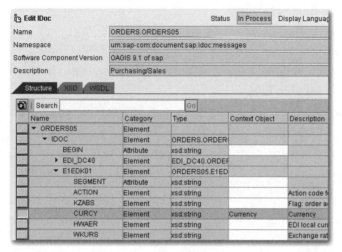

Figure 2.15 Definition of a Context Object

Figure 2.16 Assignment of a Context Object

The example in Figure 2.16 shows the assignment of the context object **Currency** to a specific field in the IDoc ORDERS.ORDERS05. With this assignment the context object **Currency** refers to the XPath expression ORDERS05/IDOC/E1EDK01/CURCY. If you need to specify a condition based on this object, you can replace the complete XPath expression with the context object. For example, instead of the condition ORDERS05/IDOC/E1EDK01/CURCY = 'EUR', you can simply write Currency = 'EUR'. Context objects can be used during the processing of process steps within Integration Processes and during the configuration of the receiver determination in the Integration Directory.

2.3.4 Mappings

As discussed in Section 2.3.2 Message Inteface Objects, data types and message types (along with external definitions and SAP imported objects) are used to define the structure of the messages. *Mapping programs* are used to define structural mappings between these message types to transform one message structure to another.

Figure 2.17 gives an overview of the objects used to define a mapping program.

▶ The *operation mapping* is used to register the mapping program that is to be used between a pair of service interface operations. Within the operation mapping you need to specify the *source operation*, the *target operation*, and the actual *mapping* that should be performed.

▶ The actual mapping can be built within the Enterprise Services Builder as a *message mapping*. Within the message mapping you need to define the *source message*, the *target message*, and the actual *field mapping* between each individual field via a graphical mapping tool.

▶ For the actual mapping you can also use an *imported archive* that can contain an XSLT mapping or a Java mapping.

▶ In addition, you can utilize a mapping that is built using the ABAP Workbench. Because this option is typically not used in a B2B environment, we only touch on this option very briefly.

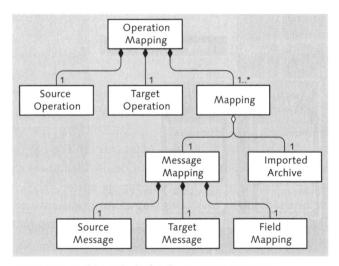

Figure 2.17 Building Blocks for the Mapping Program

Let us now take a look at the different mapping objects in more detail.

Operation Mapping

The Enterprise Services Builder provides an editor for the definition of an operation mapping as shown in Figure 2.18. You identify the source operation on the left-hand side and the target operation on the right-hand side. On the bottom you can view the messages associated with the selected source and target operations, and you need to identify the mapping program for the actual mapping.

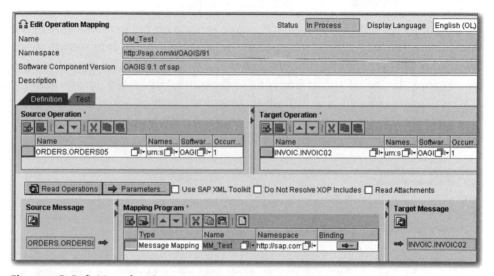

Figure 2.18 Definition of an Operation Mapping

You can choose between the following mapping types:

▸ A **Message Mapping** that is defined in the Enterprise Services Builder via a graphical mapping tool.

▸ A **Java Class** containing the Java mapping that can be imported into the Enterprise Services Repository as an **Imported Archive**.

▸ An **XSL** containing an XSLT mapping that can be imported into the Enterprise Services Repository as an **Imported Archive**.

▸ An **ABAP-Class** containing a mapping that is built using the ABAP Workbench.

▸ An **ABAP-XSL** containing an XSLT mapping that is built using the ABAP Workbench.

Message Mapping

The Enterprise Services Builder provides a graphical mapping editor to graphically define mapping rules between source and target message structures. It includes built-in functions for value transformations, queuing, and context handling. The Enterprise Services Builder also provides an interface for the creation of Java-based user-defined functions. The message mapping generates Java code to be called at runtime.

As shown in Figure 2.19, the source message appears on the left-hand side of the screen, and the target message appears on the right-hand side. Associations between fields in the source and fields in the target can be easily created by simply dragging the mouse cursor from one to the other. Functional transformations can be made using a library of built-in functions, such as `String`, `Arithmetic`, `Statistical`, `Node`, and `Conversion`, functions. There is also a function editor for the creation of user-defined Java functions.

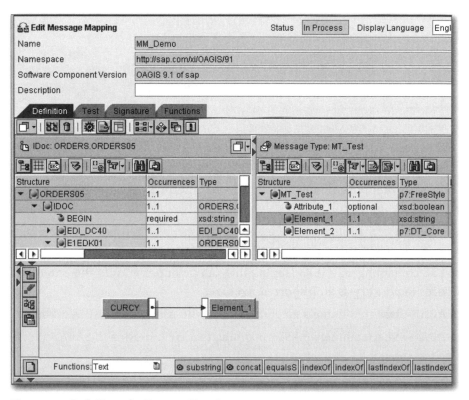

Figure 2.19 Definition of a Message Mapping

The graphical editor includes a **Test** tab that lets you load an instance of the source document and test the mapping as you work on it. These features are discussed in more detail in Section 8.4.1 Operation Mapping and 8.4.2 Message Mapping, as well as in Appendix A.

Imported Archive

To leverage existing investments, the Enterprise Services Builder allows you to import externally built XSLT or Java mappings into the Enterprise Services Repository for execution at runtime.

ABAP Mapping

ABAP mappings are mapping programs in ABAP Objects that can be implemented using the ABAP Workbench. At runtime, these programs are executed on the ABAP Engine of SAP NetWeaver PI on which the integration server is running. These mapping programs must be registered in the Enterprise Services Repository using operation mappings.

2.3.5 Integration Processes

An *integration process* is an executable, cross-system process. Integration processes enhance message-based process integration with the stateful processing of messages where the status of an integration process is persisted on the Integration Server. This means you can specify how long an integration process must wait for further messages to arrive. You can also group certain messages together and then send them in a particular order.

Integration processes are objects in the Enterprise Services Repository and are integrated with other objects, for example, service interfaces. Integration processes are integrated into all building blocks of SAP NetWeaver PI:

▶ **Design time**
To define an integration process at design time you use the graphical process editor in the Enterprises Services Builder.

▶ **Configuration time**
At configuration time, you configure the receiver determination for the integration process in the Integration Directory.

▶ **Runtime**
At runtime, the Business Process Engine (BPE) executes the integration processes. The BPE is part of the Integration Server. You monitor the execution of
business processes by using the monitoring functions of the Integration
Engine.

Integration processes are discussed in detail in Chapter 6 Business Process Management Capabilities.

2.3.6 Process Integration Scenarios

Process integration scenarios in the Enterprise Services Repository provide structured, visual documentation for a process. They can be used as the basis for the
top-down approach to the development work or can be created bottom-up when
the development is finished. Process integration scenarios are used as a basis for
communication in the Integration Directory.

Figure 2.20 shows an example of a process integration scenario for the Order Creation process in the RosettaNet standard scenario. Each scenario is built using the
following elements:

▶ **Swim lanes**
The swim lane contains the different parties involved in the scenario. A party
can be an external party, a business system, or an integration process.

▶ **Actions**
The action contains a specific step within the process. Within each action you
define the service interface operations for the communication between different actions.

▶ **Connections**
The connection describes the type of interaction between different actions.
Here you identify if the communication takes place in an asynchronous or synchronous mode, and you specify the operation mapping if the service interface
operations are not identical.

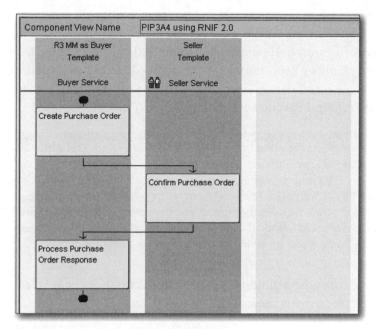

Figure 2.20 Definition of a Process Integration Scenario

2.3.7 Enterprise Services Definition

Enterprise services are highly integrated Web services with an enterprise-level business value. These are structured according to a harmonized enterprise model based on business objects, process components, and *global data types* (GDTs) and ensure a stable interface for future versions, providing backward compatibility. Enterprise services are based on open standards, and the interfaces are described according to WSDL.

All SAP services are defined and maintained in the Enterprise Services Repository and are based on a governance process that ensures quality and supports reuse. Customers can enhance SAP service descriptions with custom services relevant to their own business needs and environment. SAP NetWeaver offers a set of tools to enhance enterprise service interfaces without modifying the original enterprise service. This is discussed more in detail in Appendix C.

Whereas the definition of service interfaces including its operations and related messages in the Enterprise Services Repository always follows the WSDL-based model (compare Figure 2.8 and Figure 2.9), SAP allows more flexibility when it comes to the definition of the message structures in order to allow the reuse of message structure definitions (e.g., from external standard organizations) that don't follow the services approach. However, for the definition of enterprise services in the Enterprise Services Repository, SAP has defined a strict governance process to ensure that all enterprise services delivered by SAP are compliant to the Core Component Technical Specification (CCTS) by UN/CEFACT.

Core Component Technical Specification (CCTS)

The *United Nations/Centre for Trade Facilitation and Electronic Business* (UN/CEFACT) is a chartered activity of the *UN Economic Commission for Europe* (UN/ECE). ISO 15000-5 CCTS developed by UN/CEFACT and ISO Technical Committee provides a methodology for semantic data modeling that achieves a common understanding of data structures and message types on a syntax-independent level. CCTS-based data representation has become more and more popular and is gaining momentum in the area of B2B.

Figure 2.21 shows how data type definitions are used to ensure such compliance. In detail, the following hierarchy is used:

▶ **W3C built-in XSD types**
The W3C built-in XSD types are defined by the XML schema language as simple types that are built into the XML schema definition. They are built into the Enterprise Services Repository as well and can be utilized in the definition of any type of data types.

▶ **CCTS core data types**
CCTS core data types are data types without any business semantics and are built based on the W3C built-in XSD types. In the Enterprise Services Repository they are always represented by core data types.

▶ **Global data types**
Global data types (GDTs) are SAP-wide primary and reusable data types representing business-related content built according to the UN/CEFACT Core Component Technical Specification (CCTS). They have been approved SAP-wide by a special governance process for business content. All elements of enterprise SOA services are described by GDTs. They are defined in the Enterprise Services Repository and based on data types "core data types" or "aggregate data types."

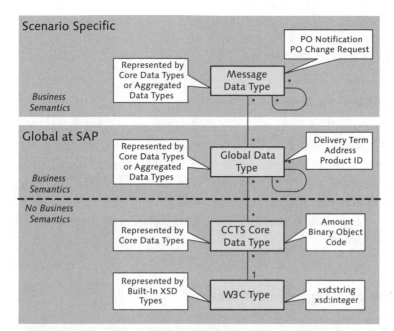

Figure 2.21 Data Type Hierarchy for the Definition of Enterprise Services

There are essentially two ways of creating enterprise services: the inside-out approach and the outside-in approach.

▶ **Inside-out approach**
In the inside-out approach the service already exists in an application system. You create a WSDL document for an existing function such as BAPI in the application system and then import the service description into the Enterprise Services Repository. The service description can then be used by any number of callers for communication using the integration server.

▶ **Outside-in approach**
In the outside-in approach no service exists in the system. It starts with the development of service interfaces in the Enterprise Services Repository. After

modeling the service interfaces and the underlying data types, a WSDL document is automatically generated for that interface. This WSDL document then becomes the basis for generating proxies for the provider and the consumer.

2.3.8 Enterprise Services Registry

A Services Registry, compliant with the Universal Description, Discovery, and Implementation,[3] (UDDI) acts as a catalog for the services within an enterprise SOA and enables the easy discovery, reuse, and management of services. It includes metadata that can be used to search for services by name, ID, category, type, and so on and contains the deployment (end point) information that is required to invoke the service. It also enables management and governance of service-enabled applications.

2.4   Overview of Integration Directory

For both B2B transactions and A2A communications along your organization's value chain, you will have individual and special requirements that concern execution and security. Individual agreements between you and your business partners must be managed centrally so that they can be made available across your entire system landscape. This is the job of the *Integration Directory* of SAP NetWeaver PI. Agreements regarding connectivity, security, and other essential operations that take place between you and your business partners are kept in the Integration Directory.

The configuration in the Integration Directory describes how the incoming messages should be processed by the Integration Server and to which receiver or receivers the messages must be sent. The process integration scenarios that were designed and created in the Enterprise Services Repository were configured using the configuration objects such as collaboration profiles, routing rules, and collaboration agreements for the cross-company or cross-system processes of your entire system landscape.

Figure 2.22 gives you an overview of the configuration objects to be maintained in the Integration Directory. You can also see that the Integration Builder pro-

---

3 UDDI is an open industry standard, sponsored by OASIS. It defines a standard method for publishing and discovering the network-based software components of a service-oriented architecture.

vides a number of wizards and editors for the maintenance of configuration objects.

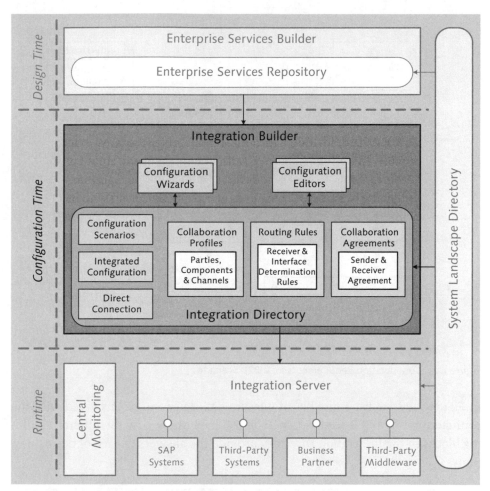

Figure 2.22 Building Blocks of the Configuration Objects

Within the Integration Directory you define the configuration for both intra-company and cross-company (B2B) collaboration scenarios. As illustrated in Figure 2.23, the configuration of a B2B scenario has some different requirements than other scenarios because you don't have the visibility on the complete system landscape.

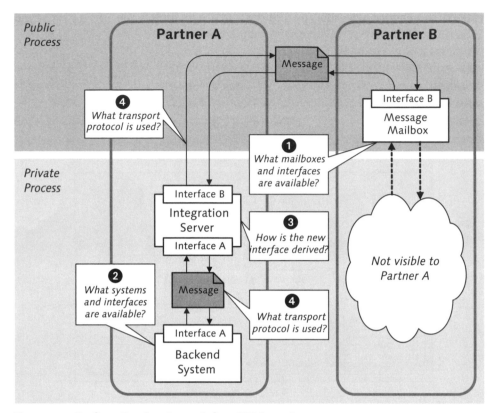

Figure 2.23 Configuration Requirements for a B2B Scenario

In Figure 2.23 we list a number of questions that need to be answered with the configuration of a B2B scenario. In Table 2.11 we show how the different building blocks in the Integration Directory provide the answers to each of these questions.

Topic	Description
❶	The external partner does not disclose his internal system landscape. Instead he provides a number of mailboxes that are maintained as part of the collaboration profile.
❷	The internal systems with its interfaces are maintained as part of the collaboration profile.

Table 2.11 Topics Handled within the Integration Directory

Topic	Description
❸	The derivation of the target interface and its receiver is maintained as part of the logical routing.
❹	The transport protocols are selected as part of the collaboration agreements.

Table 2.11 Topics Handled within the Integration Directory (cont.)

After an introduction to the Integration Builder we discuss each of the building blocks listed in Figure 2.22 and in Table 2.11 in detail.

2.4.1 Integration Builder

As shown in Figure 2.22, the Integration Builder provides various visual tools that allow you to create all necessary configuration objects for a given scenario:

▶ **Configuration wizards**
A number of configuration wizards in the Integration Builder help automate the process of configuring the objects for a given scenario. It takes you through the configuration process step-by-step, utilizing templates for the automatic generation of the configuration objects.

▶ **Configuration editors**
The configuration editors in the Integration Builder allow you to define each of the configuration objects manually and separately.

Figure 2.24 shows the overall layout of the Integration Builder, which is very similar to the layout of the Enterprise Services Builder as described in Section 2.3.1, Enterprise Services Builder. The Integration Builder contains the following main areas:

▶ The *main menu bar and standard tool bar* are located on top of the screen, offering the same features as the Enterprise Services Builder.

▶ The *navigation bar* is located on the left-hand side and consists of two tabs that serve different purposes.

  ▶ Under the **Objects** tab all configuration objects of the Integration Directory are displayed in a tree structure. The concept is the same as with the Enterprise Services Builder, but the tree structure itself differs from the one in the Enterprise Services Builder.

▶ Under the **Change Lists** tab you find all the objects that you have changed. The functionality of change lists is identical to the change list functionality of the Enterprise Services Builder where you can activate and transport objects.

▶ The *object editor* in the right-hand side is similar to the object editor in the Enterprise Services Builder and serves as the edit and display area for the configuration objects.

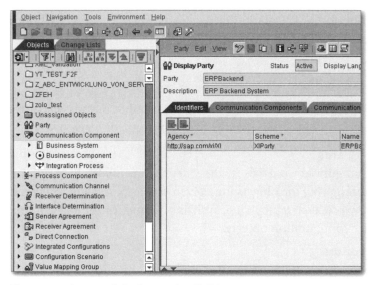

Figure 2.24 Layout of the Integration Builder

Tree Structure for Display of Configuration Objects

The tree structure used in the Integration Builder is not as deep as the one used in the Enterprise Services Builder because configuration objects are not assigned to software components and namespaces. The tree structure is shown in Figure 2.24 and consists of the following levels:

▶ Configuration objects can be placed within a structure of folders and subfolders analogous to the folder concept in the Enterprise Services Builder. The first level within the tree structure is different from the Enterprise Services Builder folders.

▶ Configuration objects that are not assigned to a folder are listed by object type underneath the list of folders.

Configuration Wizards

The Integration Builder offers a number of configuration wizards to guide you through the configuration steps for a specific connection. In particular, the following wizards are available:

▶ **Model Configurator**
The Model Configurator guides you through the configuration process step-by-step based on a model defined in the Enterprise Services Repository. You can access the wizard from the main menu of the Integration Builder via the menu path **Tools · Apply Model from ES Repository**.

Within the wizard you can choose from the following models:

▶ A *process integration scenario* defined in the Enterprise Services Repository. When you choose such a scenario, it will serve as a configuration template for automatically generating the configuration objects for a given scenario. The objects required for the configuration are created, and existing objects are checked to ensure that they can be used before including them in a configuration scenario.

▶ An *SAP process component interaction model* or an *SAP process variant type model*, which are both defined in the Enterprise Services Repository as part of the ARIS business modeling tool. For B2B scenarios these options are not yet fully supported and therefore are not discussed in more detail.

This wizard speeds up the process of setting up new business partner connections in B2B scenarios. The Integration Builder shows the results in a generation progress window showing the progress of the objects being generated. The generation log can be used to analyze and understand the configuration. We will take a closer look at the model configurator in Section 9.6 Use of the Model Configurator.

▶ **Configuration Wizard**
The Configuration Wizard also guides you through the configuration process, but it doesn't utilize a model as a template for the configuration. Based on the scenario you want to implement (B2B communication, A2A communication, or direct connection), it provides you with step-by-step instructions on the objects that need to be configured.

2.4.2 Collaboration Profiles

In the *collaboration profile* you model the units that send or receive messages including the possible means of transportation. The sending or receiving unit of a message can be any of the following:

► **External party**
An external party (trading partner) with whom you exchange messages. In a B2B collaboration scenario one of the end points is defined as an external party. In the Integration Directory the trading partner information is defined using the following objects:

  ► Your trading partners are defined via a *communication party*. Typically you represent a whole company as one party. For large enterprises you may need to define multiple parties representing different business units of the enterprise.

  ► Each trading partner can possess multiple mailboxes to or from which messages can be sent. Each of these mailboxes is represented by a *communication component* underneath the party. Within the communication component you also specify which service interfaces (service interface operations) can be processed by the mailbox.

  ► Each mailbox can allow communication using different protocols. Each of these protocols is represented by a *communication channel* underneath the communication component.

► **Application system**
An individual application system within your system landscape. In a B2B collaboration scenario one of the end points is defined as an application system within your system landscape. The following objects must be maintained in the Integration Directory:

  ► Each application system participating in a collaboration scenario is represented by a *communication component*. Note that the communication component representing an actual system requires a different type of information than the mailbox information of an external party.

  ► Each application system can allow communication using different protocols. Just as for the external party, each of these protocols is represented by a *communication channel* underneath the communication component.

▶ **Integration process**

An integration process defined in the Enterprise Services Repository. You can execute an integration process as part of your scenario. An integration sends and receives messages and must be configured in the Integration Directory just like the other end points using the following objects:

▶ Each integration process executed as part of an integration scenario must be represented as a *communication component* in the Integration Directory.

▶ Because communication with an integration process is handled internally within the Integration Server, you do not need to specify a communication protocol underneath the communication component.

Figure 2.25 gives an overview on the configuration objects used for the collaboration profile and how they relate to each other. Let's now take a look at the individual objects in more detail.

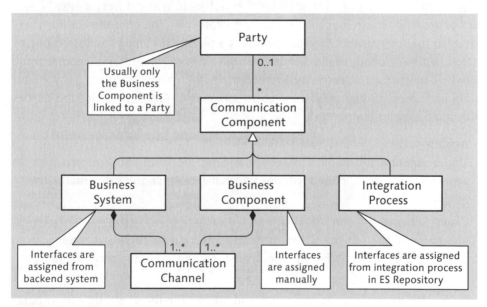

Figure 2.25 Configuration Objects of the Collaboration Profile

Communication Party

A communication party (short party) is set up for each trading partner involved in the B2B processes, which represents the external company or a larger business unit within the company. Trading partners involved in the B2B integration need

85

to agree upon a common identification scheme between them such that they can recognize each other. A number of organizations offer unique identifiers for businesses such as the D-U-N-S number provided by Dun & Bradstreet.

> **Note**
>
> UN/CEFACT has defined a unique identification code methodology that is supported by SAP NetWeaver PI. Any agency issuing party identification codes can be registered at UN/CEFACT and will receive a unique code as an agency issuing code lists (listed in UN/CEFACT data element 3055). Examples for code list issuing agencies are:
>
> ► 009 – GS1 (formerly EAN International)
> ► 016 – D&B (Dun & Bradstreet Corporation)
> ► 166 – NMFTA (National Motor Freight Classification Association)
> ► 310 – SAP AG

Trading partners may need to identify themselves in many different ways based on the specific requirement from the B2B protocols. The communication party editor in the Integration Directory provides a place where you can assign one or many similar globally valid identifiers (alternative identifiers) agreed upon between the parties. Alternative identifiers in the communication party editor allow you to assign unique identification schemes to the communication parties with the following properties:

► **Agency**
Under **Agency** you enter the agency issuing the code list. You can pick an agency from a predelivered list, but you can also enter any value manually.

► **Scheme**
Under **Scheme** you enter the name of the scheme used by the selected agency. The name of the scheme is automatically filled if you choose an agency from the predelivered list. Otherwise you can enter any scheme name manually.

► **Name**
Under **Name** you specify the unique identifier for the communication party within the specified scheme. The name is always entered manually.

Figure 2.26 shows an example of a party defined in the Integration Directory. You can see the name given to the party listed under the **Agency** http://sap.com/xi/XI and **Scheme** XIParty. We also refer to this name as the *XI party* or the *normalized name* of the party.

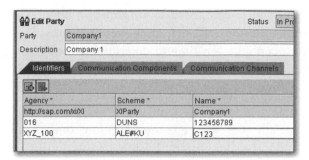

Figure 2.26 Definition of a Party with Alternative Identifiers

In the example in Figure 2.26, a couple of alternative identifiers of the party have been maintained. As mentioned above, you can pick from a predelivered list of agencies or enter the agency and scheme manually. The agencies and schemes of the predelivered list are listed in Table 2.12.

Agency	Scheme	Name
016	DUNS	D-U-N-S number to be entered manually
009	GLN	Unique identifier to be entered manually
166	SCAC	Unique identifier to be entered manually

Table 2.12 Agencies and Schemes for Alternative Party Identifiers

In addition, the IDoc adapter requires the use of alternative identifiers to link to the partner profiles as they are set up in the SAP application systems. We will take a closer look at the party configuration for IDoc communication in Section 9.2.1 Communication Party.

Communication Component

A *communication component* is used to address the application systems or business entities as senders or receivers of messages. Because in B2B collaboration scenarios the end points are defined on different levels (see also Figure 2.23), a communication component can be defined as one of the following types:

▶ **Business system**
The business system addresses a specific business (application) system in the internal system landscape as the sender or receiver of messages. It must have a

corresponding entry in the SLD and is composed of information about the inbound and outbound interfaces and the software component versions. This helps the Integration Builder at configuration time to determine which interfaces the business system supports. One of the end points in a B2B scenario is normally set up using a business system.

► **Business component**

The business component is typically used as the communication component linked to an external party. It addresses an abstract business entity (business partner) as the sender or receiver of messages and is mainly used in cross-company or B2B processes. In cross-company processes you can specify an entire company unit as the sender or receiver, with each company unit providing a multitude of services for communicating with other companies. Unlike the business system, business components do not have corresponding entries in the SLD. Business partners involved in the cross-company processes mask their internal system landscapes (business systems) by using the business components and make only the interfaces available to the partners involved.

You need to pick the interfaces associated to the business component out of all service interface definitions available in the Enterprise Services Repository. If the service interface contains multiple operations, you can add the operation to the service interface definition in the form `<Service interface>.<Operation>`. Figure 2.27 shows an example of the definition of a business component with a number of service interfaces assigned to it. The first entry consists of a specific operation within the service interface.

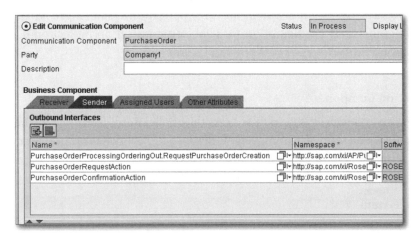

Figure 2.27 Definition of a Business Component

▶ **Integration process**
The integration process defined as a communication component addresses an integration process defined in the Enterprise Services Repository as the sender or receiver of messages. An integration process can send or receive messages using its abstract interfaces. They can be used for stateful tasks such as merging or splitting messages or for sending an asynchronous message to the process and using it to trigger a synchronous call. Integration processes are used in internal company or cross-company processes. In the Integration Directory the integration process must be configured as the sender or receiver of messages just like any other end point. The definition of an integration process within the Integration Directory is supported by a wizard that automatically assigns all service interfaces used in the integration process as defined in the Enterprise Services Repository.

Communication Channel

The *communication channel* specifies the transport mechanism for the inbound and outbound processing of a message and contains information such as adapter type, message protocol, transport protocol, security-specific configuration, and adapter-specific configuration. A communication channel is always assigned to a business system or a business component. Depending on the direction of the message, processing of the assigned communication channel can be one of the following two types:

▶ **Sender**
The sender communication channel defines the data for the sender adapter, which transforms the inbound message for further processing in the Integration Engine.

▶ **Receiver**
The receiver communication channel defines the data for the receiver adapter, which transforms the outbound message for further processing in the receiving application system or the receiving business partner.

Figure 2.28 illustrates the connection between sender and receiver communication channels and the inbound and outbound processing during the runtime. Note that we use the terms *inbound process* and *outbound process* from the viewpoint of the integration server whereas the interfaces are defined from the viewpoint of the sender system or receiver system. Therefore, the *outbound interface* is used in an *inbound process*, whereas the *inbound interface* is used in an *outbound process*.

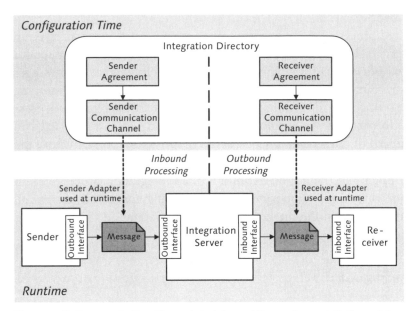

Figure 2.28 Communication Channels in Inbound Processing and Outbound Processing

Within the maintenance screen for the communication channel are a number of tabs that serve different purposes:

▶ **Parameters**

Under the **Parameters** tab you define the type of adapter you want to use for processing (check Chapter 3 Adapter Concepts for a detailed discussion of the available adapters). After you pick the type of adapter, you need to define a number of parameters for your communication channel. The parameter list consists of a non-adapter-specific area and an adapter-specific area. The non-adapter-specific parameters are the following:

▷ In the **Transport Protocol** you specify the technical transport protocol, such as HTTP or SMTP. The transport protocol available depends on the type of adapter you have chosen.

▷ In the **Message Protocol** you specify the protocol of your message. For example, the message protocol determines the definition of the message header.

▷ In the **Adapter Engine** you choose the adapter engine on which your communication channel should. We will learn in Section 2.5.1 Integration Server that you can choose from multiple adapter engines.

The adapter-specific parameters are discussed for each type of adapter in Chapter 3 Adapter Concepts.

▸ **Identifiers**
Under the **Identifiers** tab you can specify which alternative party ID should be used to identify your communication party.

▸ **Module**
Under the **Module** tab you can insert additional Java modules to be executed during runtime. This feature is discussed in more detail in Chapter 3 Adapter Concepts.

Figure 2.29 shows an example of the definition of a communication channel using the XI adapter. Based on the type of adapter you choose, you may need to configure a fairly large number of parameters for your communication channel. To avoid the need for manual input for each of these parameters, SAP NetWeaver PI offers *communication channel templates* consisting of default settings to help you configure the communication channel during the configuration of an integration scenario. These templates are defined in the Enterprise Services Repository and can be imported into the Integration Directory during the definition of a communication channel via the menu path **Communication Channel · Apply Template**.

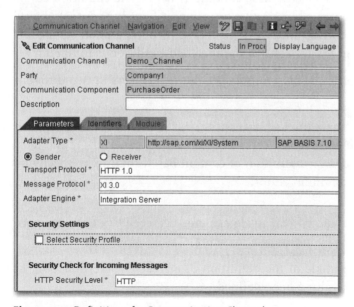

Figure 2.29 Definition of a Communication Channel

2.4.3 Logical Routing

In the collaboration profile we defined a number of end points, the service interfaces available for each end point, and the communication channels allowed for each service interface. In the *logical routing* we now need to determine for a specific scenario the end points of this scenario and the service interfaces used for communication. In this step we do not specify the transport protocol used for communication yet. In the Integration Builder the logical routing is split into two steps: the *receiver determination* and the *interface determination*.

Receiver Determination

In the receiver determination you define one or more receivers as the targets for a message based on the available sender information. The receiver can be a communication component within a communication party or a communication component without a party (representing an internal system or an integration process).

In addition to the sender information, you can also use the content of the actual message to determine the party and communication component of the receiver. For example, the receiver can be dependent on the sold-to party specified in the incoming message. You can specify these conditions within the condition editor for each receiver in the form of an XPath expression or by using context objects (see Section 2.3.3 Context Objects). During runtime, the integration server forwards the message to the receiver only if the specified condition is fulfilled.

Within the receiver determination you can specify the receivers in two different ways:

▶ **Standard**
The **Standard** option allows you to manually enter the receivers of the messages. This also includes the definition of content-based routing by specifying conditions using the condition editor.

▶ **Extended**
The **Extended** option allows you to determine the receiver of the message dynamically at runtime by means of a mapping.

Figure 2.30 shows an example of the definition of a receiver determination. In this example no conditions have been defined.

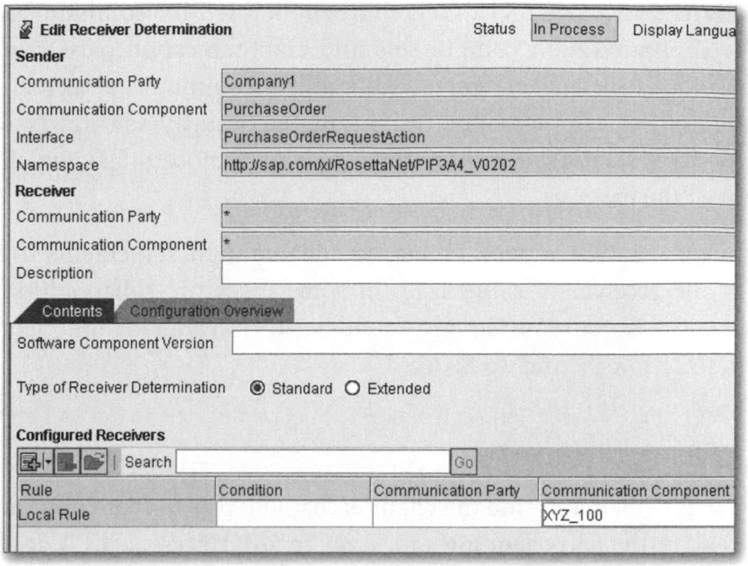

Figure 2.30 Definition of a Receiver Determination

Interface Determination

In the interface determination you define one or more service interfaces that are used for the message on the receiver side. This determination is based on the sender information and on the sender's collaboration profile. Because the service interfaces of the sender and the receiver are usually different, it is necessary to have a mapping program between these two interfaces. If a mapping is necessary, you can select the mapping program in the form of an operation mapping from the Enterprise Services Repository to be used to process this message. The mapping is not necessary when the sender and receiver use the same message structure.

You are also able to assign multiple interfaces on the receiver side. In this case the messages are forwarded to the receivers according to the quality of service specified for this scenario. If the quality of service *exactly once in order (EOIO)* is selected, the order in which the interfaces are entered determines the order in which the messages are received.

2.4.4 Collaboration Agreements

In a *collaboration agreement* you define which communication channels are to be used for a specific sender-receiver pair. In other words, in the collaboration agreement you determine the actual channels that will be used for communication purposes. The communication components and communication parties in the collaboration profile are usually assigned with multiple communication channels. Senders and receivers can also agree on additional security settings (see Chapter 10 Security Considerations for more details on security settings), which refer to the content of the message.

As you can see in Figure 2.28, we need to specify collaboration agreements for the sender and for the receiver of a message. In some cases the collaboration agreement for the sender is not required if the sender interface already uniquely specifies the communication channel to be used.

Sender Agreements

In the sender agreement you determine the channel that will be used for communication with the sender (the party sending a message to SAP NetWeaver PI). It is used in the outbound message processing to transform a message so that it can be understood and processed by the integration engine. As part of the sender agreement, you must specify the following properties:

▶ **Sender communication channel**
Here you must specify an available **Sender Communication Channel** out of the collaboration profile.

▶ **Schema validation**
As of release 7.1 of SAP NetWeaver PI, you can validate XML messages against the associated schema definition. Within the sender agreement you specify where the **Schema Validation** should take place.

  ▷ If the validation takes place in the adapter, a synchronous response is sent to the sender when an error occurs.

  ▷ If the validation takes place in the Integration Engine, the message is set to error status (in the case of an error) and can be processed by the administrator in the ABAP monitor or in the Runtime Workbench.

The necessary configuration steps for schema validation are discussed in detail in Appendix E.

▶ **Adapter-specific attributes**
Based on the selected communication channel and the attributes selected within this channel, you may need to maintain a number of **Adapter-Specific**

Attributes. These attributes are mainly related to security settings. See Chapter 10 Security Considerations for details on the security settings.

Figure 2.31 shows an example of the attributes you need to maintain for a sender agreement. Note that the security-related information is only available if the communication channel has security settings required within its attributes.

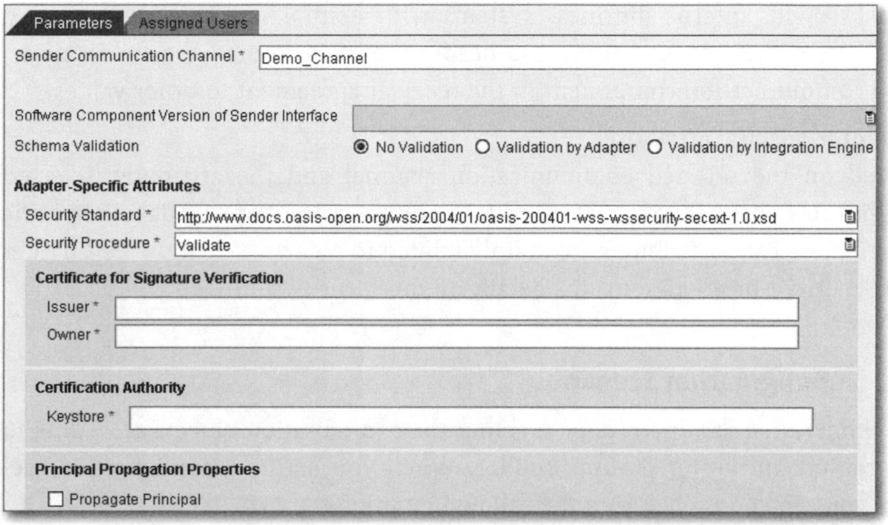

Figure 2.31 Example of the Attributes of a Sender Agreement

Receiver Agreements

In the receiver agreement you determine the channel that will be used for communication with the receiver (the party receiving a message from SAP NetWeaver PI). It is used in the inbound message processing to transform a message so that it can be understood and processed by the receiver. As part of the receiver agreement, you must specify the following properties:

▶ **Receiver communication channel**
Here you must specify an available **Receiver Communication Channel** out of the collaboration profile.

▶ **Schema validation**
As of release 7.1 of SAP NetWeaver PI, you can validate XML messages against the associated schema definition. Within the receiver agreement you specify if the **Schema Validation** should take place. In contrast to the sender agreement,

the validation can only take place in the Integration Engine. In case of an error, the message is set to error status and can be processed by the administrator in the ABAP monitor or in the Runtime Workbench.

▶ **Header mappings**
The **Header Mapping** is particularly important for the configuration of business-to-business processes when the business partner wants to replace the names of his internal business systems with neutral representatives (party, business component). You use the header mapping to map the fields, party, and communication component in the receiver agreement to other values.

▶ **Adapter-specific attributes**
Based on the selected communication channel and the attributes selected within this channel, you may need to maintain a number of Adapter-Specific Attributes. These attributes are mainly related to security settings. See Chapter 10 Security Considerations, for details on the security settings.

2.4.5 Configuration Scenarios

The *configuration scenario* groups together the configuration objects according to their content in the Integration Builder. When you define a configuration scenario, you can choose between the following options:

▶ With the option **No Model** you manually maintain all objects under the configuration scenario. There are no restrictions on the type of objects you assign to the configuration scenario.

▶ With all other options (**Process Integration Scenario**, **SAP Process Variant Type Model**, and **SAP Process Component Interaction Model**), you start the Model Configurator (see Section 2.4.1 Integration Builder). All objects defined via this configurator are assigned to the specified configuration scenario.

2.4.6 Integrated Configuration

The *integrated configuration* is used for defining the message processing locally in the Advanced Adapter Engine (AAE). Local message processing can be used for adapter-to-adapter communication within the advanced adapter engine to gain a substantial improvement in performance. The AAE provides mapping and routing locally for this purpose, and the integrated configuration provides an "all in one" configuration editor for the definition of these objects. Message processing is executed only on the Advanced Adapter Engine without the involvement of the Integration Engine. All adapters on the AAE (with the exception of the RNIF and CIDX adapters) can be configured for local processing.

Integrated configuration cannot be used for more complex configuration scenarios. For example, context-based message routing or multiple massage mappings are not supported.

2.4.7 Direct Connection

You can use a *direct connection* to configure direct communication between two business systems. This is mainly used in internal company processes. Because B2B communication does not use direct connections, we discuss this topic only very briefly.

In direct communication, one system calls another system directly without using the Integration Server as a central instance. The communication takes place using the Web services runtime. For two business systems to be able to communicate directly with one another using the Web services runtime, the receiver system must be configured as the Web service provider and the sender system as the Web service client. You can make the necessary configuration settings centrally in the Integration Directory rather than having to make them locally in the involved backend systems. When one system can communicate with another system, without going through middleware, the performance can be improved significantly. With the use of SAP NetWeaver PI, the administration, support, and maintenance activities for such scenarios can be centralized.

2.4.8 Value Mapping Groups

In B2B configuration, the same object can have different representations on the sender and receiver side. For example, a trading partner can be represented with different ID numbers in different systems. In SAP NetWeaver PI the representation of such identifiers is defined by an issuing agency and an identification scheme, just like the representation of alternative party identifiers (see the discussion on agencies and schemes in Section 2.4.2 Collaboration Profiles). Value mappings are defined in two steps:

▶ You use the **Value Mapping** function provided in a message mapping (and in Java mapping) in the Enterprise Services Repository to identify the agency and scheme for the representation of an object.

▶ You maintain a value mapping table containing the actual mapping values in the Integration Directory at configuration time.

Value mappings are discussed more in detail in Section 9.7.2 Data Conversions.

2.5 Process Integration Runtime

In the *process integration runtime* the processes are executed based on the configuration defined in the Integration Directory. In this section we first discuss the Integration Server with its different engines, followed by a discussion of the proxy runtime. We conclude this section with a closer look at some specific topics related to the runtime, in particular the message protocol used in SAP NetWeaver PI, the different pipeline steps during the execution of a message, and the different options on the quality of service.

Another central feature related to the runtime is the ability to monitor the processing of messages in your systems and to track messages that are in error status. Monitoring features are discussed in Chapter 5 Central Monitoring.

2.5.1 Integration Server

The Integration Server in SAP NetWeaver PI provides a runtime infrastructure for secure XML-based communication between applications in heterogeneous system landscapes and for mapping and routing. It acts as a hub for a set of senders and receivers of messages. As shown in Figure 2.32, the Integration Server consists of three different engines, which are discussed in more detail next.

Integration Engine

The *Integration Engine* is a central distribution engine of the Integration Server and is used for receiving, processing, and forwarding messages. It processes the XML messages received from the Adapter Engine or from the Proxy Framework. It is responsible for logical and technical routing, as well as for the transformation of the message content between sender and receiver systems. The Integration Engine processes messages according to the configuration defined in the Integration Directory.

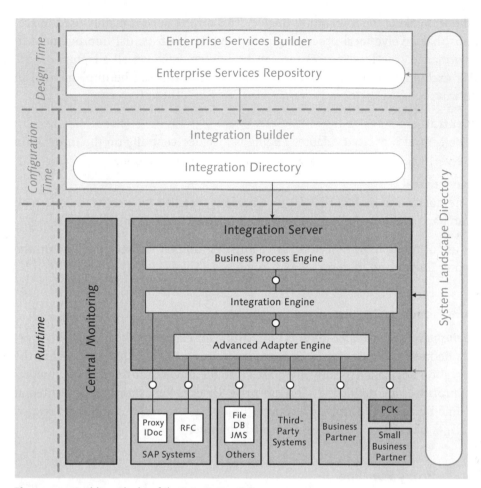

Figure 2.32 Building Blocks of the Integration Server

Adapter Engine

The *Adapter Engine* is used to connect the Integration Engine to SAP and non-SAP systems. Different kinds of adapters in the Adapter Engine are used to convert XML-based messages to the specific protocol and format required by these systems. The Adapter Engine is based on the Adapter Framework, which provides interfaces for configuration, management, and monitoring of these adapters.

The *Advanced Adapter Engine* (AAE) has evolved out of the Adapter Engine of previous releases of SAP NetWeaver PI. In addition to the adapter engine capabilities, it provides an end-to-end message processing locally within the adapters without invoking the Integration Engine. This new feature is mainly used in scenarios that involve local processing and provides a substantial improvement in performance. The local processing can be implemented on all adapters on the AAE, excluding the RNIF and CIDX adapters. The AAE can be implemented in two ways:

▸ **Central**
The central Advanced Adapter Engine is installed centrally on the Integration Server. The central AAE is always available in an installation.

▸ **Noncentral**
The noncentral Advanced Adapter Engine is installed on a separate host. You can have multiple noncentral Advanced Adapter Engines in place.

The use of multiple Advanced Adapter Engines can help balance the load on the Adapter Engine and to improve performance.

Business Process Engine

The *Business Process Engine* (BPE) is responsible for executing the integration processes defined in the Enterprise Services Repository. It is tightly connected to the Integration Engine and is fully integrated into the Integration Server. The integration processes are defined in the Enterprise Services Repository and executed at runtime by the BPE. During execution, the BPE also correlates and links related messages based on a unique user-defined identifier.

2.5.2   Proxy Runtime

The proxy model represents a programming paradigm for SAP systems and is an important element of the enterprise service-oriented architecture (enterprise SOA). Proxies allow you to expose arbitrary application functionality via web interfaces. These proxies separate business application logic from the integration logic of SAP NetWeaver PI.

Proxies are interfaces that provide connectivity to application systems, and users only need to focus on the implementation of the business application logic. Service interfaces in the Enterprise Services Repository are the basis for proxies and are generated in the Enterprise Services Repository. Proxy generation in the Enterprise Services Repository converts non-language-specific interface descriptions in WSDL into executable interfaces. The service interface determines which proxy objects are generated. There are two kinds of proxies, namely, *consumer proxies* and *provider proxies.*[4]

The proxy runtime options are different depending on the implementation language. SAP NetWeaver PI supports Java proxies and ABAP proxies as shown in Figure 2.33:

- ► **ABAP proxy runtime**
  ABAP proxies can be used to connect to SAP NetWeaver Application Server ABAP. They are generated on the AS ABAP (release 6.20 or higher) using the ABAP transaction SPROXY, based on the WSDL representation of the service interface. ABAP proxies are value-added ABAP programs that are called for execution by the Integration Engine at runtime. The ABAP proxy runtime can be used in two different ways:

  - ▶ For the exchange of messages via the Integration Server using ABAP proxies. A *consumer proxy* is used for sending messages to the Integration Server. A *provider proxy* is used to provide a service on the application server that can be addressed by messages from the Integration Server.

  - ▶ For the call of a Web service in the Internet. A *consumer proxy* is generated for this purpose. This communication is always synchronous and point-to-point.

- ► **Java Proxy Runtime**
  The Java proxies are used to integrate Java applications with the SAP NetWeaver PI Integration Server. Using the Java proxy runtime (JPR), you can receive or send messages to the Integration Server. The JPR supports Java EE applications on the AS Java using Enterprise JavaBeans 3.0. Synchronous and asynchronous outbound and inbound communication is possible with proxy beans.

  The JPR can be installed on the AS Java release 6.40 or higher. The *messaging system* must also be installed on the AS Java. The messaging system is part of the Adapter Framework and is used by the JPR to send messages to the Integration Server. The messaging system implements queuing services, persistence services, and monitoring services.

  On the receiver side the JPR proxy server listens for inbound messages from the messaging system. The JPR proxy server forwards the message to the cor-

---

4 In prior SAP NetWeaver PI releases the consumer proxy is called a "client proxy," and the provider proxy is called a "server proxy."

responding server bean using the Java proxy runtime. This bean must be registered in the JPR registry to determine the server bean that is assigned to the service interface. It calls the implementing class on the AS Java using the generated provider proxy interface.

On the sender side, users need to develop a Java client that makes use of the proxy interface to send or receive messages from the Integration Server. The Java proxy generation generates all Java classes necessary for a consumer proxy including the Enterprise Java class bean. To send messages, you use the EJB calls. The consumer proxy bean calls the corresponding method of the consumer proxy class for communication. This method generates a message from the call and forwards it to the Integration Server by using the messaging system via HTTP.

2.5.3   XI Message Protocol

In SAP NetWeaver PI application systems are connected using XML messaging and web standard protocols. Internally an SAP-specific implementation of SOAP is used. Messages received at the Integration Server are processed through a defined series of steps called *pipeline services*. When a message is received at the Integration Server, the message is examined and all of the valid configurations maintained in the Integration Directory for that message are executed.

SAP NetWeaver PI uses an SAP-specific implementation of SOAP with header extensions and payloads. The XI message protocol is based on the note "SOAP Message with Attachments" from the W3C organization. Figure 2.34 shows the structure of an SAP NetWeaver PI message.

By extending the SOAP standard, SAP NetWeaver PI is able to enhance the basic capabilities of Web services to include additional value-added functionality. SAP NetWeaver PI messages contain extensions to the basic SOAP header such as an **Error Header** or **Hop List** that allow SAP NetWeaver PI to augment the basic functionality offered by the SOAP systems.

The SOAP header of a message contains all of the important information that the Integration Server requires to forward the message, whereas the payload contains the actual business data. The *payload (trace)* traces the processing of the message. You can also append an unlimited number of attachments to the message before it is sent. Attachments are optional and typically composed of non-XML data, for example, pictures, text documents, or binary data.

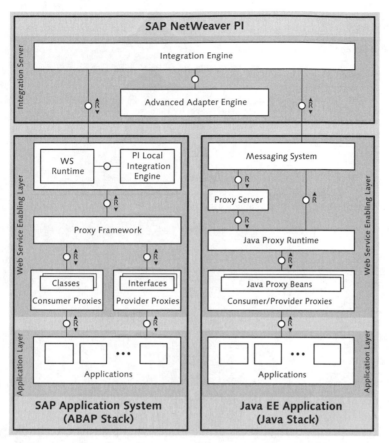

Figure 2.33 Proxy Runtime in the ABAP Stack and in the Java Stack

The information in the message header must have the correct format for the message to be processed on the Integration Server. The payload is not touched unless a mapping needs to be executed.

2.5.4 Pipeline Steps in SAP NetWeaver PI

In the Integration Server, SAP NetWeaver PI messages are passed through a series of processing steps called *pipeline steps*. *Pipeline* is the term used to refer to all the steps that are performed during the processing of a message in the Integration Server. The individual processing steps of a pipeline are called *pipeline elements*. A *pipeline service* is an ABAP object class that performs a particular processing step on a message. All of the messages that are received at the Integration Server are

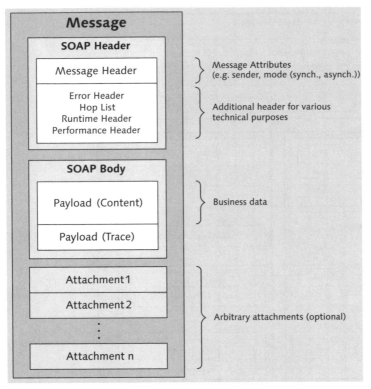

Figure 2.34 Structure of a Message in the Integration Engine

processed in a consistent way regardless of the underlying platform, technology, or vendor of the application systems involved in the message exchange.

SAP NetWeaver PI messages are processed through the set of pipeline steps as listed below, each of which performs a specific operation on the message.

- The *XML validation inbound request* step performs schema validation on the inbound message.

- The *receiver determination* step determines which system should participate in an exchange with the incoming message.

- The *interface determination* step determines which interface should receive a message for each receiver system.

- The *receiver grouping* step groups the receivers in case multiple receivers have been configured.

- The *message split* step instantiates a new message for each receiver if multiple receivers are found.

- The *request message mapping* step calls the mapping program to transform the message structure to the receiver format.

- The *technical routing* step binds a specific destination and protocol to the message.

- The *XML validation outbound request* step performs the schema validation on the outbound message if the XML validation is configured.

- The *call adapter* step sends the transformed message to the specified adapter or proxy.

The messages that have been processed through the pipeline can be monitored using SAP Transaction SXMB_MONI as shown in Figure 2.35.

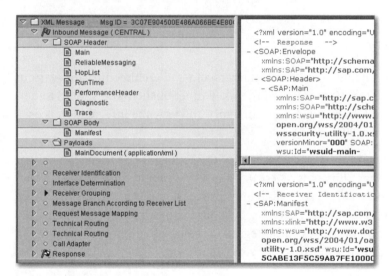

Figure 2.35 Monitoring of an SAP NetWeaver PI message via Transaction SXMB_MONI

2.5.5 Quality of Service

In SAP NetWeaver PI the sender of a message uses the attribute *quality of service* to determine how a message is delivered. The following types of quality of service are supported:

▶ **Best Effort (BE)**
In this quality of service the message is sent synchronously. The sender waits for a response before it continues processing and further processing is blocked until a response is received.

▶ **Exactly once (EO)**
In this quality of service the message is sent asynchronously. All asynchronous messages are persisted on the Integration Server and can be resent if there is a problem with the initial send. The Integration Engine and Adapter Engine guarantee that the message is sent and processed exactly once.

▶ **Exactly once in order (EOIO)**
The quality of service EOIO is used in scenarios where the sequence of message matters. It ensures that asynchronous messages arrive in exactly the same order at the receiver as they were sent from the sender.

2.6 Summary

At the end of this chapter you should understand the architecture and various components of SAP NetWeaver PI and their key functionality. You should understand the concept of System Landscape directory and how the information is used in the SAP NetWeaver PI.

You should understand the basic concepts of the Enterprise Services Repository and the various design time-objects created in it. You should understand the service interface objects, data types, modeling concepts, and the various mappings available in SAP NetWeaver PI. This chapter should also helps you understand the concept of integration processes and integration scenarios and how to import and export various objects in Enterprise Services Repository.

You should understand the various configuration-time objects and activities of SAP NetWeaver PI and how to configure collaboration profiles, logical routings, and collaboration agreements using various configuration wizards.

You should understand the basic concepts of message processing, XI-SOAP message format, and various runtime engines available within SAP NetWeaver PI.

This chapter covers the concepts of adapters and the Adapter Framework within SAP NetWeaver Process Integration and discusses in detail the Java EE Adapter Engine and the connectivity to various systems (SAP and non-SAP) using different technical and third-party adapters.

3 Adapter Concepts

SAP NetWeaver Process Integration provides a wide range of adapters that allow communication with many SAP and non-SAP systems using various protocols. Applications based on the SAP Web Application Server 6.20 or higher can communicate with SAP NetWeaver PI via the native XI-SOAP (see Figure 2.34) format using proxies. All other applications can communicate with SAP NetWeaver PI via adapters. These adapters can be used to convert XML-based messages to the specific protocols and formats of the respective external systems and vice versa.

3.1 Overview

SAP NetWeaver PI provides an *Adapter Framework* for effecting this communication. The Adapter Framework enables the Integration Engine of SAP NetWeaver PI to talk to different application components and industry standards. It provides interfaces for configuration, management, and monitoring of the adapters. The Adapter Framework is also open to customers and partners to develop their own adapters.

The *Adapter Engine* is based on the Adapter Framework and is the runtime component for adapter communication. During installation, the Adapter Engine is automatically installed on the Integration Server and is called the *central Adapter Engine*. The majority of the adapters run on the central Adapter Engine. It covers the conversion of the majority of collaborative processes within a system landscape. The Adapter Engine can also be installed separately on another host (*noncentral Adapter Engine*) and still be configured, managed, and monitored centrally. The noncentral Adapter Engine can be used in scenarios that require working closer to the application systems. This may be necessary if a system is separated from the Integration Server by a firewall. Both the central and noncentral Adapter Engines can be configured centrally in the Integration Directory of SAP NetWeaver PI.

As discussed in Section 2.5 Process Integration Runtime, the *Advanced Adapter Engine* (AAE) has evolved out of the Adapter Engine of previous releases of SAP NetWeaver PI. In addition to the standard Adapter Engine capabilities, it provides end-to-end message processing locally within the adapters without invoking the Integration Engine. The AAE provides mapping and routing for these processes locally. This enhanced feature is mainly used in scenarios that involve local processing and provides a substantial improvement in performance. The local processing can be implemented for all adapters of the AAE apart from the RNIF adapters and the CIDX adapter.

> **Note**
>
> As of release 7.1 of SAP NetWeaver PI we refer to the Adapter Engine as the Advanced Adapter Engine.

Adapters allow connectivity to SAP and non-SAP applications in a heterogeneous landscape. These adapters are used to integrate not only existing SAP solutions through IDoc and BAPI interfaces, but also non-SAP systems through file, messaging, database, and Web service interfaces.

The Integration Server comes with three built-in adapters (IDoc, HTTP, Web services runtime), whereas all other adapters are hosted by the Advanced Adapter Engine. The adapters in SAP NetWeaver PI are divided into the following categories depending on their integration approach:

- ▶ **Application adapters**
  Application Adapters are used to integrate with popular industry applications that can be easily reused. Examples of such adapters are IDoc and RFC adapters that allow integration with SAP systems.

- ▶ **Technical adapters**
  Technical adapters are not application specific but protocol specific. These adapters are more generic and reusable and are meant for integration using the open communication protocols. Examples of such adapters are JDBC, JMS, File/FTP, Mail, Marketplace, SOAP, and others.

▶ **Industry standard adapters**
Industry standard adapters facilitate communication using vertical industry standards such as RosettaNet, Chem eStandards, and others. Examples of such adapters are the RNIF adapter and the CIDX adapter.

▶ **Third-party adapters**
In addition to providing different adapters for connectivity, SAP also relies on an ecosystem of partners to provide adapters for other applications or industry standards. These partner adapters are sold and delivered through SAP. Examples of such adapters are application, technical, and industry standard adapters from SEEBURGER, iWay, and Informatica.

SAP also provides a *Partner Connectivity Kit* (PCK), which uses the Adapter Framework for enabling smaller business partners to communicate in the native XI-SOAP format.

In this chapter we discuss all adapters delivered by SAP as well as the PCK in more detail, followed by a discussion of integration with other EAI tool providers. We start with a closer look at the architecture of the Adapter Engine and the underlying Adapter Framework.

3.2   Architectural Overview

In Section 2.5.1 Integration Server, we discussed the different engines available within the Integration Server. In Figure 2.32 we saw an overview of the high-level architecture and the connection points to the different external systems. Now we want to drill down into the *Advanced Adapter Engine* (AAE) in more detail as it is shown in Figure 3.1. Here we can see that any communication between the Integration Server and external systems (SAP and non-SAP) takes place via adapters. These adapters can reside in a number of different places:

▶ **Adapters built within the Plain Java SE Adapter Engine**
The Plain Java SE Adapter Engine was already available with release 2.0 of SAP NetWeaver XI and is still supported for upgrade compatibility purposes. Because these adapters play no role in any B2B collaboration scenarios, we do not discuss them further.

▶ **Adapters built within the Integration Engine**
A few adapters have been built within the Integration Engine. We will discuss each of these adapters in detail in Section 3.4.1 Adapters on the Integration Server.

▶ **Adapters built within the Adapter Framework**
The majority of adapters are built within the Adapter Framework. As you can see in Figure 3.1, the Adapter Framework is used both in the Advanced Adapter Engine (AAE) and in the Partner Connectivity Kit (PCK). Therefore, the AAE and the PCK both offer the same set of adapters with the same functionality. As you can also see in Figure 3.1, the *central* Advanced Adapter Engine is always installed as part of the Integration Server, although additional *noncentral* installations of the AAE are also possible.

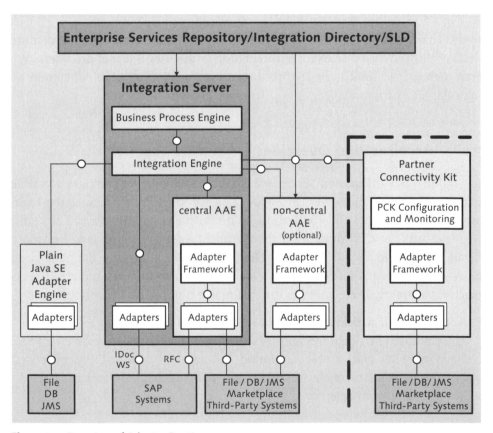

Figure 3.1 Overview of Adapter Runtime

In our architectural discussion we only focus on the concepts of how adapters are built and processed within the Adapter Framework for a number of reasons:

▸ The majority of adapters available are built using the Adapter Framework, including all certified adapters provided by third-party vendors.

▸ The Adapter Framework provides a concept for custom enhancements without any modifications. This capability can be important for implementation projects using industry standards with specific message protocol requirements.

▸ You can build your own adapters using the Adapter Framework.

Because we discuss the PCK separately in Section 3.5 Partner Connectivity Kit, we focus here on the Adapter Framework used within the Advanced Adapter Engine.

3.2.1 Advanced Adapter Engine

The Advanced Adapter Engine (AAE) is the central configuration tool for all the adapters used within SAP NetWeaver PI. The Adapter Engine provides connectivity between the SAP NetWeaver PI runtime and other application systems. You use different adapters in the Adapter Engine to convert various protocols and data formats into the message format used by the Integration Server and vice versa. Because the Adapter Framework has its own queuing and logging services, the Adapter Engine can run temporarily without a connection to the Integration Server and still provide guaranteed messaging to and from connected application systems.

The message queue and the message store of the Adapter Engine provide support for guaranteed delivery. The configuration of the Adapter Engine is done centrally in the Integration Directory, using meta-data of the adapters stored in the Enterprise Services Repository. There are interfaces for configuring and administering the Adapter Engine and built-in security features.

The Adapter Engine is fully integrated with the SAP NetWeaver PI landscape. It has central configuration of connections to application systems through appropriate adapters. It has central administration and monitoring capabilities over adapters through the Runtime Workbench and the SAP NetWeaver Administrator.

3.2.2 Adapter Framework

As we can see in Figure 3.1, the *Adapter Framework* is part of the Advanced Adapter Engine and the PCK and provides common functionality for both of them. The Adapter Framework is responsible for communication between the SAP NetWeaver PI Integration Server and any SAP or non-SAP system. It provides interfaces for configuring, managing, and monitoring adapters. The Adapter Framework is used to connect any external system to SAP NetWeaver PI.

The Adapter Framework is based on AS Java and the J2EE Connector Architecture (JCA). JCA is a widely accepted standard, making it easier for partners to develop adapters for SAP NetWeaver PI. The Adapter Framework offers a consistent interface for configuring connections through adapters and provides comprehensive integration for central configuration, administration, and monitoring of deployed adapters. The Adapter Framework inherits properties and features such as scalability, clustering, high availability, thread management, and others. It can operate temporarily disconnected from the Integration Server and still provide exactly-once messaging to and from a connected application system. Both the configuration and the administration are handled centrally, allowing working with all the deployed adapters from one single point of access. Figure 3.2 gives an overview of the architecture of the Adapter Framework.

Let's now take a look at the building blocks and the process flow within the Adapter Framework in detail:

❶ As mentioned above, the Adapter Framework is based on AS Java and the J2EE Connector Architecture (JCA). Therefore, all adapters in the Adapter Framework must be J2EE Connector Architecture 1.0-compliant. The Adapter Framework communicates with an adapter using JCA connections and the JCA Common Client Interface (CCI) via the *JCA 1.0 Framework*. JCA does not define the communication direction from adapter to Adapter Framework. Therefore, the Adapter Framework is called by the adapter with a standard Enterprise Java-Bean (EJB) 2.0 session bean.

❷ When a message from the Integration Server is received in the Adapter Framework by the messaging service, the corresponding module chain is selected in the module processor for further processing based on the receiver information. The Adapter Framework contains two default module chains:

▸ One for the sender/inbound direction
▸ One for the receiver/outbound direction

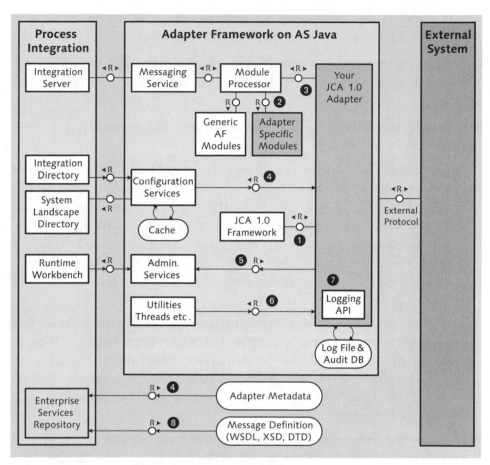

Figure 3.2 Architecture of the Adapter Framework

You can use these default module chains for your adapter if the entire message processing is executed within the adapter. You can enhance the default module chains with customer-specific modules. The module processor controls the steps in the module chain by calling generic and, if defined, adapter-specific modules.

❸ The last module in the module chain forwards the message to the adapter using JCA CCI. The adapter transfers the message to the connected system. Message processing in the sender/inbound direction proceeds in a similar way. In this case, the adapter calls the module processor in the form of an EJB local session bean and transfers the message object either as an SAP NetWeaver PI message or in its own format. In the latter case, conversion to an SAP NetWeaver PI message must then take place in an adapter-specific module.

In addition to the message exchange, the Adapter Framework provides other interfaces. Some of them must be supported by each adapter some of them are optional.

❹ The *Configuration Services* access the configuration data of the adapter and the information from the SLD:

▶ The configuration data for the adapter is managed in the Integration Directory. It contains technical data for the adapter and collaboration agreements for B2B scenarios. The configuration data is synchronized with the Adapter Framework using the CPA cache. Adapters can poll their configuration data or subscribe to data changes. To use a new adapter type, the adapter must first be described in the form of adapter metadata, which is then loaded into the Enterprise Services Repository. This must be done before the adapter can be used.

▶ The System Landscape Directory manages and saves data from all (SAP and non-SAP) components that a customer has in its system landscape. The synchronization with the SLD is executed principally in the configuration service. The respective adapter does not have to be able to communicate with the SLD. An Adapter Framework service registers the adapter with the SLD based on the adapter metadata.

❺ The *Administration Services* use the Runtime Workbench as a central tool for monitoring and administration in SAP NetWeaver PI. Monitoring covers the monitoring of message processing and the status of communication channels, processes, and components. Administration covers the scheduling of jobs such as archiving jobs, the periodic and manual starting and stopping of communication channels, and the restarting of messages.

❻ The Adapter Framework provides various service APIs such as thread manager and transaction manager as *utilities* that support adapter implementation.

❼ The Adapter Framework includes a message audit log API as part of the *Logging API*, which is used internally by the Adapter Framework components. Audit log entries can be written to a database table.

❽ Messages that are transported through the Adapter Framework contain the business document in an XML-encoded format. The describing XSD, DTD, and WSDL documents (message metadata) are related to the sender business system. If the structure of the document in the sender system differs from that of the receiver system, the message must be mapped. The message metadata is required to perform the mapping at design time. This data is usually located in the Enterprise Services Repository. Before message exchange, you must load the message metadata to the Enterprise Services Repository manually.

3.3   Interoperability with other EAI Tools

In today's world of emerging and evolving technologies, interoperability is one of the most challenging issues facing enterprises. The success of an *enterprise application integration* (EAI) relies on the set of interoperable technologies that determine how well various applications in an organization can be implemented, interfaced, and integrated. Interoperability it is the ability of diverse systems or components to exchange information and to use the information that has been exchanged.

3.3.1   Interoperability and EAI Products

Web services along with standards such as XML, SOAP, UDDI, and WSDL have gathered interest in many enterprises as a mechanism to flexibly integrate applications. In this integration process applications expose services to other applications, which use these services without any knowledge of how the other application is implemented. These Web services have grown in response to the need for a standardized way to cope with heterogeneity and create interoperability and compatibility among various web applications. They provide interoperability between software components that can communicate between different companies and can reside on different infrastructures.

The business functionalities available from SAP can easily be exposed by mere configuration as Web services via its traditional standard interfaces from the Java as well as the ABAP world, such as BAPIs, EJBs, Java classes, IDocs, function modules, and so on. Once application functionality has been made available as a Web service, any service consumer including those using a different platform can make use of this functionality by calling the Web service provider. On the other hand, SAP can also act as the client to consume external Web services running on different platforms (such as IBM and Microsoft). SAP NetWeaver thus allows companies to extend their solutions by exposing as well as integrating Web services. These Web services can be consumed in a point-to-point fashion where business functionality is directly exposed to a Web service consumer. When a Web service call that results in a more complex scenario in which the service call has to be brokered with additional routing and mapping steps, the mediated scenario can be used.

SAP NetWeaver PI offers several interoperability options with other EAI products such as IBM WebSphere Business integrator, Microsoft BizTalk, BEA WebLogic integration, SeeBeyond Egate Integrator, Tibco Active Enterprise, Vitria Business-Ware, and so on. SAP NetWeaver supports the same technology and Web service standards as other EAI products such as XML, SOAP, WSDL, and UDDI. One of the main interoperability options provided with SAP NetWeaver PI is the exchange of metadata using open standards. With this option SAP NetWeaver PI allows you to export and import metadata, which is stored in the Enterprise Services Repository, such as interface descriptions (WSDL) and business process descriptions (BPEL).

The other interoperability option is the usage of adapters. SAP NetWeaver PI delivers much of its openness through technical adapters that facilitate interoperability with other enterprise application integration infrastructures. Some of these adapters (such as JMS, SOAP, and HTTP(S)) are ideally suited for interoperating out-of-the-box with the runtime environment of other EAI products. The JMS adapter connects to all JMS-enabled messaging systems (such as MQSeries or Sonic MQ) to the Integration server. The SOAP adapter enables the exchange of SOAP messages between the Integration Server and remote clients or providers of Web services. The plain HTTP(S) adapter enables application systems to communicate with the Integration Server and to exchange business data via HTTP without a SOAP envelope around the HTTP payload.

SAP NetWeaver supports open standards, industry de facto standards, and a variety of specifications associated with Web services to interoperate with other EAI products. Among others, the Web service specifications are built on top of XML and SOAP standards and provide interoperable protocols for security and reliable messaging. These standards and protocols play a key role in providing interoperable solutions in the most demanding IT environments of SAP customers. The following standards bodies mainly deal with these standards:

► **World Wide Web Consortium (W3C)**
The World Wide Web Consortium is the international standards organization

for the World Wide Web. It plays a major role in standardizing the basic specifications for Web services including XML, SOAP, and WSDL. SAP along with other vendors has been involved in driving the SOAP specification, the Web Services Description Language, Web Services Addressing, and the Web Services Architecture Working Group.

▶ **Organization for the Advancement of Structured Information Standards (OASIS)**
OASIS focuses on developing and adopting Web service specifications such as Web Services Business Execution Language (WSBPEL), Web Service Security (WSS), and UDDI. SAP collaborates with other industry leaders on the technical aspects of these interoperability issues.

▶ **Web Services Interoperability Organization (WS-I)**
SAP is one of the founding members of WS-I, along with Microsoft, IBM, and other industry leaders. This group primarily promotes interoperability across platforms. WS-I promotes the use of Web services by helping companies select and interpret Web services specifications and develop best practices. These specifications and best practices are used to develop, deploy, and integrate interoperable business applications. WS-I provides interoperability guidance for core Web Services specifications such as SOAP, WSDL, and UDDI.

SAP NetWeaver PI supports the existing or upcoming Web service standards from these standard bodies with the goal of enabling interoperability with other applications. Some of these standards are discussed in detail below:

▶ **Web Services Policy (WS-Policy) and WS-Policy Attachment**
WS-Policy is an initiative undertaken by a number of industry leaders including SAP, with the goal of addressing interoperability issues surrounding the description and communication of Web services policies. A policy is a collection of policy assertions that describe one or more characteristics that a Web service provider requires from a Web service consumer. By using the XML, SOAP, and WSDL extensibility models, WS-Policy provides a general-purpose model and a corresponding syntax to describe and communicate the policies of a Web service. The *WS-Policy Attachment* defines how to attach WS-Policy assertions to WSDL documents and UDDI descriptions.

▶ **WS Addressing and WS Reliable Messaging**
WS Addressing defines two interoperable constructs that convey information that is typically provided by transport protocols and messaging systems. These constructs normalize this underlying information into a uniform format that

can be processed independently of transport or application. *WS Reliable Messaging* describes a protocol that allows messages to be delivered reliably between distributed applications in the presence of software component, system, or network failures.

▶ **WS Metadata Exchange**

Web services use metadata to describe what other end points need to know to interact with them. SAP and other industry leaders collaborate on the *WS Metadata Exchange* initiative, which ensures interoperability for the exchange of Web services metadata. By using the XML, SOAP, and WSDL extensibility models, WS Metadata Exchange provides a general-purpose metadata exchange model and bindings to most prominent Web services description formats such as XML, XML Schema, WSDL, and WS-Policy.

▶ **WS Security and WS Security Policy**

WS Security describes extensions to SOAP that allow for message-level authentication using binary tokens, digital signatures for integrity, and content encryption for message confidentiality. *WS Security Policy* defines security assertions detailing a Web service's requirements that the Web service consumer can meet.

▶ **Security Assertion Markup Language (SAML)**

SAML is a suite of specifications that define interoperability between different security domains. It enables XML-based exchange of security information related to a user between servers over HTTP. The information for authentication and authorization can be exchanged using SAML in the backend without users noticing the exchange. SAML acknowledges that each platform has its own mechanism for authentication and authorization. Consequently, user security information is exchanged in a standard XML-based structure.

SAP NetWeaver supports these and many other open standards and provides complete interoperability with the Microsoft .NET, Microsoft BizTalk Server, and IBM WebSphere development platforms. The interoperability with IBM WebSphere and Microsoft BizTalk Server is discussed in detail in the following sections.

3.3.2 Interoperability with IBM WebSpere

The process integration offering of SAP includes an open, standards-based integration broker and comprehensive business process management. IBM's offering includes a variety of products combined under the brand name WebSphere Business Integration. The JMS adapter and the SOAP adapter are suitable for IBM WebSphere Business Integration, providing off-the-shelf technical interoperability with the runtime environment of two integration solutions at the message level. The following list shows various interoperability options of SAP Netweaver PI with IBM WebSphere:

- ▶ **JMS-based interoperability**
  The SAP NetWeaver PI JMS adapter allows interoperability with JMS-enabled messaging systems such as IBM WebSphere MQ. By applying JMS and using WebSphere MQ, a business application that runs on SAP NetWeaver can be integrated with one that runs on IBM WebSphere. The JMS adapter supports next-to message parsing and serialization, which means a message will be delivered only once, and in a queue arranged according to when it was created. JMS provides for asynchronous, bidirectional delivery of messages between SAP NetWeaver PI and WebSphere MQ.

- ▶ **SOAP-based interoperability**
  To be able to interoperate with WebSphere Interchange Server (formerly Crossworlds), SAP NetWeaver PI offers an adapter that allows connectivity via SOAP. SOAP mainly provides a synchronous way to interact between the two integration infrastructures. Like the JMS adapter, SOAP allows bidirectional messaging. Best-of delivery and guaranteed-exactly-once delivery options are available when asynchronous usage occurs. The benefits of interoperability in both cases include a minimum number of point-to-point connections, centralized integration knowledge, allowance for ease of change, and the orchestration of processes that span many technologies.

- ▶ **JCA-based interoperability**
  SAP NetWeaver PI offers an Adapter Framework based on JCA that allows third-party providers, major software vendors, and others to develop resource adapters that plug into it. IBM WebSphere Business Integration offers a number of JCA adapters for connectivity to non-SAP backend systems. The IBM WebSphere adapters can easily and seamlessly accept the Adapter Framework. IBM and SAP will jointly evolve this technology and architecture to ensure open, standards-based connectivity not only between SAP NetWeaver PI and WebSphere Business Integration but also to other SAP and non-SAP applications.

▶ **Business process management**
Business process management (BPM) includes the orchestration, design, execution, and monitoring of business processes that span multiple systems or applications. The challenge for software vendors is to come up with business processes that include applications built by other vendors. As various BPM tools adapt to the standards, business process design that involves applications from multiple vendors becomes possible. SAP NetWeaver PI supports the open standard Business Process Execution Language for Web Services (BPEL4WS). It will give BPM tools the capability they need to import and export descriptions of business process sequences to and from other BPM tools and facilitate interoperability between SAP NetWeaver and IBM WebSphere.

3.3.3 Interoperability with the Microsoft BizTalk Server

SAP NetWeaver and Microsoft .NET support advanced Web services protocols, and this support is the basis of technical interoperability between the two architectures. The principal focus of interoperability is on SAP NetWeaver PI and on the Microsoft BizTalk Server. Both products offer interoperability based on existing open standards such as Web Services Reliable Messaging (WS-RM), SOAP, and BPEL4WS.

The enterprise services support makes it possible to integrate both SAP NetWeaver and Microsoft BizTalk Server in an enterprise service-oriented architecture without having specific SAP NetWeaver PI or Microsoft BizTalk Server adapters in place. The Adapter Framework in SAP NetWeaver PI and on .NET in the Microsoft BizTalk server extends the value of both products to a variety of industry-specific solutions, such as RosettaNet and CIDX, as well as to horizontal (EDI) solutions such as ANSI X12 and EDIFACT. The following list shows various interoperability options of SAP NetWeaver PI with Microsoft BizTalk Server:

▶ **SOAP-based interoperability**
To be able to interoperate with the Microsoft BizTalk Server, SAP NetWeaver PI offers an adapter that allows connectivity via SOAP. SOAP mainly provides a synchronous way to interact between the two integration infrastructures and allows bidirectional messaging. Best-of delivery and guaranteed-exactly-once delivery options are available when asynchronous usage occurs. Reliable messaging can be achieved using the WS-RM protocol with the exactly-once (EO) and exactly-once-in-order (EOIO) delivery of messages.

▶ **HTTP-based interoperability**
Besides the SOAP adapter, SAP NetWeaver PI offers a plain HTTP adapter that allows connectivity via HTTP without a SOAP envelope around the HTTP payload to interoperate with the Microsoft BizTalk server. This way of communication covers a synchronous message transfer without transaction support avoiding the overhead of SOAP data. BizTalk with the accompanied HTTP adapter enables data exchange with XML payload in both directions.

3.4 Adapters

The adapters offered by SAP NetWeaver PI allow communication with different kinds of application systems using various protocols. In this section we give you a brief introduction of the features and capabilities of each of these adapters. These adapters can be used for connectivity and exchange of information between various SAP and non-SAP applications. For more information on these adapters go to the SAP Help Portal under *http://help.sap.com*.

3.4.1 Adapters on the Integration Server

As we saw in Figure 3.1, some adapters are not built using the Adapter Framework but within the Integration Engine. Apart from the HTTP adapter, these adapters are used for communication with SAP application systems.

Plain HTTP Adapter

Many application systems can communicate using the Hypertext Transfer Protocol (HTTP). The plain HTTP adapter enables application systems to communicate with the Integration Server and to exchange business data using HTTP without a SOAP envelope around the HTTP payload.

The *plain HTTP adapter* is part of the Integration Engine. It receives XML messages from an external business system by means of plain HTTP. It converts this message into the SAP NetWeaver PI message protocol and forwards the message to the Integration Server for further processing. To forward a message to an external business system, the HTTP adapter receives the XML message from the Integration Server and converts it into a message with plain HTTP, which is then sent to the external business system.

HTTP is an open and widely used protocol, which allows SAP NetWeaver PI to communicate with any other HTTP Server via the plain HTTP adapter.

The capabilities of the HTTP adapter are listed in Table 3.1.

Feature	Capability
Mode	Synchronous and asynchronous
Message protocol	XI payload (see Figure 2.34) in HTTP body
Transport protocol	HTTP, HTTPS
Quality of service	Best effort (BE)
	Exactly once (EO)
	Exactly once in order (EOIO) if a GUID is specified in the URL
Attachments	Not supported

Table 3.1 Capabilities of the HTTP Adapter

IDoc Adapter

IDocs (intermediate documents) are an SAP proprietary data format used to exchange business data with external systems. The IDoc adapter enables the exchange of IDoc messages with connected SAP applications.

The *IDoc adapter* resides on the ABAP stack of the Integration Server. In addition to the application data, IDocs also contain control information such as logical system name, port definition, partner information, and others for technical processing. The IDoc adapter uses this information to build a SOAP message header with information for the Integration Server.

For an inbound message the IDoc adapter converts an incoming IDoc to the IDoc XML format and forwards it to the Integration Engine for further processing. For an outbound message the IDoc adapter converts the IDoc XML to the native IDoc format and sends the IDoc to the identified receiver system using the standard IDoc interface. The IDoc adapter also enables IDocs to be sent in batch mode. It is capable of splitting IDocs sent in batch mode into individual IDocs and forwarding them to the Integration Engine for further processing.

The capabilities of the IDoc adapter are listed in Table 3.2.

Feature	Capability
Mode	Asynchronous
Message protocol	IDoc
Transport protocol	IDoc
Quality of service	Exactly once (EO)
	Exactly once in order (EOIO) for systems based on SAP NetWeaver Application Server 6.40 and higher
Attachments	Not supported

Table 3.2 Capabilities of the IDoc Adapter

XI Adapter

The *XI adapter* supports the native message protocol used by the Integration Engine of SAP NetWeaver PI and is used to exchange XML messages between Integration Engines or between the Integration Server and the Partner Connectivity Kit (PCK). It is used for communication using the proxy runtime and supports both XI3.0 and XI2.0 protocols. The XI2.0 protocol is used for communication between the Integration Engine and the Adapter Engine based on the SAP NetWeaver XI 2.0 release (earlier version of the SAP NetWeaver PI). For all other communications the XI3.0 protocol is used.

The capabilities of the XI adapter are listed in Table 3.3.

Feature	Capability
Mode	Synchronous and asynchronous
Message protocol	XI2.0, XI3.0
Transport protocol	HTTP, HTTPS
Quality of service	Best effort (BE)
	Exactly once (EO)
	Exactly once in order (EOIO)
Attachments	Supported

Table 3.3 Capabilities of the XI Adapter

WS Adapter

SAP NetWeaver PI introduces a new adapter type for Web services with release 7.1 of SAP NetWeaver PI. The *WS adapter* resides on the Integration Engine of SAP NetWeaver PI. The Web services runtime translates between the XI protocol and Web service messages, which rely on the Web service reliable messaging (WS-RM) protocol. The WS adapter is used to exchange messages between the systems that use the Web services runtime to communicate with each other.

The capabilities of the WS adapter are listed in Table 3.4.

Feature	Capability
Mode	Synchronous and asynchronous
Message protocol	WS
Transport protocol	HTTP, HTTPS
Quality of service	Best effort (BE)
	Exactly once (EO)
	Exactly once in order (EOIO)
Attachments	Supported

Table 3.4 Capabilities of the WS Adapter

With the WS adapter it is possible to configure a direct communication between service providers and service consumers without having the messages routed through the Integration Server. If you require the enhanced routing and mapping characteristics of the Integration Server, you can configure the WS adapter such that the messages are routed through the Integration Server.

3.4.2 Adapters on the Advanced Adapter Engine

As discussed in Section 3.2 Architectural Overview, the following list of adapters on the Advanced Adapter Engine is built using the Adapter Framework. These adapters are available in both the central AAE and the noncentral AAE, as well as in the PCK.

RFC Adapter

A remote function call (RFC) is an application programming interface native to SAP applications that allows you to invoke function modules remotely. It allows remote calls between two SAP systems, or between an SAP and a non-SAP system. Because SAP systems up to release 4.6 are not able to exchange data by using XML messages and HTTP, you can only connect such systems to the Integration Server by using the RFC adapter or the IDoc adapter.

The *RFC adapter* converts RFC data to an XML message format (RFC-XML) or the other way around. It supports existing SAP systems from release 3.1I or higher. When receiving an RFC call from the SAP system, the RFC adapter transforms the RFC data into a RFC-XML message and forwards it to the integration engine or PCK for further processing. In the outbound processing, the RFC adapter accepts the RFC-XML message from the integration engine, or the PCK transforms it into a valid RFC call and executes the call.

Unlike the IDoc adapter, the RFC adapter resides on the Adapter Engine and not on the Integration Engine. In addition to the monitoring tool on the Integration Server, the messages sent by the RFC adapter can also be monitored via adapter monitoring and communication channel monitoring in the Runtime Workbench of SAP NetWeaver PI.

The capabilities of the RFC adapter are listed in Table 3.5.

Feature	Capability
Mode	Synchronous and asynchronous
Message protocol	RFC-XML
Transport protocol	RFC
Quality of service	Best effort (BE)
	Exactly once (EO)
	Exactly once in order (EOIO)
Attachments	Not supported

Table 3.5 Capabilities of the RFC Adapter

SOAP Adapter

SOAP is an XML-based protocol to exchange messages between business applications over HTTP. A SOAP message is an XML document that consists of a SOAP envelope with a header and a body. The structure of the message and the connection parameters are stored in a Web services definition language (WSDL) file. SAP NetWeaver PI allows you to generate a WSDL file from an interface definition or upload an existing WSDL file from other applications. The message exchange is performed by the *SOAP adapter,* which can transform a SOAP message to a SAP NetWeaver PI message and the other way around.

The SOAP adapter allows the exchange of SOAP messages between remote clients or Web service servers and the Integration Server or the PCK. It provides a runtime environment that includes various SOAP components for the processing of SOAP messages. The SOAP adapter receives a message from the remote client or Web services provider, converts SOAP into the XI message protocol, and forwards the message to the Integration Server for further processing. In the outbound processing, the SOAP adapter receives the message from the Integration Server, converts it into a SOAP message, and forwards it to the remote client or Web services provider.

With release 7.1 of SAP NetWeaver PI, the Axis Framework[1] is supported in the SOAP adapter. You can use Axis version 1.4 in the SOAP adapter for exchanging SOAP messages. Handlers of the Axis framework process steps at runtime that process and forward a message. You can assemble them into processing chains like modules in the module processor.

The capabilities of the SOAP adapter are listed in Table 3.6.

Feature	Capability
Mode	Synchronous and asynchronous
Message protocol	SOAP, Axis
Transport protocol	HTTP, Servlet, task as sender
	HTTP, SMTP, file, generic as receiver

Table 3.6 Capabilities of the SOAP Adapter

---

1 The Axis (Apache extensible Interaction System) framework is provided by the Apache Software Foundation.

Feature	Capability
Quality of service	Best effort (BE)
	Exactly once (EO)
	Exactly once in order (EOIO)
Attachments	Supported

Table 3.6 Capabilities of the SOAP Adapter (cont.)

File/FTP Adapter

Many external and legacy systems cannot exchange data by means of XML and HTTP. However, they can exchange data via a file interface. The *File/FTP adapter* in SAP NetWeaver PI enables you to connect to such systems and exchange data with the Integration Server or the PCK by means of a file interface or an FTP server. This adapter resides on the Adapter Engine of SAP NetWeaver PI.

When reading a file from a legacy system, the file content can be sent to the Integration Server unaltered. If the data contains a format other than an XML file, it has to be converted to an XML message. The file adapter converts this message to an XML message and forwards it to the Integration Engine or the PCK for further processing. In the outbound processing, the file adapter accepts an XML message from the Integration Engine or the PCK and forwards it to the file interface of the legacy or external system. In this process, the file adapter can put the XML message into a file unchanged or it can convert it to the text file format specific to the receiving system. The conversion rules for transforming the message from text file to the XML message and vice versa can be defined as part of the communication channel definition in the Integration Directory.

The Integration Server or the PCK can only process text files based on the UTF-8 code page. The file adapter can convert any code page sent from the legacy or external systems into UTF-8 and can convert the code page sent from the Integration Server into any code page recognized by the receiving system. FTP connections of the file/FTP adapter can be secured by using FTPS, which is FTP over Secure Socket Layer (SSL)/Transport Layer Security (TLS). Other capabilities of the File/FTP adapter are listed in Table 3.7.

Feature	Capability
Mode	Synchronous and asynchronous
Message protocol	File, file content conversion
Transport protocol	File, FTP
Quality of service	Best effort (BE)
	Exactly once (EO)
	Exactly once in order (EOIO)
Attachments	Supported in the sender adapter

Table 3.7 Capabilities of the File/FTP Adapter

JDBC Adapter

Java database connectivity (JDBC) is used to connect Java applications with databases. It allows you to establish a connection with the database, send SQL statements, and process the results. The *JDBC adapter* of SAP NetWeaver PI enables the connection of database systems with the Integration Server or the PCK. The adapter converts database content to XML messages and the other way around.

To connect to a database system using the JDBC adapter, you must first install the JDBC driver for that database. The database content can be retrieved with any SQL statement including stored procedures. For content from the Integration Server or the PCK, a specific XML format is specified that allows SQL-insert, update, select, delete, or stored procedure statements to be processed. Any number of statements can be grouped together in one message. The content of a message is always retrieved or stored inside one database transaction.

The capabilities of the JDBC adapter are listed in Table 3.8.

Feature	Capability
Mode	Synchronous and asynchronous
Message protocol	XML SQL, native SQL
Transport protocol	JDBC

Table 3.8 Capabilities of the JDBC Adapter

Feature	Capability
Quality of service	Best effort (BE)
	Exactly once (EO)
	Exactly once in order (EOIO)
Attachments	Not supported

Table 3.8 Capabilities of the JDBC Adapter (cont.)

JMS Adapter

The Java messaging service (JMS) interface is used for accessing enterprise messaging systems. Using this interface, you can invoke the messaging services of WebSphere MQSeries, SonicMQ, and other popular messaging products. The *JMS adapter* of SAP NetWeaver PI is a JMS interface that enables you to connect messaging systems to the Integration Server or the PCK in order to exchange messages with these messaging products. Before you can use the JMS adapter, you must first install the relevant JMS driver.

External or legacy systems that are already connected to the JMS provider such as SonicMQ can be connected to the Integration Engine of SAP NetWeaver via the JMS adapter. In a typical scenario the JMS adapter receives the message from the JMS provider and forwards it to the Integration Engine or PCK for further processing. In outbound processing the JMS adapter receives the message from the Integration Engine or PCK and forwards it to the external receiver system via the JMS provider.

The capabilities of the JMS adapter are listed in Table 3.9.

Feature	Capability
Mode	Asynchronous
Message protocol	JMS
Transport protocol	Various JMS providers (e.g., SonicMQ, WebSphere MQ Series, Access)

Table 3.9 Capabilities of the JMS Adapter

Feature	Capability
Quality of service	Exactly once (EO)
	Exactly once in order (EOIO)
Attachments	Not supported

Table 3.9 Capabilities of the JMS Adapter (cont.)

Marketplace Adapter

The *Marketplace adapter* can be used to connect the Integration Server of SAP NetWeaver PI to marketplaces. It allows the exchange of messages by converting the SAP NetWeaver PI message format to the marketplace format Marketset Markup Language (MML), and vice versa.

The capabilities of the Marketplace adapter are listed in Table 3.10.

Feature	Capability
Mode	Synchronous and asynchronous
Message protocol	MML
Transport protocol	HTTP, HTTPS, JMS Sonic MQ
Quality of service	Best effort (BE)
	Exactly once (EO)
Attachments	Supported

Table 3.10 Capabilities of the Marketplace Adapter

Mail Adapter

The *Mail adapter* connects email servers to the Integration Server. The receiver Mail adapter converts SAP NetWeaver PI messages to emails and uses the Simple Mail Transfer Protocol (SMTP) or the Internet Message Access Protocol (IMAP) to transfer them to the email server. The sender Mail adapter uses the Internet Message Access Protocol (IMAP) or the Post Office Protocol Version 3 (POP3) to collect emails and convert them to SAP NetWeaver PI messages.

The capabilities of the Mail adapter are listed in Table 3.11.

Feature	Capability
Mode	Synchronous and asynchronous
Message protocol	XIALL, XIPAYLOAD
Transport protocol	IMAP4, POP3 as sender
	IMAP4, SMTP as receiver
Quality of service	Best effort (BE)
	Exactly once (EO)
	Exactly once in order (EOIO)
Attachments	Supported for message protocol XIPAYLOAD

Table 3.11 Capabilities of the Mail Adapter

SAP Business Connector Adapter

The *SAP Business Connector adapter* supports the B2B protocol of the SAP Business Connector, a middleware application based on the B2B Integration Server from WebMethods, which is based on HTTP. It enables you to replace a Business Connector with the Integration Server or PCK in scenarios where several SAP Business Connectors are used. It performs the translation between XI messages and HTTP calls of an SAP Business Connector that contain RFC calls in an XML format.

The capabilities of the SAP Business Connector adapter are listed in Table 3.12.

Feature	Capability
Mode	Synchronous and asynchronous
Message protocol	RFC XML, IDoc XML
Transport protocol	HTTP, HTTPS
Quality of service	Best effort (BE)
	Exactly once (EO)
Attachments	Not supported

Table 3.12 Capabilities of the SAP Business Connector Adapter

RosettaNet RNIF Adapters (RNIF, RNIF11)

The RNIF adapters[2] enable the execution of business transactions between RosettaNet trading partners based on Partner Interface Process[3] specifications. It is used for sending messages between the Integration Server and a RosettaNet-compliant system by transforming the SAP NetWeaver PI message format into RosettaNet message format and vice versa. The adapters implement the transport, packaging, and routing of RosettaNet business messages and signals as defined in the RosettaNet Implementation Framework versions 1.1 and 2.0.

SAP NetWeaver PI has two RosettaNet adapters:

▶ The *RNIF 1.1 adapter* is used to exchange messages between the Integration Server and a RosettaNet-compliant system that supports RNIF version 1.1. It supports execution of asynchronous RosettaNet transactions by using the RNIF1.1 message protocol.

▶ The *RNIF 2.0 adapter* is used to exchange messages between the Integration Server and a RosettaNet-compliant system that supports RNIF version 2.0. It supports execution of asynchronous RosettaNet PIPs using the RNIF2.0 message protocol, including 1-action and 2-action business transactions.

The capabilities of the RNIF adapters are listed in Table 3.13. They are discussed more in detail in Chapter 4 B2B and Industry Standard Support.

Feature	Capability
Mode	Asynchronous
Message protocol	RNIF 1.1, RNIF 2.0
Transport protocol	HTTP, HTTPS
Quality of service	Exactly once (EO)
Attachments	Supported with RNIF 2.0

Table 3.13 Capabilities of the RNIF Adapters

---

2 The RNIF protocol (RosettaNet Implementation Framework) is defined by the RosettaNet organization.

3 A Partner Interface Process (PIP) defines business processes between trading partners.

CIDX Adapter

The CIDX adapter[4] supports the Chem eStandard, which is used for collaborative commerce on the Internet in the chemical industry. The CIDX adapter is based on the Chem eStandards envelope and security specifications, which refer to an extended subset of the RosettaNet Implementation Framework (RNIF) version 1.1 with certain deviations from this framework.

You use the CIDX adapter for message exchange between the Integration Server and a Chem eStandards business transaction-compliant system in a cross-company process. The capabilities of the CIDX adapter are listed in Table 3.14. They are discussed more in detail in Chapter 4 B2B and Industry Standard Support.

Feature	Capability
Mode	Asynchronous
Message protocol	RNIF 1.1
Transport protocol	HTTP, HTTPS
Quality of service	Exactly once (EO)
Attachments	Not supported

Table 3.14 Capabilities of the CIDX Adapter

3.4.3 Third-Party Adapters

In addition to the standard adapters listed above, the open Adapter Framework of SAP NetWeaver PI allows the use of third-party adapters to extend connectivity options to legacy and packaged applications as well as to proprietary technology platforms. These third-party adapters are sold and delivered through SAP. SAP NetWeaver PI has reseller agreements with the following third-party adapter vendors who provide adapters that run completely within SAP NetWeaver PI:

▶ **iWay Adapters**
The adapters provided by iWay can be categorized into mainframe and transaction adapters, application adapters, technical adapters, and industry standard adapters. The iWay adapters are installed, configured, used, and monitored

---

4 The message protocol requirements for the Chem eStandards are published by the Chemical Industry Data Exchange (CIDX).

within SAP NetWeaver. All adapters run on the SAP NetWeaver PI Adapter Framework, based on the JCA (compare with Section 3.2.2 Adapter Framework). The adapter configuration is carried out in the Integration Builder of SAP NetWeaver PI.

You can find more information on adapters provided by iWay in Section 7.4 Choosing the Right Adapter.

▸ **SEEBURGER Adapters**
SEEBURGER has developed many EDI adapters, including predefined mappings and several EDI communication protocols, for different scenarios in various industries. Each package contains basic EDI process functions, mappings of SAP XML to a native EDI format for certain common business documents, and supported communication protocols for that particular industry. All of these adapters run on the SAP NetWeaver PI Adapter Framework, based on JCA. The adapter configuration is carried out in the Integration Builder of SAP NetWeaver PI.

The SEEBURGER adapters ensure best effort (BE), guaranteed exactly once (EO), and exactly once in order (EOIO) delivery of messages. They also provide an automatic retry mechanism and automatic switching to alternative communication channels for all kinds of communication. All adapters are bidirectional, and a broad range of international codepages and character sets such as Unicode, ASCII, and EBCDIC are supported.

You can find more information on adapters provided by SEEBURGER in Section 7.4 Choosing the Right Adapter.

▸ **Conversion Agent by Informatica**
To complete the integration capabilities of SAP NetWeaver PI, SAP in partnership with Informatica has developed the SAP Conversion Agent. The Conversion Agent can convert unstructured, semistructured, and structured formats to XML, and the other way around.

The Conversion Agent is composed of the Conversion Agent Studio and the Conversion Agent Engine. In the Conversion Agent Studio you can develop and configure data conversions. The Conversion Agent Engine executes the data conversions. The Conversion Agent can be called from SAP NetWeaver PI by using an adapter module in the module processor of the SAP adapters such as the File/FTP adapter. The Conversion Agent can only be used in conjunction with SAP adapters of the Advanced Adapter Engine.

The Conversion Agent enables the transformation of message payloads from a document such as Word or Excel into XML and vice versa. Formats that can be transformed by the Conversion Agent include unstructured data (such as ASCII, HTML, Microsoft Excel, Microsoft Word, PDF) as well as semistructured data (such as HL7, COBOL, SWIFT) and XML formats (such as LegalXML, ebXML, ACORD XML). New data formats are continually being added.

3.5   Partner Connectivity Kit

The *Partner Connectivity Kit* (PCK) is a toolset for enabling small business partners or subsidiaries with no XML messaging capabilities to communicate with SAP NetWeaver PI. The PCK is an AS Java-based application and is based on the Advanced Adapter Engine. It offers an easy way to exchange messages between an application system and SAP NetWeaver PI without sophisticated services (routing and cross-component BPM) and design of collaboration knowledge.

The PCK offers a graphical editor that enables you to define mappings between source and target message structures. It includes some standard adapters and can also be used by customers to develop their own adapters. The configuration and administration of the PCK are always done locally. Typically, smaller partners of a SAP NetWeaver PI customer use the PCK to integrate with their partner.

The SAP PCK allows your business partner to provide you with data by enabling him to convert information from remote clients or Web services; information from files, databases, and messaging systems; and information from SAP ECC systems to the SAP XI messaging protocol. Conversely, your business partner can convert data that he receives from you into other formats so that he can use it in his own applications.

The PCK adapts the native message interface of the partner system to the SAP NetWeaver PI messaging format and provides HTTP connectivity to the URL of the central Integration Server.

The conversion of the message format to XI message protocol is made possible using various adapters. The PCK contains the following adapters:

▶ RFC adapter
▶ File adapter

- ▶ JMS adapter
- ▶ JDBC adapter
- ▶ SOAP adapter
- ▶ SAP Business Connector adapter
- ▶ Mail adapter
- ▶ XI adapter

The message flow for a typical scenario in PCK, where an SAP business system needs to send a message to the smaller business partner, involves the following steps:

1. The message from the Integration Sever is sent to the PCK via the XI message protocol.
2. The PCK receives the message and converts it into the format required by the receiver application of the smaller business partner.
3. The message is then forwarded to the receiver systems using the appropriate adapter.

3.6 Summary

After reading this chapter you should understand the architecture of the SAP NetWeaver PI Adapter Framework and the functionality of the Adapter Engine. You should be able to distinguish between the various adapter types provided by SAP NetWeaver PI and third-party vendors and understand the features and capabilities of each of these adapters in detail. You should now be able to configure different adapters to send and receive messages from the SAP NetWeaver PI Integration Server and the Advanced Adapter Engine (AAE). You should understand the various interoperability options provided with SAP NetWeaver PI to connect to other EAI tools.

In addition, you should understand the concept of the Partner Connectivity Kit (PCK) provided by SAP NetWeaver PI to connect to small integration partners or subsidiaries with no XML messaging capabilities.

This chapter gives you an overview of the industry standards supported by SAP NetWeaver PI and discusses the predefined content provided by SAP and third-party vendors. It also gives you a detailed overview and key features of the industry standard adapters provided by SAP NetWeaver PI.

4 B2B and Industry Standard Support

Today's business and economic environment presents organizations with a wide range of challenges such as globalization, extreme competition, and distributed supply chain networks. Organizations are under enormous pressure to keep costs down and productivity up. The key to achieving this is to replace redundant manual processes with repeatable, automated technologies.

In an attempt to communicate effectively and more efficiently with business partners, enterprises are driving the adoption of e-business initiatives for both internal and external integration. Because many of these business transactions with trading partners involve the transfer of legally binding documents representing a high monetary value, organizations are forced to address more stringent requirements for partner communication processes such as data and process validity, reliability, and security.

To address this in a unified approach, companies need to have support for industry standards to electronically communicate with their trading partners. These industry standards are the foundation for business process interoperability between SAP and non-SAP applications and platforms.

4.1 Overview

Standards define a common business language, which is a requirement to cost-effectively enable business process integration between systems, both inside an organization and across the value chain. Industry standards enable business process flexibility by providing concrete rules for integration that have been developed by representatives of the respective industries. These industry standards for automating business processes and for true system-to-system communication have become a critical requirement for many organizations. They are quickly moving from nice to have to being mandatory requirements for business-to-business integration. This is also because the vertical industry market is growing at such a high rate and the drive to adopt standard processes has become a prerequisite for effective collaboration.

As described in Section 2.1 Overview, SAP NetWeaver provides one platform to centrally manage the design, configuration, and execution of business processes running within and beyond the company's boundaries. The functionality provided in SAP NetWeaver PI for business-to-business integration includes the means to maintain and manage the collaboration profiles and collaboration agreements between business partners: a Partner Connectivity Kit to enable XML document exchange between a smaller business partner and a bigger partner. It provides support for technical and business standards for various industries through preconfigured, industry-specific business content and out-of-the-box support for XML-based data exchange standards. This includes offerings for the high-tech and chemicals industries, providing native support for RosettaNet and CIDX, and preconfigured mappings for the most common EDI standards. With the support of business process management, SAP NetWeaver PI enables model-driven process flexibility and automation within and across systems.

The key capabilities that can be used for B2B integration with SAP NetWeaver PI include the following:

▶ **Industry standards support**
SAP NetWeaver PI supports various industry data exchange standards such as RosettaNet for high tech, Chemical Industry Data Exchange (CIDX) for the chemical industry, Petroleum Industry Data Exchange (PIDX) for the oil and gas Industry, 1Sync for retail and consumer products, Health Layer 7 (HL7) for healthcare, SPEC 2000 for aerospace and defense, SWIFT for financials, AIAG, Odette for automotive, PapiNet for mill products, ACORD for insurance, HR-XML for human resources, RAPID for agriculture, STAR for automotive, ANSI ASC X12, and so on.

SAP is also a major contributor to ebXML Core Components[1] and believes that broad adoption of these specifications will help increase interoperability of IT systems and applications across industries. The adoption of these specifications by the United Nations Centre for Trade Facilitation and Electronic Business (UN/CEFACT) paves the road for next-generation XML-based e-business standards.

▶ **Predefined integration content**

SAP NetWeaver PI provides an open business process integration technology platform that supports process-centric collaboration between SAP and non-SAP systems and applications, both within and beyond the enterprise. It defines the interfaces and XML mappings required for specific business scenarios to manage message exchange and transform message contents between sender and receiver systems for efficient cross-system collaborative processes. It also offers the ability to deliver industry standard-compliant business scenarios as well as the ability to orchestrate industry standard-adherent business processes.

SAP NetWeaver PI delivers predefined integration content for B2B solutions to facilitate the implementation process and thus reduce the total cost of ownership for the customers. It provides predefined integration content for SAP applications such as Supplier Relationship Management (SRM), Supply Chain Management (SCM), radio frequency identification devices (RFID), Master Data Management (MDM), Event Management (SAP EM), and so on.

In addition, it provides predefined integration content in the form of business packages for different industry standard verticals such as the RosettaNet business package for the high-tech industry and the CIDX business package for the chemical industry. These business packages contain the collaboration knowledge as defined by the industry standards. The content includes data structures, interfaces, mapping programs, integration scenarios, integration processes, and communication channel templates and is synchronized with the related business applications and versions.

▶ **Central interface repository**

As discussed in Section 2.3 Overview of Enterprise Services Repository, SAP NetWeaver PI provides the Enterprise Services Repository as the central inter-

---

1 ebXML is an XML-based standard sponsored by OASIS and UN/CEFACT, and its Core Components Technical Specification provides a way to identify, capture, and maximize the reuse of business information to support and enhance information interoperability across multiple business situations.

face repository for B2B integration. This repository acts as the central storage for all data structures, interfaces, mapping programs, integration scenarios, and integration processes that are necessary for B2B integration.

▶ **Trading partner collaboration**
SAP NetWeaver PI provides functions to enable you to create and manage collaboration profiles and agreements centrally between business partners for B2B integration. The collaboration profile contains all the technical options that are available to communication parties for exchanging messages. A collaboration agreement specifies the technical details for message exchange that have been agreed for a particular sender-receiver pair.

▶ **Adapter partner ecosystem**
SAP NetWeaver provides out-of-the-box technical B2B adapters for high tech, chemical, and oil and gas. These adapters are based on the RosettaNet Implementation Framework (RNIF) and include the RNIF 2.0 adapter for RosettaNet and the PIDX standard, and the CIDX adapter for CIDX standard message exchange. These adapters are used to do the actual routing, transport, and packaging of the industry standard messages and business signals based on the information retrieved at runtime from the Enterprise Services Repository and Integration Directory.

In addition to providing these industry standard adapters, SAP also relies on an ecosystem of partners to provide adapters for third-party applications and certain industry standards. These partner adapters from iWay, SEEBURGER, Informatica, and others are sold and delivered through SAP. These partner adapters provide support for other application vendors such as Oracle, Peoplesoft, Baan, Siebel, Broadvision, and so on. In addition, these adapters also provide support for industry standards such as EDI, EDIINT (AS2), SWIFT, UCCnet, and so on.

▶ **Secure messaging and routing**
SAP NetWeaver PI leverages the security capabilities of SAP NetWeaver to provide secure message exchange for B2B scenarios. These features include data stream encryption via Secure Sockets Layer (HTTPS), security based on the Web service standard (WS-Security), digital signatures to authenticate sending partners and to ensure data integrity of the business document carried by a message, S/MIME support for RosettaNet scenarios, and message-level encryption for keeping the message content confidential not only on the communication lines but also in the intermediate message stores.

4.2 Industry-Specific Standard Support

SAP NetWeaver PI supports business semantic standards that provide the common understanding necessary to execute a business process, such as order-to-cash. These standards can be cross-industry or industry-specific. Cross-industry semantic standards are used to define business semantics for business messages and business objects that can be used across multiple industries, whereas industry-specific standards are defined and used by those in the specific industries. Table 4.1 lists some of the key industry-specific business semantic standards supported by SAP NetWeaver PI in the area of B2B integration either by SAP directly or via certified partner solutions. All of these standards are explained in more detail in the following section.

Standard/Data Pool	Available Content	Available Adapter
RosettaNet	Support of selected processes	RNIF 1.1, RNIF 2.0
CIDX	Support of selected processes	CIDX adapter
PIDX	Support of selected processes	RNIF 2.0
1SYNC	Support via industry-specific solutions	AS2
ACORD	Support via industry-specific solutions	ACORD-compliant adapter
STAR	Support of selected processes	ebXML, AS2, and others
HL7	Support of selected processes	HL7-compliant adapter
SWIFT	Support via financial solutions	SWIFT-compliant adapter
SPEC 2000	Support of selected processes	EDI- and XML-based adapters

Table 4.1 Examples of Industry-Specific Standards Supported by SAP

4.2.1 RosettaNet (High Tech)

RosettaNet is a subsidiary of GS1 US[2] and is a nonprofit standards organization aimed at establishing standard processes for sharing of business information. It

---

2 GS1 is a leading global organization dedicated to the design and implementation of global standards and solutions to improve efficiency and visibility in supply and demand chains globally and across multiple sectors. GS1 US, formerly the Uniform Code Council, Inc., is the GS1 member organization in the United States.

has over 500 members from a wide range of industries such as semiconductor manufacturing, telecommunications, information technology, electronic components, and logistics. RosettaNet standards form a common e-business language, aligning processes between supply chains on a global basis. These standards offer a robust nonproprietary solution, covering Partner Interface Processes, the RosettaNet Implementation Framework, and business and technical dictionaries for e-business standardization.

RosettaNet PIPs

The *Partner Interface Processes* (PIPs) are specialized system-to-system XML-based dialogs that define business processes between trading partners. PIPs apply to the core processes such as order management, inventory management, marketing information management, service and support, manufacturing, product information, and so on. RosettaNet divides the entire e-business supply chain domain for which PIPs are specified into *clusters*. Each cluster is further subdivided into two or more *segments*.

Each segment is composed of several PIPs. Each PIP contains several *activities,* and each activity contains one or more actions. For example, the Manage Purchase Order PIP is part of cluster 3 (Order Management), and that there it is fourth in sequence in the Quote and Order Entry (segment A). Hence, the Manage Purchase Order PIP is identified by the name PIP3A4. Figure 4.1 shows the layout of the RosettaNet PIP message.

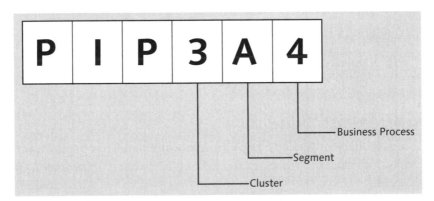

Figure 4.1 Layout of the RosettaNet PIP Message

Each PIP specification is composed of three major parts:

▶ **Business Operational View (BOV)**
The BOV specifies the semantics of business entities and the flow of business information between roles involved in the exchange as they perform business activities.

▶ **Functional Service View (FSV)**
The FSV is derived from the BOV and specifies the network component design and the interactions between the network components during execution of the PIP.

▶ **Implementation Framework View (IFV)**
The IFV specifies the action message formats and communication requirements required to run the PIP. The communication requirements include specifications on the requirement for secure transport protocols such as SSL and digital signatures.

The messages involved in a PIP business document exchange are classified as follows:

▶ **Business action messages**
Business action messages are messages with contents that are of a business nature such as a purchase order or an invoice. They can further be classified into the following activities:

  ▶ A *single-action activity* that involves the initiator sending a request action to the responder and the latter returning a business signal.

  ▶ A *two-action activity* that involves the initiator sending a request action to the responder and the responder returning a receipt acknowledgement to the initiator. This is followed by the responder returning a response action to the initiator and the initiator returning a receipt acknowledgement to the responder.

Single-action and two-action activities can also use either one or both of the synchronous and asynchronous modes of interaction, as prescribed by their corresponding PIP specifications.

▶ **Business signal messages**
Business signals are positive and negative acknowledgement messages that are sent in response to business actions for the purpose of aligning PIP states between the partners.

RosettaNet Implementation Framework (RNIF)

The RosettaNet Implementation Framework defines how to transport the PIP messages. Its core specification includes the packaging, routing, transport, and security standard of RosettaNet PIP messages and business signals. The RNIF standard is based on the XML, MIME, and HTTP standards. There are two versions of RNIF, namely, RNIF 1.1 and RNIF 2.0. Both RNIF 1.1 and RNIF 2.0 rely on HTTP, SSL, and HTTPS for message transport. Business content could also be transferred over SMTP, using an S/MIME envelope for confidentiality. It uses the S/MIME construct for packaging. The RNIF core specification for security includes the authentication, authorization, encryption, and nonrepudiation requirements essential for conducting secure electronic business over the Internet.

A RosettaNet Business Message always contains a preamble header, a delivery header, a service header, and service content. Service content is composed of an action message or a signal message. If service content is an action message, one or more attachments may be included. The headers, service content, and attachments are packaged together using a MIME multipart/related construct. A RosettaNet Business Message can optionally be signed digitally, in which case the S/MIME multipart/signed construct is used to attach the signature.

4.2.2 CIDX (Chemical)

The *Chem eStandards* were established by the trade association and standards body *Chemical Industry Data Exchange* (CIDX) to accelerate collaborative processes in areas such as logistics, order management, and invoicing. These standards align business processes between trading partners in a supply chain and are developed specifically for the buying, selling, and delivery of chemical products. Their business transactions include specification of partner business roles such as buyer, seller, and so on; activities conducted between the roles and type; content; and sequence of documents exchanged by the roles while performing these activities.

The Chem eStandards adopted the RosettaNet Implementation Framework (RNIF) at the messaging layer and are based on the RNIF 1.1 specifications. Thus, the messages themselves are enveloped as RNIF action and signal messages as specified in the RNIF 1.1 specification. The CIDX standard leverages the transport, routing, packaging, and security aspects of RNIF. CIDX messages use the message structure as specified by the RNIF 1.1 specification and contains a preamble header, a service header, and the service content stored as a multipart

MIME document as well as length fields and optional digital signature information. CIDX messages can be categorized as follows:

▶ An *action message* contains the business content such as Order Create.

▶ A *signal message* is a positive or negative message sent in response to an action message.

Each transaction in the CIDX is assigned an alphanumeric code. Table 4.2 illustrates some of the CIDX transaction codes corresponding to the CIDX requesting message. This alphanumeric transaction code indicates the Global Process Indicator code of Chem eStandard transactions.

Requesting Message	Transaction Code
OrderCreate	E41
OrderChange	E45
OrderResponse	E42
ShipNotice	E72
Invoice	E81

Table 4.2 Example of CIDX Messages

4.2.3   PIDX (Oil and Gas)

The *Petroleum Industry Data Exchange* (PIDX) standard was developed by the *American Petroleum Institute* (API) committee on electronic business standards and processes. The core mission of PIDX is to improve business efficiency within the oil and gas industry by promoting interoperability between information systems. The PIDX Complex Products and Services Task Group (Com.Pro.Serv) has developed a set of XML schema files that enable automation of various aspects of oil and gas supply chains.

The components of a basic PIDX business message are encased in a multipart/related envelope containing headers and the business process payload. It contains a preamble header, a delivery header, a service header, and service content as specified by the RNIF 2.0 standard. RNIF 2.0 supports attachment handling by allowing attachments to be encoded as separate MIME parts in the MIME multipart/related entity. Similar to RosettaNet and CIDX messages, PIDX messages can be classified into the following:

▶ An *action message* contains the business data such as purchase order data.

▶ A *signal message* is a positive or negative acknowledgement in response to a PIDX action message. Signal messages can be positive *receipt-acknowledgement* messages or negative *general exception* messages.

Each transaction implemented by PIDX is assigned an alphanumeric PIP code. Table 4.3 illustrates the PIP number corresponding to the PIDX XML Schema. This alphanumeric is the PIP identifier and indicates the Global Process Indicator code in the PIDX transactions.

PIDX XML Schema	PIDX PIP Number
FieldTicket	P11
FieldTicketResponse	P12
Invoice	P21
InvoiceResponse	P22
OrderCreate	P31
OrderChange	P32
OrderResponse	P33
QuoteRequest	P41
Quote	P42
QuoteNotification	P43
RequestRequisitionReturn	P51

Table 4.3 Examples of PIDX Messages

PIDX schemas are originally based on the RosettaNet naming standards followed by the CIDX standard. XML schemas use the PIDX namespace for all the PIDX element names. They use the PIDX namespace prefix `pidx:` to indicate that they belong to the PIDX namespace with the following attribute assignment for the schema element: `xmlns:pidx="http://www.api.org/pidXML/v1.2"`.

PIDX XML Transport, Routing, and Packaging (TRP) requirements are based on the RNIF 2.0 specifications and are used to securely and reliably transport PIDX messages to the trading partners involved in the message exchange. These requirements include authentication, authorization, confidentiality, data integrity, nonrepudiation, reliability, and so on.

4.2.4 1SYNC (Retail and Consumer Products)

The Global Data Synchronization Network (GDSN) is the process by which trading partners exchange product and service information on an ongoing basis. It is a network of certified data pools and GS1 Global Registry for communicating standardized product information between trading partners in a secure environment conforming to global standards. The Global Registry acts as a central global data repository allowing suppliers and retailers to publish and subscribe to product information.

1SYNC, a subsidiary of GS1 US, is a GDSN-certified data pool that interacts with the GS1 Global Registry and other data pools to exchange and synchronize product data information with other trading partners. It offers a data synchronization solution to aid companies in the elimination of costly data errors and increase supply chain efficiencies. It was formed in 2005 as a data synchronization organization for both retailers and manufacturers, combining the *UCCnet* and *Transora* technology platforms.

The product information that is exchanged through GDSN contains a 14-digit Global Trade Item Number (GTIN), a 13-digit unique location identifier Global Location Number (GLN), and the core attributes that define the characteristics of a trade item or product such as description, effective date, net weight, and so on. To exchange this information, suppliers first need to assemble all product information in a GDSN format and publish the information to 1SYNC or other data pools. 1SYNC then uploads this information about each item to the Global Registry on behalf of the supplier. Customers search the Global Registry through the data pool of their choice and subscribe to the information they need. The trading partners can then engage in a pub/sub process, and the information is synchronized through their respective data pools.

The 1SYNC (UCCnet) Data Synchronization Suite uses XML schemas for standard messaging, which complies with the GDSN standards. GDSN governs the communication and data synchronization between the global registry and individual company catalogs. This establishes common electronic communication architecture for companies around the world to do business with each other more efficiently and effectively. The confidential product and service attribute information is transmitted between the trading partners using secure EDIINT AS2-based communication.

4.2.5 SPEC 2000 (Aerospace and Defense)

SPEC 2000 is a set of e-business specifications administered by the *Air Transport Association* (ATA) to support the airline industry. It is the product of 12 international associations representing airlines, manufacturers, suppliers, and repair agencies. The SPEC 2000 suite of standards includes three categories of standards and the ATA Aviation Marketplace:

▶ **E-commerce standards**
E-commerce standards provide the formats, data structure, and rules for exchanging electronic order administration, quotation process, customer invoices, repair orders, warranty claims placement, and so on.

▶ **File standards**
File standards define the specifications for the transfer of large files between aircraft operators and suppliers. They provide specifications for provisioning, inventory consumption data exchange, performance reporting, delivery configuration, and reliability data collection and exchange.

▶ **Traceability standards**
The traceability standards are bar code/RFID-based standards and include specifications for customer receipt processes, repair agency receipt processes, RFID parts identification, and traceability data.

▶ **ATA Aviation Marketplace**
The ATA Aviation Marketplace is a virtual market for airline industry trading partners to display and find parts pricing, repair, and availability information. The Aviation Marketplace consists of five databases, namely, Procurement Database; Repair Database; Surplus Database; Tools, Test & Ground Equipment Database; and the Needs Database. These databases allow companies to list their products and repair services on a central file, which is accessed primarily by the world's airlines.

The traditional SPEC 2000 standard has been adopted by EDI standards such as ANSI X12 and UN/EDIFACT and is frequently exchanged over ARINC/SITA. Today, there are many XML representations of SPEC 2000 e-commerce transactions that allow trading partners to exchange information and conduct e-business over the Internet.

4.2.6   ACORD (Insurance)

The *Association for Cooperative Operations Research and Development* (ACORD) is a global, nonprofit insurance association whose mission is to facilitate the development and use of standards for the insurance and related financial services industries. ACORD standards allow different companies to transact business electronically with agents, brokers, and data partners in the insurance industry. ACORD develops and maintains XML standards for life and annuity, property and casualty/surety, and reinsurance industry segments. ACORD XML for Life, Annuity & Health is based on the ACORD Life Data Model and provides a robust, industry-tested XML vocabulary. The ACORD XML for Property & Casualty/Surety standard addresses the industry's real-time requirements. It defines property and casualty /surety transactions that include both request and response messages for accounting, claims, personal lines, commercial lines, specialty lines, and surety transactions.

4.2.7   AIAG (Automotive)

The *North American Automotive Industry Action Group* (AIAG) is a globally recognized organization that allows OEMs and suppliers unite to address and resolve issues affecting the world-wide automotive supply chain. It provides a forum for member cooperation in developing and promoting industry solutions. AIAG does not publish standards but rather works with other standards consortia, particularly the Open Applications Groups (OAGis) to develop and publish XML schema specifications. It has recommended the use of ebXML messaging and the use of OAG Business Object Documents (BODs) for exchange XML documents. The BOD message architecture is independent of the communication mechanism. It can be used with simple transport protocols such as HTTP and SMTP as well as with complex transport protocols such as SOAP, ebXML Transport, and Routing.

4.2.8   STAR (Automotive)

The *Standards for Technology in Automotive Retail* (STAR) is a nonprofit, IT standards organization that develops open, voluntary standards for the retail automotive industry. These standards are designed to support business information needs and provide secure and reliable means for dealers, manufacturers, and retail system providers to communicate with each other. The XML standards that STAR creates are referred to as Business Object Documents (BODs) and are based on the Open Application Group Inc. (OAGi) development methodology. The STAR BODs are developed to support multiple areas of business including customer relationship management, parts management, vehicle management, service and repairs, warranty, and others.

The transport methods recommended by STAR include the following two specifications for transporting the STAR messages in a secure and reliable way:

▸ **STAR ebMS Stack**
ebXML provides a complete set of services for business-to-business integration. STAR specifies a reduced set of ebXML that uses message services and collaboration protocol to meet transport requirements. The STAR ebMS communication stack includes BODs as the messaging layer; ebMS as the security, encryption, and reliability layer; XML; SOAP as the XML messaging layer; and HTTP, TCP, FTP, SMTP, MQ, and so on as the transport layer.

▸ **STAR Web Services Stack**
STAR adds a few more layers to the Web Services Stack to provide support for OEM-to-DMS communication in a well-defined way. The communication stack includes STAR BODs as the messaging layer; STAR Web service specifications as the Web service transport layer; WS-Security and WS-Reliable messaging as the security, encryption, and reliability layer; XML; SOAP as the XML messaging layer; and HTTP, TCP, FTP, SMTP, MQ, and so on as the transport layer.

4.2.9 HL7 (Healthcare)

Health Level Seven (HL7) is an ANSI-accredited standards organization that focuses on the interface requirements of the entire healthcare organization, including clinical and administrative data. It develops standards for the electronic interchange of administrative, clinical, and financial information among independent healthcare-oriented systems and to support clinical patient care and the management, delivery, and evaluation of healthcare services. HL7 focuses on object models and message structures for healthcare information that needs to be exchanged between systems.

In general terms, HL7 is an application protocol for electronic data exchange of information in healthcare environments. It is a collection of standards used by vendors of hospital information and clinical laboratory, enterprise, and pharmacy systems. HL7 develops conceptual standards (HL7 Reference Information Model), document standards (HL7 Clinical Document Architecture), application standards

(HL7 Clinical Context Object Workgroup), and messaging standards (HL7 v2.x and v3.0). Messaging standards define how information is packaged and communicated from one party to another and set the language, structure, and data types required for seamless integration from one system to another.

4.2.10 papiNet (Mill Products for Paper and Forest)

papiNet is a global communication XML standard for the paper and forest products industries. papiNet facilitates the automation of the business processes within the industry, making it easier for business partners to agree on data definitions and formats. The set of standards is referred to as the papiNet standard.

The papiNet standard is developed and maintained by a dedicated, international team of business and technical experts. These standards include common terminology and standard business documents such as request for quotation, purchase order, order confirmation, goods receipt, planning, product quality, scale ticket, business acknowledgement, and invoice.

The papiNet Interoperability Guidelines (IOGs) discuss the common elements related to the packaging of the message. A message that is packaged according to the papiNet IOG can be sent via any communication protocol. The message service can be viewed as a wrapper around a particular protocol (FTP, SMTP, or HTTP) that is used to transmit the message. papiNet uses the SOAP-ebXML protocol for safe and secure message delivery of messages. In addition, it also uses the S/MIME encryption standard. The papiNet IOG provides complete guidelines for safe and secure message exchange in the paper and forest industry.

4.2.11 RapidNet (Agriculture)

Responsible Agricultural Product and Information Distribution (RAPID) is a non-profit organization formed by the National Agricultural Chemical Association that develops and promotes commonly supported standards, transaction sets, directories, processes, and databases to enable electronic connectivity throughout the agriculture industry. RAPID's expertise is centered on the electronic commerce needs of agricultural businesses involved in crop and plant protection products, plant nutrients, grain, feed, seed, agricultural machinery, agricultural petroleum, animal health, other agricultural products, and specialties industries. RAPID has developed and promoted a broad selection of standards and guidelines for EC transactions; databases to promote product, regulatory, and environmental stewardship; and network connectivity to deliver the benefits of electronic commerce. RAPID standards are focused on order to invoice, sales and inventory reporting, and bar coding.

RAPID Agricultural eStandards were developed in collaboration with the CIDX Chem eStandards to meet Agricultural Industry needs for Internet-based B2B interactions between enterprises using XML-based standards. Agricultural eStandards utilized the Chem eStandards XML documents as the message payload and leveraged the messaging aspects of ebMS 1.0. The ebXML messaging service specification (ebMS) deals with enabling secure and reliable transport, routing, and packaging of business messages across the Internet.

The ebXML Message Service, which is based on SOAP version 1.1 and the SOAP with Attachments informational document, provides the functionality needed for two or more parties to engage in an electronic business transaction. Messaging services sit above the core Internet data transfer protocols (HTTP, SMTP, FTP) and below the business application-level software that understands and processes the message.

4.2.12 SWIFT (Financials)

The *Society for Worldwide Interbank Financial Telecommunication* (SWIFT) is an industry-owned organization that provides globally supported standards, messaging services, and interface software for banks, brokers and dealers, and investment managers, as well as their market infrastructures in payments, securities, treasury, and trade.

The SWIFTNet infrastructure is the latest from SWIFT, which operates using Internet protocols and provides an application-independent, single-window interface to all of the connected applications of all the institutions participating in the global financial community. Basically, SWIFTNet provides a centralized store-and-forward mechanism, with some transaction management. It provides banks with services such as the exchange of real-time messages using XML standards (SWIFTNet InterAct), the exchange of bulk messages such as nonurgent and low-value payments (SWIFTNet FileAct), a secure browser for accessing account information (SWIFTNet Browse), and online payment initiation, payment tracking, and status reporting (e-Payments plus).

SWIFTNet FIN is a secure, reliable, access-controlled, and structured store-and-forward messaging service. It includes services such as message validation to ensure that messages are formatted according to SWIFT message standards, delivery monitoring and prioritization, message storage, and retrieval. *SWIFTNet InterAct* is an interactive messaging service that allows financial institutions to exchange messages in an automated and interactive way. SWIFTNet Interact messaging features include interactive exchange of messages in synchronous or asynchronous mode, standard XML message envelopes, XML syntax validation, store-and-forward mode, and so on. It also provides security features such as message authentication, data integrity, data confidentiality, and nonrepudiation support.

4.3 Cross-Industry Standards

Among many others, the following are some of the key cross-industry business semantic standards widely used in the area of B2B integration. Table 4.4 lists some of the cross-industry business semantic standards supported by SAP NetWeaver PI in the area of B2B integration either by SAP directly or via certified partner solutions.

Standard	Available Content	Available Adapter
ANSI ASC X12	Support of selected processes	AS1, AS2, OFTP, and other EDI-compliant adapters
UN/EDIFACT	Support of selected processes	AS1, AS2, OFTP, and other EDI-compliant adapters

Table 4.4 Examples of Cross-Industry Standards Supported by SAP

In addition to the standards mentioned in Table 4.4, SAP NetWeaver also supports other cross industry standards such as Open Application Group Inc. (OAGi), Enterprise Interoperability Centre (EIC), Electronic Product Code (EPCGlobal) RFID-related EPC Standards, International Organization for Standards (ISO), Object Management Group (OMG), and many others.

4.3.1 Open Application Group Inc (OAGi)

OAGi is a nonprofit open standard consortium focusing on developing the process-based XML standards called Business Object Documents (BODs) that can be used widely for B2B and A2A integration scenarios across many different industries such as automotive, manufacturing, telecommunications, human resource management, and many other vertical industries.

Generally speaking, BODs are the business messages or business documents that are exchanged between software components or applications, between or across supply chains. Each BOD consists of an *Application Area* and a *Data Area*. The BOD informs the receiving system what kind of message is in the Data Area, as well as status and error conditions.

A Data Area is structured in two parts containing a *Verb* and one or more *Nouns*. The Noun is a common business object, and actions performed on the Noun are the Verbs. BODs are designed to be extensible, while providing a common underlying architecture for integration. The current release of OAGIS (Open Application Group Implementation Specification) has over 490 BODs that address a wide variety of business applications.

The BOD message architecture is independent of the communication mechanism. It works well with ebXML transport and routing, Web services, HTTP, SMTP, FTP, RosettaNet Implementation Framework (RNIF), and any other framework that a company chooses to transport information. OAGi provides a canonical business language partnering with other standard bodies such as AIAG, STAR, and HR-XML to leverage the existing domain knowledge that each industry has and provide an overlay of the vertical information on top of that domain knowledge.

4.3.2 ANSI ASC X12

Electronic Data Interchange (EDI) is a widely used method of exchanging business documents electronically in a structured, predefined standard format. It contains a set of standards for controlling exchange of business documents between a company and its trading partners. The standards are designed to work across industry and company boundaries. Several EDI standards are in use today, the most prevalent ones being ASC X12 and UN/EDIFACT.

The *American National Standards Institute* (ANSI) has been coordinating standards in the United States since 1918. The Institute has a number of committees including the ANSI Accredited Standards Committee (ASC) X12. The standard that has been recommended by this committee is known as the ANSI ASC X12. The ASC X12 message standard was formed in 1979 and is the predominant standard in the United States and the rest of North America. ASC X12 publishes cross-industry business standards, supporting syntax standards, technical reports, and guidelines. ASC X12 cross-industry standards include more than 300 individual EDI transaction sets that address five vertical industries, namely government, finance, transportation, supply chain, and insurance. It develops and maintains X12 EDI and XML standards for these industries. ASC X12 supporting syntax standards include messaging, enveloping, and security standards.

The ASC X12 EDI envelope consists of various components such as interchange segments, function groups, transaction sets, data segments, and data elements. The *interchange* segment begins the interchange and contains information about the sender and the recipient, date and time of transmission, and the version of X12 in use. Interchange segments starts with the ISA segment (interchange header) and end with the IEA segment (interchange trailer). Each interchange consists of one or many *functional groups*. For example, each interchange can consist of a functional group of purchase orders and a functional group of invoices. Each functional group starts with a GS (header segment) and ends with a GE (trailer segment). Each functional group contains one or many *transaction sets*. Each transaction set is a business document and starts with an ST (header segment) and SE (trailer segment) and is composed of three sections, namely header, detail, and summary. It is composed of a number of *data segments* of variable length. Each data segment is in turn composed of a number of *data elements* of variable length. For example, the transaction set is analogous to the business document such as purchase order, whereas a segment is analogous to a line item in that purchase order, and a data element is analogous to a unit of information in that line item. Figure 4.2 shows the structure of the ANSI X12 envelope.

The acknowledgements in the ASC X12 include a technical acknowledgement called TA1 and a functional acknowledgement called 997. All of the ASC X12 transaction sets are identified by a three-digit numeric value assigned by the ANSI Standards committee. Table 4.5 lists some of the important ASC X12 transaction sets.

Transaction	Description
810	Invoice
812	Credit and debit advice
820	Payment order and credit advice (REMADV)

Table 4.5 Examples of ANSI ASC X12 Messages

Transaction	Description
823	Lockbox
840	Request for quote
843	Quotation
850	Purchase order
855	Purchase order acknowledgement
856	Advance ship notification
860	Order change
862	Delivery schedule
997	Functional acknowledgement

Table 4.5 Examples of ANSI ASC X12 Messages (cont.)

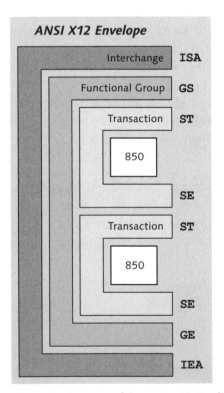

Figure 4.2 Structure of the ANSI X12 Envelope

The ASC X12 standards were designed to be independent of communication mechanism and software technologies. These can be transmitted using any methodology agreed upon between sender and recipient. This includes a variety of technologies such as value added networks (VANs), FTP, email, HTTP, Applicability Statement 1 (AS1), and Applicability Statement 2 (AS2). AS1 and AS2 are industry standard protocols for transporting the EDI and XML documents over the Internet in a secure and reliable manner.

4.3.3 UN/CEFACT

The *United Nations/Centre for Trade Facilitation and Electronic Business* (UN/CEFACT) is a division of the United Nations and is a chartered activity of the UN Economic Commission for Europe (UN/ECE). The UN/CEFACT mission is to support, enhance, and promote trade facilitation between developed, developing, and transitional economies. It has developed the international EDI standard called Electronic Data Interchange for Administration, Commerce, and Transport (UN/EDIFACT) and has defined a suite of standards to address a new paradigm in semantic interoperability. One such standard is the next-generation business information and collaborative standard called Core Component Technical Specifications (CCTS). In the next two paragraphs we look into these standards in detail.

UN/EDIFACT

UN/EDIFACT is an international EDI standard developed and maintained by the UN/CEFACT and was established in 1985. It has been adopted by the International Organization for Standards (ISO) as the ISO 9735. It is primarily used in Europe and Asia. The standard provides an interactive exchange protocol (I-EDI) and establishes the rules of syntax for the preparation of messages to be interchanged between partners. There are currently over 200 messages defined in the UN/EDIFACT, covering a wide variety of enterprises.

Similar to ASC X12 documents, the EDIFACT envelope consists of a hierarchical structure consisting of components such as interchange, functional groups, and messages. An *interchange* begins with a UNA or UNB segment and ends with a UNZ segment and contains one or many functional groups. The UNA is the optional header segment in the interchange to set structural elements such as separators, delimiters, and decimal notation. A *functional group* begins with a UNG segment and ends with a UNE segment and contains one or many messages. A *message* is equal to a transaction set in ASC X12 and begins with a UNH segment and ends with a UNT segment. Each message is composed of three sections, namely, header, detail, and summary. Each section is made up of segment groups and segments. The acknowledgement in the EDIFACT standard is called CONTRL. Figure 4.3 shows the structure of the EDIFACT envelope.

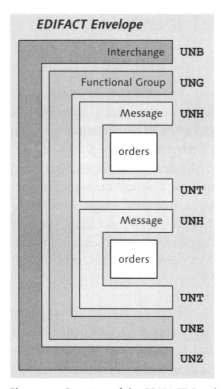

Figure 4.3 Structure of the EDIFACT Envelope

All of the EDIFACT messages are identified by a six-character message code. SAP's IDoc message types are based on the EDIFACT messages. Table 4.6 lists some of the important UN/EDIFACT messages.

Transaction	Description
INVOIC	Invoice
CREADV	Credit advice

Table 4.6 Examples of UN/EDIFACT Messages

Transaction	Description
REMADV	Remittance advice
DEBADV	Debit advice
REQOTE	Request for quote
QUOTES	Quotation
ORDERS	Purchase order
ORDRSP	Purchase order acknowledgement
DESADV	Dispatch advice
ORDCHG	Order change
DELFOR	Delivery schedule
PRICAT	Prices/sales catalog

Table 4.6 Examples of UN/EDIFACT Messages (cont.)

Similar to ASC X12, EDIFACT messages can be transmitted using a variety of technologies such as value added networks (VANs), FTP, e-mail, HTTP, Applicability Statement 1 (AS1), and Applicability Statement 2 (AS2).

Core Component Technical Specifications (CCTS)

In addition to the technical connectivity using various standards, one of the biggest challenges in B2B integration today is achieving the interoperability at the collaborative business process and data level. This lack of interoperability is addressed by the UN/CEFACT CCTS specification. CCTS offers a new paradigm in syntax-independent semantic data modeling for addressing information interoperability. It is a methodology for developing semantic-based business data structures through conceptual, physical, and logical models on a syntax-independent level.

CCTS is gaining widespread adoption by private and public sector organizations, as well as horizontal and vertical standards organizations. SAP uses CCTS to define SAP Global Data Types (GDTs) that serve as the basis for SAP business objects and enterprise services. This standard will enable SAP to provide the highest level of semantic interoperability possible between SAP and non-SAP applications.

4.4   Predefined Integration Content (SOA Business Content)

As described in Section 2.1 Overview, SAP NetWeaver PI provides an open business process integration technology platform that supports process-centric collaboration between SAP and non-SAP systems and applications, both within and beyond the enterprise. It delivers prepackaged integration content for B2B solutions in the form of *business packages*. These business packages provide business applications, technical infrastructure, and the business content all in one to match various industry standard specifications.

SAP NetWeaver provides these business packages for different industry standard verticals such as the RosettaNet business package for the high-tech industry, the CIDX business package for the chemical industry, and so on. This content includes collaboration knowledge as defined by the industry standards and contains data structures, interfaces, mapping programs, integration scenarios, integration processes, and communication channel templates and is synchronized with the related business applications and versions.

SAP NetWeaver also delivers prepackaged SOA business content that is based on the SOA design and modeling principles at SAP. This content includes Global Data Types, business objects, service interfaces, event definitions, routing conditions, mapping definitions, and implementation rules.

Predefined integration content or the SOA business content delivered by SAP can be classified into the following categories:

▶ **Content provided by SAP**
  Content delivered by SAP can be classified into two categories:

  ▷ *SAP application content* includes generic integration content provided by SAP applications. The content provides out-of-the-box integration scenarios for each application, harmonized application and integration logic, and simplified upgrade of end-to-end scenarios. SAP NetWeaver PI provides predefined integration content for application of the SAP Business Suite such as SAP Supply Chain Management (SCM), SAP Supplier Relationship Management (SRM), SAP ERP, SAP Customer Relationship Management (CRM), SAP NetWeaver Master Data Management (MDM), and so on. Predefined integration content is composed of software components, integration scenarios, Global Data Types, event definition, business objects, service interfaces, mappings between the source and target applications, and the implementation rules.

▶ *SAP business packages* provide integration content for industry standard verticals such as RosettaNet, CIDX, S95, and so on. These business packages contain the collaboration knowledge as defined by the industry standard and the technical B2B adapters that are needed for the actual transport, routing, and packaging of these industry standard messages.

▶ **Content provided by third parties**
Many SAP partners provide integration content that extends the content offering of SAP for A2A and B2B scenarios. The content provided by third-party vendors is certified by SAP. This includes content for SAP ERP, the SAP Business Suite of applications such as SAP SCM, and SAP CRM, and vertical industry standards such as EDIFACT, ANSI X12, OAGi, EANCOM, and so on.

▶ **Content to support EDI**
SAP NetWeaver PI provides support for Electronic Data Interchange (EDI) with content and adapter packages from its partner SEEBURGER. Industries such as automotive, high tech, aerospace, and defense will greatly benefit from direct EDI support and industry-specific content. Preconfigured mappings for the most common EDI standards such as ASC X12, EDIFACT, and Odette are provided as part of this content, which will significantly decrease EDI implementation costs and speed up deployments.

See also Section 7.3 Reusing Existing PI Content for more information on how to find predefined integration content.

4.5   Connectivity Using Industry Standard Adapters

SAP NetWeaver PI provides adapters that are built around the industry standards to facilitate communication among the trading partners. It provides the RNIF adapter and CIDX adapter, which support RosettaNet and CIDX based communication among trading partners. In addition to providing these standard adapters, SAP also relies on an ecosystem of partners to provide adapters for many industry standards.

4.5.1   RNIF Adapter

At a high level, the RNIF (RosettaNet Implementation Framework) adapter is based on the RNIF standard and enables the exchange of business documents among the RosettaNet trading partners. As described in Section 4.2.1 RosettaNet

(High Tech), RNIF is an open network application framework that enables business partners to collaboratively run RosettaNet Partner Interface Processes (PIPs). The RNIF standard specifies how messages should be exchanged independently of the actual message content. The Petroleum Industry Data Exchange (PIDX) standard is also based on the RNIF specifications and requires the use of the RNIF 2.0 and MIME-defined identifying wrappers.

SAP NetWeaver PI provides two flavors of the RNIF adapter: RNIF 1.1 and RNIF 2.0. These adapters meet the TRP requirements specified in the RNIF specification versions 1.1 and 2.0. The RNIF adapter executes the transport, packaging, and routing of all PIP messages and business signals based on the relevant information retrieved from the Enterprise Services Repository and Integration Directory at runtime.

The RNIF 2.0 adapter in SAP NetWeaver PI can be used for exchanging RosettaNet PIP messages as well as PIDX messages. The key features of the RNIF adapters include packing and unpacking of RosettaNet and PIDX messages, structural verification of the message headers, handling of message security, RosettaNet-defined error handling procedure, message monitoring and auditing, and reacting to failures in the backend applications. The adapters provide measures to enforce the security, authentication, authorization, nonrepudiation, and message integrity based on the RNIF 2.0 business transaction dialog.

RNIF 1.1 and RNIF 2.0 adapters are significantly different. Table 4.7 lists some of the key differences between RNIF 1.1 and RNIF 2.0.

Characteristic	RNIF 1.1	RNIF 2.0
Transport Protocol	HTTP/S	HTTP/S
Message Protocol	RNIF 1.1	RNIF 2.0
Quality of Service	Exactly once (EO)	Exactly once (EO)
Attachments	No	Yes
Message Level Encryption	No	Yes
Retries	Activity level	Action level
Digital Signature	PKCS#7	S/MIME

Table 4.7 Features of RNIF 1.1 Adapter and RNIF 2.0 Adapter

The RosettaNet Business Message is a transfer protocol-independent container that packs together business payload and the associated headers components encased in a MIME multipart/related envelope. All RosettaNet business messages must contain a preamble header, a delivery header, a service header, and a service content document. Preamble and delivery headers in RNIF 2.0 are modified and optimized versions of RNIF 1.1 equivalents. However, the delivery header is only part of RNIF 2.0.

Figure 4.4 shows the components of a basic RosettaNet message encased in a multipart/related envelope. The RNIF 2.0 message consists of the following parts:

▶ The *preamble header* identifies the message to be the RNIF message and the standard with which this message structure is compliant.

▶ The *delivery header* identifies message sender and recipient and provides the message identifier.

▶ The *service header* identifies the process layer and transaction layer information such as the PIP, the PIP instance, the activity, and the action to which this message belongs.

▶ The *service content* contains action or signal messages. If it is an action message, it may also include one or many attachments.

The RNIF adapters support the business action and business signal messages specified in the RNIF 1.1 and RNIF 2.0 standards. RNIF core specification includes the authentication, authorization, encryption, and nonrepudiation requirements essential for conducting secure electronic business over the Internet.

The RNIF 2.0 adapter 2.0 supports two levels of encryption (RNIF security settings are discussed in more detail in Chapter 10 Security Considerations):

▶ **Payload only**
In this type of encryption, the service container as well as the optional message attachment is encrypted.

▶ **Payload container**
In this type of encryption, the service header and the service container together with the optional message attachment are encrypted.

To exchange RosettaNet messages with the RNIF adapter, the RosettaNet-compliant system of the partner must be configured to send messages to the following URL: *http://<host>:<port>/MessagingSystem/receive/RNIFAdapter/RNIF*.

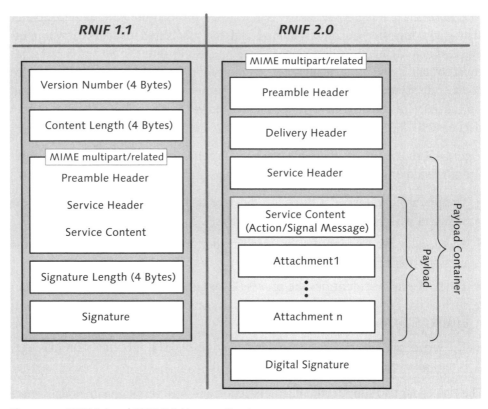

Figure 4.4 RNIF 1.1 and RNIF 2.0 Message Structure

4.5.2 CIDX Adapter

The CIDX adapter is one of the industry standard adapters provided by SAP NetWeaver PI. The CIDX adapter supports the Chem eStandards established by the standards body CIDX for exchanging business messages between trading partners involved in CIDX-based data exchange. As described in Section 4.2.2 CIDX (Chemical), the CIDX adapter leverages the transport, routing, packaging, and security aspects of RNIF and is based on the RNIF 1.1 specifications. The CIDX adapter executes the transport, routing, and packaging of all Chem eStandard messages and business signals based on the relevant information retrieved from the Enterprise Services Repository and Integration Directory at runtime.

The CIDX adapter is used for sending messages between the Integration Server of SAP NetWeaver PI and the trading partner's CIDX-compliant system by transforming the SAP NetWeaver PI message format into a CIDX message format and vice versa. The CIDX adapter supports the single-action asynchronous pattern and uses the collaboration agreements configured in the Integration Directory to manage Chem eStandard messages. The key features of the CIDX adapter include pack and unpack of Chem eStandard messages, structural verification of message headers, handling of message security, message monitoring and auditing, and message choreography of business action and business signal messages.

Table 4.8 lists some of the key characteristics of the CIDX adapter.

Characteristic	Values
Transport Protocol	HTTP/S
Message Protocol	RNIF 1.1
Quality of Service	Exactly once (EO)
Attachments	No
Message Level Encryption	No
Retries	Activity level
Digital Signature	PKCS#7

Table 4.8 Features of the CIDX Adapter

Figure 4.5 shows the components of a basic CIDX message consisting of the following parts:

► The *preamble header* identifies the message to be the CIDX message and the standard with which this message structure is compliant. The preamble header of CIDX is similar to the RosettaNet preamble header, except that the Global-AdministeringAuthorityCode is "CIDX," indicating it as a CIDX message.

► The *service header* contains the transaction routing and processing information for a given Chem eStandard transaction.

► The *service content* contains the actual Chem eStandard message. The message can be a business action or a business signal message.

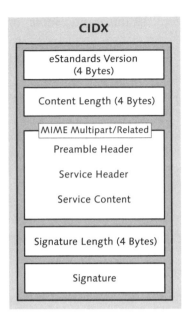

Figure 4.5 CIDX Message Structure

To exchange Chem eStandard messages with the CIDX adapter, the CIDX-compliant system of the business partner must be configured to send messages to the following URL: *http://<host>:<port>/MessagingSystem/receive/CIDXAdapter/CIDX*.

4.6   Summary

In this chapter, you have learned the various industry standards supported by SAP NetWeaver PI in detail. You have explored the predefined content provided by SAP and third party vendors and learned the key features of the RNIF and CIDX industry standard adapters.

This chapter gives you an overview of the monitoring tools available within SAP NetWeaver PI. It provides a detailed discussion of each of these monitoring tools.

5 Central Monitoring

As discussed in Chapter 2 General Concepts and Chapter 3 Adapter Concepts, SAP NetWeaver PI consists of a variety of components such as the Integration Engine, Business Process Engine, Advanced Adapter Engine, proxies, noncentral Adapter Engine, and Java SE Adapter Engine that enable the complete working of the SAP NetWeaver PI framework. The business processes represented by different messages flow through these various components, thus making the tracking of these messages an essential part of the entire process. These messages must be traceable from a single central monitoring system to enable business users and system administrators to track the messages for the successes or failures that have occurred during the process. This central system must allow you to drill down to the lowest possible level to track an error in order to find the exact problem.

5.1 Overview

SAP NetWeaver PI provides a central monitoring system that contains various monitoring tools for monitoring the flow of messages either from an end-to-end approach or at each specific message level. The purpose is to make all the required information available in one central monitoring system. Figure 5.1 shows the various components and their messages that can be viewed using the central monitoring system.

SAP NetWeaver PI provides central access to monitoring UIs (user interfaces) through the Runtime Workbench or through the SAP NetWeaver Administrator. It offers these two different approaches depending upon the SAP NetWeaver PI installations:

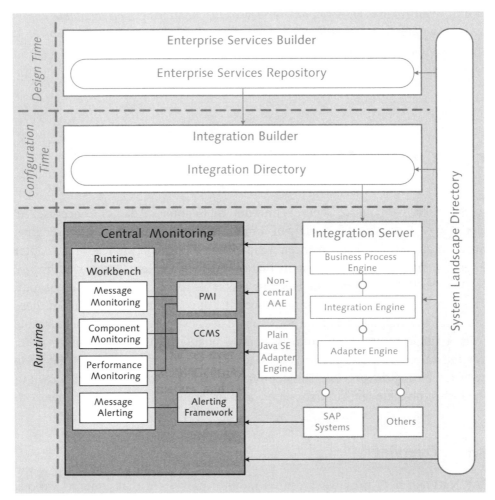

Figure 5.1 Central Monitoring in SAP NetWeaver PI

▶ **Monitoring of an individual SAP NetWeaver PI domain**
The Runtime Workbench is used to monitor individual SAP NetWeaver PI installations.

▶ **Monitoring of multiple SAP NetWeaver PI domains**
As of release 7.1 of SAP NetWeaver PI, SAP NetWeaver Administrator (NWA) can be used as an alternative to the Runtime Workbench to monitor the integration landscape. SAP NetWeaver Administrator is used for monitoring multiple SAP NetWeaver PI installations.

In this chapter, we only focus on the Runtime Workbench and the Integration Engine monitoring. For more information on message monitoring using SAP NetWeaver Administrator, refer to the SAP online documentation (*http:// help.sap.com*).

SAP NetWeaver monitoring forms the main component of the Runtime Workbench of SAP NetWeaver PI. Monitoring encompasses the traceability of all the components, the messages flowing through the components, the state transitions of the various messages, and the final state of the message flow, which represents the final state of the whole business process. Monitoring is categorized into different types based on the requirements that would enable the end user to trace the messages in a very simple way.

The Runtime Workbench offers an entry point to the SAP NetWeaver PI monitoring function and is used as a central tool for monitoring SAP NetWeaver PI, and all of its components, processes, and messages, through a Java-based user interface. It can be accessed from the Enterprise Services Builder home page or by using the URL *http://<HostName>:<Port>/rwb/index.jsp*. All of the monitoring functions are embedded as links in the Runtime Workbench page of SAP NetWeaver PI. The SAP NetWeaver PI monitoring functions can be classified into the categories described below.

- **Component monitoring**
  Component monitoring enables the viewing of the status of each of the components registered in the System Landscape Directory (SLD). It can be used to display and monitor the SAP NetWeaver PI components including the Integration Server, ABAP proxy systems, noncentral Adapter Engines, Java SE Adapter, System Landscape Directory (SLD), Enterprise Services Repository, Integration Directory, and the Runtime Workbench itself. It is also used to call the configuration data of individual SAP NetWeaver PI components and provides test tools to perform self-test on each of the components to check whether they are functioning correctly.

- **End-to-end monitoring**
  End-to-end monitoring focuses on the monitoring of a message lifecycle from a PI point of view. In other words, it enables the complete view of the message flow from the initiation of the message until the final step performed on the message. It gives a graphical representation of the message flowing through the various components of the SAP system. This helps the system administrators

monitor message processing steps in a number of SAP components and monitor the path of the individual messages flowing through these components.

▶ **Message monitoring**

Message monitoring enables the tracking of the message processing status within an SAP NetWeaver PI component and can be used for error detection and analysis. Messages can be viewed for a specific component such as the Integration Server, Adapter Engine, and so on.

Once the list of messages is displayed for the chosen component, each message status and details can be viewed, and errors in the processing of the message can be detected. Message monitoring in SAP NetWeaver PI can be done in two different ways:

▶ *Message monitoring using the Runtime Workbench* is a Java-based interface and can be used to monitor messages for a specific component such as the Integration Sever, Adapter Engine, and so on.

▶ *Message monitoring using Integration Engine Monitoring* is an ABAP-based interface where the monitoring is done on the ABAP Server using Transaction SXMB_MONI. This can be used to monitor the processing and status tracking of messages and message packages on the Integration Engine.

▶ **Performance monitoring**

Performance monitoring can be used to display statistical data on the performance of the message processing. It helps in getting the performance details either as an aggregate overview of message processing involved in a specific component or of individual messages including the message size, processing time, and so on.

In the following sections, we discuss each of these monitoring tools in more detail.

5.2   Component Monitoring

Component monitoring is used when you want to get an overview of the status of the individual components of SAP NetWeaver PI. It can be used to display the components including the Integration Server (Integration Engine, Business Process Engine, Mapping Runtime, and Adapter Engine), ABAP proxy systems, non-central Adapter Engines, Java SE Adapter, System Landscape Directory, Enterprise Services Repository, Integration Directory, and the Runtime Workbench itself.

Component monitoring provides the tabular view or the tree view to display the components:

▶ The *tabular view* displays all of the SAP NetWeaver PI components maintained in the System Landscape Directory, their current Computing Center Management System[1] (CCMS) status, and the name and type of the component.

▶ The *tree view* sorts the components by component type. You can select the component from the displayed view to check the current status such as ping and execute self-test for the selected component.

Component monitoring can also be used to check the configuration of the selected component. Figure 5.2 displays an example view of the **Component Monitoring** in the Runtime Workbench.

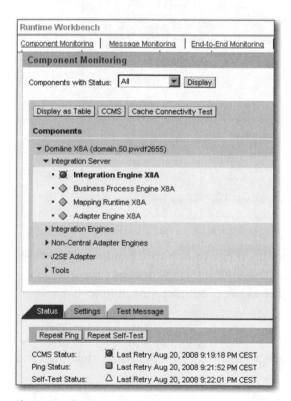

Figure 5.2 Component Monitoring

---

1 The Computing Center Management System (CCMS) consists of a set of integrated tools for monitoring and administration of SAP system landscapes.

Component monitoring can also be used to check whether the runtime components are functioning correctly, by using test messages. These test messages can be performed on the runtime components such as the Integration Engine, Adapter Engine, and Java SE Adapters. Messages can be tested by providing all of the relevant message header and message payload information in the **Test Message** tab page as shown in Figure 5.3. These test messages can also be stored in the database for later use.

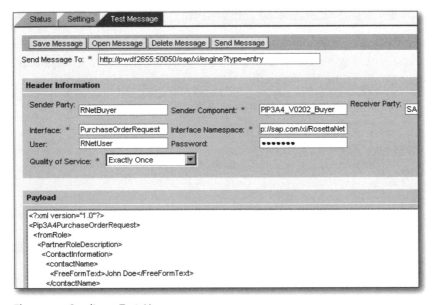

Figure 5.3 Sending a Test Message

In addition to the above monitoring functions, component monitoring provides the following monitoring functions. These monitoring functions are only available if you choose the **Adapter Engine** as the component for monitoring:

▶ **Background processing**
You use background processing for scheduling the background jobs. The features include scheduling the background jobs for archiving, deleting, and restarting the messages with errors.

▶ **Communication channel monitoring**
Communication channel monitoring is used for monitoring and administering the communication channels that are set up for a selected Adapter Engine. It can be used for checking the status of your communication channels and the

corresponding adapters. It also has a function for scheduling the stop and start of the communication channels either defining locally by **Availability Times** or by using a HTTP request. Figure 5.4 shows an example view of the **Communication Channel** monitoring.

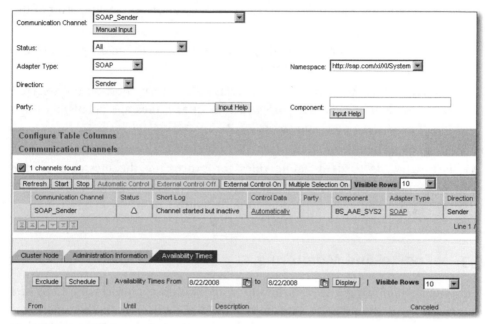

Figure 5.4 Communication Channel Monitoring

▶ **Security archiving**
This function is used to archive messages using secure S/MIME settings with a feature to set the start time and time interval for archived sessions.

▶ **JPR monitoring**
This function is used for monitoring the Java Proxy Runtime (JPR) in the chosen adapter and getting an overview of the current status of the JPR.

▶ **Engine status**
This function is used for displaying the current technical status of the selected Adapter Engine. You can also display the current technical data for several server nodes of an Adapter Engine. It has several tabs showing the status at sev-

eral nodes including the Backlog, Database Locks, Messaging Overview, and Additional Data.

▸ The **Backlog** tab displays all of the communication components for the senders and receivers that are defined for a selected adapter engine.

▸ The **Database Lock** tab displays the time of creation and locking user of the database locks.

▸ The **Messaging Overview** tab displays the status of the messages since the last restart of the Adapter Engine.

▸ The **Additional Information** tab displays the information on the selected server node in various categories such as queue, message details, message search, event handler, and so on.

▸ **Message prioritization**
This function is used to define rules for processing the messages on the Adapter Engine with low, normal, and high priorities. You can use the attributes from the message header to define such rules.

5.3   End-to-End Monitoring

End-to-end monitoring is used for monitoring the message processing steps in a number of SAP components and monitoring the path of individual messages flowing through these components. It helps the system administrators visualize the entire flow of the individual messages flowing through the various components from the beginning to the end of the message processing. Each of these components is configured for being monitored in end-to-end monitoring.

All of the SAP components that are involved in this monitoring must have a logon group of PUBLIC. The data for end-to-end monitoring is provided by the Process Monitoring Infrastructure (PMI), which is an SAP monitoring tool for monitoring end-to-end technical processes involving multiple SAP components. The runtime data of the various SAP NetWeaver PI components are assembled to form a chain of process steps by the PMI.

End-to-end monitoring requires the activation of HTTP services required for the PMI that can be configured using Transaction Code SICF on the ABAP system. You also need to ensure that the service user for the Runtime Workbench (PIRWBUSER) has been defined in each component that is to be included in end-to-end monitoring.

Figure 5.5 shows the initial screen of end-to-end monitoring in SAP NetWeaver PI.

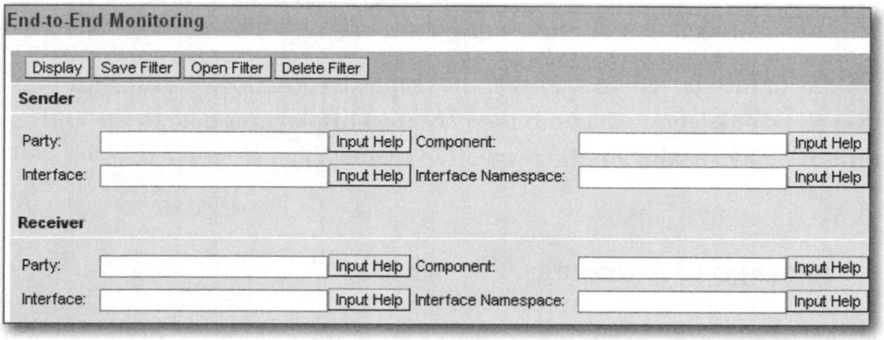

Figure 5.5 End-to-End Monitoring

End-to-end monitoring has two views for displaying the data delivered from the PMI:

▶ **Process overview**
The process overview contains the graphical representation of the components involved in the process flow and displays the total number of processed messages and number of messages with errors for each component involved.

▶ **Instance ciew**
The instance view provides the detailed data for each individual processing step in a process instance. It contains the graphical representation of the components involved in the process and displays the status of each component that the instance passes through.

The PMI collects data from various different systems by means of PMI agents, which provide the PMI with the data necessary for assembling the processes. For the industry standard adapters such as RNIF and CIDX, a set of PMI agents are invoked in the adapters. These agents include the following:

▶ The *Adapter Inbound Agent* tracks the arrival of a message in the sender adapter. It is invoked as soon as the message is received.

▶ The *Adapter Outbound Agent* tracks the outgoing message in the receiver adapter. It is invoked as soon as the message is sent out of the adapter.

▶ The *CPA Lookup Agent* tracks the data retrieved by the CPA lookup. It is invoked immediately after the successful CPA lookup.

▶ The *ID Mapping Agent* tracks the change in the message ID. It is invoked immediately after a change in the message ID.

▶ The *Status Agent* tracks the status of the message processing. It is invoked when there is an error situation or after successful sending of the message.

The invoking of the above PMI agents at the respective locations ensures the passing of the relevant adapter data onto the PMI. You display this data in the end-to-end monitoring by clicking on the respective agent call.

5.4   Message Monitoring

The message monitoring tool can be accessed from the Runtime Workbench and is used to track the status of messages that were sent and received in a selected component. Messages can be viewed for components such as the Integration Engine, the central Adapter Engine, the noncentral Adapter Engine, and the Proxy Runtime. This tool allows system administrators to track the errors in each message and to find out what caused them. You can choose between the **Database**, **Index**, and **Archive** overview for the selected component to get the current status of the message processing.

5.4.1   Message Overview

The **Message Overview** screen gives the high-level overview of the error and scheduled and successful messages in a particular time period sorted by sender and receiver attributes. These messages are grouped according to their processing status. From this screen, system administrators should be able to drill down further to the details of the message for each status group. Figure 5.6 displays the message overview in the message monitoring.

5.4.2   Message Selection

The message monitoring function is used for searching all of the messages that were sent or received in the selected component. You can select between **Database**, **Archive**, or **Index** overview for the required component to get an overview of current status of the messages.

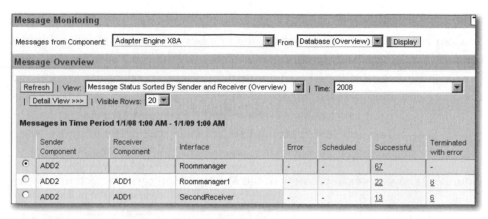

Figure 5.6 Message Overview in the Message Monitoring

You can also perform an index search for the messages that were previously indexed using the SAP Search and Classification Engine, formerly known as TREX. You need to configure the SAP Search and Classification Engine to perform this kind of search. In addition to the static header attributes, index-based search uses adapter-specific message attributes and the main payload of the message for the search. You can apply index-based message search to all indexed components such as the Integration Server, Adapter Engine, and ABAP Business systems.

SAP Search and Classification Engine

The SAP Search and Classification Engine is a search engine in the central SAP NetWeaver produced by SAP AG. It is the basic part of the SAP NetWeaver Search Integration Capabilities and is primarily used as an integral part of SAP NetWeaver products such as Business Intelligence, Enterprise Portal, Knowledge Warehouse, Process Integration, and so on. The engine's services include search and retrieval in large document collections, text mining, automatic document classification, and search and aggregation of structured data in SAP applications. The SAP Search and Classification Engine supports various kinds of text search including exact search, Boolean search, wild card search, fuzzy search, and linguistic search and can handle text from documents in numerous formats, including Microsoft Office and Adobe formats (PDF), and more than 30 languages.

5.4.3   Message Lists

You can enter filter criteria to restrict the number of messages displayed in the message list. In the **Additional Criteria** section of the tool, you can use static header attributes such as party, component, interface, interface namespace, and the processing time to search for specific messages. In addition, the adapter-specific message attributes criterion is available in the **Extended Criteria** section. The criteria **Search Text** and **Search Method** are available specifically for index-based message search to search the payload.

Figure 5.7 shows an example view of the Message Monitoring Selection Screen.

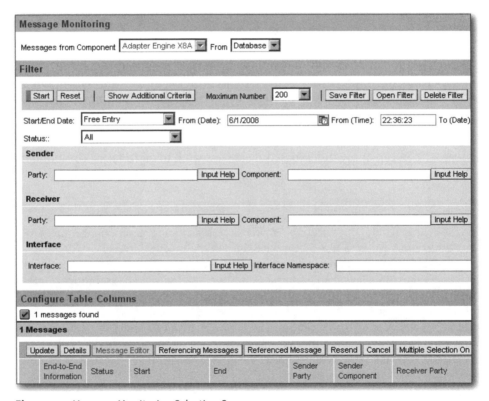

Figure 5.7 Message Monitoring Selection Screen

5.4.4   Message Details

You can get the detailed view of a selected message from the **Message** lists for the selected component by clicking on the **Details** button. The content and select options for this detailed window vary according to the type of the selected component and the type of adapter. The following options or tabs are available to both the Integration Engine and the Adapter Engine in the detailed window:

▶ **Message Data**
The message data provides all the information about a message.

▶ **Message Content**
The contents of the message such as SOAP document, payload, and attachments are displayed.

▶ **Audit Log**
The audit log for the selected message is displayed. This is displayed only if the message is from a Web service.

▶ **End-to-end Monitoring**
If the corresponding data exists for the selected message, this option takes you to the end-to-end monitoring instance view.

In addition to the above options, the following options or tabs are available only for the Integration Engine:

▶ **Inbound Adapter**
This tab page is displayed only if the message is from an IDoc adapter.

▶ **Outbound Adapter**
This tab page is displayed only if the message is going to an IDoc adapter.

▶ **Queue Monitor**
This tab is displayed only for asynchronous messages.

In addition to the options described above, the following options are available only for the Adapter Engine:

▶ **Message Security**
The system displays the security agreement and the certificates for the selected messages.

▶ **Adapter Details**
This option is available only for the messages processed by industry standard adapters such as RNIF and CIDX.

Figure 5.8 shows the detailed view of the RNIF message in the Adapter Engine.

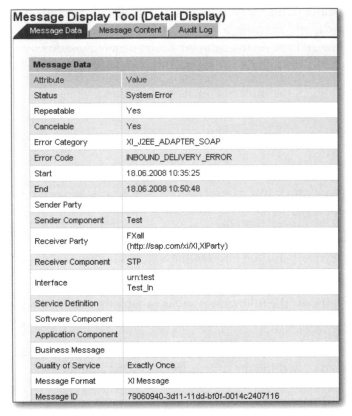

Figure 5.8 Detailed View of an RNIF Message in the Adapter Engine

5.4.5 Message Editor

As of release 7.1 of SAP NetWeaver PI, message monitoring has a new function for editing the message payload. You can use the message editor to edit the header or the payload data of a message, save changes, and process them again. Messages are blocked for other users during this processing. You need to have the required authorizations of the `edit_header` and `edit_payload` roles to edit the header and payload data of the message. You can only use message editor for asynchronous messages with errors that can be restarted. This feature is very useful when errors such as syntax, XML validation, and mapping errors occur during the processing and you want to correct and resend it instead of asking your trading partner to resend the message. For messages that are processed by an integration process, you can call the message editor from the work item display.

5.4.6 Other Features

A few other features are available as part of the message monitoring, such as the following:

▶ **Referencing messages**
This feature can be used to select messages that reference a specific message.

▶ **Referenced messages**
This feature can be used to select messages that are referenced by a specific message.

5.5 Integration Engine Monitoring

Integration Engine monitoring is used for monitoring the processing of all the *messages* and *message packages* that are processed by the Integration Engine. It can be accessed by using SAP Transaction SXMB_MONI or by using the menu path **Process Integration • Monitoring • Integration Engine Monitoring**. Monitoring contains a monitor for processed XML messages that are persisted in the database. You can also display the versions of the message in the message monitoring. The messages can be selected according to the selection criteria. It offers two different views of processed messages:

▶ **Default view**
This view displays all the messages that met the chosen criteria.

▶ **Process view**
This view displays only the messages that were processed by the Business Process Engine. The displayed messages are grouped according to the process instances involved.

You can perform the search on the messages, restricting the messages to a particular **Status Group** or **Status**. The **Standard Selection Criteria** include the selection of static header attributes such as **Party**, **Service**, **Interface Name**, and **Interface Namespace** and the **Processing Time**. The **Advanced Selection Criteria** include message attributes such as **Message ID**, **Message Type**, **Error ID**, and so on and an option for selecting acknowledgement messages. Figure 5.9 shows an example view of the message monitoring.

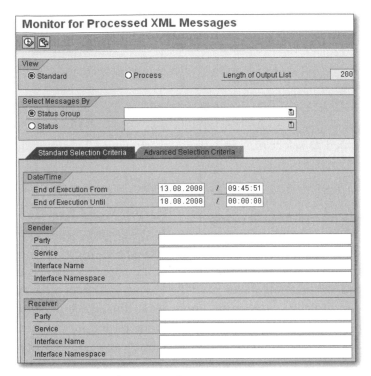

Figure 5.9 Monitor for Processed XML Messages

You have to define your selection in the selection criteria, and select **Execute** to display the messages specific to your scenario. The system displays a list of persisted messages that match your selected criteria. The system lists your messages in chronological order. The list contains information about the messages such as message status, status of acknowledgement, sender and receiver attribute information, quality of service, and so on. It also contains the information about technical inbound and outbound channels such as PE, WS, IDOC, PROXY, AENGINE, and so on. Figure 5.10 shows an example view of the message monitoring in Transaction SXMB_MONI.

The detailed view of the message shows the status of the selected message at each pipeline step in the series of pipeline steps such as XML validation, receiver identification, interface determination, message split, message mapping, technical routing, call adapter, and so on. Pipeline steps are discussed in detail in Section 2.5.4 Pipeline Steps in SAP NetWeaver PI. Figure 5.11 shows an example of a detailed view of the message in the Integration Engine message monitoring.

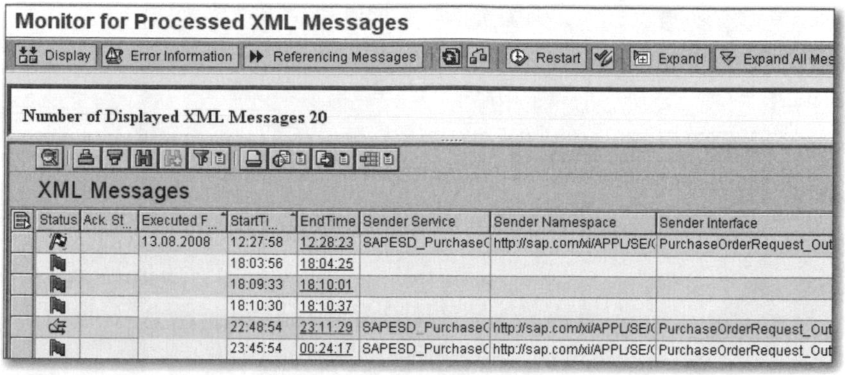

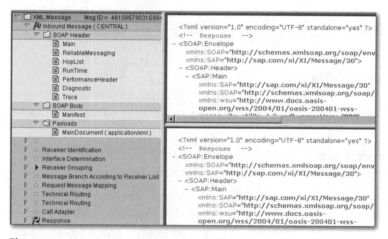

Figure 5.10 Message List in the Integration Engine Monitoring

Figure 5.11 Message Monitoring – Detailed View

5.6 Performance Monitoring

Performance monitoring is used to get the performance details or statistical data of the message processing for analysis. It offers you quick insight into the number of messages that were processed in a specific time period for a specific interface or for a specific combination of sender and receiver interfaces. It is based on the data collected from the Integration Server or from the PMI at runtime. The data from PMI informs you about the performance of the message processing on the Adapter Engine. Figure 5.12 displays a sample view of the performance monitoring in the Runtime Workbench.

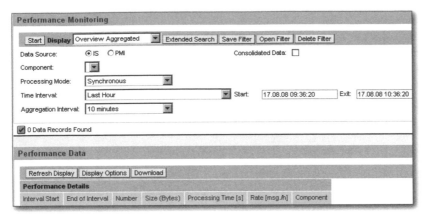

Figure 5.12 Performance Monitoring

Performance monitoring displays the following types of data in the message processing:

▶ **Aggregated overview data**
This data gives you an overview of the number of messages that were processing on the SAP NetWeaver PI component in a specific time period and in specific aggregation interval.

▶ **Individual overview data**
This data displays the overview data for each individual message.

▶ **Aggregated detailed data**
In addition to the aggregated overview data, this data displays the detailed data of the messages that were processing on the SAP NetWeaver PI component with a time stamp.

▶ **Individual detailed data**
In addition to the individual overview data, this data displays details about the time of specific processing steps for each individual message with a time stamp.

5.7 Alerting Capabilities

Alerts come into play, when business-critical situations occur within an organization. The information about the critical situation is sent to the appropriate recipients so that an action can be taken immediately in order to resolve the situation.

Alerts could occur because of a purchasing process in an ERP system or a BPM alert coming from SAP NetWeaver PI. Examples of critical situations are when a minimum inventory threshold has been reached or will occur shortly. Alert management is an ideal solution when you identify the critical business situations and want specific business recipients to be notified if these situations arise. Alerts can add a tremendous value to an organization if the timely action is taken in response to the alert notification.

5.7.1 Alert Management

The cornerstone of alert management is the central Alert Framework, the infrastructure for generating, sending, and displaying alerts. The Alert Framework is provided as part of the SAP NetWeaver Application Server. It offers a powerful framework for rapid, robust, and reliable information delivery to users. The application triggering alerts must define its own alert categories, assign them to alert classifications, and implement the triggering of the alert instances to realize alert management. When the critical situation defined in the alert category arises, the system recognizes this and sends an alert instance of the specified category to the recipients determined. The Alert Framework integrates well with a variety of information sources and channels. The user can choose which medium can be used for the delivery of the alert message. Alerts by default are routed to the user's alert inbox, but using the alert configuration, alerts can also be delivered to users via other media such as email, fax, or SMS or to the Universal Work List (UWL) within the SAP NetWeaver Portal.

For B2B scenarios, the information that is passed along with the alert enables easy identification of the message and the error that triggered the alert. For communication with industry standard adapters such as RNIF and CIDX, alerts are raised for various reasons. Several use cases representing the scenarios in which the alerts would be raised for these adapters are listed below:

▶ The system receives or sends out an exception for the RosettaNet or Chem eStandard Action message.

▶ The system receives a notification of failure due to the failure in message processing at the partner's end.

▶ The system at the partner's end fails to send a receipt acknowledgement for the RosettaNet or Chem eStandard Action message sent.

▶ The system receives a RosettaNet or Chem eStandard Action message and a system error or application error is raised.

▶ When a system initiates a RosettaNet or Chem eStandard Action message, the necessary certificates could not be found in the key store.

▶ For a signed RosettaNet Action message sent across, the receipt acknowledgement has no signature.

▶ A system sends across a RosettaNet Action message but receives no response message in a two-action scenario.

▶ In a two-action scenario, there is a failure in correlating the response message to the RosettaNet Action message.

5.7.2 Alert Configuration

To raise alerts, configuration is needed to use the Alert Framework. Alert categories can be defined using the Runtime Workbench or by using the SAP Transaction ALRTCATDEF. In both cases, you require the authorizations of the role SAP_XI_ADMINISTRATOR to configure the alerts. The steps involved in the process flow of alert configuration are listed below.

Step 1: Define Alert Classification

Alert classifications are used to group alert categories according to their subject. For example, all the B2B categories from one application could be assigned to the same classification. Figure 5.13 shows an example view of the alert classification.

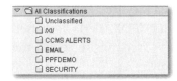

Figure 5.13 Alert Classification

Step 2: Defining the Alert Category

An alert category is used for logical administration of alerts and contains various properties and specifications such as alert text, expiry time, escalation, and so on that define the alerts in that category. Figure 5.14 shows an example view of the Alert Category screen.

Figure 5.14 Alert Categories

The properties for the alert category can be specified in the **Properties** tab of the alert category. These properties include **Description, Classification, Priority, Maximum Number of Deliveries, Expiry Time in Minutes, Escalation Recipient**, and so on. Figure 5.15 shows an example view of the properties for the alert category.

Properties	Container	Long and Short Text	Optional Subseq Activities

Alert Definition	
Description	Alerts for errors in the RNIF message processing
Alias	
Classification	Alerts for B2B messages
Priority	High
Max. No. of Dels	3
	☐ Dynamic Text
Expiry Time in Min.	1.440

Rule-Based Recipients	
Rule	

Escalation		
☐ Escalation Active	Escalation Recipient	
	Tolerance Time(Min.)	0

Figure 5.15 Properties for the Alert Category

Step 3: Defining Container Variables

The necessary information of the critical situation is passed along with the alert message to the recipients to identify and analyze the exact reason for the failure. In the **Container** tab of the alert category, you can define container variables that you want to use in the message text of the alert message. These variables can be used in the short text or long text of the alert category. You can also define other application-specific variables such as customer number, material number, company code, and so on that can be passed along with the alert message. These variables are then replaced at runtime with values from the runtime container.

Table 5.1 lists the most important available container variables that can form part of the alert long text defined in the alert category.

Container Variable	Meaning
SXMS_MSG_GUID	Message ID
SXMS_RULE_NAME	Description of the alert rule
SXMS_ERROR_CODE	Error code
SXMS_FROM_PARTY	Sender party
SXMS_FROM_SERVICE	Sender service
SXMS_FROM_NAMESPACE	Sender namespace
SXMS_FROM_INTERFACE	Sender interface
SXMS_TO_PARTY	Receiver party
SXMS_TO_SERVICE	Receiver service
SXMS_TO_NAMESPACE	Receiver namespace
SXMS_TO_INTERFACE	Receiver interface
SXMS_TO_ADAPTER_TYPE	Adapter type
SXMS_TO_ADAPTER_ERRTXT	Error text from the Adapter Engine

Table 5.1 Available Container Variables for Alert Category

In addition to the variables listed in Table 5.1, some of the error information variables that are specific to the industry standard adapters such as RNIF and CIDX are listed in Table 5.2.

Container Variable	Meaning
SXMS_AF_ERRVAL5	Process instance identifier
SXMS_AF_ERRVAL3	Proprietary document identifier
SXMS_AF_ERRVAL4	Date and time stamp of the message

Table 5.2 Container Variables Specific to RNIF and CIDX Adapters

Container Variable	Meaning
SXMS_AF_ERRVAL1	Message identifier of intiating action or response message
SXMS_AF_ERRVAL2	Message tracking identifier of the failing action or response message
SXMS_AF_ERRVAL6	Message identifier of the exception signal sent or received
SXMS_AF_ERRVAL7	Message identifier of the notification of failure
SXMS_AF_ERRVAL8	Process instance identifier of the notification of failure

Table 5.2 Container Variables Specific to RNIF and CIDX Adapters (cont.)

Figure 5.16 shows an example view of the container variables defined in the alert category.

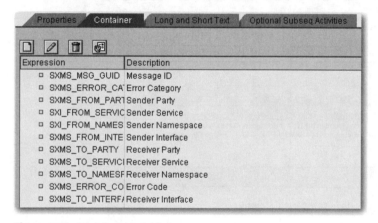

Figure 5.16 Container Variables

These variables values along with message text help the system administrators or the business users quickly identify the cause of the problem and take the necessary action.

Maintaining Alert Text

The message text in the alert category helps send a detailed message to the recipients of the message. You can maintain the alert text in the **Long and Short Text** tab of the alert category. Container elements defined in the container described above can be referenced along with the alert text and must be used in the format &<*element name*>&.

To reference the container elements in an alert text and to explode this correctly at runtime, the **Dynamic Text** field has to be selected in the **Properties** tab while defining the alert category. The text maintained in the **Message title** section is used as the subject for the email and fax and the alert title in the alert inbox. The **Short Text** and **Long Text** should indicate a possible reason and criticality of the message failure to the receiving person. The **Short Text** is used for pager and SMS messages, and the **Long Text** is used as the body text for the email, fax, or alert inbox.

Figure 5.17 shows an example view of an alert text defined in the alert category.

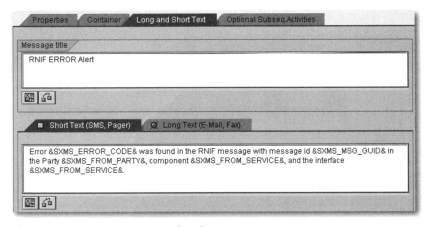

Figure 5.17 Maintaining Texts in the Alert Category

Defining Follow-On Activities

When defining alerts, you can also specify dynamic subsequent activities that could happen, based on the alert. The subsequent activities are maintained in the optional **Subsequent Activities** tab of the alert category. The subsequent activities can be defined as a URL and can trigger any program that can be rendered as a URL. For example, you can trigger an event or a program to cancel a business process.

Maintaining the List of Recipients

To notify the appropriate users about a business situation, you need to maintain those recipients in the alert category definition environment. The system administrator determines the recipients for a particular alert category and maintains the users that should receive an alert for that category using Transaction ALRTCATDEF. The recipients can be individuals or a group. The group can be defined via *User Roles* in the alert category definition. When a group is defined as a recipient, all the users with that role will have the authorization to subscribe to that category to receive the alert notifications. Figure 5.18 shows an example view of the maintain recipients screen.

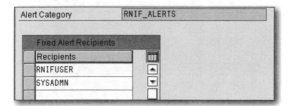

Figure 5.18 Maintenance of the Recipients

Alert Configuration

You can configure how alerts are processed. Alerts by default are routed to the user's alert inbox. For the general use of alert management, you do not have to change the default settings. However, if you want to send alerts to third-party systems or be able to confirm alerts by SMS, email, or other media, you have to configure the alert processing.

The alert configuration can be done in the alert category definition environment ALRTCATDEF, under the menu path **Settings · Configuration**. If external communication types such as email, SMS, or fax are used, these communication types must be configured correctly in the SAPconnect.[2] For detailed information on how to configure external communication types such as email, fax, or SMS, please refer to SAP Note 455140 *(Configuration E-mail, fax, paging/SMS)*. Figure 5.19 shows an example view of alert configuration for external communication.

---

2 SAPconnect enables external communication components to be connected to the SAP system. It provides a standard interface for external communication, which supports sending using telecommunication services, such as email, SMS, fax, and so on. For more information on how to configure external services using SAPconnect please refer to SAP online help at *http://help.sap.com*.

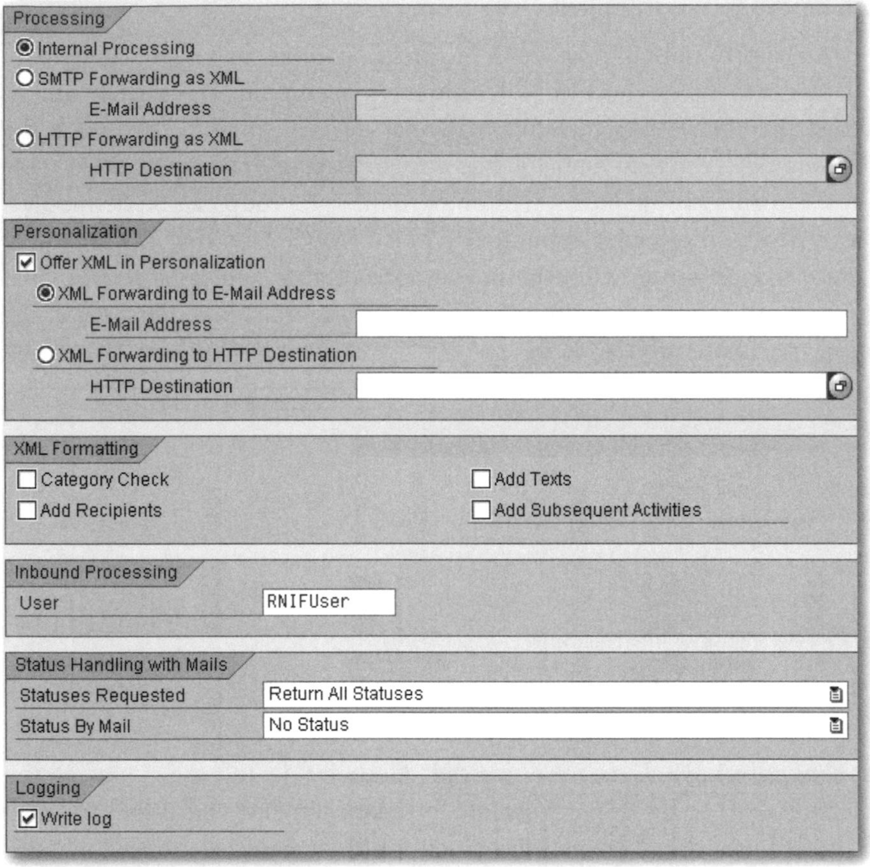

Figure 5.19 Alert Configuration for External Communication Methods

Maintaining an Alert Rule

Alert rules can be maintained for an alert category to meet the specific requirements of a business scenario. These rules can be maintained in the Runtime Workbench using the path **Runtime Workbench • Alert Configuration**. You can make these rules specific to your scenario. For example, all of the alerts for the RNIF messages can be defined to notify errors that occur in the Adapter Engine and with the adapter type RNIF. Figure 5.20 shows an example view of the **Alert Rule Definition**.

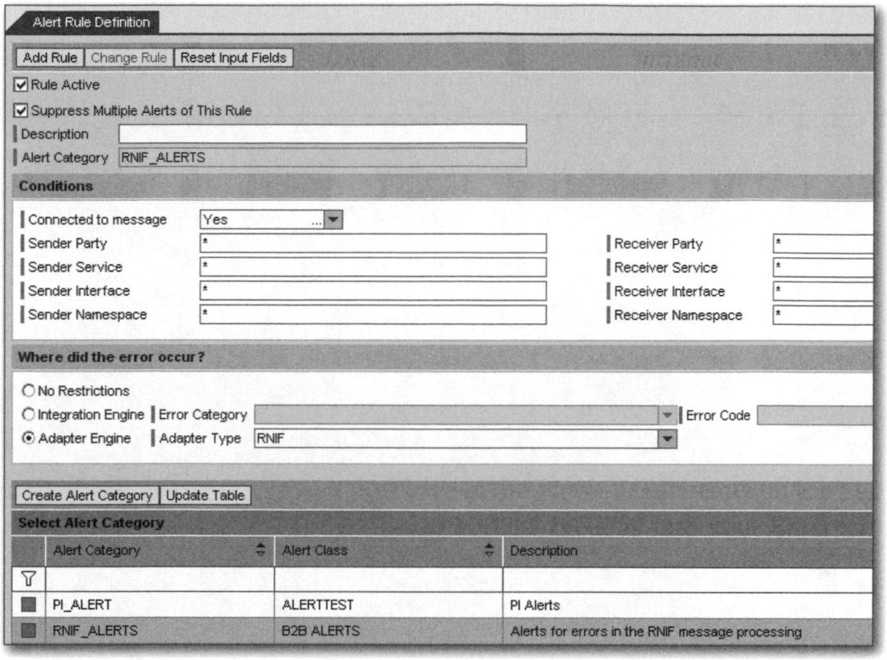

Figure 5.20 Maintenance of an Alert Rule

Alert Inbox

The alert inbox holds all of the alerts that were sent to each alert server based on the alert configuration. As described, an alert can be delivered to the recipients by means of external communication methods such as email, fax, SMS, or other media. In each case, the recipients will also find the alerts in the alert inbox, irrespective of the delivery method of the alert. The users need to subscribe to alert categories in order to receive alerts for these categories. The alert inbox in SAP NetWeaver PI can be found in the Runtime Workbench under Alert Inbox or by calling Transaction ALRTINBOX.

5.8   Summary

Having read this chapter, you should understand the various monitoring tools available in the SAP NetWeaver PI for the Adapter Engine, Integration Engine, Business Process Engine, and so on. You have learned how to track the messages to the lowest level using these monitoring tools.

This chapter gives you an overview and architecture of Business Process Management in SAP NetWeaver PI. It explains the need for BPM in an integration scenario and covers the design time, configuration time, and runtime aspects of integration processes in detail.

6 Business Process Management Capabilities

In today's ever changing competitive business environment, organizations need solutions that enable business managers and employees to effectively control their business processes including design, modeling, configuration, execution, monitoring, and analysis. Business Process Management is the solution for such organizations.

6.1 Overview

By definition, a business process is a set of process steps or linked activities that are designed to complete a business function. SAP Business Process Management (BPM) is a systematic approach to improve an organization's business processes. BPM allows companies to continuously adapt their business scenarios and processes to new business strategies and meet the demands of today's business environment. It helps companies close the gap between business and IT and enables flexible, model-driven process design, implementation, execution, and support within and across business applications. It refers to a set of activities an organization implements to optimize its processes and allows companies to model processes with different users performing different roles and tasks.

In B2B integration, Business Process Management plays a key role if an organization wants to integrate internal existing processes with trading partners in a manageable manner. Industry standards such as RosettaNet play a key role in the automation of B2B integration for both business and technology. The B2B processes can contain integration processes or broker processes that take care of the orchestration of request and response messages (for example, in a two-action RosettaNet scenario, you can correlate the response message with the original request message). These integration processes work with unique correlation identifiers (for example, purchase order numbers) that are used at runtime to detect the unique process instances.

6.1.1 Business Process Modeling Capabilities with SAP NetWeaver

Business Process Management with SAP NetWeaver and ARIS for SAP NetWeaver[1] provides procedure models, methods, technologies, and reference content for modeling, configuring, executing, and monitoring these business processes. SAP primarily divides the business processes into different subprocesses as described below:

▶ **Core application processes**

Core application processes represent the core business functionality that runs the business operations. These are delivered via SAP business applications such as SAP ERP, PLM, SCM, CRM, SRM, and so on. These processes are predefined, packaged, and can be customized in these applications.

These packaged processes are exposed as reference content in the Enterprise Services Repository of SAP NetWeaver and SAP Solution Manager to provide process insight and transparency into what is covered by business applications and how this can be used to extend the core set of highly standardized business operations.

▶ **System-centric integration processes**

System-centric integration processes are implemented to define, control, and monitor complex integration scenarios that reach beyond application systems or enterprise boundaries. An *integration process* is an executable, cross-system process for processing the messages and automating the message flow within the context of service orchestration. These processes are delivered through SAP NetWeaver PI. Typical patterns of integration processes such as collect, split, and merge or technical communication patterns such as sync/async bridge are delivered as templates to support efficient implementation.

Through system-centric integration processes, SAP NetWeaver PI supports a wide variety of business scenarios and processes, ranging from industry-spe-

---

1 ARIS for SAP NetWeaver provides various functions to evaluate, refine, and optimize business processes.

cific business scenarios such as RosettaNet to unstructured and highly structured long-running transactions owned by different business partners across multiple systems.

▸ **Human-centric composite processes**
Human-centric composite processes focus primarily on human interactions and process collaboration. These processes are mainly driven by business users and business activities and are delivered through a new building block of BPM capabilities that is integrated into SAP NetWeaver Composition Environment (CE).

6.1.2 Process Automation

Process automation is about driving processes within and across different applications. It covers the complete lifecycle of design, configuration, execution, and modeling of business processes. Process automation orchestrates the message choreography between systems and business partners using a stateful interaction model. Process automation includes two types of processes, namely, embedded processes and unbounded processes:

▸ **Embedded processes**
Embedded processes automate business processes within SAP applications. These business processes may be simple release or approval procedures or more complex business processes such as creating a material and coordinating the departments involved.

▸ **Unbounded processes**
Unbounded processes, on the other hand, automate business processes that extend across enterprise and application boundaries. These processes are mainly used to integrate third-party or legacy systems. SAP NetWeaver uses the same BPM runtime to execute both embedded and unbounded processes. It is known as the Workflow Engine in the context of embedded processes, and in the context of unbounded processes, it is known as the Business Process Engine.

SAP delivers a comprehensive solution for process automation that includes the following offerings:

▸ **Cross-component BPM**
The design and processing of integration processes is also known as cross-component BPM (ccBPM). Cross-component BPM primarily deals with structured

processes running across multiple software components. It comes with all of the necessary functionality required to design, execute, and monitor business processes that involve multiple components and systems. Cross-component BPM enhances message-based process integration with the stateful processing of messages where the status of an integration process is persisted on the Integration Server. You can group certain messages together and then send them in a particular order and can use correlations to establish semantic relationships between messages. It also provides support for handling of system exceptions and alerting.

Cross-component BPM features in SAP NetWeaver PI include the following:

▶ A graphical process editor supporting executable processes.

▶ A flexible modeling tool to design process orchestration in accordance with the Business Process Execution Language (BPEL).

▶ Process pattern templates within the Enterprise Services Builder.

▶ Wizard-based configuration of processes in the Integration Builder.

▶ Stable and secure process execution by the Business Process Engine embedded in the SAP NetWeaver PI Integration Server.

▶ Integration and interoperability with human-based workflows such as SAP Business Workflow or Adhoc Workflow.

▶ Deadline and exception handling.

▶ Process monitoring and alerting to expedite process optimization.

▶ **SAP Business Workflow**
SAP Business Workflow is concerned with structured processes embedded within the SAP applications such as SAP ERP, CRM, SRM, and so on. It delivers the tools and functionality to define flexibility within an application's process flow. You can make use of business workflows to interrupt a continuous process and transfer the responsibility for further execution to resources outside the application wherever necessary.

▶ **Universal Worklist**
The Universal Worklist (UWL) gives users a unified and centralized way to access their work and the relevant information. It aggregates all work items and notifications from multiple and different systems in one universal list. The work item inbox is where users access their work items. Work items that appear in these inboxes can span a range of business activities, from adminis-

trative processes such as a vacation request to more in-depth processes such as the evaluation of a sales opportunity.

In the remainder of this chapter we focus on the cross-component BPM tool.

6.2   Architecture

The cross-component BPM functionality of SAP NetWeaver PI primarily deals with structured processes running across multiple software components. It orchestrates messaging between systems and business partners by using stateful interactions. The components can be internal and external to the enterprise. As discussed earlier, cross-component BPM involves design and processing of the integration processes. The definition, configuration, execution, and monitoring of integration processes are all integral parts of SAP NetWeaver PI.

Figure 6.1 provides an overview of Business Process Management and how it is integrated with the various components of SAP NetWeaver PI. In the remainder of this section we discuss each of the components in more detail.

6.2.1   Design Time

The *integration process object* is incorporated in a namespace with a name and is maintained as an object in the Enterprise Services Repository. It has native access to all process-relevant design objects in the Enterprise Services Repository such as service interfaces, mappings, and so on. When modeling an integration process, users can directly link to these design objects.

An integration process receives and sends messages using *abstract interfaces*. Message interfaces of this category can perform the role of an inbound or outbound interface within integration processes, depending on whether it is used to send or receive a message. No direction is specified for these interfaces during their definition. The Enterprise Services Builder provides a graphical process modeler or *process editor* that enables users to define and edit the integration processes using various processing steps.

Integration processes adhere to standards and support open standards such as Web Services Business Process Execution Language (WS-BPEL) version 2.0 and Business Process Execution Language for Web Services (BPEL4WS) version 1.1.

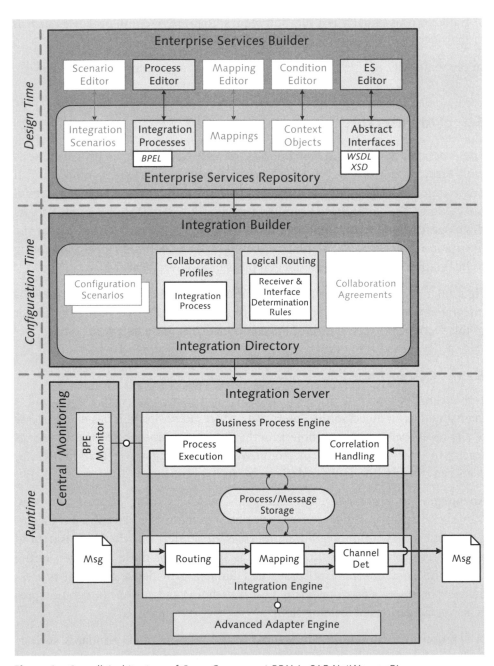

Figure 6.1 Overall Architecture of Cross-Component BPM in SAP NetWeaver PI

SAP NetWeaver PI automatically generates the WS-BPEL or BPEL4WS representation for an integration process that can be exported to a non-SAP system. Conversely, you can import representations of an integration process from a non-SAP system.

Since the release of SAP NetWeaver PI 7.1, several new modeling concepts have been introduced with the cross-component BPM. These are discussed in detail below.

▶ **Language-dependent texts**
Language-dependent texts for all modeling elements allow better documentation for all SAP-delivered processes.

▶ **Configurable parameters**
A configurable parameter is a parameter with a value that can be configured in the integration process component of the Integration Directory. This means you do not need to change the process definition if you want to change the value later.

▶ **Step groups**
You can merge frequently used sequences of steps into a step group. Step groups speed up the process modelling. The advantage of step groups is their global availability. This means that once defined, a step group can be inserted into other integration processes in the whole repository, or it can be reused several times within the same process.

▶ **Alert categories**
Another new feature is the creation of alert categories directly in the integration process. You can create an object of type *Alert Category* and use this in the control step of an integration process. After creating the alert, recipients are determined on the ABAP server using the transaction ALRTCATDEF.

▶ **User decisions**
This new step type enables a user to decide which branch of a process flow should be executed. For each decision option, a branch is entered. At runtime, the user will be notified by a dialog work item in the workflow inbox.

6.2.2 Configuration Time

Integration processes are communication components in the Integration Directory and can be assigned to a Party object. An integration process can be imported into the Integration Directory via a wizard. This integration process contains a reference link to the integration process in the Enterprise Services Repository. Integration process can be addressed as a source or target in any integration scenario in the same way as any other business system. You configure the receiver determination for the integration process in the Integration Directory.

6.2.3   Runtime

The *Business Process Engine* is responsible for executing and persisting the integration processes at runtime. It is an integral part of SAP NetWeaver PI and is embedded in the Integration Server. It communicates with the Integration Engine to execute mappings and to send and receive messages. In addition, it controls the complex and collaborative business processes and provides the necessary state management of messages exchanged between any involved components. Transaction SWF_XI_ADM_BPE, available since SAP NetWeaver PI release 7.1, allows you to start and stop the Business Process Engine in a simple and controlled way.

6.2.4   Monitoring

The execution of the integration processes can be monitored using various monitoring functions of the Business Process Engine (BPE). When an integration process is executed, the system generates corresponding work items in the workflow log similar to that of the SAP Business workflow. This workflow log enables you to see exactly what is happening in the workflow. Each work item in the workflow log represents a process or a step in the process. The BPE Transaction, SXMB_MONI_BPE can be used to display the generated work items in the workflow log and display detailed information about the status of an integration process or the individual steps.

6.2.5   Process Execution

Integration processes can be triggered by receiving a message that is assigned to a receive step or by a batch job via the job scheduling facilities of the SAP NetWeaver Application Server. Different classes of data may be accessed in a process. For messaging-relevant data, the data definition may be based on abstract interfaces, receivers, or XPATH statements to access data in the message payload. For example, define a container object based on an abstract interface to get design-time access to the structure. Data may also be based on simple XSD types and be used for controlling the flow of the process execution. For example, a counter variable is used to control a loop step.

6.2.6 Correlation Handling

A correlation joins messages that have the same value for one or more XML elements. In many business scenarios, a message may be received and must be correlated with another message. To route these messages to the correct process instance, you use the *correlation* object.

A correlation object has a name and some number of fields to match the incoming messages. For instance, line items for a purchase order may be coming from multiple places and must be appended to a purchase order create message. In this case, the purchase order number can be used as the data element to correlate the line items to the correct purchase order.

6.3 Integration Process Design with Graphic Modeler

The Enterprise Services Builder offers a special editor for the maintenance of integration processes. Figure 6.2 shows the overall layout of the Integration Process Editor with the following main areas:

▶ **Header area**
  The header area displays the name, namespace, and software component version of the integration process.

▶ **Edit area**
  The edit area is the area that allows you to create and edit the integration process. It allows you to switch between three views:

  ▶ The *Graphical Editor* is used for defining and editing steps in the integration process. It contains all the processing steps displayed in a tool bar. When a step is selected in the edit area, it becomes active in other areas.

  ▶ The *BPEL Display* displays the Business Process Execution Language representation of the integration process. Release 7.1 of SAP NetWeaver PI supports the BPEL4WS 1.1 and WS-BPEL 2.0 specifications. These definitions can be exported and imported from and to the Enterprise Services Repository.

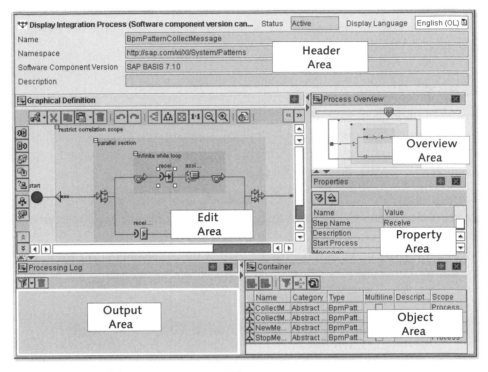

Figure 6.2 Layout of the Integration Process Editor

▶ The *Correlation Editor* is used to define the correlation data. Correlations are used to assign messages that belong together to the same process instance. For example, to ensure that the purchase order and corresponding sales order are processed in the same process instance, you define a correlation using the purchase order number.

▶ **Overview area**

The overview area shows alternative representations of the integration process. It allows you to switch between three different views:

▶ The *Process Overview* is used for displaying the section of the integration process you want to display as a tree view.

▶ The *Process Outline* view is used for displaying the integration process as a hierarchy.

▶ The *Dependent Objects* view shows the dependent objects that the integration process uses.

- **Property area**

  Each process step in the integration process has properties that can be defined and edited in the property area. These properties are specific to the type of property that is selected.

- **Output area**

  The output area is used to check whether an object is complete and works properly together with the objects referenced. It allows you to switch between four different views:

  - The *Processing Log* view displays the error, warning, and information messages.

  - The *Tasks* view displays the results of the syntax check performed on the integration process.

  - The *Search Results* view shows the results of any object searches in the Integration Process Editor.

  - The *WSDL Display* view shows the WSDL display of the data types and message types that are used in the integration process.

- **Object area**

  The object area is located right below the property area and allows you to switch between four different views:

  - The *Containers* view is the variable declaration block of the integration process and is used for defining and editing the container elements. Container elements are process variables based on the simple XSD types (date, time, integer, and string), abstract interfaces, and receivers. It can also be defined as a multiline container element for collecting messages. It carries the overall state of the integration process and can consist of an unlimited number of container elements.

  - The *Correlation Lists* view holds all of the correlations used by an integration process.

  - The *Process Signature* view shows which abstract interfaces are used in the integration process to send and receive messages.

  - As discussed earlier, the *Configurable Parameters* view is the new feature available with release 7.1 of SAP NetWeaver PI. It is used for defining the parameters that are configurable in the Integration Directory.

Any of these views in the Integration Process Editor can be maximized to the whole window or can be undocked and worked with as a separate window.

6.4   Process Step Types

The integration process is composed of several individual steps. These steps are available in the edit area of the process editor and can be inserted into the definition of the integration process by a simple drag and drop. These processing steps are mainly divided into two categories:

▶ Messaging relevant steps

▶ Processing relevant steps

The individual steps available in each category are listed in Table 6.1 and Table 6.2. Note that additional process step types can be added with future support packages.

Icon	Description
	Receive
	Send
	Transformation
	Receiver determination

Table 6.1 Messaging-Relevant Steps

Icon	Description
	Block
	Switch
	Fork
	Container operation
	User decision
	Control

Table 6.2 Process Flow Control-Relevant Steps

Icon	Description
▣	Wait
⟳	Loop
▷	Undefined

Table 6.2 Process Flow Control-Relevant Steps (cont.)

Let's now take a closer look at these individual step types used in the definition of the integration process.

6.4.1 Receive Step

As the name indicates, the receive step is used to receive messages in the integration process. This can be the first step in the process and can be used to start an integration process. The data it brings in gets transferred to the integration process. If an integration process contains further receive steps, you can correlate their messages with the message received from the first receive step.

This step can also be used to enable communication between a synchronous and an asynchronous business system, by opening a sync/async bridge in an integration process. There can be only one sync/async bridge in an integration process.

6.4.2 Send Step

The send step can be used to send asynchronous or synchronous messages from within an integration process. This step can also be used to send positive or negative acknowledgements. It can be used to close a sync/async bridge for a communication between a synchronous and asynchronous business system. Because there can be only one sync/async bridge in an integration process, there can be only one send step to close the bridge. The send step cannot be in a loop, block, or fork.

6.4.3 Transformation Step

The transformation step converts messages from one format to another and can be used to perform the following tasks:

▶ **One-to-one (1:1) transformation**
A one-to-one transformation converts one message format to another message format.

▶ **Message merge (n:1) transformation**
An n:1 transformation merges multiple messages into one message. For example, it transforms several invoices into one collected invoice. If the messages you want to merge contain several attachments, the system collects and appends them to the collected message.

▶ **Message split (1:n) transformation**
A 1:n transformation splits a message into multiple messages. For example, it transforms a combined invoice to individual invoices respecting to the original purchase orders. If the message you want to split contains attachments, the system replicates them and appends them to all the messages once they have been split.

6.4.4 Receiver Determination Step

The receiver determination step is used to get a list of receivers for a subsequent send step. This step calls the receiver determination you configured in the Integration Directory and returns the list of receivers.

6.4.5 Block Step

Some steps defined in the integration process can be combined together if they are using the same local data and need to be executed one after the other. The block step is used to for this purpose. This step can also be used to combine steps that you want to have the same deadline or exception handler or to define a local correlation. You can define the blocks in a sequence or nest them with one another.

If you want to execute the block for each line in a multiline container element, you have to define one of the following modes for that block:

▶ **Parallel for each (ParForEach)**
In the ParForEach (dynamic parallel processing) mode, an instance of the block is generated for each line of the multiline container element. All instances are processed simultaneously. For example, you can use the ParForEach mode when you want to send a message to multiple receivers simultaneously.

▸ **For each (ForEach)**
In the ForEach (dynamic sequential processing) mode, the first block runs for the first line of the multiline container element, then for the second, and so on. For example, you can use the ForEach mode, when you want to send a message to multiple receivers one after the other.

You can assign *local correlations* to a block step. This local correlation is only valid within the block and cannot be activated or used outside the block to which it is assigned. For example, you can use a local correlation in ParForEach mode to create and use a correlation with its own key for each instance created at runtime.

In a block step, you can define processing branches as *exception handlers*. Exception handlers can be defined to handle the situations such as system errors, application errors, and so on. An exception handler has the read-write access to all the data within the block. You can define multiple exception handlers for each block.

6.4.6　Switch Step

The switch step can be used to define different processing branches for an integration process. The Otherwise processing branch is created automatically. You define a condition for each processing branch that is checked at runtime. The process is continued in the branch that is first to return the value `true`. If no branch returns the value `true`, then the process is continued in the Otherwise branch.

6.4.7　Control Step

The control step can be used to terminate the current process, to trigger an exception, or to trigger an alert at runtime.

▸ **Termination of a process**
With this action, the system terminates the current process instance including all active steps and sets the status for the process to `logically deleted`.

▸ **Triggering an exception**
To trigger an exception at runtime, you have to specify the exception to be triggered. The corresponding exception handler must be defined in the same block or a super block.

▶ **Triggering an alert**

Before you can trigger an alert, you must define a corresponding alert category. You can define the alert categories in two ways:

▶ As of release 7.1 of SAP NetWeaver PI you can define alert categories directly in the Enterprise Services Builder. With this new feature, you have to create an object of type Alert Category and use this in the integration process. After creating the alert, recipients are determined in the ABAP server using Transaction ALRTCATDEF.

▶ You can define alert categories on the alert server by defining them using Transaction ALRTCATDEF on the ABAP server.

6.4.8 Loop Step

The loop step is used to repeat the execution of the steps within the loop. The loop continues to run until the end condition returns a `true` value. The end condition can be specified using the condition editor in the integration process.

6.4.9 Fork Step

The fork step is used to execute a process in branches that are independent of each other. The branches of the fork join in a union operator.

You can specify the required number of branches and then define whether the process must run through all branches or just a particular number of the branches. You can also define an end condition for the fork. The fork step is complete when the process has run through the required number of branches or when the specified end condition has returned a `true` value.

6.4.10 Wait Step

The wait step is used to incorporate a delay in a process. You can define a delay for either a point in time or a period of time. At runtime, the step waits until the specified point in time is reached or the specified period of time has passed. The system then continues the process by proceeding with the next step.

6.4.11 Container Operation Step

The container operation step is used to set a value for a target container element at runtime. The target container element and the assigned value must have the same data type. You have to use the expression editor to specify value.

You can assign a value to a single-line or multiline container element. For example, you can use this container operation to count a counter variable. You can also append a value to a multiline container element. For example, you can use this container operation to append individual messages to multiline container elements when collecting messages.

6.4.12 User Decision Step

The user decision step enables a user to decide which branch of a process flow should be executed. The system inserts a processing branch for each decision option. You then insert the required processing steps in these processing branches. The intended user receives a dialog work item in the workflow inbox at runtime. The dialog work item displays a corresponding button for each decision option that you defined. As soon as the user chooses a button, the system resumes the integration process in the relevant processing branch.

You can use local variables to define the text to be displayed for the user. A configurable parameter of type agent needs to be defined in order to determine which user should be notified at runtime. At configuration time, this configurable parameter is assigned to the relevant user in the Integration Directory. As a result, this user becomes the agent for all user decisions in which the corresponding configurable parameter is used.

6.4.13 Undefined Step

An undefined step is used as a place holder for a step that has not yet been defined and is normally used for test purposes.

6.5 Process Patterns

As discussed earlier, an integration process is composed of multiple steps. Some combinations of steps such as collecting messages or sending messages in a particular order are most commonly used functionality in an integration process. These combinations of steps are known as *process patterns*.

SAP NetWeaver PI delivers these process patterns as well as the examples for each pattern as part of the predefined integration content. These process patterns and examples are available in the Enterprise Services Repository under the namespace *http://sap.com/xi/System/Patterns* of software component version **SAP Basis**. You can use the appropriate pattern from these patterns as the basis for your own business process, configuring the steps and extending the functionality. Let's now take a look at some of these process patterns in detail.

6.5.1 Collect

The collect pattern is used for collecting several messages and merging them into one message, for example, collecting individual invoices into one collected invoice. Collecting messages can be done by using a receive step within a loop. The first message received starts the process and activates the correlation by using a correlation ID. Each subsequent message uses this correlation and is attached to a multiline container element. Once all the messages have been received, a transformation step bundles the messages in the container to a new message. This message is then forwarded to the receiver or receivers in a subsequent send step.

The following are different ways to stop collecting messages:

▶ **Payload-dependent collect pattern**
Each message that is received in the loop contains a number in the payload, which corresponds to the total number of messages to be received. The loop continues to run until all of the messages equal to the number in the payload are received.

▶ **Time-dependent collect pattern**
Messages are collected until a predefined deadline is reached. Once the deadline is met, it stops collecting and the process continues with the subsequent steps.

▶ **Message-dependent collect pattern**
Messages are collected until a stop message is received.

In addition to these options, you also have the option of collecting and bundling messages from different interfaces and stopping collecting based on a condition.

Figure 6.3 shows an example message-dependent collect pattern. In this example, the loop for receiving the message is defined as an infinite loop. The infinite loop forms a branch within a fork. A receive step is defined in a parallel branch to receive the message that ends the process. The fork is complete when both branches return `true`. However, because the infinite loop always returns `true`, the fork is only complete when the message that ends the process is received.

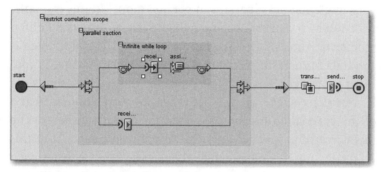

Figure 6.3 Message-Dependent Collect Pattern

6.5.2 Multicast Pattern

In some cases, you may have to send messages to multiple receivers and wait for a response from each of these receivers. This procedure is known as *multicast*. The number of receivers does not need to be known at design time. The receivers are determined at runtime from the receiver determination that is configured in the Integration Directory.

The process is started when the message in the message container element is received in the first receive step. A subsequent receiver determination step calls the receiver determination that is configured in the Integration Directory and gets the receiver list. In a dynamic block, the messages are sent to the receivers either in a parallel or in a sequential mode:

▶ **Parallel mode (ParForEach)**
In the parallel mode, the block is defined as a ParForEach. A block instance is generated for each receiver in the receiver list. A send step in the block sends the message to the receiver and activates the correlation. A subsequent receive step uses this correlation and receives the response message from this receiver. The block is complete once all block instances that were generated in parallel are complete.

▶ **Sequential mode (ForEach)**

In the sequential mode, the block is defined as a ForEach. Within this block, the send step sends a message to the first receiver in the receiver list and creates the correlation. A receive step uses this correlation and receives the response message from the first receiver. If this receive step is complete, the message is sent to the next receiver list and so on.

Figure 6.4 shows an example multicast pattern in parallel mode. In this example, the receiver determination step determines and gets the list of receivers configured in the receiver determination of the Integration Directory. The block step is defined for dynamic parallel processing (ParforEach), and a block instance is generated for each receiver in the receivers list. The send step in the block sends the message to the subsequent receiver step and activates the correlation so that a separate instance of the correlation can be processed for a block instance. The receive step uses this correlation and receives the response message from this receiver. The parallel processing is complete once the response message has been received from all of the receivers in the receiver list.

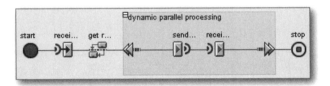

Figure 6.4 Multicast Pattern in Parallel Mode

6.5.3 Serialization Pattern

The serialization pattern is used for defining the sequence in which an integration process sends received messages. You can specify that the process must wait for an acknowledgement from the receiver each time it sends a message.

▶ **One trigger**

In the one trigger process, the process starts once the first step receives the message. When a message is received, the receive step activates the correlation. All of the subsequent steps use this correlation ID to correlate the messages. Once all of the messages have been received, the process sends the messages in the reverse order. Once a message is sent, the process waits for the acknowledgement from the receiver to arrive before sending the next message.

▶ **Multitrigger**

In the Multitrigger process, any of the messages can start the process. At the design time, it is not known which of the messages will arrive first. Therefore, the receive steps are arranged in a fork. If one of the receive steps receives its message, it starts the process and activates the correlation. This correlation is used by the subsequent steps. Finally, the process sends the received messages in the specified sequence. Each send step waits for the corresponding acknowledgement once it has sent its message.

Figure 6.5 shows an example serialization pattern with multiple triggers. In this example process, three receive steps are defined, and any of these messages can start the process. Because it is not known which of the messages will arrive first during the design time, these receive steps are arranged in a fork. The receive step that receives the message first starts the process and activates the correlation. This correlation is used by other receive steps. The fork should be complete once all three messages have been received. Finally, the process sends the received messages in the specified sequence.

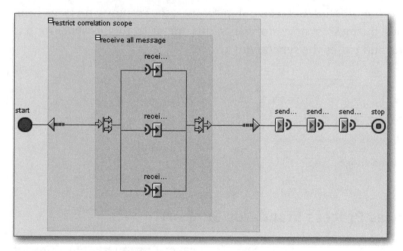

Figure 6.5 Serialization Pattern with Multiple Triggers

6.5.4 Sync/Async Bridge

Sync/async communication enables a synchronous sender system to communicate with a receiver system that cannot process synchronous messages. The central component of sync/async communication is the *sync/async bridge*, which enables the Integration Server to receive synchronous messages from a sender and send them to a receiver as asynchronous messages. Conversely, it can send the asynchronous response from the receiver back to the sender as a synchronous response.

To do this, you define an integration process, which is started as soon as a synchronous message is received from the sender system. The process uses a special receive step to open the sync/async bridge, sends the received message to the receiver system asynchronously, and waits for the asynchronous response to arrive from the receiver. The Business Process Engine receives the asynchronous response from the receiver, correlates it with the corresponding query, and activates the waiting process, which then sends the response back to the sender synchronously.

Figure 6.6 shows an example sync/async bridge process. In this example, the process gets started when the first receive step receives the request message from a synchronous business system. This receive step opens the sync/async bridge. The subsequent send step sends this message asynchronously to an asynchronous business system. The subsequent receive step receives the response message from an asynchronous business system, forwards this message to the synchronous business system, and closes the sync/async bridge.

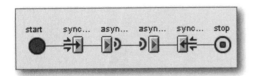

Figure 6.6 Sync/Async Bridge

6.6   Business Process Standards Support

As discussed in the previous sections, SAP NetWeaver PI supports functions for design, configuration, and execution of integration processes for the stateful exchange of messages on the Integration Server. To support portability and interoperability of business process definitions, SAP embraces industry standards that are widely adopted in the customer base. It supports the industry standard exchange formats such as BPEL4WS 1.1 and WS-BPEL 2.0 and plans to support BPEL4People. Let's now take a look at these standards in detail.

6.6.1 BPEL4WS

The *Business Process Execution Language for Web Services* (BPEL4WS) version 1.1 is one of the most widely adopted standards for the design and execution of system-centric business processes. It supports modeling of two types of business processes, namely, abstract and executable processes.

▶ **Abstract process**
An abstract process is a business protocol specifying the message exchange behavior between two parties without revealing their internal behavior.

▶ **Executable process**
An executable process specifies the execution order of a number of activities or steps that constitutes the process, the partners involved in the process, the messages exchanged between these partners, and the fault and exception handling required in case of errors and exceptions.

BPEL4WS defines the model and grammar for describing the behavior of a business process based on the interaction between the process and its partners. The interaction between these partners and their relationship is defined by a partner *link*. Each partner link is characterized by a *partner link type*. Multiple *partner* links can have the same partner link type; for example, a procurement process can interact with multiple vendors but use the same partner link type for all vendors.

The BPEL4WS process defines how multiple service interactions with these partners are coordinated to achieve a business goal, as well as the state and the logic necessary for this coordination. It also introduces systematic mechanisms for dealing with business exceptions and processing faults. It is layered on top of several XML specifications such as WSDL, XML Schema, and XPATH.

6.6.2 WS-BPEL

The *Web Services Business Process Execution Language* (WS-BPEL) version 2.0 is the successor of BPEL4WS version 1.1 and has emerged as a model for business processes based on Web services. It is considered one of the key building blocks of SOA. This version includes a lot of new features and improvements compared to BPEL4WS 1.1, but the scope remains the same.

WS-BPEL focuses on two parts:

▶ The model for executable business processes that is used to specify automated business processes that can be interpreted and executed by compliant engines

▶ The observable behavior of Web services

The language encompasses features needed to describe complex process-control flows, including error handling and compensation behavior. WS-BPEL version 2.0 is provided as a preview version through cross-component BPM of SAP NetWeaver PI.

6.6.3   BPEL4People

The *WS-BPEL Extension for People* (BPEL4People) standard is an extension of WS-BPEL for business process scenarios to enable human interactions. In addition to the orchestration of Web services, many business process scenarios require people as an additional possible type of participant, because they can also take part in business processes and can influence the execution of processes. BPEL4People is layered on top of the BPEL language so that its features can be composed with the BPEL core features whenever needed. SAP has jointly defined and developed this standard with partners to support the human interaction gap for system-centric processes.

6.6.4   Import and Export of WS-BPEL and BPEL4WS

To support the portability and interoperability, the process definitions of BPEL4WS and WS-BPEL in SAP NetWeaver PI can be used as an exchange format to import and export integration processes from and to a non-SAP system.

▶ **Export of integration processes**
The *export* function in the graphical modeler of the integration process exports the integration process definition in the WS-BPEL or BPEL4WS format. All data types, message types, and operations referenced in the process definition are exported as a WSDL description. The export generates default entries for partner link type, partner link, and role.

▶ **Import of integration processes**
The *import* function in the graphical modeler imports the WS-BPEL or BPEL4WS definition of an integration process. It imports only the definitions

and expects that all the other referenced objects in the process definition (such as the data types, message types, and message interfaces) are already available in the relevant namespace. SAP recommends that you create these objects prior to the import and assign these objects during the import in the wizard.

6.7   Monitoring and Trouble Shooting

In addition to providing general monitoring functions as discussed in Chapter 5 Central Monitoring, SAP NetWeaver PI provides specific monitoring functions for the monitoring of integration processes. There are many transaction codes in the Business Process Engine to monitor the workflow execution. The Business Process Engine is the same as the SAP Business Workflow Engine. Even though the design layer of workflows has some unique features for SAP NetWeaver PI, the runtime layer is the same as the normal workflow runtime layer. When an integration process is executed, the system generates corresponding work items in the workflow log. Each work item in the workflow log represents a process or a step in the integration process.

You can display and analyze the runtime version of an integration process in the runtime cache using Transaction SXI_CACHE. The runtime version of the integration process is created automatically from the definition of the integration process in the Enterprise Services Repository. It is created as soon as the integration process is activated in the Enterprise Services Repository. The Business Process Engine can process the integration process only when its runtime version is created without errors.

Figure 6.7 shows an example of an integration process defined in the Enterprise Services Repository and its corresponding workflow in the workflow engine.

Transaction SXMB_MONI_BPE is the entry point for all of the BPE monitoring transactions. All of these monitoring transactions take you to the same workflow log. The primary difference is the selection criteria used to get to the workflow log.

You can also use Transaction SXMB_MONI to find messages invoking an integration process. As shown in Figure 6.8, the value PE (Process Engine) in the *outbound* column of the message monitoring indicates that an integration process is involved. You can navigate to the Business Process Engine by double-clicking on this value. Figure 6.8 shows an example of an integration process displayed in the message monitoring.

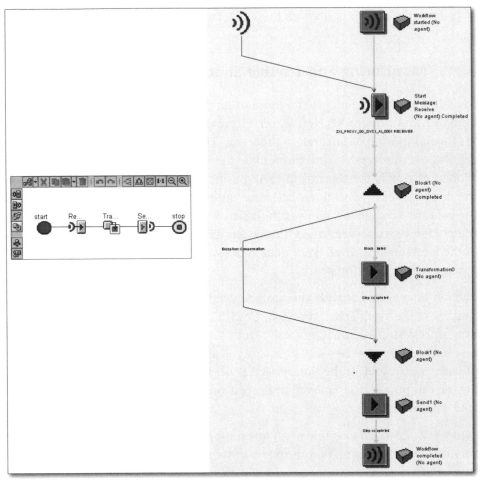

Figure 6.7 Integration Process and its Generated Workflow

Different views of the workflow log are available in the Business Process Engine. The *graphical view* of the workflow log displays the actual process flow of the workflow execution. The *technical view* displays the details of the selected step in the integration process.

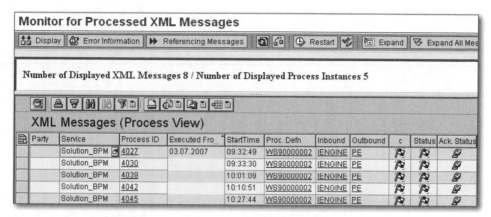

Figure 6.8 Integration Process in the Message Monitoring

6.8 Summary

At the end of this chapter, you should understand the basic concepts and architecture of Business Process Management in SAP NetWeaver PI. You have learned about the design time, configuration time, runtime, and monitoring aspects of the BPM and the different process steps used in the design of integration processes. You have learned about various business process standards and the portability and interoperability of business process definitions available in SAP NetWeaver PI.

PART II
Process Integration Implementation Aspects

This chapter explains how to implement a B2B integration scenario at a customer site. Typical system landscapes are discussed, as well as different options for how to obtain the actual SAP NetWeaver PI content and how to choose the right adapter.

7 Implementation

In the first part of the book we learned about the features and capabilities of the SAP NetWeaver Process Integration platform regarding B2B collaboration scenarios. In the second part we focus on how to utilize these features in an implementation of such a scenario.

7.1 Overview

In this chapter we discuss the major decisions you need to make when you plan to implement a B2B collaboration scenario. To guide you through this process, let's first have a look at two basic scenarios[1] that need to be taken care of from a pure business (application) point of view before we start the discussion of the technical details:

▶ **Inbound scenario**
Your trading partner sends you a message that you need to process in the correct application system. Such a scenario is called an inbound scenario. Typically your application system requires the message to be in a different format than it was sent to you by your trading partner (see Figure 7.1 for an example).

▶ **Outbound scenario**
Your application system creates a message that needs to be sent out to your trading partner. Such a scenario is called an outbound scenario. Typically you

---

[1] Within the context of our discussion we can break up other scenario patterns such as "request-confirm" or "query-response" into these basic scenarios.

have agreed with your trading partner on a message format that is different from the one used by your application system.

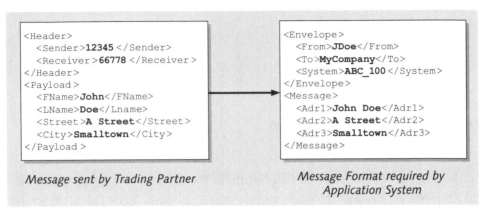

Figure 7.1 Example of a Message Sent by a Trading Partner and Processed by the Application System

Any message that is exchanged consists of two parts that will be handled in different ways:

▶ **Message header**
The message header contains, as a minimum, information about the *sender party* or the *receiver party*. Usually the receiver information is not yet complete when a message is received. For example, your trading partner cannot know your internal backend system that this message needs to be routed to and hence cannot provide this information in his message.

▶ **Message payload**
The message payload contains the actual content of the message. Usually the format of the message payload used by the trading partner is different from the format required by the application system such that the message payload needs to be transformed.

SAP NetWeaver PI takes care of the transformation of both the message header and the message payload in a number of steps. Figure 7.2 shows the high-level flow of these transformation steps.[2]

---

2 In this chapter we look at the process flow more from a conceptual level. Issues such as the transport protocol to be used for communication are discussed at the appropriate places within the book.

1. A message is received in SAP NetWeaver PI with a specific message header format and a specific format of the payload. The receiver information is not final yet, as it lacks some information (for example the URL of the trading partner or the specific system information of the application system).

2. The message is picked up by an inbound adapter in the Adapter Engine. The adapter reads the message header information and transforms it into a standard form that is used in the SAP NetWeaver PI Integration Engine.

3. The message with a standardized message header is picked up by the SAP NetWeaver PI Integration Eengine. Here the receiver information is finalized and the message payload is transformed into the format that is required by the receiver.

4. The message is then picked up by an outbound adapter in the Adapter Engine. The adapter transforms the message header into the format required by the receiver. In addition, the adapter takes care of other protocol-related issues such as security settings and authentications or the actual transport of the message.

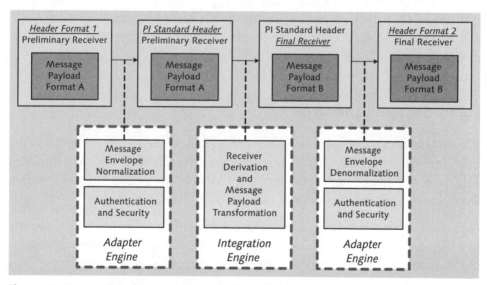

Figure 7.2 Message Transformation Steps in SAP NetWeaver PI

In addition to the transformation of the message, several other requirements need to be considered with the implementation of a B2B collaboration scenario, for example:

▶ **Security considerations**
By definition, B2B collaboration scenarios have to cross company boundaries and therefore go beyond the intra-company network that is secured by firewalls. Therefore, security issues are an important part of any implementation of a B2B scenario. We need to look at different system landscape setups because they can address different security requirements. In addition, the choice of the right adapter is important because different adapters offer different security features.

▶ **Backend application capabilities**
Any message that is exchanged between trading partners originates in a backend application system on one side and ends in a backend application system on the other side. As part of each B2B implementation project, we also need to ensure that the backend systems can process these messages correctly.

In the next sections we discuss how the requirements listed above are addressed by a number of decisions you need to make, such as the system landscape that is available for communicating with your trading partners, any predefined content you may be able to reuse, and the adapters you plan to use for communication. In addition, we discuss how you can enhance your backend capabilities if the backend is not able to support all of the features required for your B2B communication.

7.2 System Landscape

The system landscape you choose for your B2B implementation project is based to a large extent on the security requirements of your company and its related cost. Let's first have a look at the building blocks of the system landscape before we discuss the different options in the system landscape topology.

Figure 7.3 shows the building blocks that are typically involved with an incoming message using the SAP NetWeaver PI Integration Server. The picture only depicts the main building blocks; it does not show other parts such as firewalls yet. As a minimum, the following objects are involved:

▶ **Reverse proxy**

The URL of the reverse proxy is published to the Internet and hence serves as a gateway for any message requests from the outside. When the reverse proxy receives a message, it performs some security checks and then forwards the message to the actual HTTP server (represented by the Integration Server in SAP NetWeaver PI) based on predefined rules. This way the IP address of the actual Integration Server is not public outside your company borders. In Chapter 10 Security Considerations, we discuss security checks in more detail.

▶ **Integration Server**

The message is forwarded from the reverse proxy to the Integration Server in SAP NetWeaver PI. Here it is first picked up by the Adapter Engine, where some additional security checks can take place before it is handed over to the Integration Engine. Within the Integration Engine the ultimate receiver information is determined. At this point the URL of the application system is exposed. This is one of the most sensitive pieces of information that we need to keep as secure as possible. The Business Process Engine is involved only if the ccBPM tool is used (see Section 8.6 Integration Processes for more information).

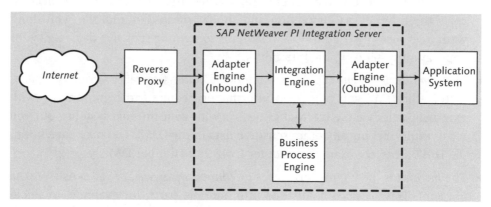

Figure 7.3 Process Flow for an Incoming Message

Figure 7.4 shows the building blocks that are typically involved with an outgoing message. The building blocks are essentially identical to the building blocks for an incoming message with the exception of the proxy. Instead of a reverse proxy an *Internet proxy* or forward proxy is used to send the message out to the external party.

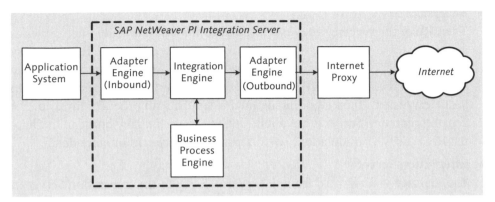

Figure 7.4 Process Flow for an Outgoing Message

Let's now look at the different options for how to place the building block we just discussed into our system landscape. Each company has a number of firewalls in place to protect their data. With the firewalls a number of different zones are created:

▶ The *Internet* is outside of any firewall of your company. Any data exposed here are available to everybody. Therefore, you need to protect data that need to cross the Internet via encryption and similar means. In addition, you don't want to expose any IP addresses of systems containing sensitive data (e.g., your application systems) in the Internet.

▶ The *demilitarized zone* (DMZ) is behind the outer firewall of your company. Within the DMZ you only keep information required to communicate with external parties via the Internet as well as with your internal systems, but you try to avoid keeping any other sensitive data in the DMZ. You may have multiple DMZ areas, for example, an outer DMZ and an inner DMZ.

▶ The *intranet* is the high-security area of your company, where all sensitive data are kept. This area can be divided into multiple parts, for example, to shield any HR-relevant data such as payroll information from the rest of your operations.

When you design the topology of your system landscape, you need to balance a number of goals that can conflict with each other. We discuss briefly some of these goals:

▶ **Security**
You want to keep any sensitive data secure and protected from the outside world. The minimal security requirements for each company are typically the following:

- ▶ You keep any sensitive data in the intranet including the URL information of the servers (usually your application systems) that contain these data. For your application-to-application (A2A) communication you always have an Integration Server (i.e., an SAP NetWeaver PI system) in your intranet area.

- ▶ To communicate with the outside world you must provide some IP address as a destination for your message exchanges. This URL should be assigned to a server that does not contain any sensitive data. Therefore, you always use a proxy server as your first point of contact with the outside world.

In your company you may have additional security requirements that can be addressed by moving some of the security checks and other checks that are performed by the adapter engine and the integration engine into the DMZ area; that is, they are performed before a message enters your intranet zone.

▶ **Total cost of ownership**
Any company is interested in a low total cost of ownership (TCO). Obviously this largely depends on the number of systems you plan to install in your system landscape. The more systems that are required, the higher the TCO. The TCO considerations can also result in a decision to outsource your communication processes to an external hub provider. Such a scenario leads to different issues and questions that are not addressed in this book.

▶ **Performance**
Performance can be impacted by the number of steps (systems) a single message needs to go through before it reaches its ultimate destination. The more steps that are required, the more overhead is created for the execution of each message. On the other hand, performance can also be improved by adding additional systems to balance the work load. For example, you can have multiple SAP NetWeaver PI systems in place for the handling of messages.

Other goals such as high availability of the system can also play an important role. The relevance of such goals depends largely on the specific customer requirements.

Let's now have a look at different system landscape options with the main focus on security requirements. Keep in mind that the complete system landscape architecture can be more complex based on your specific requirements and your already existing system landscape. For example, we recommend that you always use a *web dispatcher* right after the proxy server for load balancing purposes.

7.2.1 Minimal System Landscape Architecture

As we discussed in the previous section, the minimal requirements for a system landscape supporting B2B communication are the existence of a proxy server in the DMZ and an SAP NetWeaver PI system as the integration server in the intranet. Such a system landscape is shown in Figure 7.5.

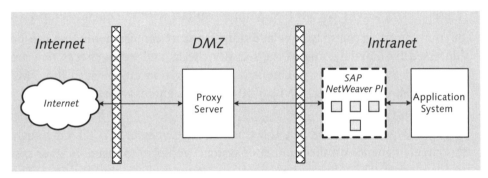

Figure 7.5 System Landscape Architecture with Limited Security

In this scenario we only have a *proxy server* placed in the DMZ that serves as a first point of contact to your external trading partners. Only the IP address of the proxy server is known to the outside world while it shields the URLs of all other systems from being exposed to the outside. The proxy server handles the translation to or from the IP addresses of the systems in your internal landscape.

7.2.2 Medium-Security System Landscape Architecture

For the next level of security we place a decentralized Adapter Engine in the DMZ as shown in Figure 7.6. The Adapter Engine communicates directly with the Integration Engine of the SAP NetWeaver PI Integration Server in the intranet.

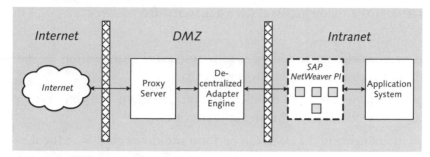

Figure 7.6 Medium-Security System Landscape Architecture

With this scenario the following issues are addressed from a security point of view:

▶ The *proxy server* shields the IP addresses of your internal systems from the outside world just as discussed in the previous scenario.

▶ The *Adapter Engine* in the DMZ handles user authorizations and takes care of certificates. Therefore, it is ensured that only messages from authorized users are passed into the intranet area.

7.2.3 High-Security System Landscape Architecture

In our last scenario the complete Integration Server of SAP NetWeaver PI is placed in the DMZ as shown in Figure 7.7. It is important to note that we still have an Integration Server in the intranet area for our A2A communication. In addition, messages coming from the Integration Server in the DMZ are received by the Integration Server in the intranet area before they are passed on to the application systems.

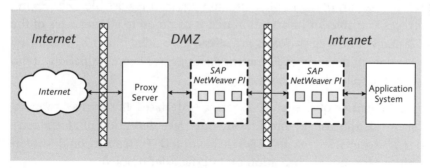

Figure 7.7 High-Security System Landscape Architecture

With this scenario the following issues are addressed from a security point of view:

▶ The *proxy server* shields the IP addresses of your internal systems from the outside world just as discussed in the previous scenario.

▶ The *Adapter Engine* in the DMZ handles user authorizations and takes care of certificates just as discussed in the previous scenario.

▶ The Integration Engine in the DMZ can perform additional checks on the message payload, such as schema validations. In addition, the transport protocol can be changed to a *Secure Network Communication* (SNC) protocol.

7.3   Reusing Existing SAP NetWeaver PI Content

Figure 7.2 illustrates on a high level how a message needs to change its format between the sender and the receiver. For a successful transformation of such a message, some additional information is required. This type of information can be divided into the following categories:

▶ Information that is trading-partner specific, for example, the URL of your trading partner.

▶ Information that is specific to your system landscape, for example the system ID of your backend system.

▶ Information that is common to all messages of the same type, for example, the rules on how to transform the message payload between different formats (message mapping rules).

Whereas information that is trading-partner specific or system landscape-specific must be provided as part of the implementation phase, it is possible to have predefined packages available for information that is common to all messages of the same type. A number of such packages are already provided either by SAP or by third-party vendors in the form of *PI content packages*. A PI content package typically consists of the following elements:

▶ The *interface definitions* of all involved message interfaces. In packages supporting B2B scenarios this usually includes the interface definition of an industry standard (e.g., RosettaNet) via an XSD schema or a DTD (see Section 8.3 Interface Definitions for more information on interface definitions).

▶ The *message mapping* that converts the message payload from the sender message payload format to the receiver message payload format (see Section 8.4 Mapping Techniques for more information on message mappings).

▶ Generic information that is required by the involved adapters (inbound and outbound). This information can be delivered via *communication channel templates* (see Section 9.2.4 Communication Channel Template for more information on communication channel templates).

▶ A high-level description of the message flow and the involved components via *process integration scenarios*. These scenarios can be used during the configuration phase of the implementation project (see Section 8.5 Process Integration Scenarios for more information on process integration scenarios).

▶ Sometimes it is necessary to provide a more advanced business process for many different reasons. If required, these advanced processes can be delivered via integration processes, called ccBPM (see Section 8.6 Integration Processes for more information on integration processes).

For PI content packages that are built by third-party vendors, SAP offers a number of certification options that are part of the *Powered by SAP NetWeaver* partner program. If you use a PI content package from a third-party vendor that is Powered by SAP NetWeaver (PBNW) certified, SAP ensures that messages will pass the SAP NetWeaver PI layer successfully when using this package.

PBNW Certification of PI Content Packages

SAP offers two options for PI content packages to receive the Powered by SAP NetWeaver (PBNW) certification:

▶ **XI Content (NW-XI-CNT)**
PI content packages are certified that usually connect a partner product to the SAP backend (predominantly used in A2A scenarios).

▶ **XI Content based on Industry Standards (NW-XI-CNT-IS)**
PI content packages are certified that involve the use of an industry standard (predominantly used in B2B scenarios).

More details about the certification process can be found at the SAP Integration and Certification Center at *http://www.sdn.sap.com/irj/sdn/icc* (choose the integration scenario **Exchange Infrastructure**).

Based on the availability of a predefined PI content package, you have different options on how to implement the required transformation of your message payload:

▶ You can utilize an existing PI content package out of the box without any changes. In most cases each implementation requires some customer-specific data; therefore, this option is not feasible for most implementation projects.

▶ You can use an existing PI content package as the starting point for your implementation and make some adjustments to fit the specific needs of your customer. We highly recommend this approach, provided a relevant PI content package is available.

▶ You can build everything from scratch during your implementation project. Obviously, this is the only option if no existing PI content packages are available for the scenario you want to implement. However, if a PI content package exists, its use can considerably reduce the implementation effort for your project.

In the following we look at each of the options listed above in more detail. Because multiple options are available if a PI content package for our scenario exists, we first discuss where you can find a list of such packages either provided by SAP or certified by SAP.

7.3.1 How to Find Existing PI Content Packages

The most comprehensive information on existing PI content packages can be found on the SAP Service Marketplace (*http://service.sap.com*). However, you need to request a user from SAP for accessing this marketplace.

The following packages are listed on this site:

▶ PI content packages provided by SAP

▶ PI content packages provided by third-party vendors that are PBNW certified by SAP

You can find the information on PI content packages on the SAP Service Marketplace as follows[3]:

---

3 This information is accurate as of the print date of this book. However, information on web sites and navigation within these sites may change over time.

1. Open the site *http://service.sap.com/solutions*.

2. Navigate along the following path: **SAP NetWeaver • SAP NetWeaver in Detail • Process Integration • SAP Exchange Infrastructure • SAP XI in Detail • Content Catalog**.

3. Under **Content Delivered by SAP** you can find PI content packages that are delivered by SAP.

4. Under **Content Delivered by 3rd-Party Vendors** you can find the PI content packages from third-party vendors that are PBNW certified by SAP.

In case you do not have an SAP user available, you can find PI content packages from third-party vendors on the following public site: *http://www.sap.com/ecosystem/customers/directories/SearchSolution.epx*. To find PI content packages only, you should limit your search to **NW-XI-CNT** and **NW-XI-CNT-IS** under the category **Third-Party Defined Integration Scenarios**.

7.3.2   Implementation of Existing PI Content Packages

For accessing PI content packages provided by SAP, you must have a valid user assigned to you by SAP. Then you can download these packages from the SAP Service Marketplace and import them into the Enterprise Services Repository of your PI system as follows:

1. Open the site *http://service.sap.com/swdc*.

2. Navigate along the following path: **SAP Software Distribution Center • Download • Support Packages and Patches • Entry by Application Group**.

3. In the main window choose the area **SAP Content** and then **ESR Content (XI Content)**.

4. You will now see a list of all PI content packages available to you. Note that some packages may require a separate license from SAP. In this case the package is only visible to you after you have obtained this license.

5. Pick the package you are interested in. You also need to decide on the version and potentially the database you want to have supported (usually PI content packages are database independent) until you are provided with the option to download the PI content package in the form of a ZIP file.

6. You can either click on the object directly and the ZIP file will be downloaded to your computer or you can add it to the download basket (in case you want to download multiple packages).

7. The ZIP file you just downloaded contains a file with the extension *.tpz*. You can import this file into your Enterprise Services Repository using the path **Tools • Import Design Objects...** in the Enterprise Services Repository.

If you want to implement a PI content package that is provided by a third-party vendor, you need to check with the vendor on how to obtain this package.

7.3.3 Adjusting Existing PI Content Packages

Although you may be able to find an existing PI content package, you most likely will need to adjust such a package for your specific implementation project. You can still considerably lower your TCO by using the existing PI content package as a starting point and only add project-specific adjustments to this package.

You can adjust an existing PI content package without modifying the delivered content by following these steps:

1. Import the existing PI content package as described in the previous paragraph. The software component versions contained in the PI content package will then be available in your Enterprise Services Repository. Let's call this software component version SWCV1.

2. Create a new software component and software component version for the adjusted PI content (see detailed description in Section 8.2.2 Software Catalog). We call this software component version SWCV2.

3. Create a dependency from SWCV2 to SWCV1 (see detailed description in Section 8.2.2 Software Catalog). Then you will find in SWCV2 a link to all objects that are available in SWCV1.

4. Adjust the content as required in SWCV2. Once you change an object, a copy of this object is created while the original object in SWCV1 remains unchanged. In Chapter 8 Development we discuss in detail how Enterprise Services Repository objects can be created or changed.

Following these steps, you can take advantage of the objects provided in the PI content package, without creating any modifications to the existing objects.

7.3.4 Building New PI Content

If no existing PI content package is available for your scenario or you choose not to take advantage of it, you need to build all of the PI content (i.e., objects in the Enterprise Services Repository) as part of your implementation project. We discuss the details on how to create objects in the Enterprise Services Repository in Chapter 8 Development.

7.4 Choosing the Right Adapter

When you implement a B2B collaboration scenario, you have to take care of the communication with your trading partner as well as the communication with your internal backend application systems. For this purpose a number of adapters are available in the Adapter Engine that are built using the Adapter Framework of SAP NetWeaver PI. The adapters are made available either from SAP directly or from third-party vendors (certified by SAP). The adapters can be divided into the following categories:

- **Application adapters**
  Application adapters are used to communicate with your backend applications. For example, with an SAP backend system you can communicate via the *IDoc adapter* (for IDocs) or the *RFC adapter* (for BAPIs or RFCs). Note that the IDoc adapter is the only adapter delivered by SAP that is not part of the adapter engine.

- **Industry standard adapters**
  Industry standard adapters are used to communicate with your trading partner via an industry standard-specific protocol. Examples are the *RNIF adapter* and different *EDI adapters*.

- **Technical adapters**
  Technical adapters can be used for external and internal communication. Examples are the *AS2 adapter* and the *SOAP adapter*.

In addition, other communication methods such as proxy communication and Web Services Reliable Messaging (WSRM) are available. Chapter 3 Adapter Concepts discusses in detail the different communication methods as well as the adapters that are available from SAP.

The most comprehensive information on existing adapters can be found on the SAP Service Marketplace. However, you need to request a user from SAP for accessing this marketplace. You can access the information on the SAP Service Marketplace as follows:

1. Open the site *http://service.sap.com/solutions*.

2. Navigate along the following path: **SAP NetWeaver** • **SAP NetWeaver in Detail** • **Process Integration** • **SAP Exchange Infrastructure** • **SAP XI in Detail** • **Connectivity** • **Connectivity SAP NetWeaver 7.0 (2004s)/SAP NetWeaver 2004**.

3. In the main window you can find the list of all adapters available from SAP and from third-party vendors that are PBNW certified by SAP.

7.5   Backend Adoption

During any B2B implementation project you will probably face some issues related to integration with your backend systems. We start with a discussion of the potential types of issues independent of the backend system that is used, followed by a discussion of how to resolve these issues for some specific examples with an SAP ERP system as the backend.

7.5.1   Outbound Scenario

Figure 7.8 gives you an overview of the most common issues you may face related to the backend system when you implement an outbound scenario. Keep in mind that the solution to these issues does not necessarily need to be done in the backend system itself. For example, some issues can be resolved in the message mapping.

The following issues are typical in an outbound scenario:

▶ **Issue A: Required information not available in the backend system**
It is possible that your business partner requires some information in the message you send to him that is not available in the backend system. For example, if your business partner expects a message in the RosettaNet format, a D-U-N-S number[4] is required as the partner ID. Such a number is not maintained in the SAP ERP system.

---

4 D-U-N-S numbers are discussed in Sectiom 2.4.2 Collaboration Profiles.

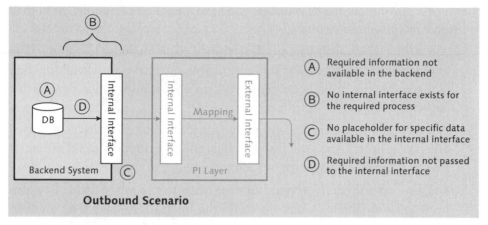

Figure 7.8 Potential Issues Related to the Backend in an Outbound Scenario

There are a number of possible solutions for this issue, for example:

▶ You can hardcode the value in the message mapping if it is a fixed value. For example, you may be able to hardcode your own D-U-N-S number in case you need to provide this information.

▶ You can maintain additional information in an add-on in your backend system or in any other external system and access these data through an additional system call in your message mapping.

▶ You can maintain additional information in an add-on in your backend system and extend the internal interface and the logic on how to fill the interface in order to provide these additional data.

▶ **Issue B: No internal interface exists for the required process**
For the message exchange you must have a communication interface available in the backend as well as the logic for filling it with the required data. If the complete interface (e.g., a BAPI, IDoc, or enterprise service) is missing for your scenario, you must define the interface as well as the programming logic on how to fill this interface. In the SAP ERP system the preferred method for resolving this issue is the generation of client proxies, which were discussed in Section 2.5.2 Proxy Runtime.

▶ **Issue C: No placeholder for specific data available in the internal interface**
For any data you want to send to your business partner, you must have a placeholder (field) available in the internal interface that can hold this type of data.

If such a placeholder is not available, you have a number of options for how to resolve this issue, for example:

- ▸ You use an additional system call in the message mapping to add the data to the external interface. For this option you must have a backend function in place that can provide the required data or you must implement such a backend function.

- ▸ You can utilize a different field in your internal interface that is not used otherwise. In this case you need to adjust the logic on how to fill the interface to reflect the new usage of such a field.

- ▸ You can extend your internal interface with the required field. You also need to adjust the logic on how to fill the interface to have the new field filled as well.

▸ **Issue D: Required information not passed to the internal interface**
Even if the required data is available in the backend and the internal interface has a place to store this information, that the program logic (e.g., the function module that fills an IDoc) may not pass this data to the internal interface. In this case you typically try to extend the program logic to handle these data as well.

7.5.2 Inbound Scenario

Figure 7.9 gives you an overview of the most common issues you may face related to the backend system when you implement an inbound scenario. Based on your specific needs, you may have additional requirements that can cause an issue with your backend. For example, if you want to ensure that all information coming in via the external interface is always stored in the backend, you can face the issue that no placeholder is available for some if this information in your backend system or in the internal interface.

The following issues are typical in an inbound scenario:

▸ **Issue E: No internal interface exists for the required process**
For the message exchange you must have a communication interface available as well as the logic for processing it in the backend. If the complete interface (e.g., a BAPI, IDoc, or enterprise service) is missing for your scenario, you must define the interface as well as the corresponding processing logic. Within the

SAP ERP system the preferred method for resolving this issue is the generation of server proxies, which were discussed in Section 2.5.2 Proxy Runtime.

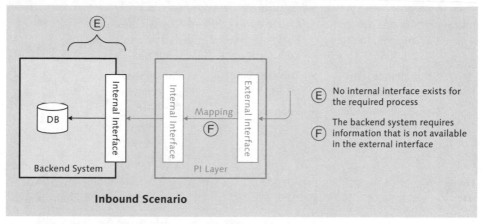

Figure 7.9 Potential Issues Related to the Backend in an Inbound Scenario

Issue F: The backend system requires information that is not available in the external interface

In some scenarios the backend system requires some information to process an incoming message in the backend that is not being provided in the external interface. Because we cannot adjust the external interface (typically defined by an industry standard), we need to find different ways to deal with this issue, for example:

▶ You can define and maintain rules in an add-on in your backend system or in any other external system and access these rules through an additional system call in your message mapping.

▶ You can define and maintain rules in an add-on in your backend system and extend the logic for processing such a message.

Next we look at how to resolve the issues listed above for the most common communication methods used in an SAP backed system. Before we go into the details we give you an overview on the solution strategy, assuming you want to solve the issues in the backend itself (see Table 7.1).

	IDoc Message Exists?	BAPI Exists?	Enterprise Service Exists?	No Interface Exists?
Issue A	▶ Create add-on in backend to store additional data ▶ Enhance IDoc interface ▶ Enhance IDoc processing logic	▶ Create add-on in backend to store additional data ▶ Enhance BAPI interface ▶ Enhance BAPI processing logic	▶ Create add-on in backend to store additional data ▶ Enhance enterprise service interface ▶ Enhance enterprise service processing logic	—
Issue B	—	—	—	Create a client proxy
Issue C	▶ Enhance IDoc interface ▶ Enhance IDoc processing logic	▶ Enhance BAPI interface ▶ Enhance BAPI processing logic	▶ Enhance enterprise service interface ▶ Enhance enterprise service processing logic	—
Issue D	▶ Enhance IDoc processing logic	▶ Enhance BAPI processing logic	▶ Enhance enterprise service processing logic	—
Issue E	—	—	—	Create a server proxy
Issue F	▶ Create add-on in backend to store rule information ▶ Enhance IDoc processing logic	▶ Create add-on in backend to store rule information ▶ Enhance BAPI processing logic	▶ Create add-on in backend to store rule information ▶ Enhance enterprise service processing logic	—

Table 7.1 Handling of Backend Issues

In the next sections we take a closer look at the different interfaces used in an SAP ERP system and the corresponding enhancement options.

7.5.3 IDoc Enhancements

IDocs (*intermediate documents*) are the standard SAP interfaces for asynchronous communication prior to the introduction of enterprise services. They continue to play an important role if you need to connect to an SAP backend system that is not yet service enabled (or the services are not utilized yet).

For a message exchange via IDocs a number of objects and configuration settings must be in place. We only give a short introduction to the main parts that are relevant for our discussion: the actual message (IDoc file) and the function module in the backend for processing the message (inbound scenario) or for creating the message (outbound scenario).[5]

The IDoc file is the actual message that is exchanged with the backend system. Besides the content itself, it always contains the information on the IDoc type and the message type assigned to the message:

- ▶ **IDoc type**
  The IDoc type contains the information about the interface definition of the message from a technical point of view. Each IDoc type is composed out of *IDoc segments* that contain the actual field definitions of the message. An IDoc type can be assigned to multiple message types.

- ▶ **Message type**
  The message type describes the business context of the message, for example, Order Creation or Order Change. A message type can be assigned to exactly one IDoc type.

The IDoc file is normally prepared (outbound scenario) or processed (inbound scenario) in the backend system by a function module. The link between the actual message (based on the attached IDoc type and message type) and the function module is provided by the *process code* (see Figure 7.10) and can be maintained using Transaction WE64. The process code is assigned to a message type and carries the information on the function module to be used. Instead of a function module, a workflow or a task can also be used. Because IDoc processing is

---

5 A detailed description of the involved objects can be found in the SAP library at *http:// help.sap.com*. Choose the documentation for **SAP R/3 Enterprise Release 4.6C** and follow the path **Basis Components • Basis Services/Communication Interfaces (BC-SRV) • The IDoc Interface (BC-SRV-EDI) • IDoc Interface/Electronic Data Interchange (BC-SRV-EDI)**.

usually handled by a function module, we will not discuss the use of a workflow or a task in detail.

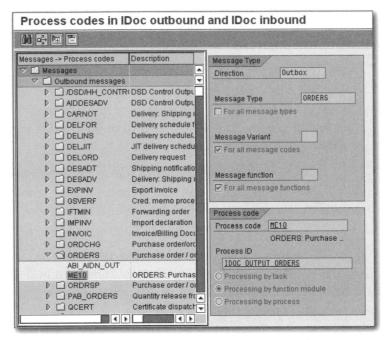

Figure 7.10 Connecting Process Codes to Message Types and Function Modules for Processing an IDoc

Enhancing the IDoc Interface

The IDoc interface is defined via IDoc types. SAP delivers a set of basic IDoc types that are configured for communication via IDocs. If you need to extend one of the interfaces defined by a basic IDoc type, you can create an extension to the IDoc type via Transaction WE30 (or the menu path **Tools • ALE • ALE Development • IDoc • IDoc Type Development • IDoc Types**). Figure 7.11 shows an example of this transaction. You can create your own IDoc segments with the fields you need to add to your IDoc interface and add these segments to your IDoc type extension.

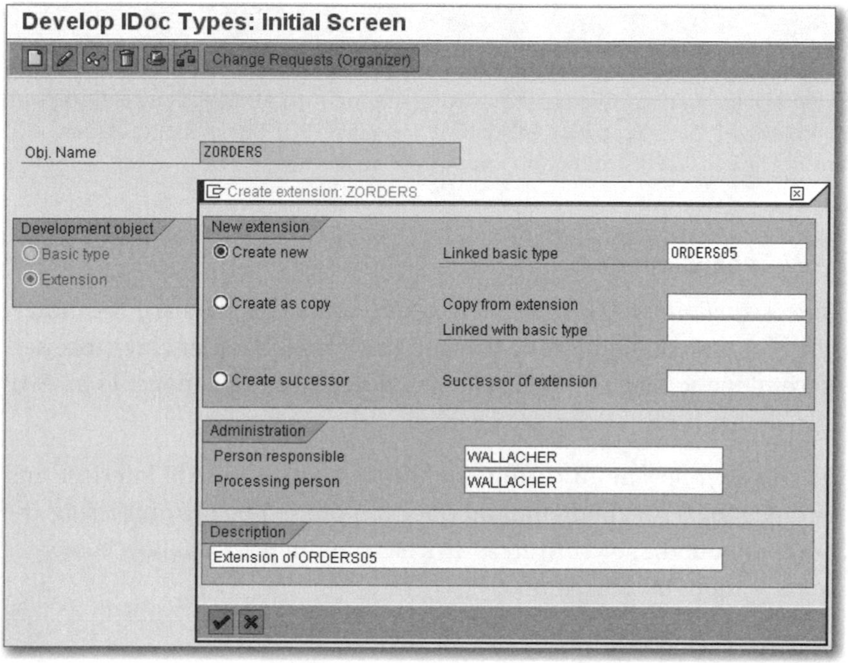

Figure 7.11 Creating an Extension of a Basic IDoc Type

Enhancing the Function Module (Outbound or Inbound)

Different options are available to find the relevant function module associated with an IDoc message, depending on the information you have available:

▸ If you search for the function module for a specific *process code*, you can use Transaction WE41 (outbound scenario) or Transaction WE42 (inbound scenario).

▸ If you know the message type and want to find the associated process codes and function modules, you can use Transaction WE64 for both outbound and inbound scenarios (see also Figure 7.10 for an example).

Each function module used for IDoc processing has a number of exits in place that can be used to enhance the programming logic. Depending on the release of your SAP backend, different methods for providing the enhancement may be realized. We discuss the different methods and how they can be implemented in detail in the following Section 7.5.6 Enhancement Options in SAP Function Modules.

Note

Detailed information on how to enhance IDoc capabilities can be found in the SAP Help Portal at *http://help.sap.com*. Choose the documentation for **SAP ERP Central Components** and follow the path **Scenarios in Application • ALE/EDI Business Processes**. At the bottom is a link to **ALE Introduction and Administration**.

7.5.4   BAPI Enhancements

BAPIs (*Business Application Programming Interfaces*) are the standard SAP interfaces for synchronous communication prior to the introduction of enterprise services. They continue to play an important role if you need to connect to an SAP backend system that is not yet service enabled.

Two major areas are relevant for customer enhancements: the BAPI interface and the programming logic for filling the interface (outbound) or for processing the additional data (inbound). For both areas SAP has tools in place to allow customer enhancements without modifications.

Enhancing the BAPI Interface

Like any function module interface, a BAPI interface is composed out of IMPORT parameters, EXPORT parameters, and TABLE parameters. Under the TABLE parameter list you can find one or both of the following parameters:

▶ The parameter EXTENSIONIN, which can be used for the import of additional data

▶ The parameter EXTENSIONOUT, which can be used for the export of additional data

Both of these parameters have a specific format that is based on the data structure BAPIPAREX. This structure offers a section of 960 Bytes[6] (divided into 4 blocks) where the actual data record can be stored as a simple string without any context information. In addition, you can specify a data structure that provides the context information on the table structure to which the data record refers. Figure 7.12 shows you the structure BAPIPAREX used for the BAPI extensions; you can view the table structure of the structure BAPIPARX using Transaction SE11. The context information is not required but makes it easier to identify the informa-

---

6 You can have multiple entries within the EXTENSIONIN and EXTENSIONOUT parameters. This actually gives you unlimited space for the extension of the BAPI interface.

tion in the data record when you need to manipulate them in the extensions of your BAPI programming logic.

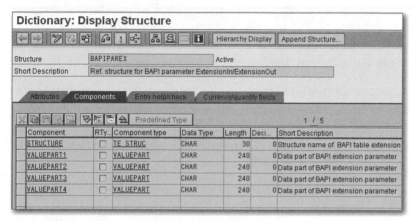

Figure 7.12 Structure of the BAPI Extension Tables

Enhancing the BAPI Programming Logic

Depending on the interface enhancements available in the BAPI, a number of exits should be available in the programming logic of the BAPI:

▶ If the interface parameter EXTENSIONIN is available, a corresponding exit should exist in the programming logic of the BAPI that can be used to fill the parameter EXTENSIONIN with the required data.

▶ If the interface parameter EXTENSIONOUT is available, a corresponding exit should exist in the programming logic of the BAPI that can be used to process the data of the parameter EXTENSIONOUT accordingly.

▶ In addition, other exits can be available in the BAPI, depending on its specific requirements.

The exits can be made available in a number of different ways that are discussed in detail in Section 7.5.6 Enhancement Options in SAP Function Modules.

Note

Detailed information on how to enhance BAPI capabilities can be found in the SAP Help Portal at *http://help.sap.com*. Choose the documentation for **SAP ERP Central Components** and follow the path **Cross-Application Components • Business Framework Architecture (CA-BFA)**.

7.5.5 Enterprise Service Enhancements

With the shift in SAP towards an enterprise service-oriented architecture (enterprise SOA), all communication with service-enabled SAP applications (both synchronous and asynchronous) will take place via enterprise services. For example, SAP ERP Central Component 6.0 already contains many enterprise services, and additional services are delivered with each enhancement package.

As with any other communication interface, the two areas relevant for enhancements are the enterprise service interface and the programming logic for filling the interface (outbound) or for processing the additional data (inbound). For both areas SAP has tools in place to allow customer enhancements without modifications.

Enhancing the Enterprise Service Interface

SAP offers a set of tools to enhance enterprise service interfaces without modifying the original enterprise service. Because enterprise service interfaces are modeled in the Enterprise Services Repository, you need in-depth knowledge of the underlying data types and their associated software components in order to understand how these interfaces can be enhanced. Because we discuss these objects in detail in Chapter 8 Development and Chapter 9 Configuration, we defer the discussion on how to enhance enterprise service interfaces to Appendix C Enterprise Service Enhancements.

Enhancing the Enterprise Service Programming Logic

Enterprise services utilize the same techniques for enhancing the programming logic as BAPIs. Among other exits, each enterprise service provides a BAdI (business add-in) with one or both of the following methods:

▶ The `inbound_processing` method is used to adjust the data that are transferred to the backend system for further processing, for example, the creation of a sales order.

▶ The `outbound_processing` method is used to adjust the data that will be returned to the caller.

See also the following Section 7.5.6 Enhancement Options in SAP Function Modules for a detailed discussion of the different types of exits.

7.5.6   Enhancement Options in SAP Function Modules

For both IDocs and BAPIs you may be required to enhance the processing logic (function module) by utilizing some of the enhancement techniques available in SAP. A number of different concepts are in place; which ones are relevant for you depends on the release of your SAP backend and the actual function module you need to enhance. The following concepts are available in SAP[7]:

► *Customer exits*, which have been available as early as release SAP R/3 3.1

► *Business add-ins (BAdIs)*, which were introduced with release SAP R/3 4.6

► The *Enhancement Framework*, which is available for systems that use SAP NetWeaver 7.0 as the underlying platform, for example, SAP ERP 6.0

We will touch briefly on each of these concepts, focusing on how to identify the exit points. We cannot discuss in detail how to implement these exits, but extensive information is available, for example in the SAP Help Portal under *http://help.sap.com* (**SAP NetWeaver by Key Capability**; follow the path **Application Platform by Key Capability** • **ABAP Technology** • **ABAP Workbench (BC-DWB)** • **Enhancement Framework**).

Customer Exits

Different types of customer exits are available for the extension of menus, of screens, and of actual coding. In our scenarios only the extension of actual coding is relevant. For this purpose function module exits are available that add additional function calls to the programming logic. These exits can be identified via the ABAP statement CALL CUSTOMER-FUNCTION followed by a three-digit number (e.g., '001') used to number the customer exits.

To implement a customer exit you first need to identify the actual function module used for the customer exit. You can get there by double-clicking on the three-digit number after the ABAP statement CALL CUSTOMER-FUNCTION. The function module only contains an INCLUDE statement to an object that does not exist yet. Figure 7.13 shows customer exit 001 within program SAPLEINM as an example. To activate the customer exit you just need to create the include object and add your source code to it.

---

7 Additional enhancement techniques are available that are used in specific applications only, such as business transaction events (Open FI). Details of these additional techniques can be found in the SAP Help Portal.

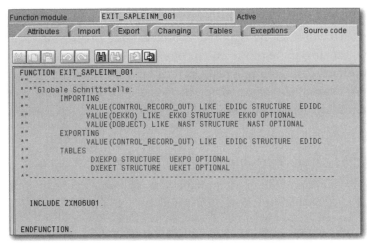

Figure 7.13 Example of a Customer Exit Used in IDoc Processing

Business Add-Ins

Similar to customer exits, BAdIs can address different types of enhancements. Because UI related enhancements are not relevant for B2B integration scenarios, we only need to look at BAdIs for extending the source code. BAdIs were introduced in SAP prior to the Enhancement Framework, but have been incorporated into this framework concept since then. Therefore, we need to distinguish between the following two BAdI concepts:

▶ **Classic BadI**
The framework for classic BAdIs is based on ABAP Objects and uses method calls to derive the actual instance of a BAdI implementation. The calling program uses the following method call to determine if there is an active implementation of the BAdI:

```
CALL METHOD cl_exithandler=>get_instance
 EXPORTING exit_name = 'BADI_NAME'
 CHANGING  instance  = bd.
```

If an active implementation is found (in the parameter `instance`), the relevant method is then executed via `CALL METHOD bd->method`.

▶ **New BadI**
The new BAdI concept is included in the Enhancement Framework and uses the ABAP statements `GET BADI badi` to search for an active implementation of the BAdI and `CALL BADI badi->method` to call a method of the active BAdI

implementation. Each new BAdI (or a group of new BAdIs) is assigned to an *enhancement spot* (see next section, Enhancement Framework). You can find the name of the enhancement spot by double-clicking on the name of the BAdI in the source code.

You can implement BAdIs from the ABAP Workbench, following the menu path **Tools • ABAP Workbench • Utilities • Business Add-Ins • Implementation** (Transaction SE19). This transaction allows you to implement the classic BAdI as well as the new BAdI (see also Figure 7.14).

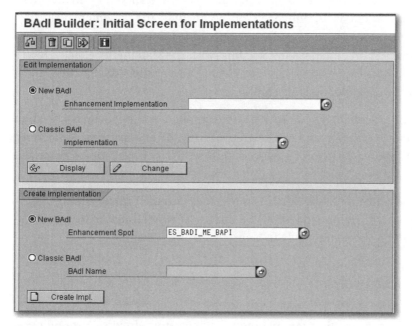

Figure 7.14 Initial Screen for Implementation of a BAdI (Transaction SE19)

Enhancement Framework

The Enhancement Framework was established to better support modifications and enhancements to SAP objects. We focus on changes to the source code only, because other options are not relevant for our scenarios. SAP allows you to modify the source code at predefined areas in the source code, called enhancement options. Two types of enhancement options are available:

▶ **Implicit enhancement options**
There are a number of implicit enhancement options, for example, after the last line of the source code of executable programs, function groups, module pools, subroutine pools, and include programs or at the end of the implementation part of a class. These enhancement options are always available and don't need to be mentioned explicitly in the SAP-delivered code.

▶ **Explicit enhancement options**
Each program can contain explicit enhancement options that are marked in the coding by specific statements. A position in a coding (called an enhancement spot) can be marked as an enhancement point (with the statement ENHANCE-MENT-POINT) where additional coding can be added or a section of the coding can be marked as an enhancement section (with the statements ENHANCEMENT-SECTION and END-ENHANCEMENT-SECTION) where this section of the coding can be replaced by customer-specific coding.

A realization of an enhancement option (both implicit and explicit) is called an *enhancement implementation* and can be created with the *Enhancement Builder* out of the ABAP Workbench. It can be viewed in the ABAP source code between the statements ENHANCEMENT and ENDENHANCEMENT.

In addition, the concept of new BAdIs is integrated into the Enhancement Framework and allows you to enhance the SAP coding at predefined areas (enhancement spots) within the source code in a very controlled manner.

Locating Enhancement Points

For both IDocs and BAPIs you potentially want to enhance the processing logic that is provided by a function module by utilizing customer exits. Although you always can browse through the function module source code to identify the customer exits, SAP also provides support in identifying all customer exits within a certain area by following these steps:

1. Identify the package in which the function module you want to enhance is located. You can find this information in the **Package** field under the **Attributes** tab of your function module maintenance screen (Transaction SE37).

2. Within the SAP menu follow the path **Tools · ABAP Workbench · Utilities · Enhancements · Project Management**.

3. On the next screen choose **Utilities • SAP enhancements**. You do not need to enter a project name.

4. Limit your search to the package your function module is located in. You identified this information in the first step.

5. After you execute the program, a list with all exits in the package is returned. Identify the exit relevant for you based on the description of the exit.

6. Double-click on the relevant exit in the list. All customer exits that are available in the specified exit are displayed. Figure 7.15 shows an example for the exit MM06E001, which is used for IDoc processing of purchasing documents.

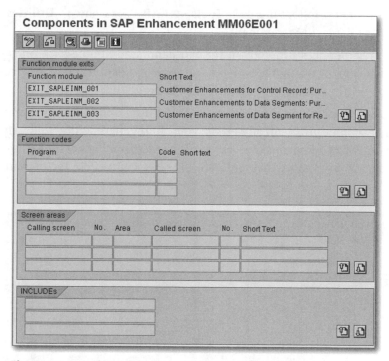

Figure 7.15 List of SAP Enhancements for Exit MM06E001

To identify the customer exits you can search the coding of the function module for the statement CALL CUSTOMER-FUNCTION. As an alternative you can use the search capabilities for customer exits provided by SAP. Section 7.5.5 Enterprise Service Enhancements discusses the search capabilities offered by SAP in detail.

7.5.7 Proxy Development

From Table 7.1 we know that proxy development is the best option for dealing with a gap in the backend if no interface for the required process exists. Because proxy development is highly integrated with the Enterprise Services Repository, we already discussed the creation of proxies in Section 2.5.2 Proxy Runtime. If you made an enhancement to the service interface used by the proxy (see Appendix C Enterprise Service Enhancements), you need to generate an enhancement proxy by following these steps:

1. Start Transaction SPROXY in the application backend system.

2. Within the SAP menu follow the path **Tools • ABAP Workbench • Utilities • Enhancements • Project Management**.

3. In the Enterprise Services Browser on the left-hand side double-click on the data type enhancement within the software component version and namespace for which you want to create the enhancement proxy.

4. If the enhancement proxy does not exist yet, the system will ask you to create it. If the enhancement proxy already exists, you can regenerate it by following the menu path **Proxy • Regenerate**. The result of the proxy generation is displayed in the main window on the right-hand side (see Figure 7.16 for an example).

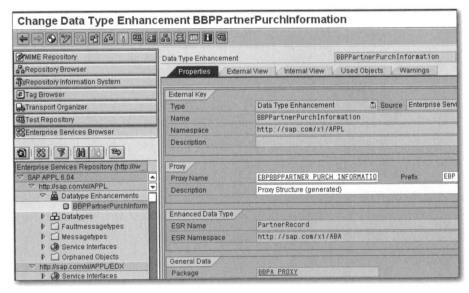

Figure 7.16 Example of an Enhancement Proxy

7.6 Summary

After reading this chapter you should understand the major decisions you need to make when setting up a B2B integration scenario. You should also understand that the implementation of a B2B integration scenario affects many different areas within your company, ranging from very technical aspects such as security considerations to business aspects such as functional gaps in your backend application systems.

In addition, you have gotten an overview of the different options for resolving functional gaps by utilizing the enhancement options provided by the backend application systems.

This chapter explains how to develop a PI content package in the SAP NetWeaver Process Integration repository. It contains step-by-step instructions for the creation of the main objects.

8 Development

In Chapter 7 Implementation we showed the overall message flow in a B2B environment, and we discussed different options for how to implement such scenarios using the SAP NetWeaver Process Integration platform. A central piece of any configuration was shown in Figure 7.2, where a message is handed over from the inbound adapter to the integration engine and then handed back to the outbound adapter.

In this chapter and in Chapter 9 Configuration we show in detail how each step along the process discussed in Figure 7.2 is configured.

8.1 Overview

Figure 8.1 shows a more detailed view of the message flow between the adapters and the integration engine. In particular we see the objects that are utilized out of the Integration Directory, the Enterprise Services Repository, and the System Landscape Directory. These areas contain all of the information that is required to transform the message header and the message payload as described in Figure 7.2. From an implementation point of view these areas can be distinguished as follows:

▶ **Integration Directory**
The Integration Directory stores all of the information that contains data specific to one trading partner. This information needs to be maintained separately for each trading partner, so it cannot be predelivered.

▶ **Enterprise Services Repository**
The Enterprise Services Repository contains all of the information that can be reused among different trading partners except for system-specific data. As dis-

cussed in Section 7.3 Reusing Existing SAP NetWeaver PI Content, this type of information can potentially be predelivered by SAP or another vendor.

▶ **System Landscape Directory**
The System Landscape Directory of SAP NetWeaver contains information that is specific to the systems used in the implemented system landscape.

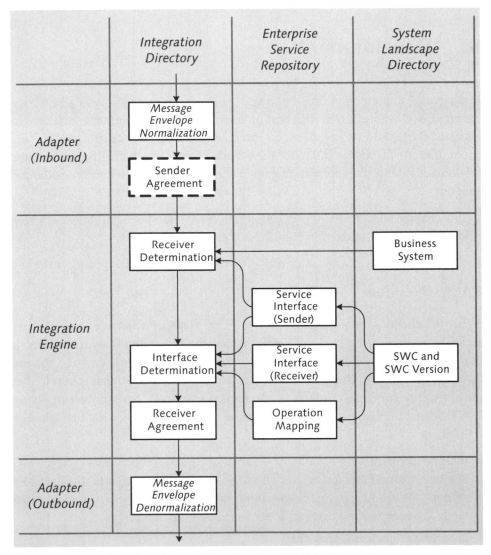

Figure 8.1 Process Steps for a Message Transformation in SAP NetWeaver PI

Let's first take a closer look at the process flow described in Figure 8.1:

▶ **Inbound adapter processing**
Any message that is sent to the SAP NetWeaver PI platform is first received by an inbound adapter. The adapter converts the message envelope into the standard XI format. An important part for this conversion is the *partner normalization*, utilizing information that is maintained in the Integration Directory. Some adapters also use information provided in the *sender agreement* such as security settings for the normalization of the message envelope.

▶ **Processing in the Integration Engine**
The message is then handed over to the integration engine, where the final receiver is determined and the message payload is transformed into the format required by the receiver via the following steps:

▶ In the *receiver determination* the final information on the receiver is derived. If the receiver is an internal system (inbound scenario), the information is provided by the system landscape directory.

▶ In the *interface determination* the structure of the message payload required by the receiver is derived and the mapping program to execute the message payload transformation is determined. A number of objects relevant for this step can be predelivered out of the Enterprise Services Repository, such as the *service interfaces* and the *operation mapping* program.

▶ In the *receiver agreement* you determine the adapter that is to be used for transporting the message to the receiver along with some adapter-specific information, such as security settings.

▶ **Outbound adapter processing**
The transformed message is finally handed over to the outbound adapter identified in the receiver agreement. The adapter converts the message envelope to the format required by the receiver. An important part of this conversion is the partner denormalization, utilizing information that is maintained in the Integration Directory.

In this chapter we discuss the objects from the Enterprise Services Repository and from the System Landscape Directory in detail, whereas in Chapter 9 Configuration we discuss the objects from the Integration Directory.

8.2 System Landscape Directory

In Figure 8.1 we can see that the System Landscape Directory (SLD) of SAP NetWeaver contains a number of objects that play a role in the configuration of a collaboration scenario. Whereas Section 2.2 System Landscape Directory provided an overview of the features and functions of the SLD, we now focus on the implementation of the objects in the SLD as far as they are relevant for the configuration of a collaboration scenario. We need to take a closer look at the following two areas:

▶ The description of the *system landscape* as it is installed at your site including the technical information on the different systems. We need this information, for example, for the routing of an incoming message to the actual backend system where it is processed.

▶ Information on all *software components* available in the systems that are installed in the system landscape. This information is important because all Enterprise Services Repository content is organized by software components.

To start the SLD, call Transaction SXMB_IFR in your SAP NetWeaver PI system and select **System Landscape Directory** in the next screen. Then the entry screen for the SLD appears as shown in Figure 8.2.

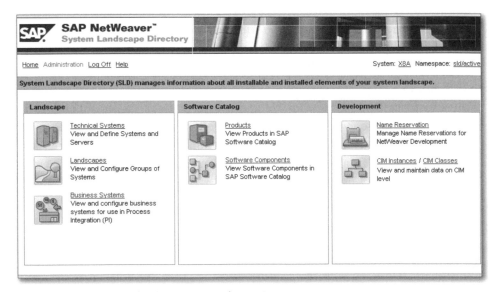

Figure 8.2 Entry Screen for the System Landscape Directory

8.2.1 Landscape Description

As discussed in Section 2.2.1 Landscape Description, the landscape description consists of the definition of the technical systems and the definition of the business systems. Whereas Figure 8.1 shows on a high level the use of the business systems as defined in the SLD for the receiver determination in the Integration Directory, we see a more detailed picture of this particular step in Figure 8.3 involving the following steps:

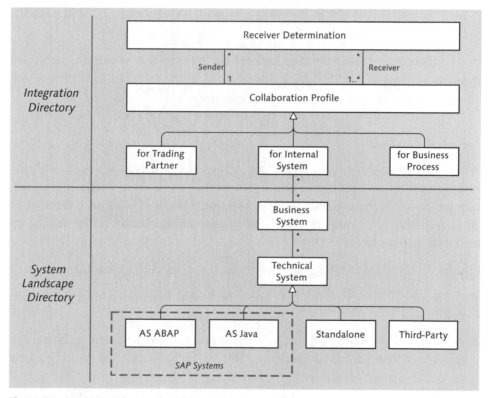

Figure 8.3 System Assignments to the Receiver Agreement

► The *receiver determination* uses information from the *collaboration profile* of the sender and of the receiver in the determination process of the receiver. The objects used within the collaboration profile are discussed in detail in Section 9.2 Collaboration Profiles. If the partner (as described by the collaboration profile) is represented by an internal system, the link to the actual technical system must be provided.

► The internal system within the Integration Directory is defined by a *business system* that is a logical view of the actual internal system. The business system itself is maintained in the SLD and copied from there into the Integration Directory. Because only a logical view of the systems is carried over to the Integration Directory, this part of the configuration does not need to be changed if the system data of the application system change; for example, if it is moved to a different server.

► Within the definition of the business system in SLD, a link to a *technical system* is provided. The technical system is also maintained in the SLD and contains the actual system data.

In the following we take a detailed look at how to set up the technical systems and business systems in the SLD. The steps required in the Integration Directory will be explained in detail in Chapter 9 Configuration.

Technical Systems

When setting up the system landscape in the SLD, you typically start with the technical systems where the technical information of all the systems in your system landscape is maintained. Because this information is used in a number of areas, you should coordinate with your system administrator before setting up technical systems in the SLD.

For the set up of a technical system in the SLD you need to follow these steps:

1. On the entry screen of the SLD select **Technical Systems** within the section **Landscape**.

2. A list with all available technical systems appears. To create a new technical system select **New Technical System...** This starts the wizard for creating a new technical system (see Figure 8.4).

3. As the first step in the wizard you must pick the type of technical system you want to create. If you want to create the technical system for an SAP backend system (e.g., SAP ERP or SAP CRM), you need to select **AS ABAP**. See also Section 2.2.1 Landscape Description for a short introduction to the different types of technical systems.

4. Follow the wizard and provide the required information (marked with a red asterisk). Based on the type of technical system you picked, the information required can be different.

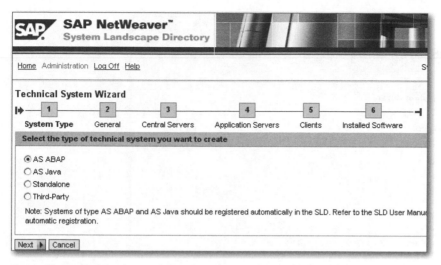

Figure 8.4 Wizard for the Creation of a New Technical System

Business Systems

As discussed in Section 2.2.1 Landscape Description the business system is a logical view at an actual technical system. The business system is also the integration point toward the Integration Directory (see Figure 8.3), omitting the need to change the configuration within the Integration Directory if any of the technical system data has changed. For the set up of a business system in the SLD, follow these steps:

1. On the entry screen of the SLD select **Business Systems** within the section **Landscape**.

2. A list of all available business systems appears. To create a new business system, select **New Business System…**. This starts the wizard for creating a new business system (see Figure 8.5).

3. As the first step in the wizard you must pick the type of technical system with which your business system will be associated.

4. Follow the wizard and provide the required information (marked with a red asterisk). Based on the type of technical system you picked, the information required can be different.

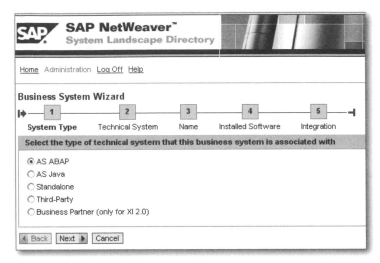

Figure 8.5 Wizard for the Creation of a New Business System

8.2.2 Software Catalog

In Section 2.2.2 Software Catalog we discussed the different objects that are maintained in the SLD. From Figure 8.1 it is clear that we need to have a number of Enterprise Services Repository objects in place for the configuration of a B2B integration scenario. Figure 8.6 shows in more detail the assignment of all Enterprise Services Repository objects to a software component version. With the exception of imported objects (see Section 8.3.6 Imported Objects), all Enterprise Services Repository objects are bundled under a namespace, and the namespace is then assigned to a software component version.

As we discussed in Section 7.3 Reusing Existing SAP NetWeaver PI Content, there are a number of options for how to obtain the required Enterprise Services Repository objects. In particular, you have the following choices:

▶ You can create the required Enterprise Services Repository objects from scratch. In this case you first need to create a product and a version with a number of software units and a software component and a version. Then you need to import the software component version from the SLD into your Enterprise Services Repository and add a number of namespaces before you can start creating the Enterprise Services Repository objects.

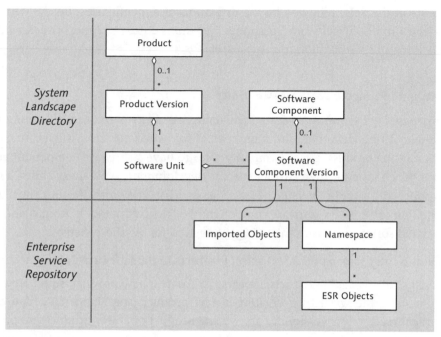

Figure 8.6 Assignment of Enterprise Services Repository Objects to a Software Component Version

▶ You can utilize an existing PI content package and use the required Enterprise Services Repository objects of this package. In this case you need to import the software component versions assigned to the package in the form of files with the extension *.tpz* into your Enterprise Services Repository.

▶ You can utilize an existing PI content package and adjust the Enterprise Services Repository objects to your specific needs. In this case you first need to import the software component versions of the existing PI content package in the form of files with the extension *.tpz* into your Enterprise Services Repository. Then you need to create a new software component version with all related objects (product, software unit, etc.) and create a dependency to the software component versions of the existing PI content package. After that you need to import the new software component versions from the SLD into your Enterprise Services Repository before you can start adjusting the Enterprise Services Repository objects.

In the following we cover all of the aspects mentioned above in detail. We start with the discussion of the creation of products, software units, and software components in the SLD, followed by the definition of dependencies, before we discuss the import of software component versions into the Enterprise Services Repository and the creation of namespaces.

Creation of Products and Software Units

As discussed in Section 2.2.2 Software Catalog, a *product* is an installable unit that is delivered to a customer, and a number of *software units* are assigned to each version of the product. Even if you only want to have a software component version in place for your own custom specific developments, you always must have a product and product version, as well as at least one software unit, in place before you can create a software component. For the creation of a product and its associated software units in the SLD, you need to follow these steps:

1. On the entry screen of the SLD select **Products** in the **Software Catalog** section.
2. A list of all available products appears. To create a new product, select **New...**. This starts the wizard for creating a new product (see Figure 8.7). You can either create a new version for an existing product or a new product and product version.
3. In the second step you must maintain the following information:
    - ► The name of your **Product**. You can give your product any name. However, some naming conventions are in place if you seek a PBNW certification (see Section 7.3 Reusing Existing SAP NetWeaver PI Content) for your product.
    - ► Your **Vendor** name. As a naming convention, you should use a URL as the vendor name, for example, *mycomany.com*.
    - ► The **Version** of your product. You can choose any value for your version number. However, some naming conventions are in place if you seek a PBNW certification for your product.
4. In the third step you must define a **Software Unit**. In the wizard you can only define one software unit. If you want to assign multiple software units to your product version, you need to do this in a separate step as described below.
5. In the last step you must define one software component and version that is assigned to the product version. If you only need to have one software component version assigned to your product version, you have now finished the complete process.

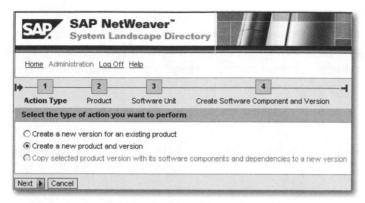

Figure 8.7 Wizard for the Creation of a Product and a Software Unit

In step 4 of the wizard for the creation of a product, you had to define one software unit. For the creation of additional software units you need to go to the detailed view of the product and add a new software unit on the **Software Components** tab (see Figure 8.8).

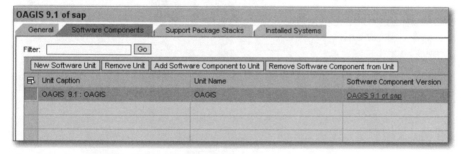

Figure 8.8 Detailed View of a Product in the SLD

Creation of Software Components

The *software component version* is the object that ultimately needs to be imported into the Enterprise Services Repository. For a new product or product version, you have already created one software component version in the previous step. Therefore, you only need to execute this step if you want to create additional software components and versions to an existing product version.

1. On the entry screen of the SLD select **Software Components** in the **Software Catalog** section.

2. A list of all available software component versions appears. To create a new software component select **New...**. This starts the wizard for creating a new software component. You can either create a new version for an existing software component or a new software component and software component version.

3. In the second step you must maintain the following information (see Figure 8.9):

   ▶ The **Product Version** and **Software Unit** to which you want to assign the software component version.

   ▶ The **Vendor** of the product.

   ▶ The **Name** and **Version** of the new software component.

   In addition, you need to set the **Production State** for the software component version. You should set it to **released** if you want to be able to use this software component version in the enterprise services repository.

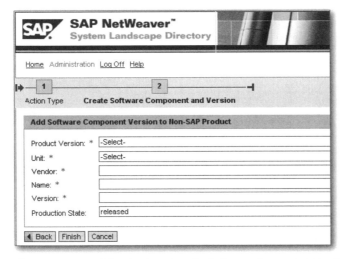

Figure 8.9 Wizard for the Creation of a Software Component Version

Dependencies

We briefly touched on dependencies of software component versions in Section 2.2.2 Software Catalog. When you create a dependency from software component SWCV1 to software component SWCV2, all objects of SWCV2 are visible within SWCV1. There are two major use cases for the creation of dependencies:

▶ You can reuse objects of one software component version in another one by building software component hierarchies using dependencies. For example, SAP offers the complete message interface definitions of the CIDX standard in the software component version CIDX 1.0. If you want to build mappings against this standard, you can create your own software component and create a dependency to CIDX 1.0. Then you can reuse all message interface definitions in your software component.

▶ The creation of dependencies between software component versions is an important building block for the enhancement concept of SAP. We will discuss such a use in Section 8.3.7 Message Types and Data Types, with the enhancement of a data type.

Dependencies between software component versions are maintained in the SLD. If you want to have all objects of software component SWCV2 available in software component SWCV1, you need to create a dependency as follows:

1. On the entry screen of the SLD select **Software Components** in the **Software Catalog** section.

2. A list of all available software component versions appears. Click on the software component version **SWCV1,** and in the detailed screen open the **Dependencies** tab (see Figure 8.10).

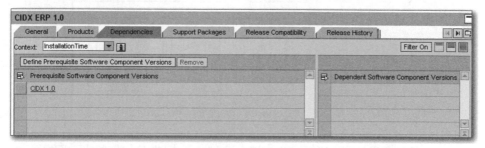

Figure 8.10 Definition of Dependencies Between Software Component Versions

3. Ensure that the **Context** is set to **Installation Time**. This setting means that software component version SWCV1 does not function properly without the dependent software component versions being installed as well.

4. Click on **Define Prerequisite Software Component Versions**. A list of all available software component versions appears.

5. Select all software component versions to which you want to create a dependency (in our case SWCV2) and click on **Define as Prerequisite Software Components**. The dependencies have been created.

Now we know how to set up dependencies between software component versions, but we still need to understand how the system handles dependencies in the Enterprise Services Repository. Figure 8.11 shows an example of how dependent objects are treated in the system. In this example we have a software component version SWCV1 that is dependent on SWCV2. In SWCV1 the following Enterprise Services Repository objects are available:

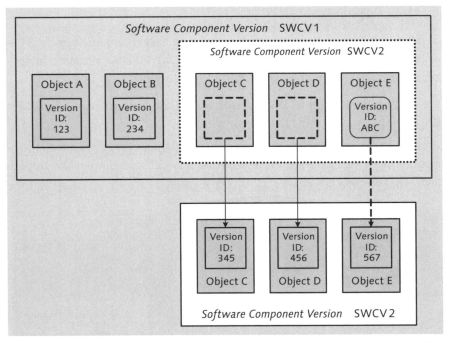

Figure 8.11 Visibility of Enterprise Services Repository Objects Between Dependent Software Component Versions

▶ Objects A and B are created in SWCV1 and therefore are only visible in this software component.

▶ Objects C and D are originally created in SWCV2. Because all objects in this software component are also visible in SWCV1 (due to the dependency), you can see these objects in SWCV1 under the entry **Basis Objects**. However, logically you only have a pointer to the original objects. Each object is identified by an object ID and a version ID, and you can see that both IDs are identical, independent of the software component. If object C or D is changed in SWCV2, the change will automatically be reflected in SWCV1 as well.

▶ Object E is originally created in SWCV2. Like objects C and D, it is also visible in SWCV1. However, in this case we have changed object E in SWCV1, which created a different version of this object in SWCV1 compared to SWCV2. If object E is now changed in SWCV2, the system will not overwrite the object in SWCV1 but report a potential conflict instead. The enhancement concept for Enterprise Services Repository objects[1] is based on this process.

Import of Software Component Versions from the SLD and Creation of Namespaces

Once all objects related to the software catalog have been created in the SLD, you can import the relevant software component versions into your Enterprise Services Repository by following these steps:

1. In the Enterprise Services Repository follow the menu path **Object** • **New**. Alternatively, you can right-click in the navigation window and select **New**.

2. In the popup that is displayed select **Work Areas** • **Software Component Version**, select the option **Import from SLD**, and click on **Display** (see Figure 8.12).

Figure 8.12 Importing a Software Component Version into the Enterprise Services Repository from the SLD

---

1 As discussed in Section 2.3 Overview of Enterprise Services Repository, the Enterprise Services Repository objects Data Types and Business Objects have their own enhancement objects in place, allowing more advanced enhancement features.

3. A list of all available software component versions appears. Select the software component version you want to import into the enterprise services repository and click on **Import**.

4. The **Name**, the **Vendor**, and the **Version** of the software component are filled into the display area of the popup screen. Click on **Create** to import the software component version into the Enterprise Services Repository (see Figure 8.13 for the result of the import step).

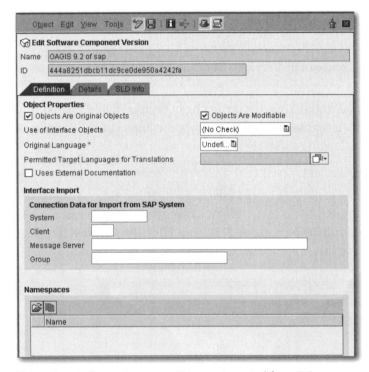

Figure 8.13 Software Component Version Imported from SLD

Now we have imported a software component version into the Enterprise Services Repository that has been created in the SLD. Such software component versions do not contain any content yet, but are the empty containers for the development you plan to carry out as part of your implementation project. Figure 8.13 shows the software component version after the import from the SLD. As you can see, the properties **Objects Are Original Objects** and **Objects Are Modifiable** are both marked, indicating that this software component version is open for development in your system.

In Figure 8.14 you can also see that no namespaces exist yet in the software component version you just imported from the SLD. As the next step you must create namespaces within your software component version by following these steps:

1. In the Enterprise Services Repository follow the menu path **Object • New**. Alternatively, you can right-click in the navigation window and select **New**.

2. In the popup that is displayed choose **Work Areas • Namespace** and enter the namespace you want to create in your software component version.

3. The editor as shown in Figure 8.14 is displayed, and the namespace is added to the list of namespaces of your software component version. You can also add additional namespaces within this editor.

4. Save and activate your changes.

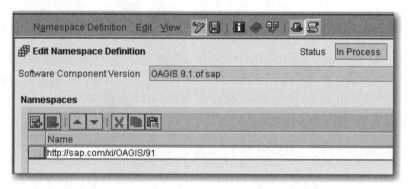

Figure 8.14 Creation of Namespaces for a Software Component Version

Import of Software Component Versions as File

So far, we have discussed the import of software component versions that have been created in your system as new objects. Now we want to look at the import of existing PI content packages that can be provided by SAP or third-party vendors. Such existing PI content is always delivered in the form of an export file with the extension *.tpz*. You can import software component versions carrying actual content by following these steps:

1. Obtain the export file containing the required PI content. For PI content delivered by SAP you can retrieve these export files from the SAP Service Marketplace as described in Section 7.3.2 Implementation of Existing PI Content Pack-

ages. These files must be copied either into your local machine or into the import directory of the Enterprise Services Repository.[2]

2. In the Enterprise Services Repository follow the menu path **Tools · Import design objects….**

3. You are asked in a popup if you want to import a file from your local machine (client) or from the server. Choose the appropriate destination based on the location you picked for the export file in the first step.

4. Select the appropriate export file (with the extension *.tpz*) either from your local machine or from the list of files available in the import folder of your server. The software component version and its content is then imported into the Enterprise Services Repository.

8.3   Interface Definitions

The definition of the message interfaces used in the communication with your trading partners is one of the crucial tasks in the implementation of a collaboration scenario for a number of reasons. Message interfaces play an important role in all phases of the implementation process.

▶ **Service interfaces in the scoping phase**
During the *scoping phase* you must agree with your trading partner on the messages you want to exchange as well as on the corresponding message structure. In addition, you must come to an agreement on the semantics of the message definition. These topics are covered in more detail in Chapter 11 Testing Considerations.

▶ **Service interfaces in the implementation phase**
During the *implementation phase* of the scenario the message definitions (often provided by an industry standard organization) must be implemented in the Enterprise Services Repository. Because a number of technical standards are used by the different standard organizations, the Enterprise Services Repository must support these different technical standards.

▶ **Service interfaces in the configuration phase**
During the *configuration phase* (onboarding of a new trading partner) the rout-

---

2 The import directory of the enterprise services repository can be found in the path *<systemDir>\xi\repository_server\import*, where *<systemDir>* denotes the path for the system directory of the host.

ing rules must be set up for communication with the specific trading partner. As you can see in Figure 8.1, the information from the interface plays an important role in the determination of the receiver of the message. We want to have a harmonized view on the message interface such that the configuration step does not depend on the underlying technical standard used for the definition of the message structure.

▶ **Service interfaces during runtime**
During the message exchange you must expose the name of the message interface to your trading partner. This information must be platform independent because you cannot expose any implementation specific information to your trading partner. Otherwise you would need to notify him of any changes to your internal implementation.

To accommodate all of the requirements listed above, SAP NetWeaver PI offers a hierarchy of objects for the definition of message interfaces as discussed in Section 2.3.2 Message Interface Objects: We have an outer shell consisting of a harmonized view of the interfaces based on the WSDL definition of Web services as shown in Figure 2.9. Underneath, a number of different technical standards are supported, as well as SAP proprietary formats such as the interface descriptions of IDocs and BAPIs (see Section 7.5 Backend Adoption for a discussion of these interfaces).

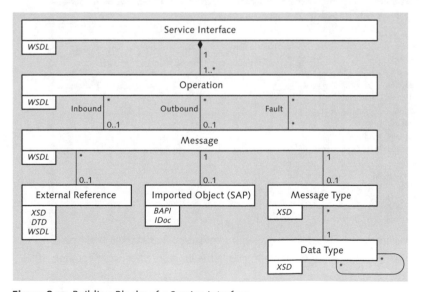

Figure 8.15 Building Blocks of a Service Interface

In the following we take a closer look at the definition of message interfaces, with a special focus on external definitions because they are used frequently in B2B environments. Figure 8.15 shows an overview of all message interface-related objects we need to discuss.

8.3.1 Service Interfaces, Service Operations, and Messages

As discussed in Section 2.3.2 Message Interface Objects, the *service interface* is a logical container for a service with one or more *operations* assigned to it. Each operation must be assigned to at least one *message* that carries the actual message structure. Within the Enterprise Services Repository you define all of these objects in one transaction as follows:

1. In the Enterprise Services Repository follow the menu path **Object • New**. Alternatively, you can navigate to the software component version and namespace where you want to create the service interface and select **New** after right-clicking on the namespace.

2. In the popup that is displayed select **Interface Objects • Service Interface** and enter the name, namespace, and software component version for the service interface you want to create (see Figure 8.16).

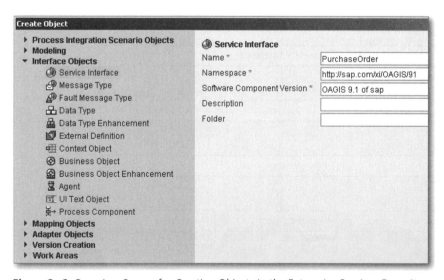

Figure 8.16 Overview Screen for Creating Objects in the Enterprise Services Repository

3. The maintenance screen for the service interface is displayed as shown in Figure 8.17. Specify the service interface attributes **Category** and **Interface Pattern**. Check Table 2.6 and Table 2.7 for possible values.

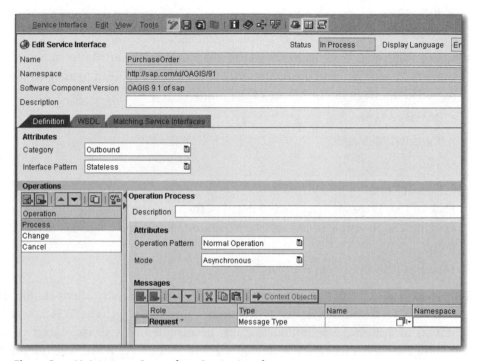

Figure 8.17 Maintenance Screen for a Service Interface

4. Define the operations that are associated with the service interface in the list labeled **Operation**. One operation with the same name as the service interface is added to the list by default. You can delete it if you don't want to use an operation of this name.[3]

5. For each operation specify the attributes **Operation Pattern** and **Mode**; check Table 2.8 and Table 2.9 for possible values. In a B2B environment you would typically choose **Normal Operation** as the **Operation Pattern**.

---

3 If you use the interface pattern **Stateless (XI30-Compatible),** you cannot change the default settings for the operations.

6. Based on the attributes you have chosen, for each operation one or more of the following **Roles** appear under the header **Message**:

▶ Request

▶ Response

▶ Fault

Check Table 2.10 for a list of roles available based on the attributes chosen for the service interface and the operation. For each role you need to assign a message. The message can be of one of the following types:

▶ Message Type

▶ External Message

▶ IDoc

▶ RFC Message

Each of these types is discussed in detail in the next sections. The message you assign must be visible in the software component version of the service interface.

7. Save and activate the service interface.

We just saw in step 6 of the definition of a service interface that each operation in the service interface is associated with one or more messages. The WSDL representation of a message definition that can be assigned to a service interface is shown in Listing 8.1 (compare with Figure 2.9 in Section 2.3.2 Message Interface Objects). In this definition you can see that you need to provide a link to the actual definition of the message structure via the attribute element.[4] The element can be defined by a message type, an IDoc, an RFC, or an external definition in the form of an XSD, a DTD, or a WSDL. In the next sections we discuss each of these options in detail.

```
<wsdl:message name="Message">
    <wsdl:part name="Part" element="MessageStructure">
</wsdl:message>
```

Listing 8.1 WSDL Representation of a Message Definition

---

4 In the WSDL specification the message structure can also be identified by the type attribute. However, in SAP NetWeaver PI the element attribute is always used.

8.3.2 External Definitions via XML Schema Definitions

In today's world the *XML Schema Definition* (XSD) is the preferred method of defining the underlying message structure of an XML document. Therefore, the import of XSDs is well supported within the Enterprise Services Repository. We just saw in Listing 8.1 that each message of a service definition must carry the definition of the actual message structure via the attribute `element`.

An XSD usually contains many `element` definitions that can potentially be used for the definition of a message. Therefore, you can specify which of these `element` definitions should actually be made available as a `message` definition in the generated WSDL representation of the XSD (and hence can be used as a message definition within a service interface operation). For each imported XSD you can choose between the options as listed in Table 8.1 via the list field **Message** (see Figure 8.18 for the maintenance screen of this field).

Selection Option for Message	Meaning
Do Not Extract Messages	No WSDL representation is created, and therefore no element definitions are made available as a message.
All Elements Contained	All element definitions in the XSD are made available as a message.
All Unreferenced Elements	Only element definitions that are not referenced by another element are made available as a message.

Table 8.1 Select Options for the Message List Field for an XSD

Let's now take a look at the tools provided in the Enterprise Services Builder for the import of XML schema definitions. In particular, we discuss the following features:

▶ The import of an individual XML schema definition.

▶ The ability to link individual XML schema definitions together.

▶ The mass import of XML schema definitions that also automatically provides the link between the imported schemas.

We start with a short discussion of XML schema definitions as far as it is relevant to understanding how they can be linked in SAP NetWeaver PI.

XML Schema Definitions

SAP NetWeaver PI provides tool support for working with XML schema definitions (XSD) so that you don't need to be familiar with the syntax of schema definitions when working with them in the Enterprise Services Builder. However, it is beneficial to understand at least the concept of how to form an XSD by reusing other schema definitions as building blocks.

In a XSD you can use the following two elements for linking schemas to each other:

▶ **Include element**
The `include` element is used to reuse an existing XSD in another definition within the same namespace. The attribute `schemaLocation` determines the actual location of the included schema.

▶ **Import element**
The `import` element is used to reuse an existing XSD in another definition that can be assigned to a separate namespace. The attribute `namespace` defines the namespace used with the imported schema, whereas the attribute `schemaLocation` determines the actual location of the imported schema.

The syntax for the `include` element and the `import` element can be found in Listing 8.2. Both elements use the attribute `schemaLocation` to determine the actual location of the included or imported schema. This location is provided in the form of a *Uniform Resource Identifier* (URI). The URI can be provided as an *absolute URI* or as a *relative URI*. With the relative URI you need to know the context in which it is used, which can cause some issues with the implementation in SAP NetWeaver PI when you link multiple schema definitions to each other. We will see an example of such an issue and its resolution in Section 8.3.3 Example of the Import of a XML Schema Definition.

```
<xsd:import id="id" namespace="ns " schemaLocation="anyURI"/>
<xsd:include id="id" schemaLocation="anyURI"/>
```
Listing 8.2 Syntax for Import and Include Statement in XSD

Import of Individual XSDs

Let's now take a look at how to import an individual XML schema definition (XSD) file. We assume that you have the XSD available on your local machine. Most standard organizations offer a download section for their schema definitions so you can store them locally on your machine. Then the import can be done very easily by following these steps in the Enterprise Services Repository:

1. In the Enterprise Services Repository follow the menu path **Object • New**. Alternatively, you can navigate to the software component version and namespace where you want to create the external definition and select **New** after right-clicking on the namespace.

2. In the popup that is displayed select **Interface Objects • External Definition** and enter the **Name**, **Namespace**, and **Software Component Version** for the service interface you want to create. The maintenance screen for the external definition is displayed.

3. In the **Category** list field, select **xsd** (because we want to import a file of type XSD).

4. In the **Messages** list field select the appropriate option. Check Table 8.1 for possible values.

5. Use the dialog under the **File** list field to find the location of the schema you want to import from your local machine and select this file.

6. Save and activate the external definition.

After completing these steps you will see the imported XML schema definition as shown in Figure 8.18. Within the external definition you have the following tabs available:

▶ On the **Imported Document** tab the imported XML schema definition is displayed.

▶ On the **Messages** tab all `element` definitions of the XSD are listed that are made available as a `message` definition in the corresponding WSDL representation. The WSDL definitions for a `message` are shown in Listing 8.1 and in Figure 2.9. You can influence the creation of `message` definitions as discussed in Table 8.1.

▶ On the **WSDL** tab the imported XSD is represented as a WSDL file. This representation is generated automatically for each imported XML schema definition.

▶ On the **External References** tab all schemas that are referenced via the `include` statement or the `import` statement are listed. The values contained in the attribute `schemaLocation` are listed here.

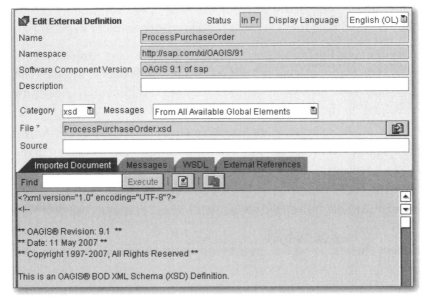

Figure 8.18 Import Screen for an XML Schema Definition (XSD)

Source Maintenance of XSDs

Now we know how to import individual XML schema definitions. Because these schemas often reference other schemas via an `include` or an `import` statement, we need to know how we can provide this link in the Enterprise Services Repository. For this purpose each external definition in the Enterprise Services Repository has a **Source** list field available that is used to maintain information on the location of the schema (in WSDL terms, we maintain the `schemaLocation` of the XML schema). The overall process is described in Figure 8.19 and consists of the following steps:

❶ Each XML schema definition imported into the Enterprise Services Repository can have a reference to other schema definitions using the `include` statement or the `import` statement. Both statements contain the attribute `schemaLocation` with information on the actual location[5] of the included or imported schema. On the **External References** tab all values listed are that are used in the `schemaLocation` attribute of included or imported schemas.

---

5 The location in this context refers to the original location, not the location of the imported schema in the Enterprise Services Repository.

❷ For all values listed on the **External References** tab, the system tries to find another XML schema definition within the same software component version that has the exact value entered in the **Source** list field.

❸ If a match is found in step 2, the link between the two schemas has been established in the Enterprise Services Repository and the information is visible on the **External References** tab.

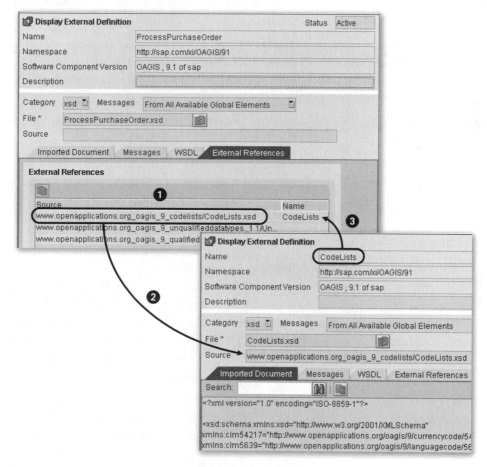

Figure 8.19 Derivation of Dependent Schema Definitions

All you need to do for the source maintenance described above is enter the required information into the **Source** list field of each imported XML schema definition. The system will then automatically find the links based on this information. You can maintain the information in the **Source** list field directly when you import the XSD, or you can first import all schemas and then update them with the required information in the **Source** list field.

It is important to keep in mind that the **Source** list field in an external definition is treated as a pure string value and not as a relative or absolute path. This can lead to some issues if the information in the attribute schemaLocation of the XSD is provided as a relative URI. The main issues are listed in Table 8.2 together with a brief description of possible solutions.

Issue	Solution
One XSD is referenced by multiple other schemas using a different schema location.	Import the XSD multiple times.
The same relative path in a schema location points to two different XSDs.	Change the XSD definition.
The schema location is longer than the available space in the **Source** list field.	Change the XSD definition.

Table 8.2 Potential Issues with the Import of XML Schema Definitions

Let's now take a look at each of these issues in more detail.

▶ **Different schema location references to one XSD**
It is possible that one XSD is imported by multiple schemas. If these schemas use a relative URI in the schemaLocation attribute to locate the imported XSD, these values (viewed as a string) are not necessarily unique. This issue does occur with some schema definitions provided by standard organizations such as RosettaNet and OAGi (see also see the example shown in Section 8.3.3 Example of the Import of an XML Schema Definition).

To resolve this issue you can import the XSD that is referenced multiple times (under different names) as often as different schema locations are used. Then you can assign a different schema location value to the **Source** field list of each instance of the XSD.

▶ **Different XSDs with the same reference information**
This scenario is best explained with an example:

Let's assume we have an XSD file *special.xsd* stored under the path */a/b1/c* and another XSD file with the same name under the path */a/b2/c*. If a schema located in */a/b1* includes the first file using the relative path, the value in the schemaLocation attribute is *c/special.xsd*. However, a schema located in */a/b2* using the same relative path would point to the second file. We have a conflict because in the Enterprise Services Repository all schemas must be located in the same namespace, and here we can import a schema with the name *special.xsd* only once.

Luckily, such scenarios are quite unusual, so this problem most likely will not occur in a real-life scenario. To resolve this issue you need to adjust the XML schema definition such that you use a different name for each occurrence of the XSD in conflict (*special.xsd* in our example) and adjust the corresponding values in the schemaLocation attribute.

▶ **Schema location reference is too long for source field**
The **Source** list field of an XSD that is imported as an external definition contains the value of the schemaLocation attribute as described in Figure 8.19. These values can become rather long, exceeding the maximum length of the **Source** list field for SAP NetWeaver PI releases prior to 7.1. Whereas the length in release 7.1 is 255 characters, release 3.0 and release 7.0 both have a limitation of 120 characters for this field. To resolve this issue you need to adjust the XML schema definition by shortening any value in the schemaLocation attribute to a length of less than the allowed number of characters.

Mass Import of XSDs

It is possible that an XML schema definition references many other schema definitions, where each of them can again reference other schemas, and so on. This is quite common in XSDs defined by standard organizations such as OAGIS and RosettaNet. In this case it is not convenient if you need to import each schema individually and provide the source information manually.

Therefore, SAP NetWeaver PI offers the capability (as of release 7.1) to mass import XML schema definitions through a wizard.[6] With the mass import the links between the schemas are defined automatically as long as the system can identify a match.

1. In the Enterprise Services Repository follow the menu path **Tools • Import External Definitions....** A wizard starts that will guide you through the process of importing a set of XML schema definitions.

---

6 The wizard for mass imports also supports definitions of the type WSDL and DTD. We discuss the mass import for each type in the respective sections.

2. After you pass the introduction you need to specify in step 2 of the wizard the source and the target information:

▸ As a **Source**, your local file system is already preselected. Currently no other choices are available.

▸ As a **Target**, select the namespace and software component version into which you want to import the schemas.

3. In the third step browse your local file system for the schema definitions or the folders that contain these definitions. Select all schemas you want to import. You can also simply select a folder, and all objects in it (including objects in sub-folders) will automatically be considered for import (see Figure 8.20).

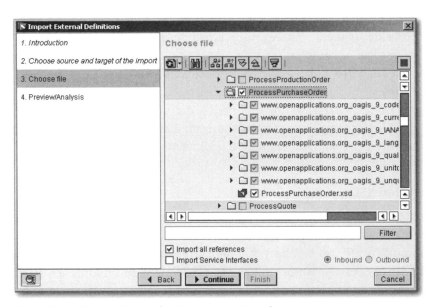

Figure 8.20 File Selection in the Mass Import Wizard

4. In the fourth step the system detects all files of a valid type (XSD, DTD, or WSDL) that are marked in the previous step, determines the references, and tries to identify the values that need to be entered into the **Source** list field of each imported schema (see Figure 8.21).

5. When you select **Finish**, all schema definitions you selected are imported into the Enterprise Services Repository as external definitions under the software component version and namespace you select in the second step. You still need to activate the external definitions in the Enterprise Services Repository.

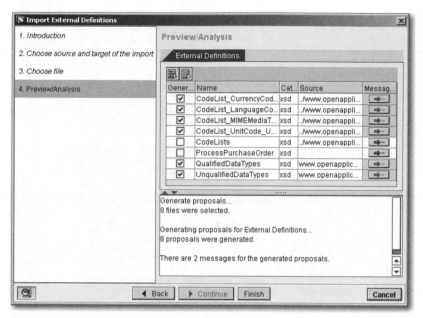

Figure 8.21 Preview of Generated Objects in the Mass Import Wizard

8.3.3 Example of the Import of an XML Schema Definition

Let's now take a look at a concrete example of the import of a set of XML schema definitions. We use the *purchase order creation* message of the OAGIS standard, because with this message we can also discuss some of the pitfalls you may experience when uploading XSD schemas.

The OAGIS standard has defined a message ProcessPurchaseOrder that is used to communicate the creation of a purchase order. The message structure is defined via XML schema definitions and utilizes a number of imported schemas as shown in Figure 8.22.

Preparation Step

Before you can import external standards into the Enterprise Services Repository, you need to download the schema definitions onto your local machine. Most standards offer a download section for the specifications of their respective standard. In our example we use the OAGIS 9.1 standard developed by the *Open Application Group* (OAGi), which can be downloaded from the OAGi website at *http://www.oagi.org*. The result of the download can be found in Figure 8.23.

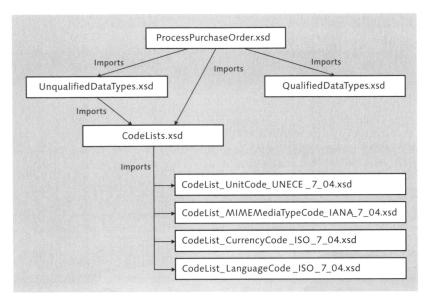

Figure 8.22 XSD Structure for OAGIS Message ProcessPurchaseOrder

Figure 8.23 Result of the Download of OAGIS Message Definitions

Import Step

For the import of the XSD representation of the purchase order creation message, we use the mass import feature as described in the previous section. The result of the mass import is shown in Figure 8.24. As you can see, not all references could be established; therefore, we need to take care of the missing links in an additional step.

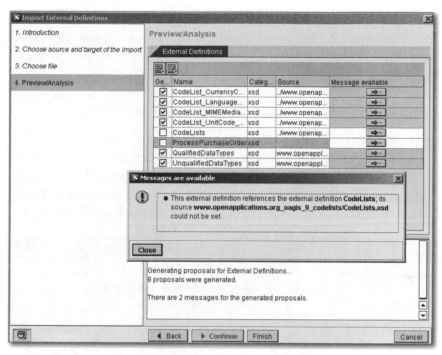

Figure 8.24 Result of the Import of the Process Purchase Order Message

Post Processing Step

As you can see in the result screen of the import (see Figure 8.24), the schema *CodeLists.xsd* has been referenced twice using different schema location values:

▶ *www.openapplications.org_oagis_9_codelists/CodeLists.xsd* is used in the `schemaLocation` attribute of the `import` statement within the schema *ProcessPurchaseOrder.xsd*.

▶ *../www.openapplications.org_oagis_9_codelists/CodeLists.xsd* is used in the `schemaLocation` attribute of the `import` statement within the schema *UnqualifiedDataTypes.xsd*.

Because the values are different, the system could only assign one of the values to the **Source** list filed of the *CodeList.xsd* schema. In our case, the link to schema *ProcessPurchaseOrder.xsd* is missing. To correct this problem we need to import schema *CodeList.xsd* a second time under a different name, for example, *CodeList2*, and maintain the **Source** list field with the schema location information used in schema *ProcessPurchaseOrder.xsd*.

8.3.4 External Definitions via Document Type Definitions (DTD)

Before the emergence of XML schema definitions, *Document type definitions* (DTDs) were widely used to define the structure of a XML message. Even though they are not commonly used any longer for the definition of new versions of message structures, many standards still in use are based on DTDs. Therefore, SAP NetWeaver PI also supports the import of DTDs as external definitions.

Just like external definitions of type XSD, we need to prepare external definitions of type DTD for use in service interfaces. The system creates a WSDL representation of the DTD and needs to know which part of the DTD it should make available as a message definition as shown in Listing 8.1. For each imported DTD you can choose between the options as listed in Table 8.3 via the list field **Message**.

Selection Option for Message	Meaning
Do Not Extract Messages	No WSDL representation is created, and therefore no element definition is made available as a message.
Message from DOCTYPE	The name of the tag DOCTYPE is made available as a message.
Message from First ELEMENT	The name of the first tag ELEMENT is made available as a message.

Table 8.3 Select Options for the Message List Field for a DTD

The tools provided by the Enterprise Services Builder for the import of DTDs are the same as for the import of XSDs. Whereas a DTD also allows the link to externally defined DTDs via the identifiers SYSTEM and PUBLIC, a DTD is typically defined as a standalone definition. Therefore, you usually only need to use the individual import of an external definition using the following steps:

1. In the Enterprise Services Repository follow the menu path **Object • New**. Alternatively, you can navigate to the software component version and namespace where you want to create the external definition and select **New** after right-clicking on the namespace.

2. In the popup that is displayed select **Interface Objects • External Definition** and enter the name, namespace, and software component version for the service interface you want to create. The maintenance screen for the external definition is displayed.

3. In the **Category** list field, choose **dtd** (because we want to import a file of type DTD).

4. In the **Messages** list field select the appropriate option. Check Table 8.3 for possible values.

5. Use the dialog under the **File** list field to find the location of the DTD you want to import from your local machine and select this file.

6. Save and activate the external definition.

After completing these steps you will see the imported DTD, similar to that shown in Figure 8.18. Within the external definition the following tabs are available:

▶ On the **Imported Document** tab the imported DTD is displayed.

▶ On the **Messages** tab all `element` definitions of the XSD are listed that are made available as a `message` definition in the corresponding WSDL representation. The WSDL definitions for a `message` are shown in Listing 8.1 and in Figure 2.9. You can influence the creation of `message` definitions as discussed in Table 8.3.

▶ On the **WSDL** tab the imported DTD is represented as a WSDL file. This representation is generated automatically for each imported DTD.

▶ On the **External References** tab all schemas that are referenced via the `SYSTEM` identifier or the `PUBLIC` identifier are listed.

8.3.5 External Definitions via WSDL

SAP NetWeaver PI also supports the import of WSDL documents as external definitions. Each WSDL definition consists of two parts:

▶ The *abstract definition* of the service operations and messages, which is provided within the WSDL element `portType`. We already discussed the abstract service definition using WSDL in Section 2.3.2 Message Interface Objects.

▶ The *binding* of the abstract operation and message definition to a concrete message structure and transport protocol. The most common type of binding is via SOAP using an HTTP(S) transport protocol. All WSDL documents generated in the Enterprise Services Repository use SOAP binding when applicable. To understand the different options provided in the Enterprise Services Repository for the import of a WSDL definition, we need to take a closer look at the syntax for the definition of a SOAP binding in a WSDL definition.

The syntax for the definition of a binding in a WSDL document using SOAP is shown in Listing 8.3.

```
<wsdl:binding name="name" type="portType">
  <soap:binding style="document|rpc" transport="URI"/>
  . . .
</wsdl:binding>
```
Listing 8.3 WSDL Syntax for a SOAP Binding

The `soap:binding` element as shown in Listing 8.3 contains two attributes[7]:

▶ The attribute `style` determines how the body of a SOAP message is to be constructed. The following two values are possible:

  ▶ With the style `rpc` each message contains a parameter or return values, where each of these elements is enclosed by a wrapper element. The syntax of these wrapper elements must follow specific rules as defined by Section 7.1 of the SOAP specification.

  ▶ With the style `document` the message can contain an arbitrary XML instance. This is the default value for the style attribute.

▶ The attribute `transport` indicates the transport protocol to be used for the SOAP message in the form of a URI. Typically, the transport protocol HTTP(S) is used, but other protocols such as SMTP or FTP are possible as well.

All WSDL documents generated in the Enterprise Services Repository (e.g., service interfaces) use the `document` style. However, you can import WSDL documents using the `rpc` style as an external reference into the Enterprise Services Repository. The system will then generate another WSDL reference based on the `document` style where applicable.

As with external definitions of type XSD and DTD, we need to prepare external definitions of type WSDL for use in service interfaces using the list field **Message**. Even though the imported definition is already of type WSDL, a new WSDL definition is generated based on the options listed in Table 8.4 for the list field **Message**.

---

7 We only can cover some of the basics of SOAP binding in a WSDL description. The detailed specification can be found in the W3C Note Web Services Description Language (WSDL) 1.1 from March 15, 2001 at *http://www.w3.org/TR/wsdl*.

Selection Option for Message	Meaning
Do Not Extract Messages	The WSDL document is not interpreted any further, and no messages are made available.
From All Available Message Definitions	All message definitions available in the WSDL document can be utilized as a message.
Using RPC Style	This option is to be used if the imported WSDL file is of style rpc.

Table 8.4 Select Options for the Message List Field for a WSDL File

The tools provided by the Enterprise Services Builder for the import of WSDL documents are the same as for the import of XSDs. Because the definition of the message structure within a WSDL definition is typically done using XSD, the same rules apply for linking together multiple definitions. Therefore, the source maintenance and the mass import typically contains a mix of one WSDL definition and a number of XSDs, which is described in Section 8.3.2 External Definitions via XML Schema Definitions. Here we only describe the individual import of an external definition using the following steps:

1. In the Enterprise Services Repository follow the menu path **Object • New**. Alternatively, you can navigate to the software component version and namespace where you want to create the external definition and select **New** after right-clicking on the namespace.

2. In the popup that is displayed select **Interface Objects • External Definition** and enter the name, namespace, and software component version for the service interface you want to create. The maintenance screen for the external definition is displayed.

3. In the **Category** list field select **wsdl** (because we want to import a file of type WSDL).

4. In the **Messages** list field select the appropriate option. Check Table 8.4 for possible values.

5. Use the dialog under the **File** list field to find the location of the WSDL document you want to import from your local machine and select this file.

6. Save and activate the external definition.

After completing these steps you will see the imported WSDL with the same information available as for imported XSDs, which is described in Section 8.3.2 External Definitions via XML Schema Definitions.

8.3.6 Imported Objects

We just covered external definitions as the first block of objects to be used for message definitions based on external standards. Figure 8.15 shows that the second important block of objects in this context is *Imported Objects*. Here you can import the following interface definitions defined in an SAP backend system:

▶ An *IDoc* consisting of the message type and its corresponding IDoc type.

▶ An interface definition provided by an *RFC*. Because BAPIs are also defined as function modules, you can import there interfaces under this option as well.

Many of the IDoc and RFC definitions provided by SAP are already made available by SAP as imported objects in the respective software component versions. Before you import an IDoc or RFC definition, you should first check if they are already made available by SAP. To check this, you need to know the software component to which the particular IDoc or RFC belongs. You can find this it information by following these steps in the SAP backend system:

1. For an IDoc, call Transaction WE30, enter the name of the IDoc you want to check, and follow the menu path **Goto • Header Data**.

   For an RFC, call Transaction SE37, enter the name of the RFC you want to check, click on **Display**, and select the **Attributes** tab.

2. In the screen displayed for the IDoc or for the RFC you will find the information of the package to which the IDoc or the RFC belongs.

3. Call Transaction SE21 with the name of the package you determined in the previous step and click on **Display**.

4. On the **Properties** tab you will find the information of the **Software Component** to which the package belongs.

Some of the common software components provided by SAP that contain IDocs and RFCs already made available by SAP are listed in Table 8.5.

Software Component	Description
EA-APPL	SAP Enterprise Extension for PLM, SCM, and Financials
EA-FINSERV	SAP Enterprise Extension for Financial Services
SAP APPL	SAP Enterprise Solution for Logistics and Accounting
SAP BBPCRM	SAP Customer Relationship Management Solution
SAP HR	SAP Enterprise Solution for Human Capital Management
SAP SCM	SAP Supply Chain Management Solution
...	...

Table 8.5 Software Components Containing IDoc and RFC Definitions

Once you have verified that the IDoc or the RFC you need is not imported by SAP in its respective software component or if you need to make your own IDoc or RFC available, you need to import this object yourself. Before you can start the import process you must ensure that your software component version is set up for the import of objects from an SAP system. We discuss both steps in detail.

Prepare Software Component Version for Import of Objects

First, ensure that the software component version you want to import objects from the SAP system into is set up to allow such imports. You can check this by following these steps:

1. In the Enterprise Services Builder select the software component version into which you want to import objects.

2. Choose the **Definition** tab and ensure that the following information is provided (see also Figure 8.25):

   ▶ Under the header **Object Properties** both flags **Objects Are Original Objects** and **Objects are Modifiable** must be selected.

   ▶ Under the header **Connection Data for Import from SAP System** the **System** and **Client** of the system you want to import the objects from must be maintained.

3. Save your data. You do not need to activate changes to the software component version.

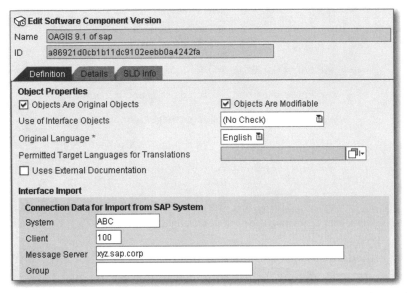

Figure 8.25 Settings of a Software Component Version to Enable Import of SAP Objects

Import Objects from an SAP System

After you have prepared the software component version for the import of objects from an SAP system you can start the process of importing objects. You need to follow these steps:

1. In the Enterprise Services Builder navigate to the software component version you want to import objects into, right-click on the entry **Imported Objects**, and select **Import of SAP Objects**. This starts a wizard guiding you through the import process.

2. In the first step of the wizard you must provide the logon information to the backend system that has been identified in the software component version.

3. In the second step of the wizard you must select the IDocs and RFCs that you want to import from the backend (see Figure 8.26). The wizard displays the list of all available IDocs and RFCs in the system you selected in the first step.

4. In the third step of the wizard the selected objects are imported from the backend system. The objects are available in the selected software component version under the entry **Imported Objects**. With this step the wizard is completed.

5. Activate the imported objects.

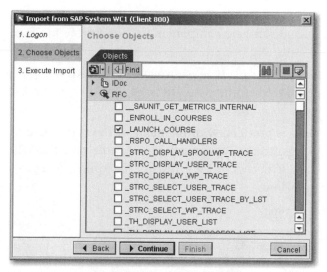

Figure 8.26 Wizard for the Import of Objects from an SAP System

8.3.7 Message Types and Data Types

We discussed message types and data types in Section 2.3.2 Message Interface Objects, where we learned that these objects play a central role in enterprise service definitions. As shown in Figure 8.15, *message types* are the third block of objects that can be used in the definition of messages within a service interface. The figure also shows that message types are always composed out of *data types*. We show for both of these objects in detail how they are created in the Enterprise Services Repository and how *data type enhancements* can be created. Because the Enterprise Services Repository generates an XSD representation for all three objects, we finish this chapter with a discussion on namespaces and how to utilize them in different scenarios.

Creation of Message Types

You create message types in the Enterprise Services Repository by following these steps:

1. In the Enterprise Services Repository follow the menu path **Object • New**. Alternatively, you can navigate to the software component version and namespace where you want to create the message type and select **New** after right-clicking on the namespace.

2. In the popup that is displayed select **Interface Objects · Message Type** and enter the name, namespace, and software component version for the message type you want to create.

3. The maintenance screen for the message type is displayed as shown in Figure 8.27. Specify the data type that determines the message structure in the list field **Data Type Used**.

4. The list field **XML Namespace** is prefilled with the name of the namespace to which the message type belongs. You can assign a different namespace that will be used in the XML message if necessary. We discuss the consequences of defining another namespace below.

5. Save and activate the message type.

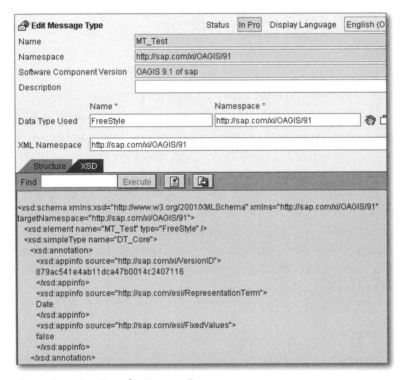

Figure 8.27 Creation of a Message Type

After completing these steps, you will see the message type definition as shown in Figure 8.27. The following tabs provide detailed information on the message structure:

▶ On the **Structure** tab is the message structure as defined by the underlying data type displayed as a hierarchical structure.

▶ On the **XSD** tab is a generated XML schema definition of the message structure.

Creation of Data Types

As discussed in Section 2.3.2 Message Interface Objects, each message type has exactly one data type assigned that contains the actual information on the attributes and elements used in the message type. You create data types in the Enterprise Services Repository by following these steps:

1. In the Enterprise Services Repository follow the menu path **Object • New**. Alternatively, you can navigate to the software component version and namespace where you want to create the data type and select **New** after right-clicking on the namespace.

2. In the popup that is displayed select **Interface Objects • Data Type** and enter the **Name**, **Namespace**, and **Software Component Version** for the data type you want to create. In addition, specify the **Classification** of the data type by selecting one of the following values:

   ▶ **Free-Style Data Type**

   ▶ **Core Data Type**

   ▶ **Aggregated Data Type**

   We discussed the different data type classifications in detail in Section 2.3.2 Message Interface Objects.

3. The maintenance screen for the data type is displayed. Based on the classification you chose in the previous step, this screen looks different.

   ▶ For a data type based on the Core Data Type classification, you must specify a **Representation Term** that is based on the CCTS specification,[8] and a template containing a number of attributes based on the representation term is provided (see Figure 2.12 as an example). You can delete some or all of the attributes but you cannot add any new attributes or elements.

   ▶ For the other data types only the top element is prefilled with the name of the data type. Additional attributes and elements must be added in the next step.

---

8 See Section 2.3.7 Enterprise Services Definition for a detailed discussion of the Core Components Technical Specification (CCTS).

4. Add additional elements and attributes (for free-style and aggregated data types only) under the **Type Definition** tab using the icon **Insert New Lines** as shown in Figure 8.28. Once you have placed the cursor on one of the existing lines, one or more of the following options are available:

▶ **Insert Element** adds a new element to the list on the same level after the selected line.

▶ **Insert Subelement** adds a new element one level below the selected line. This option is only available when you select the top node.

▶ **Insert Attribute** adds an attribute to the selected line or adds an attribute to the attribute list if the selected line is an attribute itself.

▶ **Insert Rows...** is always available. Once you select this option, all available options are listed based on the context.

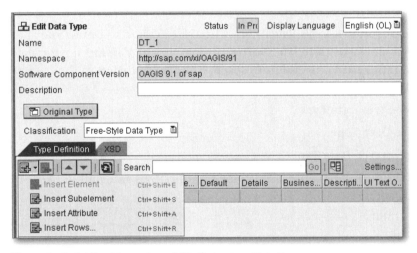

Figure 8.28 Adding Elements and Attributes to a Data Type

5. After you have added a line, the following columns are available for maintenance:

▶ In the **Name** column you define the name of the element or attribute.

▶ The **Category** column specifies if this object is an element (simple or complex) or an attribute. This value is automatically filled.

▶ In the **Type** column you must enter the reference type of this element or attribute. The reference type can be another data type or a generic XSD type such as `xsd:string` or `xsd:integer`.

▸ In the **Occurrence** column you define the minimum and maximum occurrence for an element and you specify if an attribute is mandatory or optional.

▸ In the **Default** column you can specify a default value.

▸ In the **Details** column you can specify additional attributes such as the minimum or maximum length or a pattern, define a list of possible values, and specify the handling of white spaces.

▸ The **Business Context** column is currently not used.

▸ In the **Description** column you can provide a description of the element or attribute.

▸ In the **UI Text Object** column you can assign a UI text object for display in a UI. This feature is not relevant in a B2B context.

6. Save and activate the data type.

In the maintenance screen for data types two tabs are available that display the data type structure with two different views:

▸ On the **Type Definition** tab is the list representation of the data type structure.

▸ On the **XML** tab is a generated XML schema definition of the data type structure.

Import of an XSD as Data Type

We just learned how to create data types manually on the **Type Definition** tab, which generates an XSD representation that can be viewed on the **XML** tab. You can also create data types starting with an XML representation and have the list view created out of the XML file. However, there are some restrictions to the XML files you can use in this process:

▸ The XSD file must comply with the restrictions in the XML language established for the different data type categories (free-style data types, core data types, aggregated data types).

▸ The XSD attribute `targetNamespace` must either be missing in the XSD file, or it must be identical to the namespace in which the data type resides.

▸ The name of the data type must be identical to the global data type defined in the XSD file. This implies that for XSD files containing multiple global data types, the XSD file must be imported multiple times under the respective names.

If you want to create a new data type based on an existing XSD file, you follow the same steps as described in the previous section for the creation of a data type. Once the maintenance screen for the data type is displayed, you follow the menu path **Tools · Import XSD...** to import the XSD file from your local file system. After the file is imported, you can continue to manipulate the data type definition as described in the previous section.

Data Type Restrictions

Once a data type is available in the Enterprise Services Repository, you may want to use this data type as a basis for further manipulation in one of the following ways:

▶ You want to extend the data type with additional attributes or elements. For this scenario SAP offers an *enhancement concept* that is discussed in detail in the next section.

▶ You want to eliminate some of the optional elements or attributes of the data types for certain use cases. For this scenario SAP offers a *restriction concept* that is discussed next.

Among other scenarios, the restriction concept is widely used in the definition of enterprise services in the Enterprise Services Repository. For example, the template of the order request enterprise service contains some optional elements that are never used in a purchase order created in an ERP system. To keep the message structure small, the template for this particular use case is reduced to the relevant segments of the order request template. You can create a restricted version of a data type by following these steps:

1. In the Enterprise Services Builder navigate to the data type you want to create a restriction for, right-click on the data type, and select **Copy Object....** A popup as shown in Figure 8.29 appears.

2. In the popup you must maintain the following information:

    ▶ The **Name** must contain the same name as the data type from which you copy.

    ▶ The **Namespace** and **Software Component Version** for the data type that you create. The namespace must be different from the namespace of the original data type.

    ▶ The **Save Original as Reference** flag must be checked.

▶ You can check the **With All Dependent Objects** flag if you want to create all data types that are used within the selected data type as well.

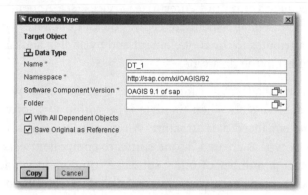

Figure 8.29 Copying of a Data Type for a Restricted Version

3. After you click on the **Copy** button, the data type is copied as a restricted version of the original data type and is displayed as shown in Figure 8.30.

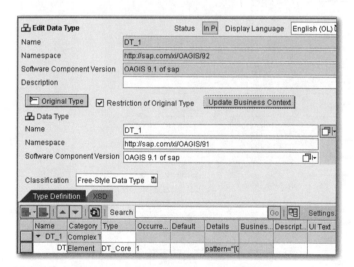

Figure 8.30 Data Type as a Restriction to Another Data Type

4. Now you can delete optional elements and attributes using the **Deleted Selected Line** icon. The system will issue a warning if you try to delete a mandatory object or if you try to add additional objects.

5. Save and activate the data type.

Creation of Data Type Enhancements

As mentioned above, SAP offers an enhancement concept for data types that is also utilized in the enhancement concept of enterprise services (see Appendix C for more details on the overall enhancement concept). You can enhance a data type by adding additional attributes to the root element and by adding additional elements (including attributes) to the data type.

You can only create data type enhancements for data types that are visible within the same software component version. Then the data type within this software component version uses the enhanced data structure. A typical use case is shown in Figure 8.31, where a data type is created in one software component version (SWCV 1) and then reused in a number of other software component versions (SWCV A and SWCV B). The reused data type is then enhanced specifically to the needs of the respective software component version.

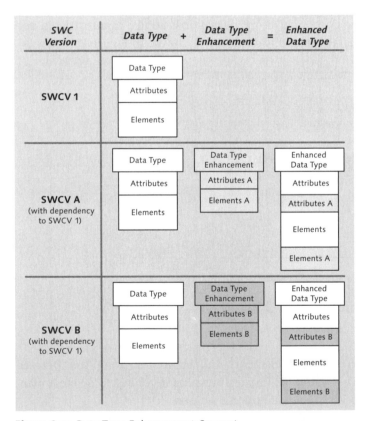

Figure 8.31 Data Type Enhancement Concept

When you create a data type enhancement, the system automatically adds a group element at the end of the definition of the data type and an attribute group at the end of the attribute list of the root node. You create a data type enhancement by following these steps:

1. In the Enterprise Services Repository follow the menu path **Object • New**. Alternatively, you can navigate to the software component version and namespace where you want to create the data type enhancement and select **New** after right-clicking on the namespace.

2. In the popup that is displayed select **Interface Objects • Data Type Enhancement** and enter the name, namespace, and software component version for the data type enhancement you want to create.

3. The maintenance screen for the data type enhancement is displayed as shown in Figure 8.32. Specify the data type you want to enhance in the **Enhancement for Data Type** list field.

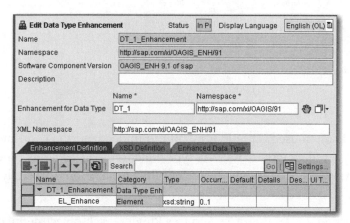

Figure 8.32 Creation of a Data Type Enhancement

4. The **XML Namespace** list field is prefilled with the name of the namespace to which the message type belongs. You can assign a different namespace that will be used in the XML message if necessary. We discuss the consequences of defining another namespace below.

5. Add additional elements and attributes on the **Enhancement Definition** tab using the **Insert New Lines** icon similarly to the creation of data types. Similar columns are available for maintenance as for data types.

6. Save and activate the data type enhancement.

In the maintenance screen for data type enhancements a number of tabs are available that display different information:

- On the **Enhancement Definition** tab is the list representation of the data type enhancement.
- On the **XSD Definition** tab is a generated XML schema definition of the data type enhancement.
- On the **Enhanced Data Type** tab is the complete data type structure with the enhancements you just defined, as shown in Figure 8.33.

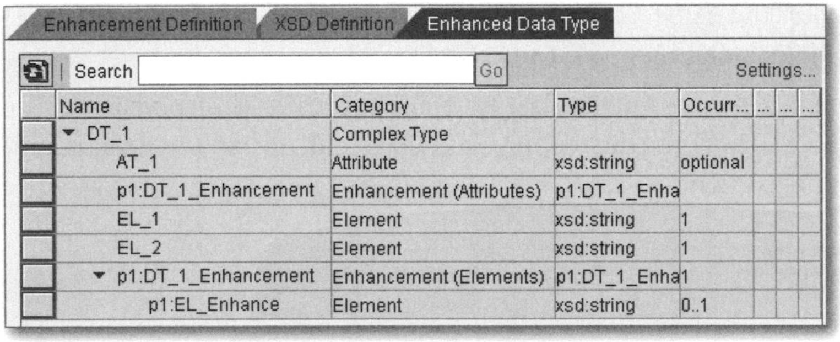

Name	Category	Type	Occurr...			
▼ DT_1	Complex Type					
AT_1	Attribute	xsd:string	optional			
p1:DT_1_Enhancement	Enhancement (Attributes)	p1:DT_1_Enha				
EL_1	Element	xsd:string	1			
EL_2	Element	xsd:string	1			
▼ p1:DT_1_Enhancement	Enhancement (Elements)	p1:DT_1_Enha	1			
p1:EL_Enhance	Element	xsd:string	0..1			

Figure 8.33 Display of an Enhanced Data Type

Namespaces

The term *namespace* is often used quite loosely, but to understand the concepts used with message types, data types, and data type enhancements as far as they are related to namespaces, we need to define this term more precisely. Namespaces are used in two separate contexts:

- As discussed in Section 2.3.1 Enterprise Services Builder, each object defined in the Enterprise Services Repository is assigned to a *repository namespace*. This namespace is used to enforce the uniqueness of the Enterprise Services Repository objects.
- Each element of an XML message is assigned to an *XML namespace*. Because an XML schema definition (XSD) is an XML file in itself, this rule also applies to XSDs.

Ultimately, we need to know which XML namespaces a XML message instance uses because these messages are exchanged between the trading partners. The trading partners must agree on the exact definition of the message structure including the namespaces used in order to pass any validation of the message content. Because each XML message is defined through message types, data types, and data type enhancements, we need to know how these objects influence the XML namespaces used in the XML message. Before we discuss the details of how the XML namespace is derived, let us take a look at the final result as shown in Figure 8.34.

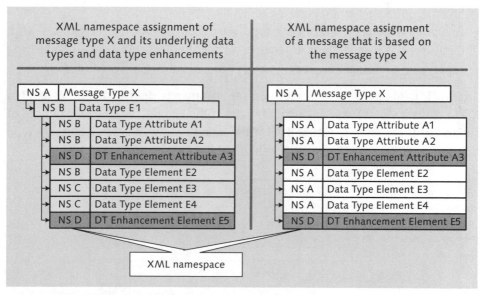

Figure 8.34 XML Namespace Assignments to a Message Instance

Here we see an example of a message type X assigned to data type E1, which consists of a number of attributes and elements assigned to different data types and data type enhancements. An example of a message based on this structure is also given in Listing 8.4.

```
<?xml version="1.0" encoding="utf-8" ?>
<n0:X A1="a1" A2="a2" n1:A3="a3" xmlns:n0="A" xmlns:n1="D">
    <E2>Element2</E2>
    <E3>Element3</E3>
    <E4>Element4</E4>
    <n1:E5>Element5</n1:E5>
</n0:X>
```

Listing 8.4 Example of a Message Instance

As we can see, only the XML namespaces assigned to the message type and the data type enhancement are reflected in the actual message instance, whereas the namespaces of the data types are not used in such an instance. Therefore, we have the following capabilities for assigning XML namespaces to these objects:

▶ For a data type the XML namespace is always inherited from the repository namespace. You cannot define the XML namespace in the data type maintenance.

▶ For a message type and a data type enhancement you can assign an XML namespace as part of the maintenance for these objects. As a default value, the repository namespace is used.

The XML namespace used in the message instance is defined in the generated XSD via the `targetNamespace` attribute within the element `xmlns`. An example of such an XSD is shown in Figure 8.35. This example shows the same message type definition as Figure 8.27, except for the field list **XML Namespace**.

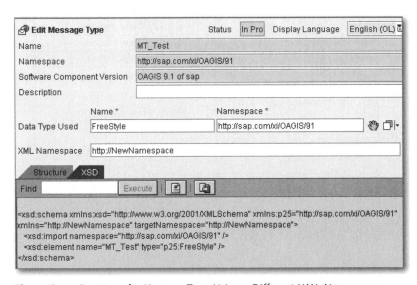

Figure 8.35 Creation of a Message Type Using a Different XML Namespace

There are a number of use cases for a separate definition of the XML namespace. One common use case that is heavily used in the definition of enterprise services is shown in Figure 8.36. Here a buyer sends a purchase order to his supplier, who receives the message and creates a sales order in his backend system. Both parties use a service-enabled SAP ERP system as their backend; the buyer utilizes a service within the Materials Management (MM) area, and the supplier uses a service within the Sales & Distribution (SD) area. The message instance exchanged between the two parties must not be altered and therefore needs to be understood on both sides. This implies that the XML namespaces used in the message definition must be identical even though the definitions of the underlying message types reside in different repository namespaces. This can be achieved by defining the XML namespace in the message type to be different from the repository namespaces of the respective message types.

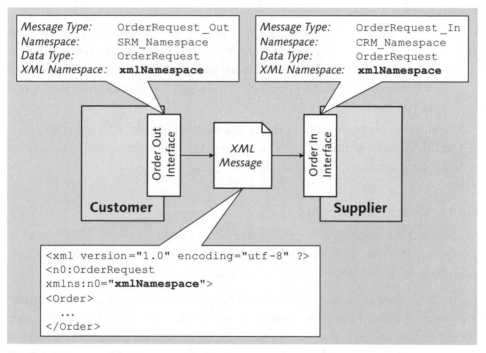

Figure 8.36 Message Flow in Regard to the Namespace

8.4 Mapping Techniques

In B2B integration scenarios the message structures of the message we exchange with our trading partner and the message we forward to our internal backend systems often differ. Therefore, the mapping between incoming messages and outgoing messages plays an important role. Before we go into more detail, let's briefly recap what we try to achieve with such a mapping.

Looking back at Figure 7.2 and Figure 8.1, we see that the adapters take care of the conversion of the message envelope, whereas with the *interface determination* step we determine the new structure of the message payload itself. Therefore, the mapping programs we discuss in this section take care of the message payload only.

We discussed mappings in Section 2.3.4 Mappings, but because B2B integration scenarios often utilize external standards, we need to extend our discussion to include such scenarios as well. As already discussed, a mapping consists of the following two parts:

▸ The *operation mapping* registers the mapping program that is to be used between a pair of service interface operations. During configuration time we need to define operation mappings as part of the interface determination step in case the message structures of the receiver operation and the sender operation do not match.

▸ The *mapping program* contains the actual mapping between the message structures that can be defined through a message type, an external definition, or an imported object.

8.4.1 Operation Mapping

In Section 2.3.4 Mappings we used Figure 2.17 to describe the building blocks of a mapping. We now need to extend this picture to also include the role that external interfaces and imported objects play in this context.

Figure 8.37 shows the building blocks of an operation mapping. As we can see, the source operation and target operation can be not only a service interface operation, but also an IDoc or an RFC in the form of an imported object. This implies that imported objects can be used as a source or target operation of an operation mapping either directly or through the service interface operation as shown in Figure 8.15.

You create an operation mapping using the Enterprise Services Builder by following these steps:

1. In the Enterprise Services repository follow the menu path **Object • New**. Alternatively, you can navigate to the software component version and namespace where you want to create the operation mapping and select **New** after right-clicking on the namespace.

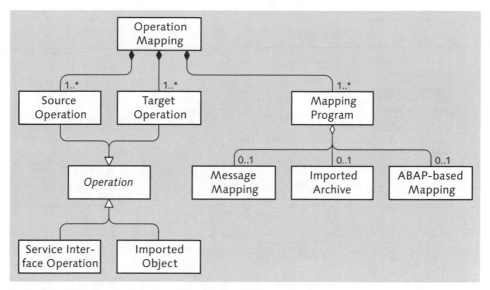

Figure 8.37 Building Blocks of an Operation Mapping

2. In the popup that is displayed select **Mapping Objects • Operation Mapping** and enter the **Name**, **Namespace**, and **Software Component Version** for the operation mapping you want to create.

3. The maintenance screen for the operation mapping is displayed as shown in Figure 8.38. Enter the **Source Operation** and the **Target Operation** of the operation mapping. These objects can reside in any software component. You can enter multiple source and target operations, which we will discuss in detail in Section 8.4.6 Multi-Mappings.

4. You can maintain the following attributes of the operation mapping. In most cases you leave these flags blank:

   ▸ The **Use SAP XML Tool** flag is only used for Java mappings and XSLT mappings and is discussed further in Section 8.4.8 Other Mapping Options.

   ▸ The **Do Not Resolve XOP Includes** flag is only relevant if an XML message contains binary data. In this case the binary data can be transmitted using *XML-binary Optimized Packaging* (XOP), which converts a message into a different format using `xop:include` statements. If your message mapping can understand this statement, the flag should be turned on for performance reasons.

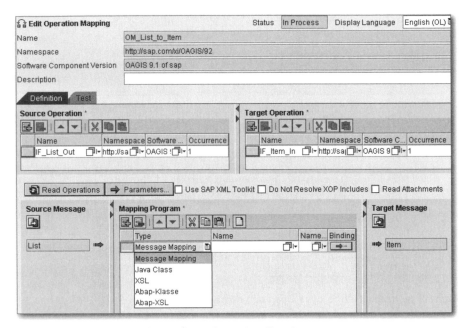

Figure 8.38 Maintenance Screen for an Operation Mapping

▷ The **Read Attachments** flag should only be set if you need to utilize attachments in your mapping program. As a default, no attachments are transferred from the Integration Engine (which resides on the ABAP stack) to the mapping processor (which resides on the Java stack) for performance reasons.

5. When you click on the **Read Operations** button, the system reads the defined source and target operations and determines the assigned message structures. As you can see from Figure 8.15, the message structure can be a message type, an external reference, or an imported object. These objects are then displayed in the lower part of the main window, where you need to assign the mapping program. Because mapping programs are based on the message structure and not on the operation itself (see Section 8.4.2 Message Mapping), we need this information to determine the mapping programs available to us.

6. Assign a mapping program to each step of the operation mapping. You only need more than one mapping program in multi-mapping scenarios as discussed in Section 8.4.6 Multi-Mappings. In the field **Type** you specify which type of mapping program you want to assign. As shown in Figure 8.37, you can choose between a message mapping, an imported archive, and an ABAP based map-

ping. The imported archive and the ABAP based mapping can refer to a number of different object types, as shown in the list in Figure 8.38.

7. Save and activate the operation mapping.

As shown in Figure 8.38, two tabs are available in the maintenance screen of an operation mapping.

▶ On the **Definition** tab you define the operation mapping and set all required attributes.

▶ On the **Test** tab you can test the operation mapping for correctness. We discuss the testing capabilities in more detail in Chapter 11 Testing Considerations.

8.4.2 Message Mapping

As mentioned in the previous section, the mapping program assigned to an operation mapping can be a message mapping developed using the graphical mapping tool of the Enterprise Services Builder or an imported archive containing different types of mappings, such as XSLT or a Java mapping. Although we give a short overview of the different imported archive options in Section 8.4.8 Other Mapping Options, we mainly focus on the message mapping tool provided with the Enterprise Services Builder. Figure 8.39 gives an overview of the building blocks for a message mapping.

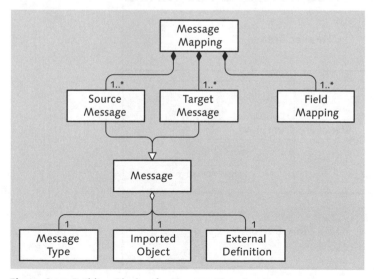

Figure 8.39 Building Blocks of a Message Mapping

As you can see in Figure 8.39, the source message and the target message of the message mapping can be assigned to any of the objects message type, imported object (RFC or IDoc), or external definition. This is consistent with the possible assignments to a message within a service operation, as shown in Figure 8.15.

The creation of a message mapping can be the most time-consuming activity within the Enterprise Services Repository if the message structures of your incoming and outgoing messages don't match very well. Therefore, we discuss the creation of message mappings in detail. Let's start with the message mapping editor provided by the Enterprise Services Builder. This editor consists of three major areas, as shown in Figure 8.40:

- The *Header Area* subscreen contains the information that uniquely identifies a message mapping.

- The *Structure Overview* screen contains a graphical representation of the selected source message and target message. It also gives you a graphical representation of fields that have been mapped, fields that must be mapped due to their cardinality, and so on.

- In the *Data-Flow Editor* you can view and define the mapping of an individual target field that you have selected from the structure overview screen. We discuss the features of the data-flow editor in the next section.

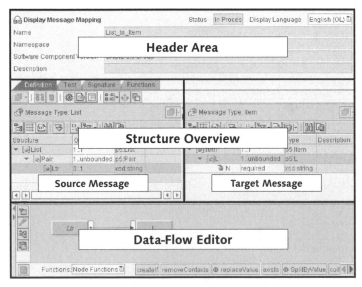

Figure 8.40 Partitioning of the Message Mapping Editor

The basic steps for the creation of a message mapping using the Enterprise Services Builder are described below. Some advanced features available with message mappings are described in the subsequent sections.

1. In the Enterprise Services Repository follow the menu path **Object · New**. Alternatively, you can navigate to the software component version and namespace where you want to create the message mapping and select **New** after right-clicking on the namespace.

2. In the popup that is displayed choose **Mapping Objects · Message Mapping** and enter the **Name**, **Namespace**, and **Software Component Version** for the message mapping you want to create.

3. The maintenance screen for the message mapping is displayed as shown in Figure 8.41. Enter the **Source Message** and the **Target Message** of the message mapping. These objects can reside in any software component. You can use the search help to identify the objects or simply drag and drop them from the list provided in the navigation bar.

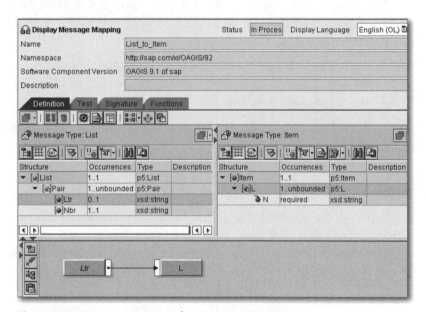

Figure 8.41 Maintenance Screen for a Message Mapping

4. For each target field that needs to be mapped, you need to create the actual mapping steps in the data-flow editor. By double-clicking on a target field in the structure overview screen the target field and its related mapping steps are

displayed in the data-flow editor and can be further edited. We discuss the details of the field mapping steps in Section 8.4.3 Field Mapping.

5. Save and activate the message mapping. With the activation of the message mapping, Java source code is generated containing the mapping for execution during runtime.

As shown in Figure 8.41, several tabs are available in the structure overview section of the maintenance screen for a message mapping:

▶ On the **Definition** tab you can view a graphical representation of your source message and your target message. In addition, you can manipulate the messages to some degree, which we discuss below.

▶ On the **Test** tab you can run a first test of the message mapping you created. We discuss the testing and debugging capabilities for message mappings in Section 8.4.4 Testing and Debugging Capabilities.

▶ On the **Signature** tab you can adjust your message mapping to support multi-mappings. We discuss multi-mappings further in Section 8.4.6 Multi-Mappings. In addition, you can introduce parameters to your mapping, which we cover in Section 9.7.1 Parameters in Mappings.

▶ On the **Functions** tab you can define user-defined functions that can be utilized in your field mapping. We discuss the creation of user-defined functions in Section 8.4.5 User-Defined Functions.

Let us now take a closer look at the structure overview screen and how to read the information provided there.

Graphical Display of Messages

The graphical display of the source message and target message in the structure overview section contains an icon in front of each line that gives you a quick overview on the type of the field and the status in regard to the field mapping. The different field types are depicted by different icons used in the list display of the messages.

Table 8.6 provides an overview of the available icons. Note that the **Variable** field type is not part of the message structure itself, but is an additional variable that can be used within the mapping process only. We discuss the creation of variables in detail below.

Icon for Field Types	Description
[●]	Element with maxOccurs = 1
[▲]	Element with maxOccurs > 1
🐌	Attribute
[●]	Recursive element with maxOccurs = 1
[▲]	Recursive element with maxOccurs > 1
𝒚	Variable

Table 8.6 Icons Used for Different Field Types in a Message Mapping

In addition, you can see the status of the target message fields in regard to the field mapping based on the color of each of the icons. Table 8.7 gives an overview of the available colors and their meanings.

Color	Description
White	No field mapping is required because the target field is not mandatory
Green	Field mapping for this target field exists
Red	Target field is mandatory, but no field mapping exists
Yellow	Field mapping for this target field is not complete yet

Table 8.7 Color Coding Based on the Status of Each Target Field

If you collapse a node in the graphical display where any node icon of the subtree is colored red, the node you collapsed will be displayed in red even if this node itself is not in a red status. This ensures that a red status is always visible, independent of the chosen display.

Mapping of Structure Nodes

To understand when a field mapping is required, we need to distinguish between the three basic node types that can be part of an XML message:

▶ **Structure nodes**
Structure nodes of an XML message are elements that contain other subelements. They can contain attributes, but they never carry a value itself.

▶ **Leaf nodes**
Leaf nodes of an XML message are elements that do not contain any subelements. Unlike the structure node, they always carry a value. They also can contain attributes.

▶ **Attributes**
Attributes are linked to structure nodes or leaf nodes and always carry a value.

The message mapping tool only requires you to create a field mapping if it doesn't have sufficient information available to create the target message otherwise. Therefore, the following rules exist for the creation of field mappings:

▶ Because *leaf nodes* and *attributes* carry a value, they always require a field mapping if you want these objects to appear in your target message. With the field mapping you specify the number of occurrences of this object in your target message and the value for each of these occurrences.

▶ Because *structure nodes* don't carry a value, they only require a field mapping in certain circumstances:

▶ If the minimum occurrence of a structure node is equal to its maximum occurrence (minOccurs = maxOccurs), the mapping tool knows exactly how many instances of this node need to be generated. Because structure nodes don't carry any value, all the necessary information for the creation of this node is available, and no field mapping is required. If a field mapping is provided, it will be ignored by the mapping tool.

▶ If the minimum occurrence of a structure node is not equal to its maximum occurrence (minOccurs < maxOccurs), the mapping tool needs to know the number of occurrences for this object. Therefore, you need to create a field mapping just like for leaf nodes and attributes that specifies the number of occurrences. However, any values provided with the field mapping will be ignored.

Manipulation of the Target Structure Display

The message mapping tool allows you to manipulate the tree display of the target structure to a certain degree in order to support all mapping requirements.

▶ **Duplicating subtrees**
By default, each object is displayed only once in the tree display of the message structure. However, if an element is allowed to occur multiple times

(minOccurs > 1) in your target message, you may need to provide a different field mapping for some of these occurrences. In this case you need to have this element with its subtree displayed more than once in the tree display of the message structure. To duplicate such a section in your display, right-click on the element you want to duplicate and select **Duplicate Subtree** from the list. The element and all subordinate nodes are then repeated in the tree display. However, you only can duplicate a subtree if you have a field mapping in place for all existing occurrences of this field.

▶ **Adding variables**
Sometimes you may want to reuse a certain value that you have derived as part of your mapping process. As of release 7.1 of SAP NetWeaver PI, you can create additional variables that are shown in the tree display of your target structure and that are treated like any other field. You can create a field mapping for a variable and reuse it in the field mapping of any subsequent field. To create a variable, right-click on the element that should contain the variable, select **Add Variable** from the list, and provide the name of the variable.

8.4.3 Field Mapping

In the previous section we discussed how to read the information provided on the *structure overview screen*. In this section we discuss how to maintain the mapping for each relevant target field in the *data-flow editor*. For each target field for which you want to create a mapping, you need to perform the following steps within the message mapping maintenance process:

1. In the structure overview screen double-click on the field of the target structure for which you want to create a mapping. The field is then displayed within the data-flow editor.

2. Move the required fields from the source structure and the required functions into the data-flow editor. This can be done by double-clicking on the required objects or by simply dragging and dropping them into the editor.

3. Some functions have properties assigned to them. Maintain these properties based on the specific mapping requirements by double-clicking the function. Alternatively, you can also right-click and then choose **Properties** from the list.

4. Maintain the required connections between the objects based on the specific mapping requirements. You create a connection by simply dragging the mouse between the two endpoints.

Although the graphical mapping tool as just described is very easy to use, it is essential to understand exactly how this tool processes the data of a message to create more sophisticated mappings. Because we cannot give a complete introduction to all of the features and capabilities of the message mapping tool, we start the discussion with an introduction of data queues and context handling, followed by a simple scenario that we enhance step by step to a more sophisticated mapping example. In addition, you can find several message mapping scenarios in Appendix A Message Mapping Examples.

Data Queues and Context Handling

Message mappings work with *data queues* that contain the complete message instance for a specific field. In addition to the pure data stream of the field, the *context* within the message structure plays an important role as well. Figure 8.42 illustrates how the context of a data queue is derived.

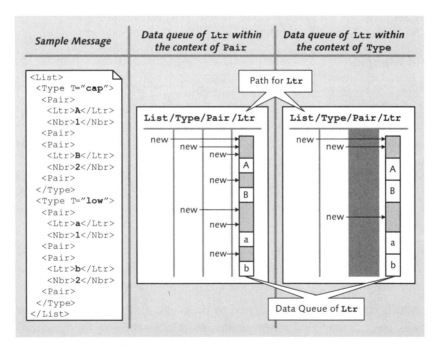

Figure 8.42 Context Changes in a Data Queue

In the example used in Figure 8.42 the data stream for the element Ltr is (A,B,a,b). This data stream is interpreted within the context of the complete message. To do that, we first need to identify the complete path for the element in question. The path is simply the hierarchy of parent nodes for an element or attribute. For the element Ltr the path is List/Type/Pair/Ltr.

The data queue can now be interpreted within the context of each of these parent nodes. We say that two elements of the data queue are within the same context if they belong to the same parent node; otherwise, a *context change* took place. In Figure 8.42 we see the data queue for the element Ltr within the context of the node Pair and the node Type.

▶ Within the context of the node Pair a context change takes place after each item in the queue, denoted by a grey box in Figure 8.42.

▶ Within the context of the node Type the subsequent node Pair is ignored. Because items A and B belong to the same occurrence of the node Type, no context change takes place (within Type) between these two items. The same holds true for items a and b, such that only one context change takes place within the context of the node Type.

The goal of the field mapping is to provide the correct input data stream to each target field including the proper context changes. Each target field requires the complete input queue with the context changes based on the preceding node. If the length of the input queue is not identical to the required length of the target field data queue, the system behaves as follows:

▶ If the input queue is longer than the target message allows (e.g., due to limitations in the maximum occurrence), the additional input values are ignored.

▶ If the input queue is shorter than the target message requires, an error is triggered. There is an exception if the input queue is filled from a standard function without any input values (e.g., the function Constant). In this case the input value is repeated as often as required.

For example, let's take a look at Figure 8.43. Here we have a source message as shown in ❶ that needs to be converted to a target message as shown in ❺ using the following mapping requirements:

▶ The values of the element Ltr of the source message must be transferred to the element L of the target message.

▶ The values of the element Nbr of the source message must be transferred to the attribute N of element L within the target message.

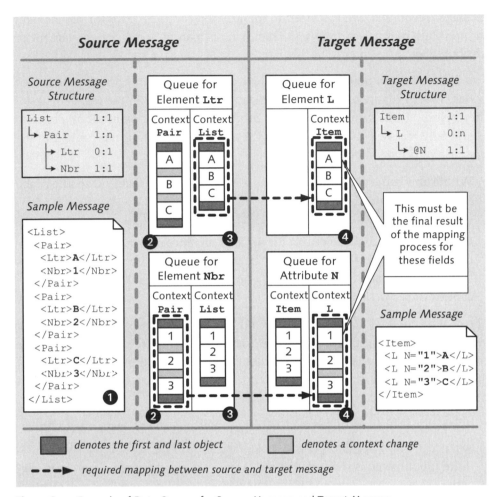

Figure 8.43 Example of Data Queues for Source Message and Target Message

The data queues for the fields of the source message are shown in ❷ (within the context of the node Pair) and in ❸ (within the context of the node List). The data queues for the fields of the target message within the contexts of the preceding node are shown in ❹. For this particular message instance we see that we can get the correct queue data for the target message fields simply from the corresponding source message fields as shown in Figure 8.44. For the source element Ltr we have to change the context to List by right-clicking on the object representing the element Ltr in the data-flow editor and selecting **Context • <context level>** from the list.

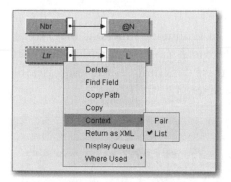

Figure 8.44 Setting the Context in a Field Mapping

This mapping works fine for the example message used in Figure 8.43, but it doesn't work correctly for all possible message instances. Figure 8.45 shows an example where the mapping creates an incorrect result in the second occurrence of the element L. The correct entry for this line should read `<L N="3">C</L>`.

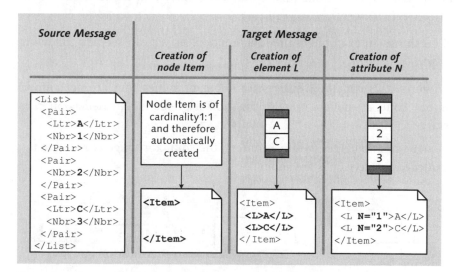

Figure 8.45 Target Message Creation Using Mapping from Figure 8.44

We can achieve this mapping by utilizing some of the standard functions provided by the graphical mapping tool. Before we complete this example, we first give a short overview of the standard functions currently available. Because a new standard function can be added with each support package, you should check the most current documentation on available standard functions.

Arithmetic Functions

The graphical mapping tools offers a variety of arithmetic functions that can be applied to numeric input values. Table 8.8 provides a list of all arithmetic functions currently available. We use some of these functions in the use cases of Appendix A Message Mapping Examples, as denoted in the table.

Arithmetic Functions	Used in Appendix
`divide`, `floor`	Section A.2 Message Splitting
`add`, `subtract`, `multiply`, `equalsA`, `abs`, `sqrt`, `sqr`, `sign`, `neg`, `1/x`, `power`, `less`, `greater`, `max`, `min`, `ceil`, `round`, `counter`, `FormatNum`	—

Table 8.8 Arithmetic Functions Available in the Graphical Mapping Tool

Most of these functions are self-explanatory. We only need to understand how these functions work with input queues that do not match in terms of number of values or context changes.

Figure 8.46 shows an example of the function `add`. As we can see, the following rules apply:

▶ If the two queues contain a different number of values (but are not empty) within one context, the last value of the shorter queue is repeated as often as necessary.

▶ If one queue has no values within a context, the context change is added to the result queue, but no values are added.

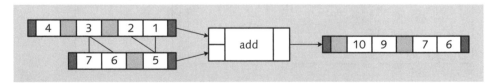

Figure 8.46 Example of the Standard Function Add

Boolean Functions

Boolean functions require Boolean values (`true` or `false`) in the input queues, or they return a queue of Boolean values as a result. Table 8.9 provides a list of all

Boolean functions currently available. We use some of these functions in the use cases in Appendix A Message Mapping Examples, as denoted in the table.

Boolean Functions	Used in Appendix
if, ifWithoutElse	Section A.3 Duplicating Nodes
And, Or, Not, Equals, notEquals	—

Table 8.9 Boolean Functions Available in the Graphical Mapping Tool

Figure 8.47 shows an example of the function ifWithoutElse. You can define in the **Properties** of this function how it should react if the input condition has the value false. The result value can be omitted, or a special value, SUPPRESS, can be added to the result queue, denoting that this item should be suppressed in further processing.

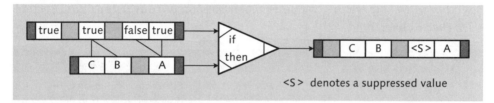

Figure 8.47 Example of the Standard Function ifWithoutElse

Text Functions

Text functions interpret the input queues as a string and perform the operations accordingly. Table 8.10 provides a list of all text functions currently available. We use some of these functions in the use cases in Appendix A Message Mapping Examples, as denoted in the table.

Text Functions	Used in Appendix
equalsS	Section A.1 Simple Looping
concat, substring, indexOf, lastIndexOf, compare, replaceString, trim, length, endsWith, startsWith, toUpperCase, toLowerCase	—

Table 8.10 Text Functions Available in the Graphical Mapping Tool

Figure 8.48 shows an example of the function `concat`. As you can see, input queues that don't match in terms of number of values or context changes are treated the same as we discussed for arithmetic functions.

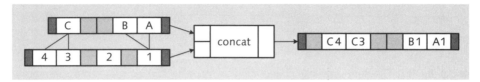

Figure 8.48 Example of the Standard Function concat

Conversion Functions

All functions in this category offer data conversion using different data sources. Table 8.11 provides a list of all conversion functions currently available. Apart from the function `FixValues`, all of them require some settings in the Integration Directory as well; therefore, we defer the discussion of conversions until Section 9.7.2 Data Conversions.

Conversion Functions	Used in Appendix
`FixValues`, `Value mapping`, `JDBC Lookup`, `RFC Lookup`	Conversion functions are discussed in Section 9.7.2 Data Conversions

Table 8.11 Conversion Functions Available in the Graphical Mapping Tool

Constants

Many functions are available that don't need any input, but provide a constant value instead. Whereas for all other functions the result queue is determined by the input queues, no input queue is available for functions of the constant function group. Therefore, the output queue needs to be determined differently. In short, these functions generate a new value whenever required as part of the mapping process. The following rules are applied:

▶ If the constant function is assigned to a target field, a value is generated as often as specified by the `minOccurs` parameter of the target field. If `minOccurs` = 0, a value is still generated once.

▶ If the constant function is used as input for another function, a value is generated as often as the other input queues require a value. If multiple input queues with different numbers of values are used, the generation is based on the queue with the most values.

Table 8.12 provides a list of all constant functions currently available. Even though the function `CopyValue` requires an input, it follows the rules of the other constant functions.

Constants Functions	Used in Appendix
Constant	Section A.1 Simple Looping, Section A.2 Message Splitting, Section A.3 Duplicating Nodes
CopyValue, sender, receiver	–

Table 8.12 Constant Functions Available in the Graphical Mapping Tool

Date Functions

You can view the date functions as a subcategory of the constant functions, related to date values. Date functions generate a value whenever required as part of the mapping process, following the same rules as constant functions. Table 8.13 provides a list of all date functions currently available.

Date Functions	Used in Appendix
currentDate, DateTrans, DateBefore, DateAfter, CompareDates	–

Table 8.13 Date Functions Available in the Graphical Mapping Tool

Statistic Functions

The statistic functions contain functions that provide you with statistical information on the input queue. For example, the sum or the average value of an input queue is returned to the function caller. Table 8.14 provides a list of all statistic functions currently available.

Statistic Functions	Used in Appendix
index	Section A.2 Message Splitting
sum, average, count	–

Table 8.14 Statistic Functions Available in the Graphical Mapping Tool

Node Functions

Many functions are available for manipulating queues of the source message fields or those created by other functions. For example, you can duplicate values, change context information, and perform other manipulations. Table 8.15 provides a list of all node functions currently available.

Node Functions	Used in Appendix
createIf	Section A.1 Simple Looping
formatByExample, collapseContent	Section A.2 Message Splitting
SplitByValue	Section A.2 Message Splitting, Section A.3 Duplicating Nodes
exists, removeContexts, useOneAsMany	Section A.3 Duplicating Nodes
replaceValue, sort, sortByKey, mapWithDefault	—

Table 8.15 Node Functions Available in the Graphical Mapping Tool

As you can see, we discuss many of the node functions in the examples used in Appendix A Message Mapping Examples. Therefore, here we give only a short introduction to some of the node functions available.

Figure 8.49 shows a common example of how the functions removeContext and SplitByValue can be used in conjunction. In this scenario the data queue already contains the correct value list, but not the correct context changes. With the function removeContext you first eliminate all context changes out of the queue, and then you reassign context changes with the function SplitByValue. For this function you can specify within the properties when a context change should take place. In our example we have a context change after each value.

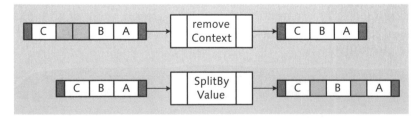

Figure 8.49 Example of the Standard Functions removeContext and SplitByValue

Figure 8.50 shows an example of how to use the function `useOneAsMany`. This function can be used to duplicate values, for example, when you need to bring header information into a line-item-based table. The function `useOneAsMany` requires three input queues:

▶ The first input queue contains the values that need to be duplicated. This queue must have a context change after each value.

▶ The second input queue contains the information on how to distribute the values. This queue must have the same number of context changes as the first input queue, and it must have at least one value within each context. This is denoted in Figure 8.50 via the solid lines between the first and the second input channel.

▶ The third input queue contains the same structure (context changes) as the result queue. Only the values of the result queue are replaced with the values from the first input queue. The third input queue must have the same list of values as the second input queue. Then the values for the result queue are derived following the dotted lines between the first input queue and the second input queue followed by the solid lines between the second and third input queues.

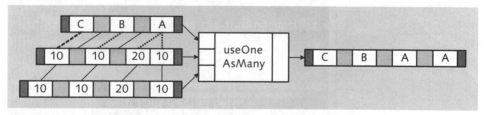

Figure 8.50 Example of the Standard Function useOneAsMany

Example of a Field Mapping

Because we now have an overview of the predefined functions provided with the graphical mapping tool, we can complete our example that we left off with the problem described in Figure 8.45. Further examples of the creation of message mappings can be found in Appendix A Message Mapping Examples.

Figure 8.51 shows the complete mapping for the attribute @C along with the data queues between messages. The mapping for this attribute consists of the following steps:

1. Because the creation of the attribute N depends on the availability of the source field Ltr, we need to use this data queue as an input for the mapping of the attribute N.

2. We need to determine if the data queue for Ltr contains a value within each context of the node Pair. The result of this check is either true or false for each context. This check is done using the function exists.

3. Only if the result of the check in the previous step is true, should the value from queue Nbr be considered. This assignment is done using the function ifWithoutElse.

4. Now we have the correct values in the result queue, but we still need to adjust the context used in this function. This can be done using the functions remove-Context and SplitByValue (see the results of the mapping as displayed in Figure 8.51).

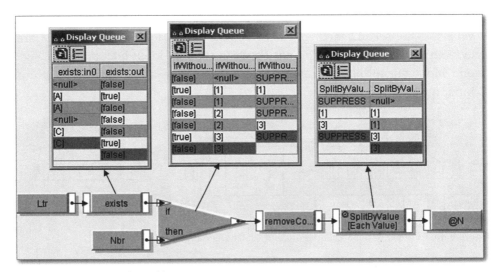

Figure 8.51 Example of a Field Mapping

8.4.4 Testing and Debugging Capabilities

The graphical mapping tool offers very comfortable test and debugging capabilities for the development of a message mapping. These features are integrated into the graphical mapping tool and can easily be accessed during the development of a field mapping itself. The following options are available:

▶ You can test the complete message mapping with a sample message instance.

▶ You can debug through a field mapping by checking the result of each step using a sample message instance.

For both options you first must provide a sample XML message. You can enter the sample message on the **Test** tab of the message mapping maintenance screen (see Figure 8.52). You can enter the sample message either in list form as shown in Figure 8.52, or you can enter it in form of an XML document. If you click on the **Start the Transformation** (▦) icon, the message mapping will be executed and the result displayed on the right-hand side of the screen, as shown in Figure 8.52.

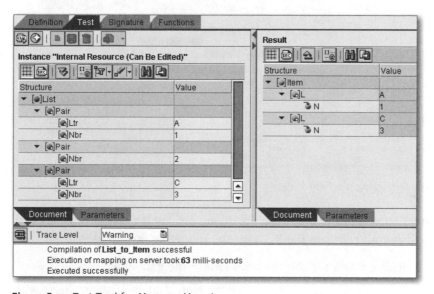

Figure 8.52 Test Tool for Message Mappings

The sample message is also the starting point for checking an individual step of your field mapping. Once you have entered a sample message and set up a field mapping, you can check this mapping using the following steps. Note that you don't have to have any of the other field mappings in place to execute this check.

1. After you have entered a sample message, select the **Definition** tab in the message mapping maintenance screen.

2. Select the target field you want to check the mapping for such that the mapping appears in the data-flow editor.

3. Right-click on the function you want to check and select **Display Queue** from the list. The data queues for the input variables and the result queue are displayed based on the sample message, as shown in Figure 8.53.

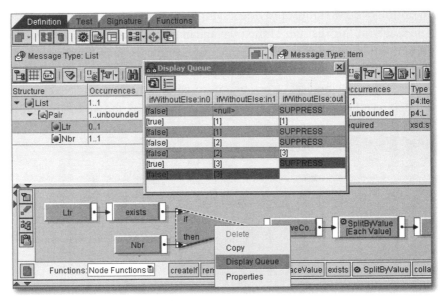

Figure 8.53 Debugging of a Field Mapping

From Figure 8.53 you can also see that the queue display list contains some color coding. The different colors in the list have the following meanings:

▶ The *white* fields contain the actual values within the data queues.

▶ The *light gray* fields denote a context change. Note that each queue starts with a context change.

▶ The *dark gray* fields denote the end of the queue.

▶ The special value SUPPRESS (if added to the queue) is displayed as a *light blue* field.

8.4.5   User-Defined Functions

In the previous section we saw that many functions are delivered with the graphical mapping tool. If these functions are not sufficient for your purposes, you can create additional user-defined functions that integrate into the graphical mapping tool. The following options are available for creating a user-defined function:

▶ **Functions in a Function Library**

Functions that are created as part of a function library are visible within the software component version where the function library resides and within any dependent software component versions. Function libraries are available as of release 7.1 of SAP NetWeaver PI.

▶ **Local User-Defined Functions**

Local user-defined functions are only visible within the message mapping where this function was created.

The actual creation of a function does not differ between local user-defined functions and functions defined in a function library. Therefore, we first discuss briefly how to set up a user-defined function in a function library and as a local function before we discuss the creation of the user-defined function itself.

Functions in a Function Library

You can define functions within a function library to make these functions available for all message mappings within the software component version. To do that you must create a function library and then make this library visible within your message mapping.

1. In the Enterprise Services Repository follow the menu path **Object • New**. Alternatively, you can navigate to the software component version and namespace where you want to create the message mapping and select **New** after right-clicking on the namespace.

2. In the popup that is displayed select **Mapping Objects • Function Library** and enter the name, namespace, and software component version for the function library you want to create.

3. The editor for the creation of user-defined functions is displayed, where you can create your functions. We discuss how to work with this editor below.

4. Save and activate the function library.

We now have created a function library within a software component version. Next, we need to assign the function library to the message mapping to utilize the functions of the library. You assign a function library to a message mapping as follows:

1. In the Enterprise Services Builder open the message mapping where you want to utilize functions out of your function library.

2. On the left-hand side of the data-flow editor click on the **Show Used Function Libraries** icon. A list of all assigned function libraries appears to the left of the data-flow editor. As a default, one entry in this list refers to the local user functions that are available for this particular message mapping only.

3. Use the **Insert Line Below Selection** icon to add the relevant function libraries to your list. If a library contains any user-defined functions, the library is added to the list of function groups that you can use in your message mapping (see Figure 8.54).

4. Save and activate the message mapping.

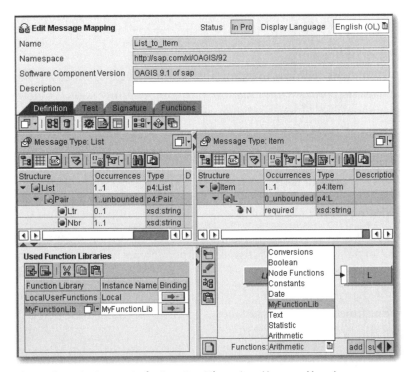

Figure 8.54 Assignment of a Function Library in a Message Mapping

Local User-Defined Functions

Within the message mapping you can create local user-defined functions that are only visible within the message mapping itself. To create local user-defined functions select the **Functions** tab within the structure overview of the message mapping maintenance screen. This tab displays the editor for the creation of user-defined functions, where you can create your local functions. We discuss how to work with this editor in the next section.

Alternatively, you can create local user-defined functions out of the data-flow editor by clicking on the **Create** icon. Although the user interface has a different look, it offers the same functionality as the editor on the **Functions** tab.

Creation of a Function

The editor for user-defined functions is identical for functions in a function library and for local user-defined functions (on the **Functions** tab of a message mapping). Figure 8.55 shows an example of the maintenance editor for user-defined functions.

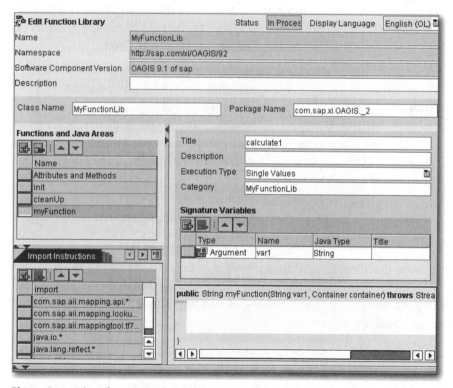

Figure 8.55 Editor for User-Defined Functions

This editor consists of the following sections:

▶ **Functions and Java area**
The functions and Java area is located on the left-hand side and consists of two lists. In the top list you can define the name of your user function. In the bottom list you can specify the Java packages that should be imported into the Java class of the specified function library.

▶ **Main Window**
In the main window you specify a number of attributes of your user-defined function and provide a list of input variables for your function. The lower part of the main window is used for the actual coding of the user-defined function.

For each user-defined function you need to specify the execution type. The following options are available:

▶ **Single Values**
A function of this type returns only one value at a time. The result is returned with the statement `return(String value);`. Similar to arithmetic functions or constant functions, this type of function is called as many times as necessary when used as part of a mapping with input queues containing multiple elements.

▶ **All Values of a Context**
A function of this type processes all values of the input fields that are within the same context at the same time. After each context change this function loads all values of the input variables that are within the same context. The result is stored in an array of type `ResultList`.

▶ **All Values of Queue**
A function of this type processes all values of the input fields of the complete queue. The result is stored in an array of type `ResultList`.

After you have specified the execution type, you need to maintain the signature variables of the function under the header **Signature Variables** (see Figure 8.55), followed by the actual coding of the user-defined function. The following types of signature variables are available:

▶ A signature variable of type **Argument** is used as an input to the function and expects the input in the form of an input queue. These variables define input variables to the user-defined function in the following way:

- For functions of type **Single Values** these variables are exposed as single values.

- For functions of all other types these variables are exposed as an array.

▶ A signature variable of type **Parameter** is used as a property of the function that needs to be maintained within the message mapping. All variables of this type are exposed as single values.

▶ A signature variable of type **Result** contains the data queue that should be returned to the mapping process as the result of the function. This type of variable does not exist for functions of type **Single Values** because in this case only one value is returned as a result of the function. The return is handled via the statement `return(String value)`.

Ultimately, the function needs to return a data queue or an individual value used in a data queue. Because the data queues can contain some special values, such as a context change, the following constants are available for you to use in user-defined functions:

▶ The constant `ResultList.CC` denotes a context change.

▶ The constant `ResultList.SUPPRESS` denotes the special value SUPPRESS.

For functions of type **All Values of a Context** or **All Values of Queue**, the return queue is always represented by an object of type `ResultList`. For this type a number of methods are available to enable you to fill this object properly. These methods are listed in Table 8.16.

Methods of ResultList	Description
void addValue(String value)	The value is added to the result list.
void addContextChange()	A context change is added to the result list.
void addSuppress()	The special value SUPPRESS is added to the result list.
void clear()	The result list is cleared.

Table 8.16 Methods of the Object ResultList

In addition, you can utilize a number of standard objects for better manipulation across multiple calls of a user-defined function. In particular, the following objects are available:

▶ **Container object**
Each user-defined function automatically has an instance of the object `Container` embedded via the parameter list of the user-defined function. During the execution of a message mapping the container object can be used to cache data for later reuse within the same function.

▶ **Global container object**
Within your user-defined function you can create an instance of the object `GlobalContainer` using the method `getGlobalContainer()` of the container object. During the execution of a message mapping the container object can be used to cache data for later reuse by any user-defined function used in the message mapping.

You can find more information on the container objects and their available methods in the SAP help documentation at *http://help.sap.com*.

8.4.6 Multi-Mappings

So far, we have discussed mappings between one source interface and one target interface. However, other scenarios are also possible, which are called *multi-mappings*. In particular, we have the following scenarios:

▶ **1:n mappings**
In a 1:n mapping one source message needs to be split into multiple target messages. This scenario is supported in the mapping tool and can be utilized in the transformation step of a cross-component BPM scenario (see Section 6.4.3 Transformation Step), as well as by adapters that are part of the adapter engine.

▶ **n:1 Mappings**
In an n:1 mapping you want to bundle multiple source messages into one target message. This scenario is supported in the mapping tool and can be utilized in the transformation step of a cross-component BPM scenario only (see Section 6.4.3 Transformation Step).

▶ **n:m mappings**
An n:m mapping is a combination of the first two scenarios. It is supported in the mapping tool and can be utilized in the transformation step of a cross-component BPM scenario only (see Section 6.4.3 Transformation Step).

▶ **Consecutive mappings**
In a consecutive mapping you create an operation mapping that utilizes multiple mapping programs consecutively.

In this section we discuss how multi-mappings can be created in the Enterprise Services Repository, and we discuss the configuration of multi-mappings in Chapter 9 Configuration.

1:n Mappings, n:1 Mappings, and n:m Mappings

You can define a multi-mapping of these types on the **Signature** tab of the message mapping maintenance screen, as shown in Figure 8.56. A multi-mapping is created if you have more than one source message or more than one target message or if the occurrence of any message is not equal to 1.

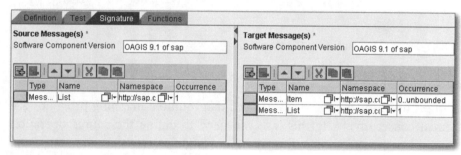

Figure 8.56 Example of a 1:n Mapping

When you return in your message mapping to the **Definition** tab, you can see that the message structure that is available for your message mapping has changed, as shown in Figure 8.57. The source and the target message now have the following structure (once for the source structure and once for the target structure):

▶ The top node **Messages** with the occurrence 1:1 is the container for all messages defined for the multi-mapping process.

▶ Underneath the node **Messages** are the nodes **Message1**, **Message2**, and so on for each message that has been added as a source (target) message. The occurrence for each of these nodes is 1:1.

▶ Underneath the nodes **Message1** and so on are the corresponding message that you have entered as a source (target) message. The occurrence of these nodes depends on the occurrence you have defined for each of these messages on the **Signature** tab (compare with Figure 8.56).

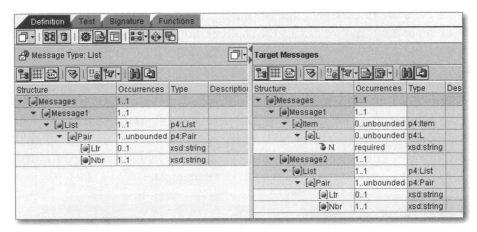

Figure 8.57 Message Structure for a 1:n Mapping

Consecutive Mappings

You can set up an operation mapping such that multiple mapping programs are performed consecutively. In this case you need to define the source operation and the final target operation as the source and target of your operation mapping. Then you assign the mapping programs to your operation mapping, which are performed in the order they are specified (see Figure 8.58 for an example). Because the message mappings can use other messages than those specified as an intermediate source or target message, you need to adjust your search criteria for applicable mapping programs accordingly.

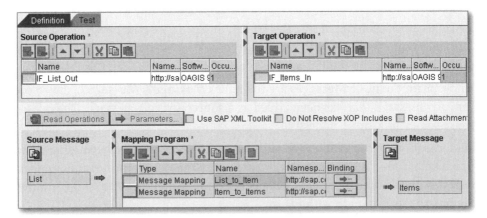

Figure 8.58 Operation Mapping with Consecutive Message Mappings

It is important that the target message of one mapping program matches exactly the source message of the subsequent mapping program because the result of the first mapping serves as the input for the subsequent mapping. This implies that either all mapping programs must be 1:1 mappings or none of them are. As soon as we have one multi-mapping in the chain of consecutive message mappings, we have its source message and its target message using the adjusted message structure definition as shown in Figure 8.57. Therefore, the preceding and subsequent mapping programs have to use the adjusted message structure as well, and so on.

8.4.7 Mapping Templates

Often certain segments of a message (e.g., address information) are reused in multiple message definitions. If the mapping of such segments between different message standards is identical, you don't want to redo this part of the mapping for each message definition. Instead you can define one mapping template for such a segment and then include this template in your message mappings.

As the source and target element for a mapping template, you can use any of the following objects:

▶ Data types

▶ Any segment of an imported object

▶ Any message segment of an external definition

Note that you cannot select a message type as the source or target element for a mapping template, because this would result in a complete message mapping. We discuss briefly how a mapping template can be created and how it can be reused in a message mapping.

Creating a Mapping Template

You can create standalone mapping templates, or you can use one part of a message mapping and expose it as a mapping template. Once the mapping template is created, you work with it the same way as with a message mapping.

▶ **Standalone creation of a mapping template**
To create a mapping template in the Enterprise Services Repository follow the menu path **Object • New** and choose **Mapping Objects • Mapping Template** in the popup that is displayed. After you have entered the mapping template

name with its software component version and namespace, the mapping template is created. You can maintain the field mappings of the template exactly the same way as for message mappings.

▶ **Exposing part of a message mapping as a mapping template**
You can expose a part of a message mapping as a mapping template. Within the structure overview section of the message mapping maintenance screen, you need to select the source field and the target field that should become the top nodes of your mapping template, right-click on the target field, and select **Create Template Based on Mapping**. A short wizard will then guide you through the creation of the mapping template.

Using a Mapping Template

After you have created a mapping template, you obviously want to use it in your message mappings. They can easily be incorporated into your message mappings by following these steps:

1. Open the message mapping in which you want to utilize your mapping template.

2. Mark the source field and the target field that should be the basis for your mapping template.

3. Select the **Show Suitable Templates** (⬥) icon. A popup appears that shows the available mapping templates based on your source and target field selection. You may need to extend the search range for available mapping templates to any source type and target type in order to find all suitable mapping templates. For example, the nodes of an IDoc message carry both the IDoc type and the segment name (e.g., ORDERS05.E1EDK01) but can be used with the specified segment for any IDoc type. The default settings in the search range would not pick up such mapping templates.

4. Select the correct mapping template from the list and select **Apply**. The mapping template is inserted into your message mapping.

Mapping templates are copied into the message mapping. This implies that changes you make to the mapping template after you insert it into your message mapping are not reflected in the message mapping.

8.4.8 Other Mapping Options

We know from Section 2.3.4 Mappings that besides message mappings there are a number of alternatives for how to create a mapping program. In particular, we have the following options:

- **Imported archives**
  You can import an external archive in the form of a *.zip* or *.jar* file. This archive can contain the following mapping types:

  - A Java mapping in the form of class files.

  - An XSLT mapping in the form of xsl files.

- **ABAP-based mappings**
  You can build mappings using the ABAP development environment.

  - An ABAP mapping using the interface IF_MAPPING of the package SAI_MAPPING.

  - An ABAP XSLT mapping built using the ABAP workbench.

Because ABAP-based mappings are not very common in a B2B integration environment, we don't discuss this type of mappings any further. Java mappings and XSLT mappings both use languages that are widely known and for which a lot of literature exists. Therefore, we only touch briefly on some SAP-related aspects of these mapping options. Imported archives are defined in the Enterprise Services Repository as its own object by following these steps:

1. In the Enterprise Services Repository follow the menu path **Object · New**. Alternatively, you can navigate to the software component version and namespace where you want to create the imported archive and select **New** after you right-clicking on the namespace.

2. In the popup that is displayed select **Mapping Objects · Imported Archive** and enter the **Name**, **Namespace**, and **Software Component Version** for the imported archive you want to create.

3. Use the dialog under the **File** list field to find the location of the ZIP or JAR file containing the Java mapping or XSLT mapping you want to import from your local machine and select this file.

4. Save and activate the imported archive. The mappings in the ZIP or JAR file are now available as mapping programs for use in your operation mappings.

Imported archives are executed on the Java engine of the Integration Server. Prior to release 7.1 of SAP NetWeaver PI, the *SAP XML Toolkit* is used to run Java mappings or XSLT mappings. As of release 7.1 it is recommended that you use version 5 of the Java Development Kit (JDK 5) instead. Because both options are currently supported, you need to decide on the runtime environment when you assign the mapping to an operation mapping. To choose between the options you need to set the **Use SAP XML Tool** flag accordingly (compare with Section 8.4.1 Operation Mapping).

Java Mappings

An API in the form of the package `com.sap.aii.mapping.api` is offered by SAP NetWeaver PI as a framework for implementing Java mappings. You must import this package into your Java mapping program and implement the required methods of this API. Some of the important classes of this API are the following (the list is not complete):

▶ `AbstractTransformation`
This class contains the method `transform()`, which is required to start the transformation process.

▶ `TransformationInput` **and** `TransformationOutput`
These classes contain methods for accessing the source message and for the creation of the target message.

▶ `AbstractTrace`
This class contains methods for writing data to the runtime trace.

Listing 8.5 shows an extract of a Java mapping program that is based on the example we used in the previous sections for the message mapping. The source and target message for the example are shown in Figure 8.41. The complete Java mapping is listed in Appendix A.3.4 Mapping Solution 3.

```
package com.sap.xi.mappings;
...
import com.sap.aii.mapping.api.StreamTransformation;
import
   com.sap.aii.mapping.api.StreamTransformationException;

public class List2ItemJava implements StreamTransformation
{
```

```
public void setParameter(Map param) {
}

public void execute(InputStream in, OutputStream out)
    throws StreamTransformationException {
    try {
        ...
        Result result = new StreamResult(out);
        Source domSource = new DOMSource(outDoc);
        transformer.transform(domSource, result);
        ...
    }
  }
}
```

Listing 8.5 Extract of Java Mapping Program

XSLT Mappings

You can build XSLT mappings using any editor and import them into SAP NetWeaver PI as an imported archive as described above. Listing 8.6 shows an example of an XSLT mapping that is based on the example we used in the previous sections for the message mapping. The source and target message for the example are shown in Figure 8.41.

```
<?xml version="1.0" encoding="UTF-8"?>
<xsl:stylesheet version="1.0"
xmlns:ns0="http://sap.com/xi/OAGIS/92"
xmlns:xsl="http://www.w3.org/1999/XSL/Transform">
<xsl:template match="/">
 <Item>
  <xsl:for-each select= "ns0:List/Pair">
   <xsl:if test="Ltr">
    <L><xsl:attribute name="N"><xsl:value-of select="Nbr"/>
    </xsl:attribute><xsl:value-of select="Ltr"/></L>
   </xsl:if>
  </xsl:for-each>
 </Item>
</xsl:template>
</xsl:stylesheet>
```

Listing 8.6 Example of an XSLT Mapping

8.5   Process Integration Scenarios

So far, we have discussed a number of objects we define in the Enterprise Services Repository as individual building blocks. Next we want to bring these building blocks together by defining a complete scenario for a B2B integration process. SAP NetWeaver PI offers two tools for the definition of such scenarios:

▶ **Process component architecture models**
The process component architecture models (also known as ARIS models) are mainly used as modeling tools for service-enabled business process models. Although they will play an important role in the future as a major building block of model-driven service development environments, they are not yet widely used outside the modeling of the enterprise service-oriented architecture.

▶ **Process integration scenarios**
The process integration scenarios provide an overview of the process flow for a collaborative scenario. These scenarios bind together all relevant objects defined in the Enterprise Services Repository and can be used in the Integration Directory for configuring an A2A or B2B scenario as described in Section 9.6 Use of the Model Configurator.

For the remainder of this section we focus on the discussion of process integration scenarios. Process component architecture models are briefly discussed in Appendix D Process Component Architecture Models.

A process integration scenario consists of a number of objects, with some of them only existing within the scenario itself. Figure 8.59 shows how a process integration scenario is modeled in the Enterprise Services Builder and gives a graphical representation of the objects involved. These objects are:

▶ **Application components**
The *application component* represents an object such as a business partner or an internal system. In Figure 8.59 we have three application components (see ❶ for an example). Application components only exist within the context of the process integration scenario.

▶ **Actions**
An *action* describes a function that can be carried out within an application component. Actions are depicted as shown under ❷ in Figure 8.59. Because

actions describe functions that may be applied to multiple scenarios, they are defined as its own entity.

▶ **Connections**

A *connection* defines the interaction between two actions. In a cross-component interaction the following modes are possible:

- ▶ An *asynchronous connection* as shown under ❸ in Figure 8.59.
- ▶ A *synchronous connection* as shown under ❹ in Figure 8.59.

Connections only exist in the context of the process integration scenario.

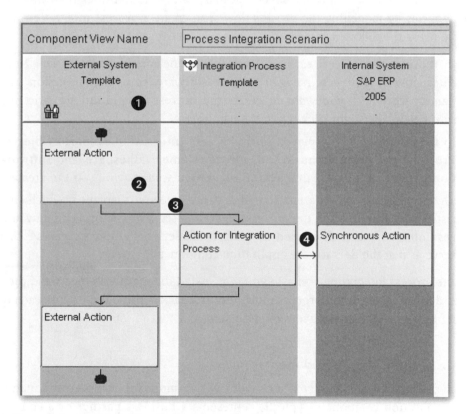

Figure 8.59 Graphical Editor for Process Integration Scenarios

One of the goals of the process integration scenario is to provide a guide for the configuration of the scenario in the Integration Directory. As we saw in Figure 8.1 the configuration utilizes a number of objects from the Enterprise Services

Repository, in particular service interfaces and operation mappings. Next we will see how these objects are linked to a process integration scenario such that this information can be utilized within a configuration wizard. The use of the process integration scenario in the model configurator is described in detail in Section 9.6 Use of the Model Configurator.

8.5.1 Definition of a Process Integration Scenario

The process integration scenario is the umbrella that brings together the objects required for the execution of a specific scenario and that identifies their interdependencies by modelling the process flow. You create a process integration scenario using the following steps:

1. In the Enterprise Services Repository follow the menu path **Object · New**. Alternatively, you can navigate to the software component version and namespace where you want to create the process integration scenario and select **New** after right-clicking on the namespace.

2. In the popup that is displayed select **Process Integration Scenario Objects · Process Integration Scenario** and enter the **Name**, **Namespace**, and **Software Component Version** for the process integration scenario you want to create.

3. The process integration scenario maintenance screen is displayed, which consists of a header area and the process integration scenario editor. For a new process integration scenario the editor consists of a series of empty swim lanes that serve as placeholders for the application components.

In the process integration scenario you now assign the required objects and their interdependencies in the process integration scenario editor. We discuss each of these objects in the respective sections below.

8.5.2 Application Components

Each process integration scenario contains two or more application components. An application component typically represents a business partner or a component within the business partner landscape. You create application components in a process integration scenario by following these steps:

1. In the process integration scenario editor right-click on the first available swim lane and select **Insert Application Component**.

2. Select the right **Application Component Type** from the following options:

   ▸ With the type **Product Version** you specify a product version from the SLD that will be assigned to your application component.

   ▸ With the type **Main Instance** you specify a software unit within a product version from the SLD that will be assigned to your application component.

   ▸ With the type **Template** you don't define any link to an object in the SLD.

   You must use the type **Template** if the application component cannot be assigned to one product uniquely, for example, it represents an external party. Otherwise you have the option to choose any of the types.

3. Select the flag **External Party with B2B Communication** if the application component represents an external party. Application components with this flag selected are displayed as shown in the first swim lane of Figure 8.59.

4. On the **Role** tab you can maintain the following information:

   ▸ The **Name** is the unique identifier for this application component in the process integration scenario.

   ▸ The **Description** is the text displayed in the graphical representation of the application component.

5. On the **Integration Process** tab you can assign an integration process that will be executed as part of the scenario. You can assign an integration process only to application components that are not flagged as external parties. Application components with an integration process assigned are displayed as shown in the second swim lane of Figure 8.59.

6. On the **Further Attributes** tab you can maintain the following information:

   ▸ The **Extended Name** can be used to further describe the application component and is displayed in the graphical representation of the application component.

   ▸ The information on the **WSCI Name** (Web Services Choreography Interface) is required by some industry standards such as RosettaNet. You can maintain this information here. This information is then added automatically to the business component when the process integration scenario is used in the model configurator in the Integration Directory (see Section 9.6 Use of the Model Configurator for more details).

8.5.3 Actions

An action is a function carried out in an application component. As mentioned earlier, we focus on the collaborative part of the process; therefore, the main information required with an action is the message interfaces it uses for communication. You can create an action by following these steps:

1. In the Enterprise Services Repository follow the menu path **Object • New**. Alternatively, you can navigate to the software component version and namespace where you want to create the action and select **New** after right-clicking on the namespace.

2. In the popup that is displayed select **Process Integration Scenario Objects • Action** and enter the **Name**, **Namespace**, and **Software Component Version** for the action you want to create. In addition you need to decide on the **Type of Usage**.

3. The editor for the creation of actions is displayed in Figure 8.60. Here you can maintain the operations executed by this action under the header **Outbound Interfaces** and **Inbound Interfaces**. The same options are available as for operations assigned to the source and target operation of an operation mapping (compare with Figure 8.37).

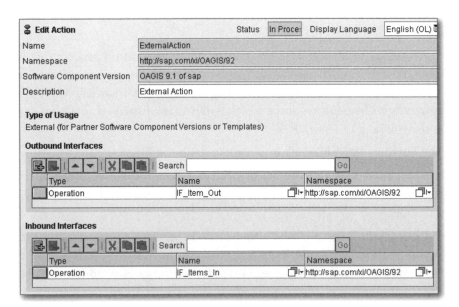

Figure 8.60 Maintenance Screen of an Action

4. First, choose the **Type** of the operation from the following list:

- ▸ **Operation**
- ▸ **Function Module**
- ▸ **IDoc**

Once you specified the type, you can select the appropriate object as the outbound interface or inbound interface.

5. Save and activate the action.

Once the actions are defined, you need to add them to the relevant application components in a process integration scenario. There are multiple options for how to add an action to an application component. For all of them the process integration scenario must be open in edit mode:

- ▸ You can drag an action from the navigation bar and drop it into the application component of the process integration scenario.

- ▸ You can right-click on the application component and select **Insert Action** from the list.

- ▸ You can right-click on the application component and select **Create Action** from the list. In this case a new action is created and added to the application component.

8.5.4 Connections

Like application components, connections are not independent objects defined in the Enterprise Services Repository, but they are part of the process integration process and are therefore maintained as part of this process. You create connections within the process integration scenario editor by connecting two actions together. The type of connection you create depends on the location of the actions in relation to each other:

- ▸ For a *synchronous connection* both actions must be placed at the same level in the application components.

- ▸ For an *asynchronous connection* the action representing the source must be placed higher than the action representing the target.

Once the actions are placed appropriately in the application components, you can create a connection by following these steps:

1. Click on the first action for which you want to create a connection. The action is now highlighted in red.

2. Click on the second action for which you want to create a connection while pressing the ⬚ key. Both actions are now highlighted in red.

3. Right-click on one of the actions highlighted in red and select **Create Connection Between Selected Actions** from the list. The maintenance screen for connections is displayed as shown in Figure 8.61.

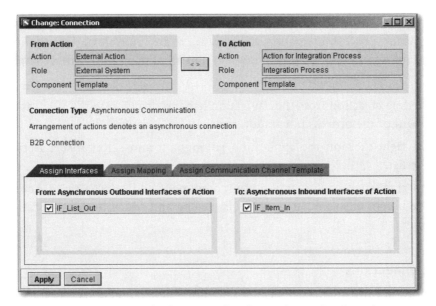

Figure 8.61 Maintenance of a Connection in a Process Integration Scenario

4. On the **Assign Interfaces** tab select the outbound and inbound interface that should be used to exchange messages between the two actions via the connection.

5. If the message structures between the outbound and inbound interfaces are not identical, you need to define an operation mapping on the **Assign Mapping** tab.

6. On the **Assign Communication Channel Template** tab you can assign a sender and receiver communication channel template. Part of the configuration process is defining the transport mechanism for the message exchange between the two actions. To a large degree, this information is partner specific and is set up under a communication channel in the Integration Directory. However,

parts of the settings can be generic and set up in a template that can be included in the communication channel. We discuss the creation of communication channels and its templates in detail in Section 9.2.4 Communication Channel Template.

8.6 Integration Processes

We discussed the different features and process patterns of an integration process in detail in Chapter 6 Business Process Management Capabilities. We saw in the previous section that an integration process can be assigned to an application component in a process integration scenario to help better orchestrate the business process. In this section we focus on how to create an integration process and discuss some of the basic features in more detail. Some use cases for integration processes in a B2B integration scenario are provided in Appendix B Integration Process Examples.

Let's now take a closer look at integration processes. As a minimum, each integration process consists of the following steps:

▶ It must contain a *receive step* as the starting point of the integration process.

▶ It typically contains a *send step* for the message exchange with the subsequent application component.

▶ It should contain additional step types for orchestrating the business process. Without any additional step, the integration process is not required because the same process can be modeled without using an integration process.

You create an integration process by following these steps:

1. In the Enterprise Services Repository follow the menu path **Object ∙ New**. Alternatively, you can navigate to the software component version and namespace where you want to create the integration process and select **New** after right-clicking on the namespace.

2. In the popup that is displayed select **Process Integration Scenario Objects ∙ Integration Process** and enter the **Name**, **Namespace**, and **Software Component Version** for the integration process you want to create.

3. The maintenance screen for the creation of integration processes is displayed as shown in Figure 8.62. As a default, the screen contains the start and end sym-

bol. Here you can define the integration process by adding the necessary steps to the process (via drag and drop) and defining all required objects such as containers. Each integration process must have one triggering step, which can only be the **Receive** step.

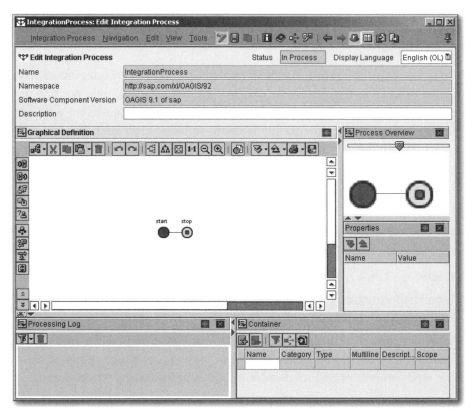

Figure 8.62 Initial Maintenance Screen for an Integration Process

For each of the step types used in the integration process you need to define a set of attributes in the **Properties** section of the integration process editor. The list of attributes to be maintained depends on the selected step types. Some of them require additional objects that need to be maintained outside the step type properties as part of the integration process. These objects are:

▶ **Container objects**
Used to hold the definition of the message structures utilized as part of the integration process.

► **Correlation lists**
The umbrella for correlating multiple messages. The details on the data that are used for the correlation are defined as part of the individual send step or receive step.

► **Configurable parameters**
Can be configured in the Integration Directory and are used in the property list of the individual steps, similar to container objects.

In the next sections we discuss how these objects are maintained. In Appendix B Integration Process Examples, we discuss some examples for the use of integration processes and show in detail how to set up these examples.

8.6.1 Container

As discussed earlier, integration processes are used for message-based process integration. Therefore, the assignment of the utilized message structures is a key element within the definition process of an integration process. They are not assigned directly to a particular step within the integration process, but they are linked to a container object. Then the container objects are assigned to a step in the integration process.

You can create a container object by following these steps (see Figure 8.63 for an example):

1. In the **Object Area** of the integration process editor (compare with Figure 6.2) switch to the **Container** view (usually this view is the default).

2. Add the name of your container element to the list and assign a message type to the container element. In the **Category** list field you can choose between these categories:

   ► In the **Abstract Interface** category you can assign any abstract interface operation available in your software component version to the list field **Type**.

   ► In the **Simple Type** category you can assign simple variables such as a counter. In the **Type** list field you assign built-in XSD types such as xsd:string or xsd:integer to a simple type.

   ► In the **Receiver** category you don't need to specify a **Type**. You only use this container type for a receiver determination step.

3. In the **Multiline** list field you can specify that the container element should be used in a multi-mapping, as discussed in Section 8.4.6 Multi-Mappings.

4. In the **Scope** list field you can decide if the container should be visible within the complete integration process or within a specific block of the process only. By default, each container is visible in the complete integration process.

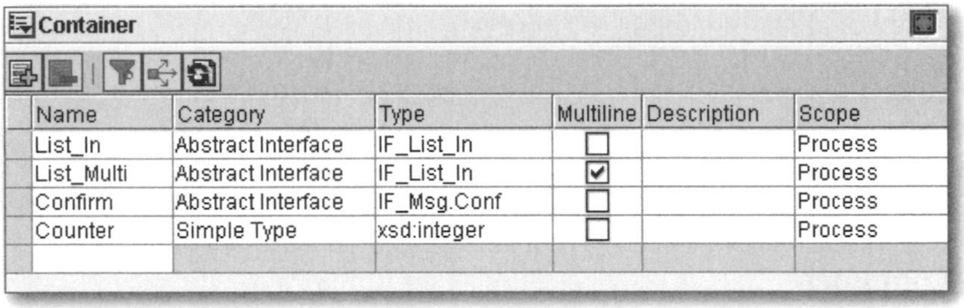

Name	Category	Type	Multiline	Description	Scope
List_In	Abstract Interface	IF_List_In	☐		Process
List_Multi	Abstract Interface	IF_List_In	☑		Process
Confirm	Abstract Interface	IF_Msg.Conf	☐		Process
Counter	Simple Type	xsd:integer	☐		Process

Figure 8.63 Definition of Container Elements

8.6.2 Correlation Handling

Because most B2B processes are handled in asynchronous mode, it is important to be able to correlate interrelated messages such as the confirmation message for a request message. You can handle such scenarios with the help of an integration process using *correlations*. Figure 8.64 describes the concept behind the correlation handling implemented as part of integration processes.

▶ You need to create a *correlation container* that holds the required information for checking a correlation. Each message that is part of the correlated business process will be linked to this correlation container.

▶ For each message participating in the correlated business process you need to define which information from the message is used as an ID to check for the correlation. Two types of interactions are possible:

  ▶ Messages *activating* a new business process. Messages sent and messages received can activate a new business process.

  ▶ Messages *using* an existing business process. Messages sent and messages received can use an existing business process, with the exception of a message received that is marked as a starting point for the integration scenario (the **Start Process** field in the properties list of a receive step).

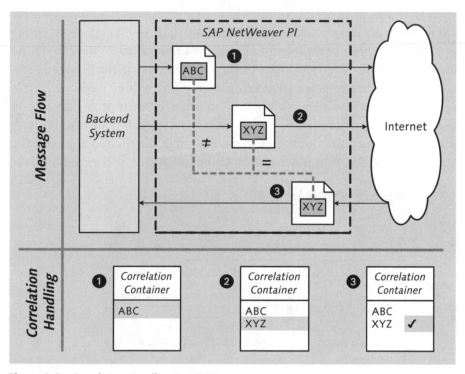

Figure 8.64 Correlation Handling in ccBPM

In Figure 8.64 all messages depicted are linked to the same correlation container. The following messages are exchanged with your trading partners:

▶ The first message (❶) is sent out and activates a new business process. The correlation ID ABC of this message is added to the correlation container.

▶ The second message (❷) is sent out and activates a new business process as well. The correlation ID XYZ of this message is added to the correlation container.

▶ The third message (❸) is received containing the correlation ID XYZ. Because this message uses an existing business process, it checks all correlation IDs stored in the correlation container and tries to find a match. In this example a match with the second message is found and the correlation is established. This particular business process can now continue based on the integration process definition. Once the business process is completed, the correlation ID of this process is removed from the correlation container.

Now that we understand the concepts behind the correlation handling, we next need to discuss how these concepts are realized in an integration process. In the next sections we explain how the required objects and settings for the correlation handling are realized, and in Section B.1 Establishing a Correlation between Messages, in Appendix B, we discuss a use case utilizing correlations. Because the creation of a correlation involves multiple steps in different areas of the integration process editor, we give an overview of all involved objects in Figure 8.65. Here you can see that the maintenance of these objects is distributed between the *graphical editor* and the *collaboration editor* of the integration process editor.

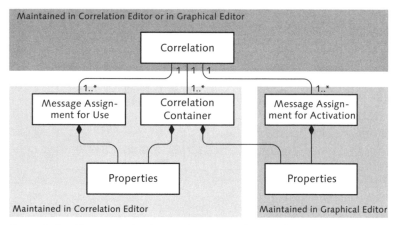

Figure 8.65 Objects Involved in Configuration of a Correlation

Creating a Correlation Container

The correlation container is defined under a collaboration object. Only a unique name is required to identify this specific container. You can create a new correlation container by following these steps:

1. In the **Object Area** of the integration process editor (compare with Figure 6.2) switch to the **Correlation List** view.

2. Add the name of your correlation to the list. This name is only an umbrella under which you can define one or more *correlation elements*.

3. In the **Edit Area** of the integration process editor switch to the **Correlation Editor** view.

4. Add the name of your correlation container to the list labeled **Correlation Container** and assign the correct **Type**.

We now have created a correlation container that is available in the integration process. So far, no messages are assigned to this correlation container.

Assign Messages for Use and Define their Properties

In the next step we identify the messages that use the correlation in an existing business process. For each message we also need to identify the content that should be used for trying to correlate this message. You make these definitions using the following steps:

1. After you have created a correlation container, you can continue and define the messages that use this correlation in the correlation editor.

2. Add the name of your message that uses this correlation to the list labeled **Involved Messages**. The message name and the correlation container now appear under the list labeled **Properties**, as shown in Figure 8.66.

Figure 8.66 Defining Involved Messages in the Correlation Editor

3. In the list labeled **Properties** click on all values that are still missing the correct information. The **Expression Editor** starts in a separate window.

4. Maintain the appropriate information in the expression editor as shown in Figure 8.67. Usually you will enter an XPath expression by either typing it in or selecting the element from the list display of the message structure.

5. So far, we have defined the correlation information for an abstract interface. Now we need to assign the correlation to a step of the integration process that is linked to this interface via the container definition. To do this, you need to switch to the **Graphical Definition** view in the integration process editor.

6. In the **Edit Area** click on the step of the integration process that you want to use for the correlation check. The properties of this step are displayed in the property area.

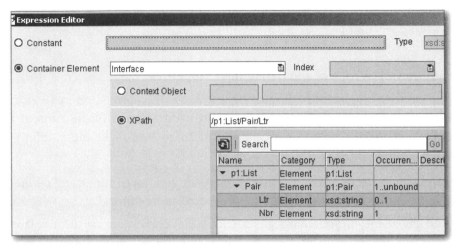

Figure 8.67 Maintaining Values in the Expression Editor

7. Add the correlation container to the **Use Correlations** list field.

Assign Messages for Activating a Correlation and Define its Properties

As a last step you need to assign the correlation to a step that will activate the correlation by starting a new business process. Typically, the start step of the integration process is used for this activation. As a prerequisite you must have defined the correlation containers in your correlation. You assign the correlation container to a step as follows:

1. In the **Object Area** of the integration process editor (compare with Figure 6.2) switch to the **Graphical Definition** view.

2. In the **Edit Area** click on the step of the integration process that you want to use for the correlation activation. The properties of this step are displayed in the property area.

3. Add the correlation container to the **Activate Correlations** list field. Underneath this list field the correlation name with its correlation containers are displayed as shown in Figure 8.68.

4. Add the appropriate value for each correlation container. You use the expression editor to define these values. Usually you will enter an XPath expression by either typing it in or selecting the element from the list display of the message structure.

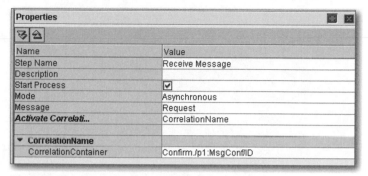

Figure 8.68 Activating a Correlation in the Integration Process Editor

8.7   Summary

After reading this chapter you should be able to create all objects required for the execution of a B2B integration scenario in the Enterprise Services Repository and in the System Landscape Directory (SLD). In particular, you should know the different options for how to define message structures based on industry standard definitions that are used in the definition of a service operation.

In addition, you should be familiar with the concepts behind the message mapping tool and understand some of the advanced features, such as process integration scenarios and integration processes.

This chapter explains how to configure B2B integration scenarios in the Integration Directory. It contains step-by-step instructions for the configuration both natively and using the Model Configurator.

9 Configuration

In the introduction to Chapter 8 Development we briefly discussed the different roles of the Integration Directory, the Enterprise Services Repository, and the System Landscape Directory. Whereas in Chapter 8 we discussed the Enterprise Services Repository and the System Landscape Directory in detail, we now switch our focus to the objects provided in the Integration Directory. This is where the trading-partner-specific information is captured and where the information required for the processing of a message during runtime is held.

9.1 Overview

Because the configuration that is set up in the Integration Directory is closely linked to the processing of a message in the runtime, we first take a look at the flow of a message between the different runtime engines, followed by a look at the required transformation steps for such a message. The transformation steps are then discussed in detail in the remainder of this chapter, starting with Section 9.2 Collaboration Profiles.

9.1.1 Message Flow

We showed a high-level picture of the message flow in Figure 7.2. In this picture we also can see that the message is passed through a number of different engines. As a minimum, the following engines are involved:

▶ **Inbound adapter**
The inbound adapter is the first point of contact for a message that reaches SAP NetWeaver PI. The inbound adapter takes care of the security and encryption

aspects and creates an XI message using an SAP-specific implementation of SOAP for consumption by the Integration Engine.

► **Integration Engine**
The Integration Engine is called by any of the inbound adapters with the newly created XI message. It can transform the message payload based on a new message structure, and it prepares the message for consumption by the outbound adapter.

► **Outbound adapter**
The outbound adapter receives the XI message from the Integration Engine and prepares a new message using the required protocol, which can be passed on to your own backend (inbound scenario) or to your trading partner (outbound scenario). Also, security and encryption considerations are taken care of in the outbound adapter.

As you can see in Figure 9.1, the message is passed from the inbound adapter to the integration engine and then from the integration engine to the outbound adapter. Let's first take a closer look at the conditions that must be met before one engine can pass the message on to the next engine.

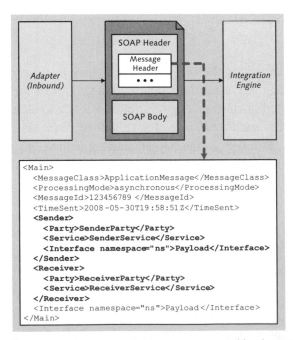

Figure 9.1 Message Header Structure Required by the Integration Engine

Inbound Adapter to Integration Engine

The Integration Engine receives an XI message from the inbound adapter. It expects a message with the message header provided in a specific format as shown in Figure 9.1. Each message sent to the Integration Engine consists of a *SOAP header* and a *SOAP body* (compare with Figure 2.34 in Section 2.5.3 XI Message Protocol). Part of the SOAP header is the *message header*, which contains a number of message attributes such as the processing mode, sender information, and receiver information. The format of the message header is shown in the bottom part of Figure 9.1.

The Integration Engine only accepts messages that use an SAP-specific implementation of SOAP. We refer to messages using this protocol as *XI messages*. If the inbound adapter receives a message in a different format, it creates a new XI message based on the information available in the incoming message and the configuration settings in the Integration Directory (see Section 9.1.2 Transformation Steps for more detail).

The format of the message header in an XI message is depicted in Figure 9.1 as well. The main information is highlighted in bold and consists of the sender information, the receiver information, and the interface used by the sender. The inbound adapter checks this information against the configuration settings in the Integration Directory before it passes the message on to the Integration Engine.

Integration Engine to Outbound Adapter

The outbound adapter receives the message from the Integration Engine. It expects the message using the same SOAP header structure as it was received by the Integration Engine, but enriched by a segment containing outbound binding information (see Figure 9.2).

The Integration Engine does not change the structure of the SOAP header, but it can alter its content. In particular, the following parts of the message can be changed:

▶ **The sender information can be adjusted.**
For example, if you send out a message to your external trading partner, you will want to replace any physical sender system information by a logical name representing your entity.

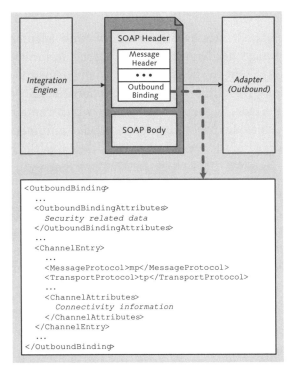

Figure 9.2 Outbound Binding Information in the SOAP Header

▶ **The receiver information can be adjusted.**
For example, for an incoming message you need to replace an abstract receiver name with an actual business system that should receive this message.

▶ **The interface information can be adjusted.**
For example, if you receive a message in the form of an IDoc from your back-end application system, but you agreed to communicate with your trading partner via an industry standard message, you need to adjust the information on the interface used for communication. In addition, the message payload must be transformed to the new message format.

▶ **The technical binding between the abstract receiver information and the concrete implementation must be provided.**
This includes information such as the physical address of the receiver (usually in the form of a URL) and security and encryption information.

The Integration Engine checks that all required information is in place before it passes the message on to the outbound adapter.

9.1.2 Transformation Steps

In Section 8.1 Overview we went through the individual configuration steps for a B2B integration scenario with a focus on the objects that need to be provided by the Enterprise Services Repository. In Figure 9.3 we refine this picture with a stronger focus on the message flow that we discussed in the previous section. Figure 9.3 also is a more detailed picture of the message flow that was given in Figure 7.2. It consists of the following steps:

▶ **Message protocol conversion (inbound adapter)**
The inbound adapter receives a message in a certain format with some information on the sender, the receiver, and the interface used for this message. This information consists only of preliminary data and not necessarily final information that is passed on to the next destination. The inbound adapter must convert the message to a message using the SAP-specific implementation of SOAP (see also Section 2.5.3 XI Message Protocol). For this conversion the inbound adapter uses the following configuration objects of the Integration Directory:

  ▶ The *collaboration profile*, against which the adapter checks the sender and receiver information.

  ▶ The *sender agreement*, which contains some information relevant to the processing of the message such as security information. The sender agreement is only required for adapters that are part of the adapter engine.

▶ **Receiver determination**
The receiver determination is the first step that takes place in the Integration Engine. Here the real receiver of the message is derived, and the message header of the SOAP body is updated accordingly. The information used for the receiver can be updated one more time to its final value.

▶ **Interface determination**
The interface determination determines the interface definition that is used when the message is passed on to the next destination. If the new message structure is different from the message structure received by the Integration Engine, a transformation of the message payload is triggered as well.

▶ **Receiver agreement**
In the receiver agreement step the outbound binding information is added to the SOAP header (compare with Figure 9.2). In addition, the sender and receiver information that will be passed on to the next destination can be adjusted to its final form.

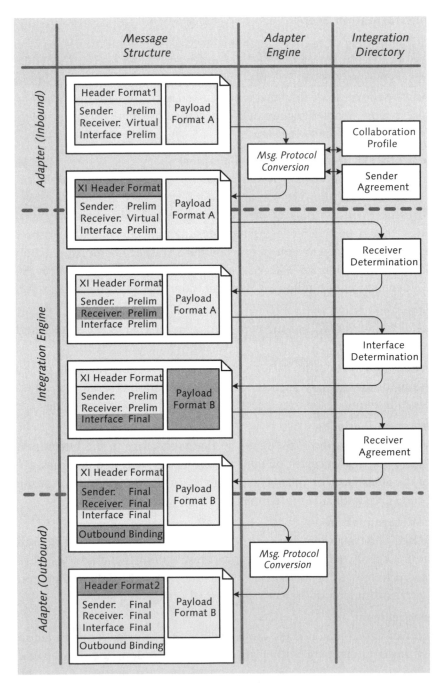

Figure 9.3 Configuration Steps in the Integration Directory

▶ **Message protocol conversion (outbound adapter)**
After the receiver agreement information has been added to the SOAP header, the message is forwarded to the outbound adapter (as specified in the receiver agreement). The outbound adapter receives the message in the SAP-specific SOAP format and adjusts the message based on the protocol that has been specified for the communication with the next destination. In addition, the outbound adapter takes care of other transport-relevant issues such as security and encryption requirements.

In the remainder of this chapter we go through each of the configuration steps listed above in detail (both natively and by using the Model Configurator), followed by a discussion of some advanced topics such as parameter handling and data conversions.

9.2 Collaboration Profiles

As discussed in Section 2.4.2 Collaboration Profiles, you model the units that send or receive messages in the *collaboration profile*. In a B2B integration scenario the following units are typically involved:

▶ **External party**
An external party represents the trading partner with whom you exchange messages.

▶ **Application systems**
One or more internal application systems that receive or send the messages you exchange with your trading partner.

▶ **Integration process**
Optionally, you can have an integration process involved in your scenario that is set up as its own unit in the collaboration profile.

The inbound adapter checks the sender and receiver information in the message header against the collaboration profile before it passes a message on to the integration engine. If any information is missing, the inbound adapter raises an error and does not pass the message on to the Integration Engine.

9.2.1 Communication Party

As discussed in Section 2.4.2 Collaboration Profiles, you need to define a *communication party* for each of your trading partners involved in B2B processes. For each trading partner you need to answer the following questions, which are addressed by the subsequent objects defined underneath the party (see also Figure 9.4):

▸ What mailboxes are provided by the trading partner, and what messages are accepted by each mailbox? Each business component represents exactly one mailbox.

▸ How can messages be delivered to each mailbox, and how are they sent out from each mailbox? This question includes topics such as:

   ▸ The physical address of each mailbox (usually provided in the form of a URL)

   ▸ The transport protocols that each mailbox can handle

   ▸ The message protocols that each mailbox can handle

   ▸ The security settings that are required to communicate with each mailbox

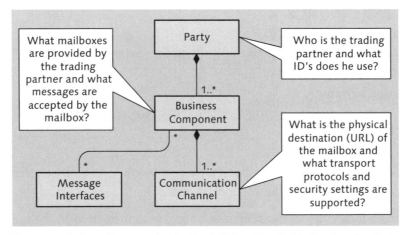

Figure 9.4 Information Provided by the Collaboration Profile for a Trading Partner

You create a communication party by following these steps:

1. In the Integration Directory follow the menu path **Object • New**. In the popup that is displayed select **Collaboration Profile • Party** and the name of the party you want to create.

2. The maintenance screen for parties is displayed as shown in Figure 9.5. On the **Identifiers** tab you can maintain additional identifiers for this party that can be required for further processing. For example, any communication via a RosettaNet message requires the use of a D-U-N-S number for all parties involved, whereas any communication with your SAP backend application system via IDocs requires special alternative identifiers as described below.

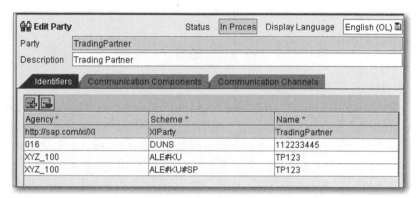

Figure 9.5 Definition of a Party with Alternative Identifiers

3. You need to save and activate the party. Only after you have saved the party can you utilize the **Communication Components** and **Communication Channel** tabs for the creation of the respective objects. We discuss the creation of these objects in the next two sections.

We discussed the use of alternative identifiers in Section 2.4.2 Collaboration Profiles, with the main focus on partner identifiers defined by standard organizations. However, alternative identifiers can be used for any type of party identifications. For example, B2B configuration settings for IDoc processes are handled using alternative identifiers.

Because IDoc messages were already used for B2B integration processes before SAP offered a separate middleware layer, some of the B2B configuration settings for IDocs are built into the SAP application systems. The counterpart to the collaboration profile in the SAP application systems in regard to IDocs is the *partner profile*, which can be mapped into the configuration settings within the Integration Directory via an alternative identifier of a communication party.

Table 9.1 shows how the partner profile information is mapped to an alternative identifier of the XI party.

Field	Description
Agency	The business system as defined in the SLD is used as an agency.
Scheme	The scheme is composed of the partner type and partner role used in the partner profile as follows: `ALE#<Partner type>#<Partner role>`
Name	The name of the IDoc partner.

Table 9.1 Alternative Identifiers for IDoc Settings

9.2.2 Communication Component

The *communication components* represent the endpoints of an integration scenario. Such an endpoint can be a logical mailbox of your trading partner, a physical system within your system landscape, or a business process that is triggered for orchestrating the process. For each of these types of endpoints, a corresponding communication component type exists (see also Section 2.4.2 Collaboration Profiles):

▶ **Business system**
A business system that usually represents a physical system in your system landscape

▶ **Business component**
A business component that usually represents a logical mailbox of a trading partner, as shown in Figure 9.4

▶ **Integration process**
An integration process that represents an integration process defined in the Enterprise Services Repository

For all communication component types you must specify all interfaces that the communication component will be able to process. Within a communication component each interface is categorized as an outbound interface (the backend sending out a message) or as an inbound interface (the backend receiving a message). In addition, you can categorize these interfaces in two classes:

▶ Real interfaces that exist under the same name in the Enterprise Services Repository. If the name you enter for the interface exists in the Enterprise Services Repository as a service interface operation, the interface is considered a real interface.

▶ Logical interfaces for which no counterpart exists in the Enterprise Services Repository.

Both of these categories can be used for configuring a B2B integration scenario within the Integration Directory; however, real interfaces are required if you need to utilize a mapping for converting the source message into the target message.

The creation of a communication component depends on the type of component you want to create. We discuss all three types in detail below.

Business System

Any business system you want to use in a collaboration profile must first be defined as a business system in the System Landscape Directory. Once it exists in the SLD, you can make it available in the Integration Directory using the following steps:

1. In the object list of the Integration Builder right-click on the **Communication Component** and select **Assign Business System...** from the list. This starts a wizard for assigning a business system from the SLD as a communication component.

   If you want to define the communication component underneath a communication party, you can also start the wizard out of the maintenance screen of the communication party by clicking the **Create** icon ( ) on the **Communication Components** tab.

2. In the wizard click on the **Continue** button to pass the **Introduction**.

3. In the second step of the wizard you select the **Party** to which the business system should be assigned (see Figure 9.6). You can leave the field empty to create a communication component without assignment to a party. Business systems are typically not assigned to a party.

4. In the third step you select from the SLD the business systems for which you want to create a communication component. If the **Create Communication Channels Automatically** flag is checked, the following communication channels are created (see Section 9.2.3 Communication Channel for more details on communication channels):

   ▶ A sender and receiver communication channel using the HTTP adapter

   ▶ A sender and receiver communication channel using the RFC adapter

▸ A sender and receiver communication channel using the IDoc adapter

▸ A sender and receiver communication channel using the XI adapter

▸ A sender and receiver communication channel using the WS adapter

The communication channels that are created may still miss some attributes that need to be maintained separately.

5. Activate the communication components and communication channels created by the wizard.

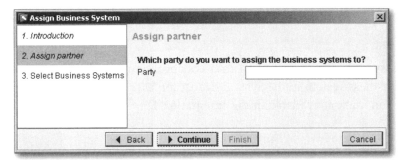

Figure 9.6 Wizard to Assign a Business System to a Communication Component

In the maintenance screen for a communication component in the form of a business system, a number of tabs are available that hold different type of information (see Figure 9.7):

▸ On the **Receiver** tab the following information is available:

▸ All **Inbound Interfaces** that are available for the business system are listed. This list is automatically derived based on the information provided in the SLD. In the SLD you link a business system to a technical system, where you specify the available software component versions for this particular technical system. All inbound service interfaces and relevant IDocs defined in the Enterprise Services Repository for these software component versions are then listed as inbound interfaces.

▸ All available **Receiver Communication Channels** are listed on this tab. If the flag **Create Communication Channels Automatically** was checked, a number of channels are automatically added to the list. You can create additional communication channels assigned to this communication component.

▶ The **Sender** tab is the counterpart to the **Receiver** tab. It displays the same information, but from a sender's point of view instead of a receiver's point of view.

▶ On the **Assigned Users** tab you can specify which application user is allowed to execute a process using this particular communication component. If no user is assigned, any user is allowed to execute this process.

▶ On the **IDoc Partner** tab is the list of parties that use this business system as an agency for identifying an alternative party for ALE communication.

▶ On the **Other Attributes** tab you can view the software component versions assigned to the business system. As discussed above, only interfaces defined in these software component versions are available within this communication component for use as a receiver or sender interface.

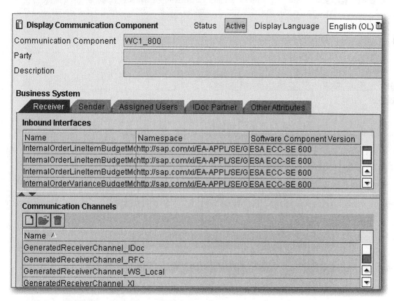

Figure 9.7 Maintenance Screen for a Communication Component Using a Business System

Business Component

Usually you use a business component in connection with a party defining the mailboxes that are provided by your trading partner (see Figure 9.4). You create a business component by following these steps:

1. In the Integration Directory follow the menu path **Object • New**. In the popup that is displayed choose **Collaboration Profile • Business Component** and

enter the name of the business component you want to create. If you want to have the business component linked to a communication party, you also need to enter the name of the party. In this case you can also start the wizard out of the maintenance screen of the communication party by clicking on the **Create** icon (⬜) on the **Communication Components** tab.

2. The maintenance screen for business components is displayed as shown in Figure 9.8. You can assign interfaces (inbound or outbound) and communication channels to the business component by maintaining on the appropriate tabs based on your specific requirements.

3. Save and activate the business component.

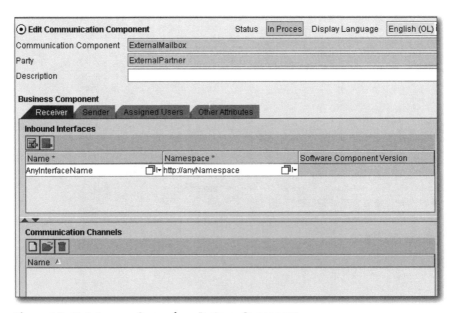

Figure 9.8 Maintenance Screen for a Business Component

In the maintenance screen for a business component a number of tabs are available that hold different types of information (see Figure 9.8):

▶ On the **Receiver** tab you can maintain the following information:

   ▶ Here you define all **Inbound Interfaces** that should be available as part of the business component. You can select interfaces that exist in the Enterprise Services Repository or define logical names without a counterpart in the Enterprise Services Repository.

► All available **Receiver Communication Channels** are listed on this tab. You can create additional communication channels assigned to this communication component either out of this list or in a separate step as described in Section 9.3.2 Interface Determination.

► The **Sender** tab is the counterpart to the **Receiver** tab. It displays the same information, but from a sender's point of view instead of a receiver's point of view.

► On the **Assigned Users** tab you can specify which application user is allowed to execute a process using this particular communication component. If no user is assigned, any user is allowed to execute this process.

► On the **Other Attributes** tab you can specify the business component either as **Third-Party Communication Component** or as **SAP Communication Component**. Business components are usually set up as third-party communication components.

Integration Process

Any integration process you want to use in a collaboration profile must first be defined as an integration process in the Enterprise Services Repository. Once it exists there, you can make it available in the Integration Directory using the following steps:

1. If you want to define the integration process as a communication component without an assignment to a communication party you right-click on the **Communication Component** in the object list of the Integration Builder and select **Integration Process** from the list. This starts a wizard for transferring an integration process from the Enterprise Services Repository to the Integration Directory as a communication component.

   If you need to have the integration process assigned to a communication party, you must start the wizard out of the maintenance screen of the communication party by clicking the **Create** icon (⬚) on the **Communication Components** tab.

2. In the wizard click on the **Continue** button to pass the **Introduction**.

3. In the second step of the wizard you select from the Enterprise Services Repository the integration process that you want to make available as a communication component (see Figure 9.9).

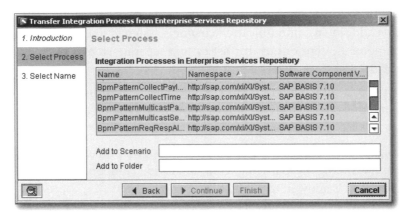

Figure 9.9 Wizard to Define an Integration Process as a Communication Component

4. In the third step of the wizard you can provide a name for the communication component that you created based on the integration process. As a default, the name of the integration process is entered.

5. Activate the communication component created by the wizard.

In the maintenance screen for a communication component based on an integration process a number of tabs are available that hold different types of information (see Figure 9.10):

▶ Under the **Receiver** tab all **Inbound Interfaces** are listed that are used in the integration process. These are all abstract interface definitions that are used in a **Receive** step of the integration process (compare with Section 8.6 Integration Processes). You cannot add or delete any inbound interfaces.

▶ The **Sender** tab is the counterpart to the **Receiver** tab. It displays all **Outbound Interfaces** used in the integration process. These are all abstract interface definitions that are used in a Send step of the integration process. You cannot add or delete any outbound interfaces.

9.2.3 Communication Channel

As you can see in Figure 9.3, each message is first picked up by the inbound adapter and as the last step is passed on to the next destination by the outbound adapter. Both adapter types require technical information, some generic and some trading partner specific. The communication channel carries this information, which can vary based on the adapter chosen for the communication.

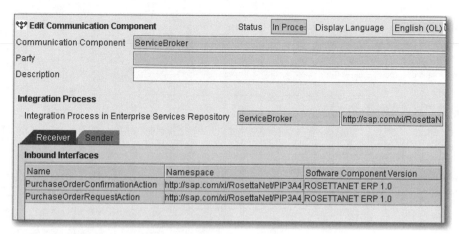

Figure 9.10 Maintenance Screen for a Communication Component Based on an Integration Process

The communication channel is always created for a specific communication component (see also Figure 9.4) by following these steps:

1. In the Integration Directory follow the menu path **Object • New**. In the popup that is displayed select **Collaboration Profile • Communication Channel** and enter the name of the communication channel you want to create, as well as the communication party and the communication component to which the communication channel belongs.

   Alternatively, you can create the communication channel out of the maintenance screen of a communication party (**Communication Channels** tab) or out of the maintenance screen of a communication component (**Sender** tab or **Receiver** tab) by clicking on the **Create** icon (🗋).

2. The maintenance screen for business components is displayed as shown in Figure 9.11. In the **Adapter Type** field you need to specify the adapter that is used to send (**Sender** flag is checked) or receive (**Receiver** flag is checked) the message.

3. Once the adapter type is specified, some adapter-specific information must be added to the communication channel. We discuss these adapter-specific settings for some of the widely used adapter types in the next sections.

4. Save and activate the communication channel.

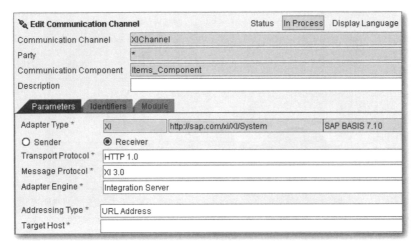

Figure 9.11 Maintenance Screen for a Communication Channel

In the maintenance screen for a communication channel a number of tabs are available that hold different types of information (see Figure 9.11):

▶ On the **Parameters** tab you specify which adapter type is used and if the adapter is used for sending or receiving messages. Based on these settings, a number of adapter-specific attributes are displayed that need to be maintained. We take a closer look at the attributes for the XI adapter below. The settings for some other adapter types are discussed in Chapter 12 Real-Life Test Scenarios.

▶ On the **Identifiers** tab you can maintain how the sender and receiver party are identified. This information is important for communication channels using the IDoc adapter. Figure 9.29 in section 9.4.2 Receiver Agreements shows an example on how these identifiers are used.

▶ On the **Module** tab you can add additional modules specific to your requirements. This tab is only available for adapters that are part of the Adapter Framework. The modules are executed as shown in Figure 3.2 under the second step.

As mentioned above, the data required on the **Parameters** tab depends to a large degree on the actual adapter used with the communication channel. An example of the XI adapter used as a receiver is shown in Figure 9.12. The communication channel settings for some other adapter types are discussed in Chapter 12 Real-Life Test Scenarios. You can find detailed information on each parameter for any available adapter type in the SAP Help Portal at *http://help.sap.com*.

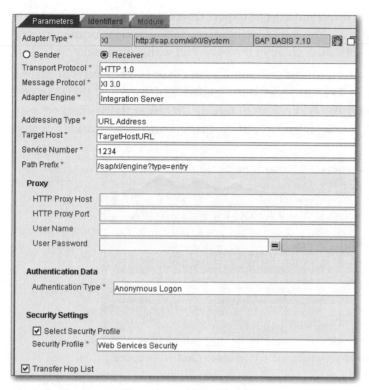

Figure 9.12 Parameters for a Receiver XI Adapter

9.2.4 Communication Channel Template

We have seen in the previous section that in the definition of communication channels a lot of adapter-specific information needs to be maintained (see also the use cases in Chapter 12 Real-Life Test Scenarios). Part of this information is partner specific such as the target host URL, whereas part of the information is generic and applies to all trading partners that we communicate with via this specific adapter. Therefore, SAP NetWeaver PI allows you to create a communication channel template in the Enterprise Services Repository where you can define all generic settings and simply apply the template to a communication channel. You create a communication channel template by following these steps:

1. In the Enterprise Services Repository follow the menu path **Object • New**. Alternatively, you can navigate to the software component version and namespace where you want to create the communication channel template and select **New** after right-clicking on the namespace.

2. In the popup that is displayed select **Adapter Objects • Communication Channel Template** and enter the name, namespace, and software component version for the communication channel template you want to create.

3. The maintenance screen for the communication channel template is displayed. Specify the **Adapter Type** used for this template and specify if the adapter is used to send (**Sender** flag is checked) or receive (**Receiver** flag is checked) messages. Figure 9.13 shows an example of the maintenance screen after this step.

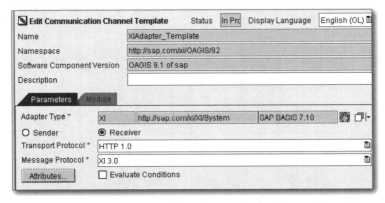

Figure 9.13 Maintenance Screen for a Communication Channel Template

4. When you click on the **Attributes...** button, a popup appears where you can specify the data you want to maintain as part of the communication channel template (see Figure 9.14).

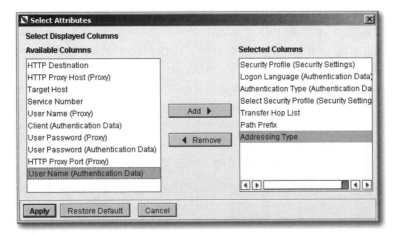

Figure 9.14 Attribute Selection Screen for a Communication Channel Template

5. After you have selected the relevant attributes, you can maintain the communication channel template as shown in Figure 9.15.

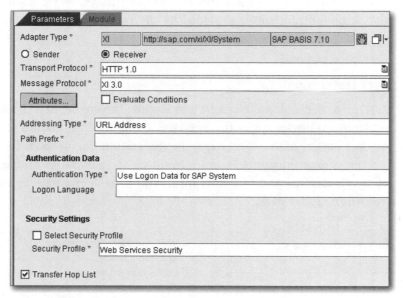

Figure 9.15 Maintenance Screen for a Communication Channel Template after Attribute Assignment

6. You need to save and activate the communication channel template.

The communication channel template can now be applied to a communication channel in the Integration Directory. In the maintenance screen of a communication channel select **Communication Channel • Apply Template** to copy the data maintained in the communication channel template to the communication channel.

9.3 Logical Routing

After the adapter has forwarded the message to the Integration Engine, the *logical routing* is the first step that takes place within the Integration Engine itself. As shown in Figure 9.3, the logical routing consists of two steps:

▶ Receiver determination
▶ Interface determination

In the logical routing you identify the actual receiver of the message and the message interface that is used for the message. The receiver information is still given on a logical level, whereas the technical specification of the receiver (which is required for the outbound binding) is provided by the receiver agreement at a later step.

9.3.1 Receiver Determination

When an XI message is received in the Integration Engine, the engine first checks if a receiver determination is set up for this message. Using the information provided in the message header of the XI message, the Integration Engine looks for a corresponding receiver determination. Figure 9.16 shows an example with a message header of an XI message and how this information must translate to the receiver determination header data.

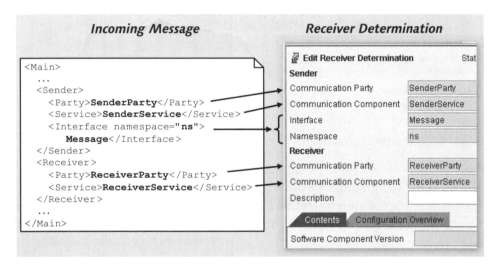

Figure 9.16 Receiver Determination Header Settings

You create a receiver determination by following these steps:

1. In the Integration Directory follow the menu path **Object · New**. In the popup that is displayed select **Configuration Objects · Receiver Determination** and enter the sender information of the receiver determination you want to create, consisting of the following data:

▶ The **Communication Party** of the sender, which must match the party information provided in the message header of the XI message (under the XPath expression `Main/Sender/Party`).

▶ The **Communication Component** of the sender, which must match the service information provided in the message header of the XI message (under the XPath expression `Main/Sender/Service`).

▶ The **Interface,** which must match the interface information provided in the message header of the XI message (under the XPath expression `Main/Sender/Interface`).

▶ The **Namespace,** which must match the namespace information provided in the message header of the XI message (under the XPath expression `Main/Sender/Interface/@namespace`).

2. The message header of the XI message can also contain receiver information. Because the receiver information available to your trading partner is usually not complete, only a virtual receiver can be added to the message header. If you want to utilize this information in your receiver determination, you need to check the **Sender Uses Virtual Receiver** flag. In this case the following receiver information becomes available as part of the key for the receiver determination (see also Figure 9.17):

▶ The **Communication Party** of the receiver, which must match the party information provided in the message header of the XI message (under the XPath expression `Main/Receiver/Party`).

▶ The **Communication Component** of the receiver, which must match the service information provided in the message header of the XI message (under the XPath expression `Main/Receiver/Service`).

For the receiver information you are also able to specify a placeholder using an asterisk (*).

3. After you have created the receiver determination, the maintenance screen for the receiver determination is displayed (see Figure 9.18). You need to select the **Type of Receiver Determination** as **Standard** or as **Extended**. Based on this choice, different data need to be maintained. We discuss both options in detail below.

387

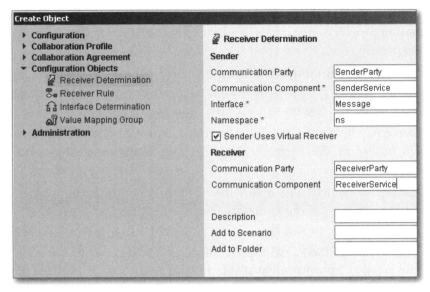

Figure 9.17 Creation Screen for a Receiver Determination

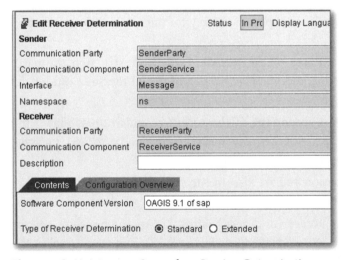

Figure 9.18 Maintenance Screen for a Receiver Determination

Standard Receiver Determination

With the standard receiver determination you specify the receiver information manually. If you need to maintain multiple receivers or if the receiver depends on certain information of the message payload, you must maintain each receiver separately. You must have at least one receiver specified within the receiver determination. Figure 9.19 shows an example of a standard receiver determination.

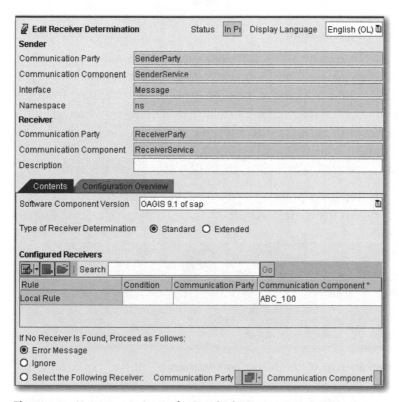

Figure 9.19 Maintenance Screen for Standard Receiver Determination

For each receiver you can also define a condition when this receiver should be triggered. A condition is defined as part of a rule, where the rule itself can be set up as one of the following

▶ A **Local Rule** is specified within the receiver determination and can only be utilized within this particular receiver determination.

▶ You can define a **Receiver Rule** as an independent object in the Integration Directory that contains the condition. You can include a receiver rule in the receiver determination by selecting the small arrow next to the **Insert Line** icon (⊞▾) and selecting **Insert Receiver Rule** from the list.

Because conditions play a role in the interface determination as well, we discuss the creation of receiver rules and conditions separately in Section 9.3.3 Receiver Rules and Conditions.

Extended Receiver Determination

With the extended receiver determination you can utilize a mapping to determine the receiver information. To use the extended receiver determination you need to have an operation mapping in place that provides a mapping from the sender interface to a predefined message structure containing the receiver information. This message structure is made available by SAP in the Enterprise Services Repository under the namespace `http://sap.com/xi/XI/System` of the software component `SAP BASIS`. In particular, the following objects are used:

▶ The message type **Receivers** pointing to the data type **Receivers**. The structure of this message type is shown in Figure 9.20.

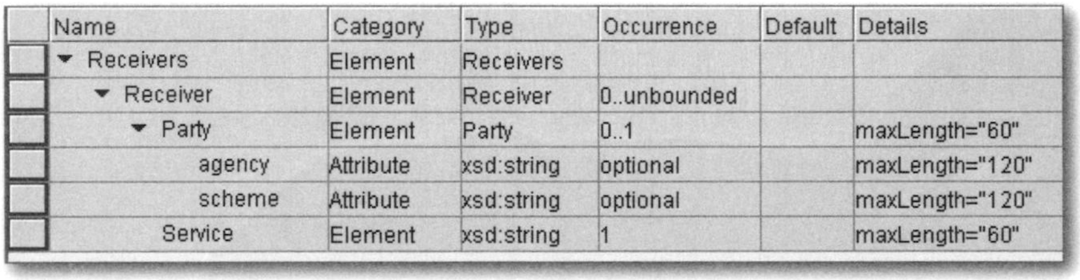

Name	Category	Type	Occurrence	Default	Details
▼ Receivers	Element	Receivers			
▼ Receiver	Element	Receiver	0..unbounded		
▼ Party	Element	Party	0..1		maxLength="60"
agency	Attribute	xsd:string	optional		maxLength="120"
scheme	Attribute	xsd:string	optional		maxLength="120"
Service	Element	xsd:string	1		maxLength="60"

Figure 9.20 Message Structure of the Message Type Receivers

▶ The service interface **ReceiverDetermination** with one operation called **ReceiverDetermination**. This operation is assigned to the message type **Receivers**.

In the message mapping you must identify the *party* and the *service* that should be used as the **Communication Party** and **Communication Component** in the receiver determination. The party can be identified either by specifying the communication party directly or by using any alternative identifier defined for the communication party.

You maintain the extended receiver determination as shown in Figure 9.21. As you can see, you maintain the extended receiver determination per interface operation, whereas the standard receiver determination does not take the operation into account.

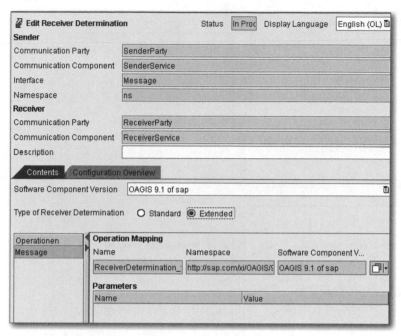

Figure 9.21 Maintenance Screen for Extended Receiver Determination

9.3.2 Interface Determination

The first step of the logical routing is the receiver determination, where the party and service of the receiver has been specified. The second step is the determination of the interface expected by the receiver. This step is handled by the interface determination. Figure 9.22 shows an example of how the message header of the XI message translates to the interface determination header data.

As you can see, the interface determination must be set up using the receiver information that was updated by the receiver determination step. You create an interface determination by following these steps:

1. In the Integration Directory follow the menu path **Object • New**. In the popup that is displayed select **Configuration Objects • Interface Determination** and enter the sender and receiver information of the interface determination you want to create, consisting of the following data:

   ▶ The **Communication Party** of the sender, which must match the party information provided in the message header of the XI message (under the XPath expression `Main/Sender/Party`).

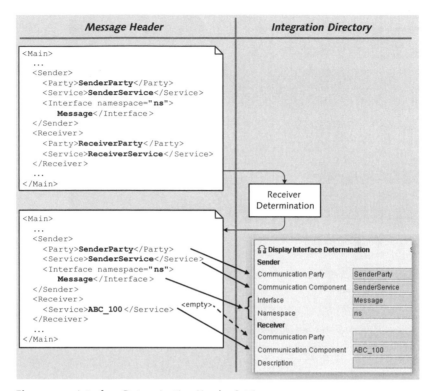

Figure 9.22 Interface Determination Header Setting

▶ The **Communication Component** of the sender, which must match the service information provided in the message header of the XI message (under the XPath expression `Main/Sender/Service`).

▶ The **Interface,** which must match the interface information provided in the message header of the XI message (under the XPath expression `Main/Sender/Interface`).

▶ The **Namespace,** which must match the namespace information provided in the message header of the XI message (under the XPath expression `Main/Sender/Interface/@namespace`).

▶ The **Communication Party** of the receiver, which must match the communication party information specified by the receiver determination rule.

▶ The **Communication Component** of the receiver, which must match the communication component information specified by the receiver determination rule.

The maintenance screen for the interface determination is displayed after you have created this object (see Figure 9.23).

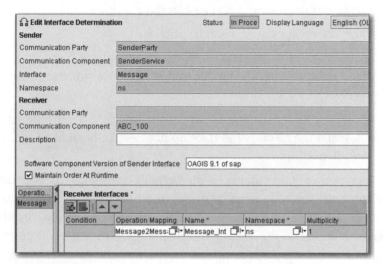

Figure 9.23 Maintenance Screen for the Interface Determination

2. In the **Software Component Version of Sender Interface** field you can specify the software component version in which the sender interface is located. The system then reads the operations of the sender interface and displays them on the left-hand side of the maintenance screen.

3. The **Maintain Order at Runtime** flag is only relevant if you define multiple receiver interfaces in your interface determination. If the flag is turned on, the quality of service exactly once in order (EOIO) is used; otherwise, the quality of service is exactly once (EO). See also Section 2.5.5 Quality of Service for a discussion of the quality of service options.

4. Under the table labeled **Receiver Interfaces** you maintain the receiver interfaces and if necessary the operation mappings between the sender and receiver interfaces. You can also define a condition for when a receiver interface should be triggered (see Section 9.3.3 Receiver Rules and Conditions for the creation of conditions).

5. Save and activate the interface determination.

When you specify the receiver interfaces within the interface determination, you can support a number of different scenarios. Let's take a short look at the most important features you need to keep in mind:

▶ If you use an operation mapping as part of the interface determination, the following objects must exist in the Enterprise Services Repository:

 ▶ The *sender interface* must exist as a service interface.

 ▶ The *receiver interface* must exist as a service interface.

 ▶ The *operation mapping* must exist as an operation mapping between the service interface representing the sender and the service interface representing the receiver.

▶ If you don't use an operation mapping as part of the interface determination, the sender interface and the receiver interface do not need to be defined in the Enterprise Services Repository.

▶ If you use an operation mapping that is set up for multi-mappings (see Section 8.4.6 Multi-Mappings), you only need to specify the operation mapping. The receiver interfaces are then determined out of the operation mapping itself. You need to keep in mind that the use of multi-mappings in the interface determination is only supported by adapters that are part of the Adapter Framework.

The interface determination with an operation mapping using parameters is discussed in detail in Section 9.7.1 Parameters in Mappings.

9.3.3 Receiver Rules and Conditions

In the definition of receiver determinations and interface determinations we were able to utilize conditions to determine when a determination should be triggered. Let's now take a closer look at the creation of conditions.

Conditions are always assigned locally to an interface determination, whereas they can be assigned to a receiver determination either locally or via a receiver rule.

Receiver Rules

A receiver rule is an independent object in the Integration Directory that contains a receiver party and a receiver service together with a condition for when this receiver should be utilized. Receiver rules can be added to a receiver determination as discussed in Section 9.3.1 Receiver Determination. You create a receiver rule by following these steps:

1. In the Integration Directory follow the menu path **Object · New** and select Configuration **Objects · Receiver Rule**. Then the maintenance screen for a receiver rule is displayed as shown in Figure 9.24.

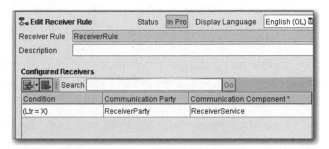

Figure 9.24 Maintenance Screen for a Receiver Rule

2. Specify a **Communication Party** and a **Communication Component** that should be selected if the associated condition holds true.

3. Define the condition by clicking on the field in the column labeled **Condition**. Then the maintenance screen for the condition appears, which is discussed further below.

4. Save and activate the receiver rule.

Conditions

You create a condition within the receiver rule or directly within a receiver determination or an interface determination simply by clicking on the field in the column labeled **Condition**. Then the maintenance screen for the condition appears as shown in Figure 9.25.

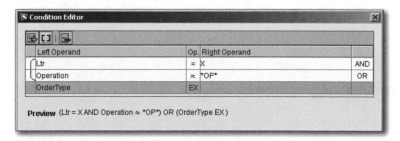

Figure 9.25 Maintenance Screen for the Condition Editor

Each line of the condition editor consists of the following elements:

- A **Left Operand**, which is an expression in the form of an XPath expression or in form of a context object. For conditions defined within a receiver rule only context objects are possible because the receiver rule is not directly assigned to a specific interface. The left operand is maintained using the expression editor, which we already discussed in Section 8.6.2 Correlation Handling. See Figure 8.69 for a screenshot of the expression editor. For conditions used in a receiver rule only context objects can be maintained. Otherwise, context objects and XPath expressions can be utilized.

- An **Operation** that compares the left operand with the right operand. The following operations are supported:

  - The **Equals** (=) operation checks if the two operands are equal.

  - The **Not Equals** (≠) operation checks if the two operands are not equal.

  - The **Contains Pattern** (≈) operation checks if the left operand contains the pattern as defined by the right operand. You can use an asterisk (*) as a placeholder for a string and a plus sign (+) as a placeholder for a single character.

  - The **Exists** (EX) operation checks if the left operand exists. In this case the right operand is not used.

- A **Right Operand** that contains a value to be checked against. Only for the **Exists** operation is the right operand not used.

You can add additional lines to the conditions by using the following icons:

- With the **Insert Expression** icon (▦) you can add a new condition using an AND clause.

- With the **Insert Group** icon (▯) you can add a new condition using an OR clause.

9.4   Collaboration Agreements

Collaboration agreements provide information on the technical binding and on security and encryption settings both for the incoming message (covered by the *sender agreement*) and for the outgoing message (covered by the *receiver agreement*). In a collaboration agreement you assign a communication component that is always linked to one specific adapter. As shown in Figure 9.3, the adapters utilize the following objects during runtime:

▶ The *inbound adapter* uses information provided by the sender agreement. The need for a sender agreement depends on the selected adapter and the specific scenario.

▶ The *outbound adapter* uses information provided by the receiver agreement. A receiver agreement is always required, independent of the adapter or the scenario that is used.

9.4.1 Sender Agreements

As mentioned above, the inbound adapter utilizes the information provided by the sender agreement. However, a sender agreement is only required under certain circumstances. The following rules exist for the definition of a sender agreement:

▶ The following adapters only require a sender agreement if you have special security setting requirements for the processing of a message:

  ▶ IDoc adapter

  ▶ HTTP adapter

  ▶ XI adapter

  ▶ SOAP adapter

  ▶ Mail adapter

▶ All other adapters always require a sender agreement, independent of the security setting requirements.

When a message is sent to SAP NetWeaver PI, it is first picked up by the *messaging system*, which has a number of different listeners for the different adapter types. Based on the information provided in the incoming message, the listeners know if they need to react to this message. If the message is relevant for a certain adapter type, the following steps are performed:

▶ Within the messaging system an algorithm is executed to determine the sender information (party, service, and interface) of the message.

▶ The messaging system passes the message to the correct inbound adapter along with the sender information that was derived above.

▶ The inbound adapter uses the information provided in the sender agreement (such as security and encryption information) to further process the message. It can find the correct sender agreement using the sender information derived by the messaging system.

The sender agreement must be set up using the same header information as used for the receiver determination (compare with Figure 9.16). You create a sender agreement by following these steps:

1. In the Integration Directory follow the menu path **Object · New**. In the popup that is displayed select **Collaboration Agreement · Sender Agreement** and enter the sender information of the sender agreement you want to create, consisting of the following data:

   ▶ The **Communication Party** of the sender, which must match the party information provided in the message header of the XI message (under the XPath expression `Main/Sender/Party`).

   ▶ The **Communication Component** of the sender, which must match the service information provided in the message header of the XI message (under the XPath expression `Main/Sender/Service`).

   ▶ The **Interface,** which must match the interface information provided in the message header of the XI message (under the XPath expression `Main/Sender/Interface`).

   ▶ The **Namespace**, which must match the namespace information provided in the message header of the XI message (under the XPath expression `Main/Sender/Interface/@namespace`).

   You can also specify a placeholder using an asterisk (*) in the definition of your sender header data.

2. Similar to the receiver determination (compare Section 9.3.1 Receiver Determination), you can check the **Sender Uses Virtual Receiver** flag. In this case the following receiver information becomes available as part of the key for the receiver determination:

   ▶ The **Communication Party** of the receiver, which must match the party information provided in the message header of the XI message (under the XPath expression `Main/Receiver/Party`).

   ▶ The **Communication Component** of the receiver, which must match the service information provided in the message header of the XI message (under the XPath expression `Main/Receiver/Service`).

You can also specify a placeholder using an asterisk (*) in the definition of your receiver header data.

3. The maintenance screen for the sender agreement is displayed as shown in Figure 9.26. In the **Sender Communication Channel** field you must specify a sender communication channel. This channel must be available in the collaboration profile of your sender party and sender service. After you have selected the sender communication channel, a number of additional attributes appear, depending on the settings in the communication channel.

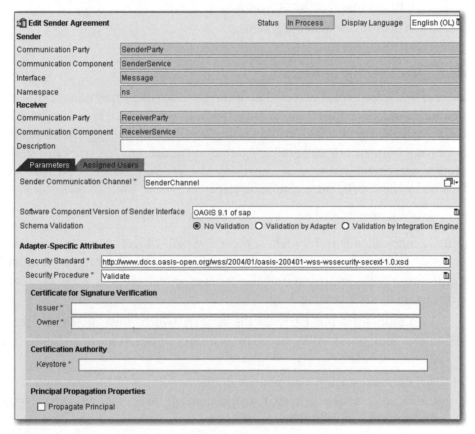

Figure 9.26 Maintenance Screen for a Sender Agreement

4. You can specify that you want to have the message that is sent to you validated. Here you can choose between the following options:

▸ With the option **No Validation** the message will not be validated.

▶ With the option **Validation by Adapter** the message will be validated by the inbound adapter. If the validation fails, the adapter sends a notification about the failed validation to the sender.

▶ With the option **Validation by Integration Engine** the message will be validated by the integration engine. If the validation fails, the message is set to an error status and an administrator can process the message further using the tools provided by the runtime workbench.

5. You can specify security-related information, which is covered in more detail in Chapter 10 Security Considerations.

6. Save and activate the sender agreement.

9.4.2 Receiver Agreements

The receiver agreement is executed after the interface determination takes place. If multiple interfaces have been identified, multiple receiver agreements must be in place as well. Figure 9.27 shows an example of how the message header of the XI message translates to the receiver agreement header data. As you can see, the receiver agreement must be set up using the receiver information that was updated by the interface determination step.

You create a receiver agreement by following these steps:

1. In the Integration Directory follow the menu path **Object • New**. In the popup that is displayed select **Collaboration Agreement • Receiver Agreement** and enter the sender information of the receiver agreement you want to create, consisting of the following data:

   ▶ The **Communication Party** of the sender, which must match the party information provided in the message header of the XI message (under the XPath expression `Main/Sender/Party`).

   ▶ The **Communication Component** of the sender, which must match the service information provided in the message header of the XI message (under the XPath expression `Main/Sender/Service`).

   ▶ The **Communication Party** of the receiver, which must match the party information provided in the message header of the XI message (under the XPath expression `Main/Receiver/Party`).

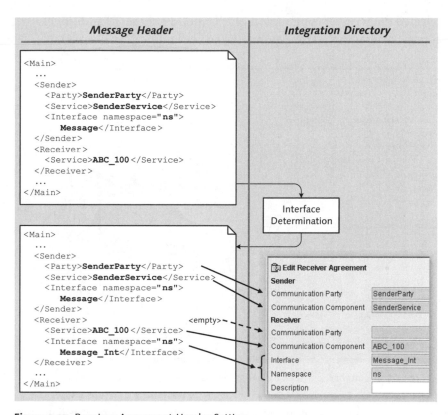

Figure 9.27 Receiver Agreement Header Setting

▶ The **Communication Component** of the receiver, which must match the service information provided in the message header of the XI message (under the XPath expression `Main/Receiver/Service`).

▶ The **Interface** of the receiver, which must match the interface information provided in the message header of the XI message (under the XPath expression `Main/Receiver/Interface`).

▶ The **Namespace** assigned to the receiver interface, which must match the namespace information provided in the message header of the XI message (under the XPath expression `Main/Receiver/Interface/@namespace`).

2. The maintenance screen for the sender agreement is displayed as shown in Figure 9.28. In the **Receiver Communication Channel** field you must specify a receiver communication channel. This channel must be available in the collaboration profile of your receiver party and receiver service. After you have

selected the receiver communication channel, a number of additional attributes appear, depending on the settings in the communication channel.

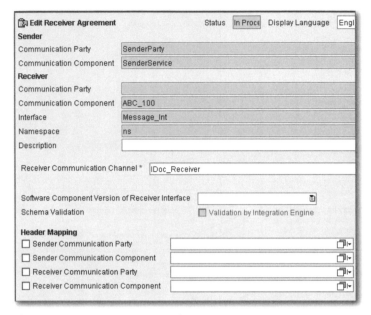

Figure 9.28 Maintenance Screen for a Receiver Agreement

3. Check the **Validation by Integration Engine** flag if you want to have the message validated before it is sent out.

4. You can change the sender and receiver information that will be send out with the message header of the XI message using the following fields:

   ▶ The value entered in the **Sender Communication Party** replaces the sender party of the message header if the checkbox for this item is checked.

   ▶ The value entered in the **Sender Communication Component** replaces the sender service of the message header if the checkbox for this item is checked.

   ▶ The value entered in the **Receiver Communication Party** replaces the receiver party of the message header if the checkbox for this item is checked.

   ▶ The value entered in the **Receiver Communication Component** replaces the receiver service of the message header if the checkbox for this item is checked.

With this logic of using a checkbox in addition to the value field, you can also delete party information from the message header.

5. You can specify a number of security-related information, which is covered in more detail in Chapter 10 Security Considerations.

6. Save and activate the receiver agreement.

With the receiver agreement using an IDoc adapter we can also see very well how alternative identifiers of a communication party are utilized in conjunction with the identifiers defined in a communication channel. Figure 9.29 shows the steps in the outbound IDoc adapter for deriving the correct inbound partner profile for the IDoc process.

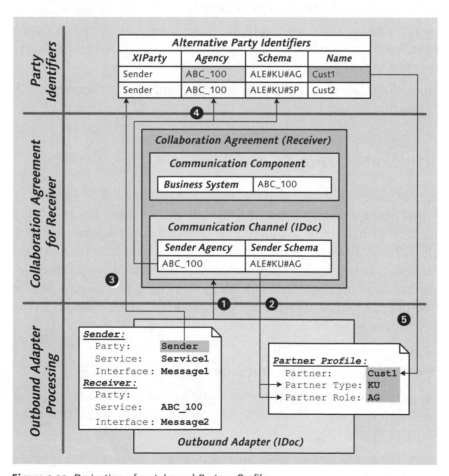

Figure 9.29 Derivation of an Inbound Partner Profile

The following steps are performed:

❶ The outbound IDoc adapter utilizes the receiver agreement to find the communication channel for the specific process. On the **Identifiers** tab of the communication channel the **Agency** and the **Schema** for the sender must be maintained.

❷ The sender schema that was found in the communication channel contains the information of the **Partner Type** and the **Partner Rule** to be used in the inbound partner profile.

❸ The XI message received by the outbound adapter contains the information of the sender party in form of an XI party. With this information we can check all alternative identifiers defined for this XI party.

❹ We need to find an alternative party identifier for the XI party (which we derived in the previous step) using the agency and schema of the sender that is maintained in the communication channel.

❺ The name of the alternative party identifier is used as the **Partner** in the inbound partner profile.

9.5   B2B Configuration Scenarios

In the previous sections we discussed the individual building blocks we need to set up as part of the configuration in the Integration Directory. The individual processing steps are performed in a fixed order, referred to as a *pipeline*, and each step is referred to as a *pipeline element*. Each pipeline element is linked to a *pipeline service* such as the receiver determination. Here we bring these pipeline elements together and discuss a typical pipeline process for a B2B message that is sent out by our company (outbound scenario) and for a B2B message that is received by our company (inbound scenario).

9.5.1   B2B Configuration of an Outbound Scenario

We can see a typical message transformation using a number of pipeline steps for an outbound B2B scenario in Figure 9.30. The following steps are performed as part of this transformation:

1. A message is created in our application system and enters the Integration Engine in the form of an XI message containing the following information:

▶ The sender information consists of the backend application system in the form of a business system and the interface used by this system.

▶ The receiver information consists of a party and service using backend application system proprietary information. For example, the party can be the internal customer or vendor number used for your trading partner.

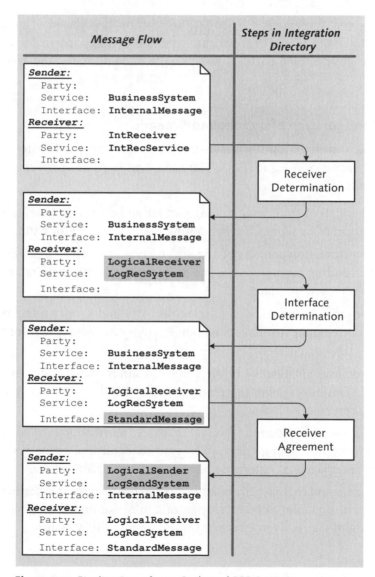

Figure 9.30 Pipeline Steps for an Outbound B2B Scenario

2. With the **Receiver Determination** the receiver information is changed to a party and service name that you want to send out as receiver information to your trading partner.

3. With the **Interface Determination** the receiver interface information is filled with the name of the interface that you exchange with your trading partner. Typically, an industry standard interface is used here.

4. With the **Receiver Agreement** the sender information is adjusted using the header mapping of the receiver agreement. Instead of sending internal system information to your trading partner, you provide a logical party and service name.

9.5.2 B2B Configuration of an Inbound Scenario

We can see a typical message transformation using a number of pipeline steps for an inbound B2B scenario in Figure 9.31. The following steps are performed as part of this transformation:

1. A message is being sent from your trading partner and enters the Integration Engine in the form of an XI message containing the following information:

   ▸ The sender information consists of a logical party and service name representing your trading partner and an interface name that typically refers to an industry standard interface.

   ▸ The receiver information consists of a logical party and service name representing your company. It does not contain any system-specific information.

2. With the *receiver determination* the receiver information is changed to a service in the form of a business system representing the backend application system that ultimately receives the message.

3. With the *interface determination* the receiver interface information is filled with the name of the interface that is expected by your backend application system. Typically, this interface is an enterprise service, an IDoc, or a BAPI.

4. Because the sender and receiver information already has the required form, the *receiver agreement* does not need to change this information. Therefore, the header mapping of the receiver agreement is not used in this scenario.

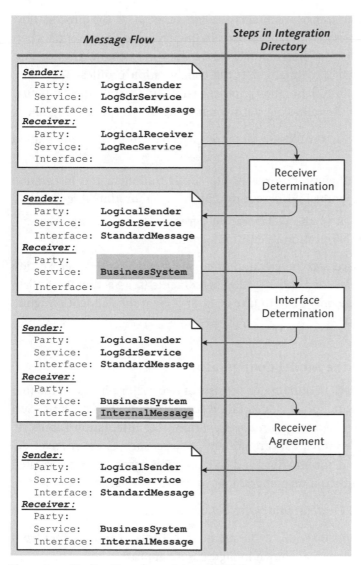

Figure 9.31 Pipeline Steps for an Inbound B2B Scenario

9.6 Use of the Model Configurator

As mentioned in Section 8.5 Process Integration Scenarios, we can take advantage of a process integration scenario to automate the required configuration settings in the Integration Directory to a large degree by using the Model Configurator.

The process integration scenario contains the information of the process flow including all service interface operations that are involved and the potential operation mappings. The process integration scenario does not contain any partner-specific information that is maintained in the collaboration profiles. Therefore, you still need to maintain collaboration profiles manually. Overall, the configuration process consists of the following steps when using the Model Configurator:

1. Create the collaboration profiles for all parties involved in the B2B integration process.
2. Start the Model Configurator to create the configuration in the Integration Directory consisting of the logical routing and the collaboration agreements.
3. Complete the settings in the collaboration agreements by adding security-, encryption-, and authentication-relevant information.

Because we already discussed the creation of collaboration profiles (see Section 9.2 Collaboration Profiles) and collaboration agreements (see Section 9.4 Collaboration Agreements), we only need to take a closer look at the Model Configurator itself.

9.6.1 Execution of the Model Configurator

The execution of the Model Configurator consists of two major phases. In the first phase you need to import a process integration scenario from the Enterprise Services Repository and create a *configuration scenario* in the Integration Directory. In the second phase the individual configuration objects such as the receiver determination, interfaces determination, and collaboration agreements are created and assigned to the configuration scenario that we created as part of the first step.

You execute the Model Configurator by following these steps:

1. In the Integration Directory follow the menu path **Tools • Apply Model from ES Repository....** A popup as shown in Figure 9.32 appears.
2. Select the option **Process Integration Scenario** and select the process integration scenario you want to import from the Enterprise Services Repository. The other options are discussed briefly in Section 2.4.1 Integration Builder.
3. In the next step you define the name of the configuration scenario that will be created in the Integration Directory. As a default, the name of the process integration scenario is proposed.

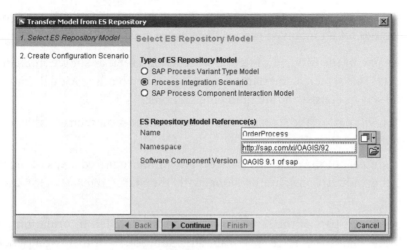

Figure 9.32 Entry Screen of the Model Configurator

4. When you finish this process, a popup as shown in Figure 9.33 appears. This marks the end of phase one of the Model Configurator. Once you click on the **Close** button, the second phase is started.

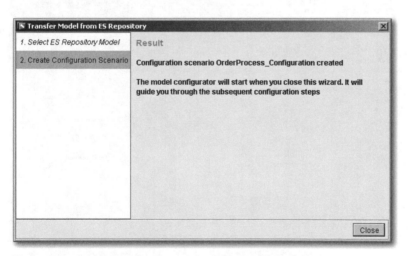

Figure 9.33 Final Screen for Phase One of the Model Configurator

In the second phase of the Model Configurator you work with the imported process integration scenario where the individual configuration objects are created in the Integration Directory based on the information provided in the process integration scenario. In the following step-by-step description we assume that the collaboration profiles for all involved parties already are created.

1. After phase one of the Model Configurator closes, a screen as shown in Figure 9.34 appears. This screen is the start screen for phase two of the Model Configurator. The screen consists of the following sections:

   ▶ In the top-left part of the screen is the process integration scenario that was imported in the first phase.

   ▶ In the right part of the screen is an overview of the required steps of phase two of the Model Configurator along with the status overview for each step.

   ▶ The bottom-left part of the screen is reserved for detailed information for each individual step. Here you can add additional information when required.

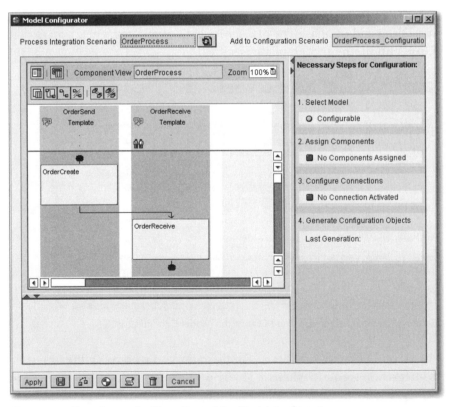

Figure 9.34 Entry Screen for Phase Two of the Model Configurator

2. If the process integration scenario consists of multiple variants, you can choose the correct variant for your scenario by clicking on the **Select Component View...** button (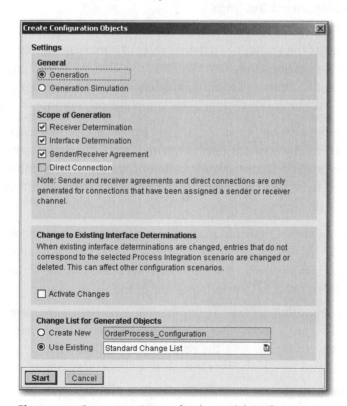).

3. Select the **Assign Component...** button ( ) to assign the parties and services to each component of the process integration scenario. The details for this step are discussed in Section 9.6.2 Component Assignment Settings.

4. Select the **Configure Connections...** button ( ) to assign communication channels to each connection. The details for this step are discussed in Section 9.6.3 Connection Settings.

5. Select the **Generate** button ( ) to generate the configuration objects. As shown in Figure 9.35, receiver determinations, interface determinations, and collaboration agreements can be created for the specified scenario. All objects are listed under the configuration scenario, as shown in Figure 9.36.

6. Save and activate the objects created with the Model Configurator.

Figure 9.35 Generation Options for the Model Configurator

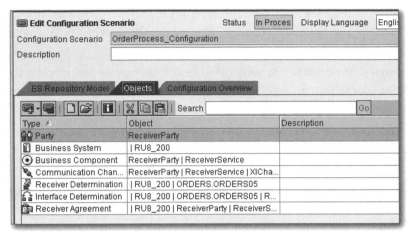

Figure 9.36 Configuration Objects Created by the Model Configurator

9.6.2 Component Assignment Settings

Depending on the scenario, each application component of the process integration scenario serves either as the sender or as the receiver of a message. Because the configuration of the Integration Directory identifies the sender and receiver of a message by a party and a communication component, we need to assign in step 2 of the Model Configurator these objects to each application component.

In Figure 9.30 and Figure 9.31 we can see how the party information and the service information (represented by a communication component) changes during each pipeline step of the process. With the information provided in the component assignments we need to be able to support each of these steps. Here we can distinguish between the following scenarios:

▶ The application component that represents our company sends out a message. For example, the sender in Figure 9.30 is represented by such a component. During the pipeline steps in Figure 9.30 the sender is identified by the actual business system and then converted into a logical party and service name.

▶ The application component that represents our company receives a message. For example, the receiver in Figure 9.31 is represented by such a component. During the pipeline steps in Figure 9.31 the receiver is identified by a logical party and service name and then converted into an actual business system.

▶ The application component that represents our trading partner sends out a message. For example, the sender in Figure 9.31 is represented by such a component. During the pipeline steps in Figure 9.31 the sender is only identified by a logical party and service name.

▶ The application component that represents our trading partner receives a message. For example, the receiver in Figure 9.30 is represented by such a component. During the pipeline steps in Figure 9.30 the receiver is identified by the internal name used in the SAP backend system and then converted into a logical party and service name.

As we can see, the application component representing our company always requires information on the logical party and service as well as on the actual business system. Therefore, we provide both sets of data in the Model Configurator, as shown in Figure 9.37. With this information the receiver determination, and the header mapping in the receiver agreement, can be created automatically.

Assign Components	Details		
Assign Components for A2A and B2B Communication			
Business System Components		Business Components for External Communication	
Party	Component	Party	Component
	RU8_200	SenderParty	SenderService

Figure 9.37 Component Assignment for Internal Parties

The application component representing the trading partner as the sender only requires the information on the logical party and service, whereas as the receiver, the internal name used in the backend system is also involved. However, the internal name only plays a role as a header input for the receiver determination. Because the Model Configurator creates the receiver determination without using the receiver information by using the asterisk (*) as a placeholder, the internal name is actually not required for setting up the configuration. Therefore, only the logical party and service are provided to the Model Configurator, as shown in Figure 9.38.

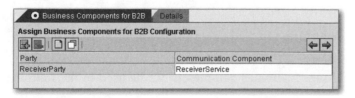

Business Components for B2B	Details	
Assign Business Components for B2B Configuration		
Party	Communication Component	
ReceiverParty	ReceiverService	

Figure 9.38 Component Assignment for External Parties

A drawback of this configuration is that you need to adjust the receiver determination settings after they are created by the Model Configurator in order to handle multiple trading partners for the same type of message. Here you need to add conditions to determine the receiver based on the internal names provided by the SAP backend system.

9.6.3 Connection Settings

In the third step of the Model Configurator we need to configure the connections between the sender of a message and the receiver of a message. Most of the information such as the interface names and the mapping programs are provided by the process integration scenario itself. The only information that needs to be added is the communication channels to be used in the collaboration agreements. Figure 9.39 shows how this information is maintained during this step of the Model Configurator.

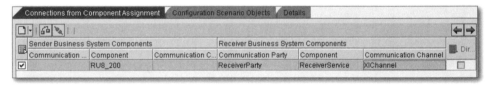

Figure 9.39 Communication Channel Assignments in the Model Configurator

9.7 Advanced Features

SAP NetWeaver PI offers a number of advanced features where the set up requires certain configuration settings in the Integration Directory and the use of specific objects in the Enterprise Services Repository. Therefore, we postponed the discussion of these features until we discussed the basics of both the Integration Directory and the Enterprise Services Repository. In this section we now discuss a few of these advanced features available in SAP NetWeaver PI.

9.7.1 Parameters in Mappings

As of release 7.1, SAP NetWeaver PI offers the ability to use parameters within its mapping programs. In message mappings parameters can be used in the following scenarios:

▶ **Import parameters**

Import parameters can be used in the property section of both standard functions and user-defined functions. To assign a parameter as an input variable to a function you can use the `Constant` function, where the property value is set to the parameter value.

▶ **Export parameters**

Export parameters can only be set up in user-defined functions, and they can only be used in a transformation step of an integration process.

Because export parameters only have limited use, we focus on the configuration of inbound parameters in our further discussion. An overview of the required steps for setting up an inbound parameter mapping can be found in Figure 9.40. The overall process includes the following steps:

▶ As part of the *message mapping* you define a set of parameters you want to use in your mapping. These parameters can be utilized in the functions used in the field mappings of your message mapping.

▶ Within the *operation mapping* you define another set of parameters and provide a link to the parameters used in the associated message mapping. This process is called *binding* of the parameters. Alternatively, you can assign fixed values to the parameters of the message mapping.

▶ In the *interface determination* you specify the operation mapping used for this determination. If the mapping contains any parameters, you need to assign values to these parameters in the form of a constant value or in the form of a container object.

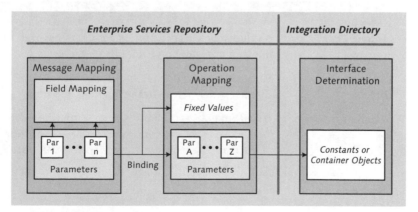

Figure 9.40 Configuration Overview on an Import Parameter Mapping

You can also set up parameter mappings for Java mappings and for XSLT mappings. The process of binding the parameters in the operation mapping and assigning values in the interface determination or in the operation mapping is identical for all message mapping types.

Parameters in Message Mappings

In a message mapping you can define parameters that can be used in the field mappings on the **Signature** tab, as shown in Figure 9.41. For each parameter you can specify the parameter type (**Import** or **Export**) and its **Category**. The different options are listed in Table 9.2.

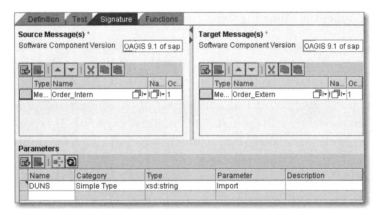

Figure 9.41 Definition of Parameters in a Message Mapping

Type	Category	Description
Import	Simple Type	A value of type string or integer is transferred to the mapping program before its execution.
	Adapter	The adapter type defined in the communication channel is transferred to the mapping program.
Export	Simple Type	A value of type string or integer is transferred for further use in an integration process after execution of the mapping program in the transformation step of an integration process.
	Adapter	n/a

Table 9.2 Parameter Types and Categories

Once a parameter is defined on the **Signature** tab of the message mapping, it can be used in the field mapping by assigning it as a property value to the appropriate functions. For example, the parameter can be assigned as the value to the `Constant` function, as shown in Figure 9.42.

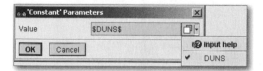

Figure 9.42 Use of a Parameter in the Constant Function

Parameter Binding in Operation Mappings

In the message mapping we defined a set of parameters that we used within the field mappings. To utilize a message mapping you must assign it to an operation mapping. As part of the operation mapping you can assign either fixed values to the parameters used in the message mapping or you can bind them to another parameter that you need to define as part of the operation mapping. Let's take a closer look at the steps you need to execute for binding the message mapping parameters to the right values defined in the operation mapping.

Figure 9.43 shows the maintenance screen of an operation mapping. When you click on the button labeled **Parameters...** you can maintain another set of parameters within the operation mapping as shown in Figure 9.44. As you can see, the same set of attributes is available as with parameters defined in a message mapping.

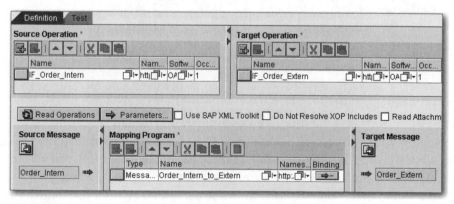

Figure 9.43 Maintenance Screen of an Operation Mapping

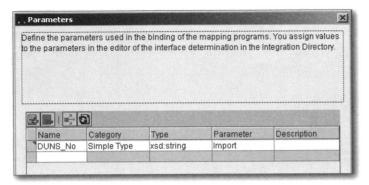

Figure 9.44 Definition of Parameters in an Operation Mapping

When you click on the button under the list field labeled **Binding** (see Figure 9.43), you can create the link between the parameters defined in the message mapping and the parameters defined in the operation mapping, as shown in Figure 9.45. Instead of a binding, you can also specify a fixed value that will be assigned to the message mapping parameter whenever the message mapping is used through this particular operation mapping.

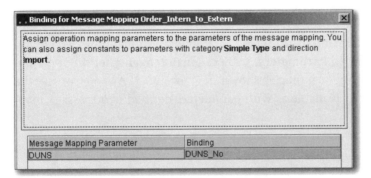

Figure 9.45 Binding Between Operation Mapping Parameters and Message Mapping Parameters

Parameter Settings in the Interface Determination

As discussed in Section 9.3.2 Interface Determination, you can specify an operation mapping within an interface determination. If the operation mapping has parameters defined as part of the mapping, these parameters are displayed within the interface determination maintenance screen (see Figure 9.46), where you can specify the values that should be used for these parameters within the context of this interface determination. The value can be defined either in the form of a constant value or through a container element, as shown in Figure 9.47.

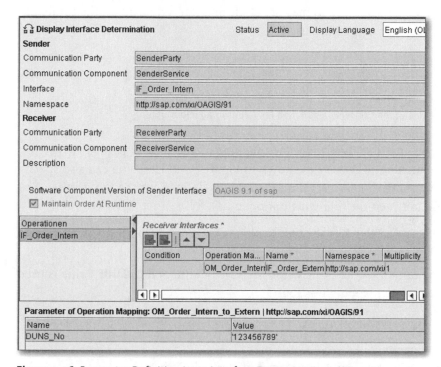

Figure 9.46 Parameter Definition in an Interface Determination

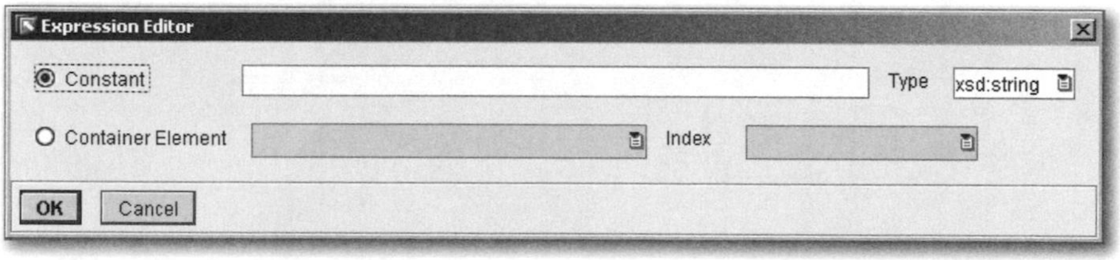

Figure 9.47 Maintenance Screen for the Value Assignment to a Parameter Within an Interface Determination

9.7.2 Data Conversions

SAP NetWeaver PI provides a number of tools for converting data from one format to another. Most of these tools require configuration settings in the Integration Directory in addition to certain objects in the Enterprise Services Repository.

Fixed Values

You can use the conversion function `FixValues` in a field mapping (see Figure 9.48) if the values you need to map are static and don't depend on the context in which the message mapping is used.

Figure 9.48 Use of the Conversion Function FixValues in a Field Mapping

The key-value pairs of the fixed value mapping are defined as part of the properties of the function `FixValues` as shown in Figure 9.49. Here you can also specify how the mapping should react if no mapping is defined for the input value. You can choose between the following options:

▶ With the option **Use Key** the input value is used as a result if no mapping was found.

▶ With the option **Use Default Value** the value defined in **Default Value** is used as a result if no mapping was found.

▶ With the option **Throw Exception** an exception is triggered if no mapping was found.

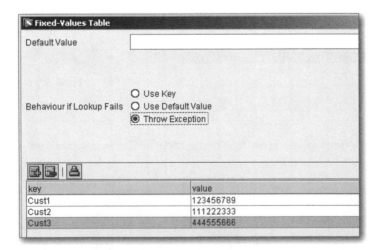

Figure 9.49 Definition of Values in the Conversion Function FixValues

Value Mapping

With the conversion function `Value mapping` you specify a set of agencies and schemas that is used for the derivation of the value mappings. The actual values for the mapping are maintained in the Integration Directory because they are considered a customer-specific configuration.

In the field mapping screen you specify that a value mapping should be used as shown in Figure 9.50. As part of the properties of the function `Value mapping` you specify the sender agency and schema as well as the receiver agency and schema for this particular mapping (see Figure 9.51).

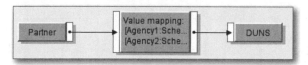

Figure 9.50 Use of the Conversion Function Value Mapping in a Field Mapping

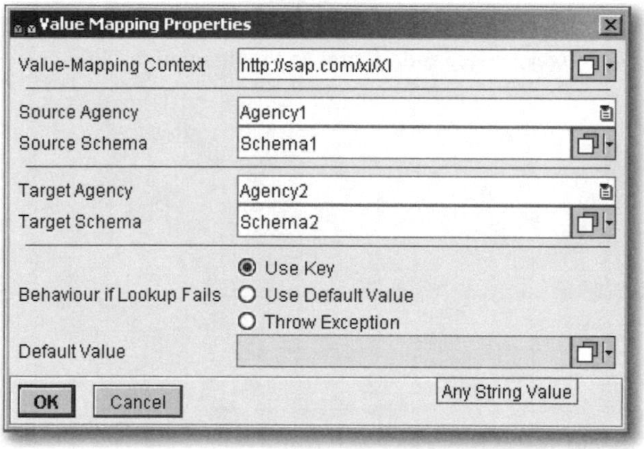

Value Mapping Properties		
Value-Mapping Context	http://sap.com/xi/XI	
Source Agency	Agency1	
Source Schema	Schema1	
Target Agency	Agency2	
Target Schema	Schema2	
Behaviour if Lookup Fails	⦿ Use Key ○ Use Default Value ○ Throw Exception	
Default Value		

OK   Cancel   Any String Value

Figure 9.51 Definition of Source and Target Agencies and Schemas in the Function Value Mapping

The actual mapping values are then defined in the Integration Directory via the menu path **Tools • Value Mapping**. There you specify which agency and schema you want to use for the source values and which agency and schema you want to use for the target values (see Figure 9.52) before you can enter the actual values as shown in Figure 9.53.

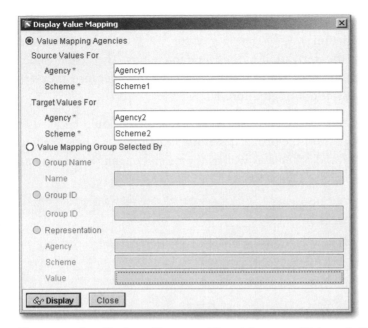

Figure 9.52 Specification of Source and Target Agency and Schema in the Integration Directory

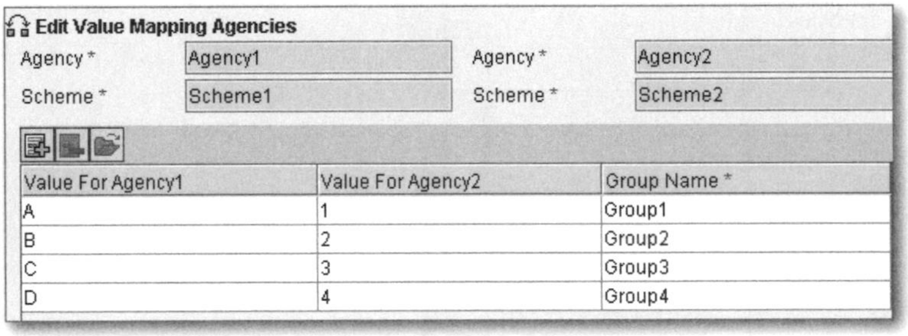

Figure 9.53 Definition of Values Used in the Conversion Function Value Mapping

Data Look-Ups

As of release 7.1 of SAP NetWeaver PI, a number of data look-ups are supported via standard functions provided in the graphical mapping tool. The following functions are available:

▶ **JDBC lookup**
With a JDBC lookup you can read data from a database table for further processing in your mapping process.

▶ **RFC lookup**

With an RFC lookup you can execute a remote function call (RFC) in the SAP backend to retrieve data for further processing in your mapping process.

Because both options have similar configuration requirements, we only discuss the RFC lookups in detail. Table 9.3 lists the steps you need to perform to set up an RFC lookup in a message mapping.

Step	Description	Source
1	Ensure that the RFC is available as an imported object under the software component of the message mapping.	Enterprise Services Repository
2	Create a communication channel for accessing the RFC in the SAP backend.	Integration Directory
3	In your message mapping create a parameter of category **Adapter** and type **RFC**.	Enterprise Services Repository
4	Create a field mapping in your message mapping containing the function RFC Lookup.	Enterprise Services Repository

Table 9.3 Steps for Creation of an RFC Lookup

In detail, the steps for the creation of an RFC lookup are as follows:

1. The RFC you want to use must be available as an imported object in the same (or a dependent) software component version as the message mapping. If the RFC is not yet available, you need to import it as described in Section 8.3.6 Imported Objects.

2. To retrieve data from the SAP backend via an RFC lookup call, we need to set up a communication channel under the business system representing the backend system where the RFC is to be executed. We discussed the creation of communication channels in Section 9.2.3 Communication Channel. This communication channel must use the adapter type RFC and be set up as a receiver communication channel as shown in Figure 9.54.

3. We need to provide a link from the communication channel we created in the previous step to the RFC lookup we want to use in our message mapping. This link is established through an import parameter of type **Adapter**, as shown in Figure 9.55. We discussed the use of parameters in detail in Section 9.7.1 Parameters in Mappings.

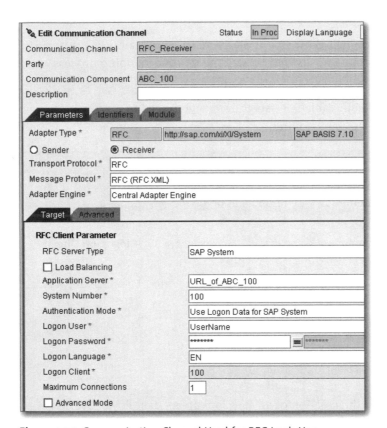

Figure 9.54 Communication Channel Used for RFC Look-Ups

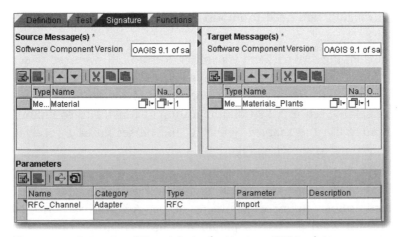

Figure 9.55 Parameter of Type Adapter for Use in an RFC Look-Up

4. As the last step in the message mapping we need to create the field mapping that contains the RFC lookup, as shown in Figure 9.56. You must specify the following properties of the RFC lookup (see also Figure 9.57):

  ▸ Under the heading **Communication Channel** you need to provide the link to the communication channel that should be used for accessing the backend. The link is established through the import parameter of type **Adapter** that we created in the previous step.

  ▸ You need to specify the RFC you want to use in this particular RFC lookup. The list of available RFCs is displayed when you click on the icon next to the text **Select an RFC module** (⬚). The text is then replaced by the name of the RFC module.

  ▸ You need to specify which information is required as input information of the function **RFC Lookup**. You can choose any combination of fields from the RFC interface, which is displayed on the left-hand side of the properties screen (see Figure 9.57). You need to mark the relevant fields and add them as an input field by clicking the **Insert Object** icon (⬚).

  ▸ You need to specify which information is required as output information of the function **RFC Lookup**. You can choose any combination of fields from the RFC interface, which is displayed on the right-hand side of the properties screen (see Figure 9.57). You need to mark the relevant fields and add them as an input field by clicking on the **Insert Object** icon (⬚).

We have completed the creation of a message mapping containing a function **RFC Lookup**. Because we had to use a parameter in the message mapping, we need to define a parameter binding in the associated operation mapping and specify the actual communication channel in the parameter assignments of the interface determination step in the Integration Directory.

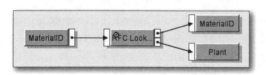

Figure 9.56 RFC Lookup in a Field Mapping

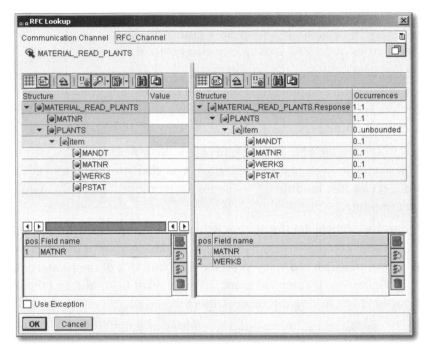

Figure 9.57 Properties of an RFC Look-Up

9.8 Summary

After reading this chapter you should be able to configure a B2B integration scenario in the Integration Directory of SAP NetWeaver PI, both manually and by using the Model Configurator. You should understand the purpose of each configuration step and understand the importance of the process integration scenarios from the Enterprise Services Repository for the Model Configurator.

In addition, you should now understand some of the advanced features crossing the Enterprise Services Repository and the Integration Directory such as parameterized mappings and different data conversion options.

This chapter gives you an overview of security concepts and explains the need for security in B2B Integration. It explains various security features provided within SAP NetWeaver PI, adapter-specific security configuration, and, in particular, configuration of B2B standard adapters.

10 Security Considerations

The emergence of the Internet has opened up several opportunities for companies involved in B2B integration. The Internet has become the most cost-effective vehicle and an important information sharing channel for businesses in B2B integration. Sharing of business data over the Internet has increased the strategic and tactical processes of any business alliance, resulting in an improved responsiveness, efficiency, and expansion of sales opportunities. Globalization, extreme competition, and distributed supply chain networks have also increased the use of the Internet in the B2B world for exchanging business information with global trading partners.

With the increasing use of distributed systems and the Internet for managing business data, the demands on electronic security are also on the rise. With the pace of change in the technology, secure exchange of confidential business data and documents over the Internet has become one of the most challenging aspects of B2B integration. To protect data against tampering, eavesdropping, and unauthorized access, communication lines as well as the storage locations of business data need to be made secure. The exchange of business-critical information with trading partners can only be protected with a security policy for the entire system landscape and appropriate security measures and strategies. These policies, strategies, and measures must be developed through an analysis of business requirements and assessment of threats, vulnerability, and risks.

In B2B relationships, partners should provide only limited access to each other's system resources and ensure that the data and processes support their business requirements without allowing unauthorized access to their business-critical information.

10.1   Overview

SAP NetWeaver PI reduces the complexity of B2B integration by providing an open integration platform that integrates collaborative business processes across SAP and non-SAP systems within and beyond enterprise boundaries. These business processes are integrated using the standards-based XML messages relying on various communication protocols such as SOAP, FTP, JDBC, RFC, JMS, File, Proxies, and Web service protocols. In addition, it uses industry standard protocols such as RNIF, AS2, and CIDX to communicate with external business partners. It also enables process integration using the standards-based enterprise SOA architecture to provide open-ended access to any number of existing applications.

With all of these integration features and capabilities, one of the most important responsibilities of SAP NetWeaver PI is to ensure that these business processes can be exchanged in a secure manner. The security requirements have to be increased while exchanging confidential business data over the Internet with trading partners. These requirements also have to be increased between numerous components of PI, because these components need to communicate with each other on a technical level to keep the infrastructure running. In addition, the security level has to be achieved at runtime at the message level and transport level by using numerous security mechanisms such as digital signatures, encryption, HTTPS, SSL, and so on to protect data integrity and against unauthorized access to the data.

SAP NetWeaver PI provides multiple levels of security at the message level and transport level for secure transmission of business information within and beyond enterprise boundaries. These measures allow you to control who can access your system, what they can see, and what they can change. It also provides auditing features, allowing you to track what has been changed and who made the changes. SAP NetWeaver PI provides security mechanisms based on open and mature standards to support interoperable solutions for secure partner integration. These standards are described in brief below.

▶ **Secure Socket Layer**
   SSL is an industry standard and is most widely used in B2B integration in protection of business transactions over the Internet. It is a cryptographic protocol that provides secure communication over the Internet. All of the HTTP-based adapters in SAP NetWeaver PI use SSL for making secure connections over the Internet.

▶ **Transport Layer Security**

TLS is another name for SSL Version 3.0 or later. TLS is defined in RFC 2246 and identifies itself in the protocol version field as SSL3.1. Many protocols such as HTTP, IMAP, POP3, SMTP, and FTP, use TLS to establish secure connections. It is composed of two layers, namely, TLS Handshake protocol and TLS Record protocol. The TLS Handshake protocol performs the key exchange using an asymmetric algorithm such as RSA. The TLS Record protocol opens an encrypted channel using a symmetric algorithm such as 3DES.

▶ **X.509**

X.509 is a standard for public key infrastructure and provides a standard format for public key certificates. This is discussed in more detail in the following sections.

▶ **Secure/Multipurpose Internet Mail Extensions**

S/MIME is an Internet standard for public key encryption and signing of email encapsulated in MIME. This standard is also used in communication protocols such as HTTPS. S/MIME provides cryptographic security features such as authentication, data integrity, nonrepudiation using digital signatures, and data security using encryption. In SAP NetWeaver PI, RNIF and mail adapters employ the S/MIME standard.

▶ **Public Key Cryptographic Standard**

PKCS#7 is a cryptographic message syntax standard used to sign and encrypt messages under a public key infrastructure (PKI). In SAP NetWeaver PI, the PKCS#7 standard is supported via the RNIF 1.1 adapter and the CIDX adapter.

▶ **WS Security**

The OASIS WS Security specification describes extensions to SOAP that allow for message-level authentication, integrity, and confidentiality. It incorporates security features in the header of a SOAP message and ensures end-to-end security. The SOAP header contains all relevant security such as security tokens to carry authentication data and a TimeStamp to protect against replay attacks, signatures against message tampering, encrypted keys, and data to protect confidential information. In SAP NetWeaver PI, message-level security for XI protocol, WS, and SOAP adapters is based on the WS Security standard.

▶ **WS Trust**

OASIS WS Trust is an extension of WS Security, and its main goal is to enable applications to construct trusted SOAP message exchanges. It enables the exchange and brokering of security tokens such as Username Token, SAML

Token, and so on as defined by WS Security. It focuses on the methods for requesting, issuing, renewing, and validating security tokens with ways to establish a trust relationship between the players in a secure message exchange.

▶ **WS SecureConversation**
WS SecureConversation is an OASIS specification to allow secure conversation between the partners using Web services communication. It works in conjunction with WS Security, WS Trust, and WS Policy.

▶ **WS SecurityPolicy**
OASIS WS SecurityPolicy provides policy assertions that are utilized by WS Security, WS Trust, and WS SecureConversation specifications.

▶ **Security Assertion Markup Language**
SAML is an OASIS XML-based standard for exchange of security information related to a user between systems. This standard is discussed in detail in Section 10.2 Authentication and Authorization.

▶ **XML encryption**
XML encryption is a W3C recommendation that specifies processing rules for encrypting data and representing the results in XML. The data can be an XML document, an XML element, or XML element content. The WS Security standard for Web services relies on XML encryption in conjunction with security tokens to ensure message-level security.

▶ **XML Signature**
XML Signature is a W3C recommendation and is used to protect a message against unauthorized modification and nonrepudiation. XML Signature can be used to digitally sign XML documents. The WS Security standard for Web services relies on XML encryption in conjunction with security tokens to ensure message-level security.

SAP NetWeaver PI provides various security mechanisms to protect the confidential business data against eavesdropping and unauthorized access. These security features are discussed in detail in the below sections.

10.2   Authentication and Authorization

Authentication and authorization are the most basic steps to protect and ensure the integrity of confidential data because these mechanisms can be used to limit access to it. All components of SAP NetWeaver PI use the solution of underlying AS ABAP or AS Java for authentication, authorization, and user administration. These concepts are discussed in detail in the following sections.

10.2.1   Authentication

Authentication is the process of verifying the identity of a person or a system component before allowing that person or system component access to the internal resources. It is the process by which a person or a system component proves that it is who it says it is. A common example is the way you authenticate yourself with your ATM card and personal identification number (PIN) to withdraw money at a teller machine. Once your identity is verified, you should be able to access the internal resources (your bank account) of the bank to withdraw money.

All of the network connections, protocols, and application systems involved in B2B integration should use strong forms of authentication. The basic authentication should be a user ID and password or something stronger. To achieve authentication that is stronger than a user ID and password, you have to use them in combination with other authentication mechanisms such as single sign-on, digital certificates, secure tokens, and so on. For B2B transactions, the authentication information should be transmitted encrypted. Several authentication mechanisms are available for authenticating users of SAP NetWeaver PI to execute a specific action. These mechanisms are discussed in detail below.

Basic Authentication

This is the simple and traditional authentication mechanism that can be implemented with the least effort. It is an HTTP method for authentication that allows users to access an application or application functionality upon entering the valid combination of user ID and password. The credentials are transported in an HTTP 1.0 header field. This mechanism does not encrypt the password when sending them over the Internet. To increase the security access to internal resources, it has to be used in combination with transport-level security mechanisms such as Secure Socket Layer (SSL).

Single Sign-On

Single sign-on (SSO) is a specialized form of authentication that allows users to access the resources on multiple systems or components based on an initial authentication. It simplifies the user login process by eliminating multiple passwords and separate application logins. SSO complements user authentication and enables users to access resources in several systems.

SAP NetWeaver PI supports session-based single sign-on for the dialog users of the PI components such as System Landscape Directory, Enterprise Services Repository, Integration Builder, Runtime Workbench, and so forth. That means the users have to login only once to get access to all of the components of SAP NetWeaver PI, provided they use the same browser session that they used to log in.

X.509 Digital Certificates

A digital certificate, or a public key certificate, is a digital identification card operating much like a driver's license or passport and is used to verify the identity of an organization or an individual. It is used in conjunction with public key cryptography and is used particularly for secure authentication of users.

Principles of Cryptography

Cryptography is a process of protecting information by transforming it into an unreadable format (encrypt) called cipher text and transforming that back into readable format (decrypt) only by a legitimate reader using a secret key. Cryptography is used to protect the company-wide business-critical information and is concerned with four main objectives: message confidentiality, message integrity, nonrepudiation, and authentication. Cryptography can be categorized into *symmetric* and *public-key (asymmetric)* cryptography.

▶ Symmetric cryptography systems use a shared secret key that the sender and the receiver can use to encrypt and decrypt a message. In such systems, the sender and receiver who want to communicate securely first agree on a secret key that allows each party to encrypt and decrypt messages. Symmetric cryptography systems use a wide range of symmetric algorithms for cryptography that use the same key to encrypt and decrypt the message. Examples of supported symmetric algorithms include the Data Encryption Standard (DES), the Triple DES (3DES), the International Data Encryption algorithm (IDEA), and the Advanced Encryption Standard (AES).

▶ Public-key cryptography systems use the cryptographic key pair: a *public key* and a *private key*. As the name suggests, the public key is shared with anyone who wants to exchange the encrypted information with you, whereas its corresponding private key is kept secret and is used for decrypting the message.

Public key cryptography systems use a wide range of asymmetric algorithms that use a key pair described above to encrypt and decrypt a message. A message encrypted by the algorithm using the public key can be decrypted by the same algorithm using the private key. Some of the most common examples of asymmetric algorithms include Rivest, Shamir, Adleman (RSA), Digital Signature Algorithm (DSA), and Diffie Helman exchange (DH).

Most modern cryptographic systems use a *hybrid approach* to benefit from both of the approaches described above. Where performance is concerned, symmetric algorithms are much faster than asymmetric algorithms. Because of this characteristic, asymmetric algorithms are typically used for data authentication, and symmetric algorithms are used for bulk encryption.

Digital certificates are issued by a trusted third party known as a *certification authority* (CA) such as VeriSign or Thawte, which guarantees the validity of the information contained in the certificate. The owner (person, computer, or organization), who possesses the public and private key pair, sends the public key to the CA for certification. The CA then verifies the public key, signs the certificate with its own private key, and issues the signed digital certificate to the owner. This digital certificate contains the information needed to ensure that the public key belongs to the person or the company indicated. The owner of the keys then distributes his public key certificate to the recipients. The recipient uses the information from the public key certificate to verify the signature of the signed document.

The most common certification standard is the X.509 standard, which has the specification for the format of the binary file that constitutes a certificate. The X.509 v3 certificate contains the information such as version, serial number, validity period, certificate issuer's name, owner's name, owner's public key, cryptographic algorithm used, and the CA's digital signature.

Message-level security in SAP NetWeaver PI relies on public and private X.509 certificates maintained in the AS Java key store, where each certificate is identified by its alias name and the key store view where it is stored. Message-level security is discussed in detail in the next section.

Digital Signatures

Digital signatures are used to sign the digital document and are based on the cryptographic hash functions together with public key cryptography-based encryption. Like traditional signatures written with ink on paper, a digital signature can be used to authenticate the identity of the signer of the data. It identifies the signer of the digital document and protects the integrity of the message and helps reveal secret or improper modification of the data.

When you apply your digital signature to a document, it is used to create a hash value exclusive to the combination of your signature and the specific document. The most commonly used hash algorithms for digital signatures include the Secure Hash Algorithm (SHA-1) and the Message Digest Algorithm 5 (MD5).

Figure 10.1 shows how the digital signature works, that is, the creation of a digital signature on the service consumer side and the verification of this signature on the service provider side. This process consists of the following steps:

❶ A cryptographic hash algorithm[1] is applied to the document or message to generate a fixed-length message digest from the variable-length message. The message digest represents a unique fingerprint for the document.

❷ This message digest is encrypted using the signer's private key to create a signed message digest. This signed message digest is then packed together with the document to create a digitally signed document and is sent to the receiver.

Upon the receipt of the digitally signed document, the receiver either accepts or denies the digital signature by verifying the identity of the sender and the integrity of the signed document. This process divides the received signed document into its components, namely, the signed message digest and the document itself.

❸ The public key from the sender is applied to the signed message digest to generate the message digest from the original document.

❹ The same hash algorithm that was used by the sender is applied to the document to be verified, to generate the message digest for the signed document.

❺ These two message digests are compared to see if they are identical. If they are identical, the document was not altered after being signed, and the signer is who you think it is.

Digital signatures are often confused with digital certificates because both of them are based on asymmetric or public key cryptography. Whereas the digital

---

1 A hash algorithm takes a message of any length as input and generates a fixed-size string called a hash value.

certificate authenticates a public key and identifies the owner of that key, the digital signature is used to authenticate a specific document and the organization or the individual that created the document.

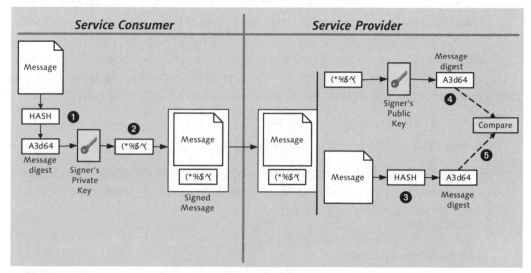

Figure 10.1 Digital Signature Using a Hash Algorithm

SAP NetWeaver PI supports digital signatures for XML-based messages through the protocols SOAP, WS, Mail, XI protocol, RNIF, and CIDX. Repudiation of order transactions by customers is a major business risk faced by many suppliers in Internet-based B2B integration. This business risk can be addressed by digitally signing the business document and providing support for nonrepudiation. The digital signatures in B2B integration with SAP NetWeaver PI authenticate the business partner signing the message and ensure the data integrity of the business document carried by that message. The industry standard adapters such as RNIF and CIDX provide support for nonrepudiation of origin and nonrepudiation of receipt of the message. In the nonrepudiation of origin, the sender signs a message so that the receiver can prove that the sender actually sent a message. In the nonrepudiation of receipt, the receiver signs the receipt back to sender so that the original sender can prove that the receiver actually received the message. Message-level security is discussed more in detail in message level security section.

Principal Propagation

Principal propagation is the authentication mechanism for securely propagating user identities across system boundaries to access all of the SAP and service-enabled enterprise applications where the user does not interact with those systems directly. The identity of the user (principal) is propagated end-to-end along the whole message flow, from a sender application to a receiver application, provided the security settings have been configured appropriately and the necessary authorizations have been granted to the user in the sender application. Principal propagation in SAP NetWeaver PI is supported by the following mechanisms:

► SAP assertion tickets
► Security Assertion Markup Language (SAML)

Propagation of user identities should not be used for B2B communication because external users cannot be distinguished from internal users. Thus, these two concepts are discussed only briefly below.

SAP Assertion Tickets

SAP NetWeaver PI offers *SAP assertion tickets* as an authentication mechanism to integrate applications running on SAP and non-SAP systems for a single sign-on. SAP assertion ticket has been available since SAP NetWeaver Application Server 6.40 and is based on the SAP logon ticket[2] mechanism. SAP assertion ticket is downward compatible with SAP logon ticket. In contrast to SAP logon ticket, SAP assertion ticket is transmitted in the HTTP header field, not as a HTTP cookie. With the assertion ticket, all of the participating applications along the way from sender to receiver require a separate authentication. The SAP assertion ticket is consumed during authentication at each participating application, and a new ticket is generated each time a message moves forward to the next application in the flow.

To use SAP assertion tickets, a trust relationship must be established between the underlying application servers based on the X.509 certificate mechanism. In SAP NetWeaver PI, SAP assertion tickets are supported by the XI protocol, SOAP, RFC, and WS.

---

2 An SAP logon ticket is a browser cookie issued and signed after initial authentication to the primary SAP system. This ticket is then used to access all of the connected SAP or non-SAP systems without any further authentication. The logon ticket is transmitted via HTTP request in the browser main memory.

The steps involved in the configuration of assertion tickets in SAP NetWeaver PI for ABAP systems are as follows:

1. Activate the principal propagation on the Integration Engine by executing the **Configure principal propagation** option using transaction SXMB_ADM (see Figure 10.2). This will create a service user `XIPPUSER` with the role `SAP_XI_APPL_SERV_USER` and an RFC destination `SAPXIPP<client number>`.

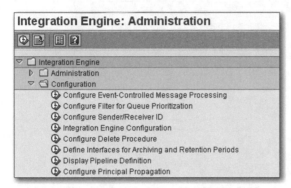

Figure 10.2 Enable Principal Propagation on IE

2. Configure the trust relationship for SAP assertion tickets between the participating systems. To configure the trust relationship on the client ABAP system, generate the public and private key pair and export the certificate using Transaction STRUST (see Figure 10.3). On the server ABAP system, import the client certificate into the secure storage and add the client to the access control lists (ACL) using Transaction STRUSTSSO2.

3. Configure the sender system. For a sender ABAP system, configure the interface filter by specifying the interface, interface namespace, and user for the message for which an assertion ticket is to be issued. Transaction SXMB_ADM can be used for this purpose.

4. Set up the configuration in the Integration Directory. Here you need to configure sender and receiver agreements to propagate user identities. This can be done by simply setting the **Propagate principal** flag (see Figure 10.4) in the sender and receiver agreement.

5. As the last step, you must maintain the users to be propagated in all of the participating components with the same name as the sender system. The users who need to be propagated must be system users with the role `SAP_XI_APPL_SERV_USER`.

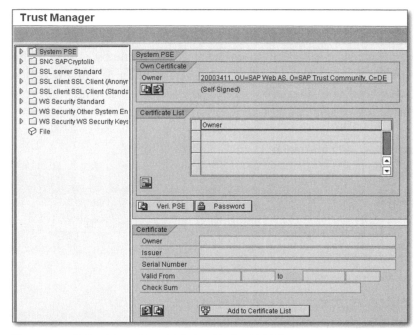

Figure 10.3 Maintaining a Trust Relationship for ABAP Systems

Figure 10.4 Configure Principal Propagation in the Sender Agreement

Security Assertion Markup Language

Security Assertion Markup Language (SAML) is an OASIS XML-based standard for exchange of security information related to a user between systems. Using SAML, the information for authentication and authorization can be exchanged in the backend without users noticing the exchange. SAML uses assertions that contain statements about a subject, authentication, authorization, and attributes. A SAML assertion containing the subject name is created and signed by a trusted attester system against which the sender system is able to authenticate the subject. This assertion also contains a signature with respect to the entire message proving the linkage of the assertion to the message contents. These assertions can be used in SOAP messages to carry security and identity information between actors in Web service transactions. The SAML specification has the following four core components.

▶ **Assertions**
Assertions are statements about a subject (user) such as authentication, attribute information, or authorization decision

▶ **Protocols**
Protocols are request-response protocols for obtaining assertions

▶ **Protocol bindings**
Protocol bindings are mappings from SAML request-response protocols into standard messaging or communication protocols. For example, the SAML SOAP binding defines how the SAML protocol can be communicated within SOAP messages.

▶ **Profiles**
Profiles define how assertions, protocols, and bindings are combined for particular usage scenarios.

SAML defines three kinds of statements that can be carried with an assertion.

▶ **Authentication**
These statements describe the particular means used to authenticate a subject at a particular time. They contain a piece of data that represents an act of authentication performed on the subject (user) by the authority.

▶ **Attribute**
These statements contain specific attribute information about a subject.

▶ **Authorization decision**
These statements define that the specified subject is authorized to access a particular resource, for example, whether the subject is permitted to buy a specified item.

As discussed previously, SAML provides assertions about aspects of identity, but just by providing assertions from an asserting party to a relying party may not be adequate for a secure system. A system can be prone to attacks such as "man-in-the-middle" that can grab the assertions to replay them later. SAML defines a number of security mechanisms that prevent or detect such attacks. The primary mechanism is to have a preexisting trust relationship between the systems typically involving a public key infrastructure (PKI). To validate and process an assertion, the receiver needs to establish the relationship between the subject of each SAML subject statement and the attesting entity. SAML assertions are used in two types, where either the sender itself sends the SAML-enriched messages to the target system (holder-of-key) or the attester forwards the message to the target system (sender vouches).

SAP NetWeaver PI supports SAML assertions based on the SAML 1.1 standard. It enables you to use the sender-vouches-subject confirmation method to confirm a subject with SAML token profile[3] authentication. For this subject confirmation method, the WS intermediary system also acts as a SAML assertion issuer. The WS intermediary authenticates the client and forwards to the backend WS provider the authentication information for the WS consumer using a SAML token profile. The WS provider, in turn, authenticates access based on its trust relationship with the intermediary system.

The configuration steps involved in the configuration of the SAML assertions in SAP NetWeaver PI for ABAP systems are as follows:

1. Enable principal propagation similar to step 1 of the assertion ticket configuration.

2. Configure a trust relationship similar to step 2 of the assertion ticket configuration.

3. To configure the trusted issuer in the consumer (sender) system, run the report WSS_INFO using Transaction SA38 on the ABAP stack. This report, when exe-

---

3 SAML Token Profile is developed by the OASIS Web Services Security (WS Security) Technical Committee as a standard to integrate and use SAML for Web Services Security.

cuted, provides information about what an issued SAML assertion will look like.

4. To configure the trusted issuer in the provider (receiver) system, run the report RSUSREXTID using Transaction SA38 on the ABAP stack, and maintain user mapping for each propagated user. You can also maintain these user mappings either in the table USREXTID or via table view VUSREXTID using the transaction SM30 on the ABAP stack.

5. As the last step, configure the communication channel and agreements in the Integration Directory. Maintain the channel for adapter type WS (see Figure 10.5) and select the authentication method **SAML 1.1 Sender Vouches Assertion**.

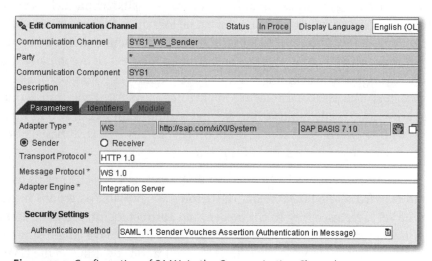

Figure 10.5 Configuration of SAML in the Communication Channel

10.2.2 Authorization

In the previous section, we discussed in detail the various authentication features provided with SAP NetWeaver PI. In this section we look into the authorization features of SAP NetWeaver PI. The terms *authentication* and *authorization* sound similar and are often confusing. Whereas authentication is the process of identifying a user, authorization restricts what a user is allowed to do. In other words, once an identity has been authenticated, the authorization process determines whether that identity has access to a given resource. Authorizations are building blocks that specify which tasks the user is allowed to perform. The authorizations can be consolidated and stored in the user role information. These authorizations are applied when the user logs on to the system to perform his activities.

The authorization concept in SAP NetWeaver PI AS ABAP is similar to that of SAP ECC systems. In SAP systems authority checks are performed at runtime to determine if the user has the right to carry out a task. These authority checks can be applied to transactions, tables, documents, and other resources. The authorizations are defined depending on the activity and responsibility of the users. Authorizations in ABAP are combined in an authorization profile, and a profile can contain one or more authorizations. The authorization profiles are then assigned to individual users via roles. Thus, these roles carry authorization information. With role-based user access, users only see the activities that they need. For example, an accountant in an organization can only see his role-specific menu such as view account balance, post payment, and so on when he logs on to the system. The role a person plays in an organization can also be used to determine their authorizations to information and applications. For example, the CFO of a company has different access rights to accounting data than the employees who work for him as administrators. The users and roles are maintained in AS ABAP via Transaction SU01 and are automatically replicated to AS Java. Authorizations can also be integrated with LDAP-based user administration. The details of LDAP based user administration are beyond the scope of this book.

The authorization concept in SAP NetWeaver PI AS Java uses AS ABAP as its user master and is based on AS ABAP roles. These roles are available as groups in AS Java. On the AS Java, a security role represents an abstract logical group of users that is defined for specific application components by the AS Java administrator. AS Java enables you to authorize access to your applications by utilizing the UME authorization concepts and the JEE authorization concepts. The authorization concept of UME is only discussed briefly below, but not in detail because it is beyond the scope of this book as well.

The user and role concept of the User Management Engine (UME) provides refined access to SAP applications that use programmatic authorization checks. The UME provides centralized user management for all Java applications in SAP NetWeaver and can be configured to work with user management data from multiple data sources. It is seamlessly integrated into the Java EE engine of AS Java and can be administered using administration tools of AS Java.

By default, any SAP NetWeaver PI developer or configurator can modify any objects in the Enterprise Services Builder and Integration Directory. In distributed teams or in a shared SAP NetWeaver PI environment, it might be necessary to limit authorization for a developer or group of developers to only one software component or objects within a software component or specific configuration objects. In both the Enterprise Services Builder and the Integration Directory, you can define more detailed authorizations that can restrict access to design and configuration objects. We discussed this in detail in Section 2.3.1 Enterprise Services Builder.

10.3 Dialog and Service Users

SAP NetWeaver PI supports two types of users for authentication and authorization: the dialog users and the service users. We discuss these two types of users in detail in the next two sections.

10.3.1 Dialog Users

The dialog users are human users who interact with SAP NetWeaver PI tools using various user interfaces (UIs) in the Enterprise Services Builder and in the Integration Builder. These users access the Enterprise Services Repository, Integration Directory, and System Landscape Directory during the design phase and configuration phase of the scenarios. The user authorization for dialog users is defined in the ABAP part of SAP NetWeaver PI and can be maintained via Transaction SU01. SAP NetWeaver PI delivers some standard roles that carry all of the required authorizations to perform the tasks of creating and maintaining the objects in SAP NetWeaver PI during the design and configuration phase. These roles are discussed in section 2.3.1 Enterprise Services Builder and are listed in Table 2.4.

Each of these roles is a composite role consisting of an ABAP role with a suffix _ABAP and a Java role with a suffix _JAVA. The ABAP role is relevant for executing the ABAP application, whereas the Java role is relevant for executing Java applications such as the Enterprise Services Repository and the Integration Directory. The newly created roles are propagated to the user groups of the User Management Engine. Using these roles, access to the object types in the Enterprise Services Repository and Integration Directory can be restricted to display or maintain access. In the Enterprise Services Repository, access to the individual objects such as software component versions, namespaces, and all of the objects underneath them can be restricted to create, change, delete or display access. In the Integration Directory, access to the objects of collaboration profiles, collaboration agreements, and logical routings can be restricted. In general, display access is granted for all general users other than the developers using the role SAP_XI_DISPLAY_USER.

10.3.2 Service Users

Unlike dialog users, service users do not log in interactively. These service users are used for dialog-free communication between various components of the SAP NetWeaver PI system and between various sender application systems and SAP NetWeaver PI. The SAP NetWeaver PI components such as the Enterprise Services Repository, Integration Directory, System Landscape Directory, and so on must have access to one another during the design, configuration, and runtime phases for obtaining the relevant information. For example, the Integration Directory needs to access the Enterprise Services Repository and the SLD during the configuration phase for obtaining the relevant design and the business system information. For this purpose, the Integration Directory reads the data for the service users PIREPUSER and PILDUSER from the exchange profile[4] and uses it to authenticate to Enterprise Services Repository and System Landscape Directory components.

The service users are set up during the SAP NetWeaver PI installation and are automatically configured. The passwords for the service users are also assigned during the installation. These users are made available in the AS Java and AS ABAP, and are referenced in the exchange profile. Each Java-based SAP NetWeaver PI component on the AS Java has read access to the service user data on the exchange profile and uses this information to connect to other SAP NetWeaver PI components. Table 10.1 shows the list of service users assigned to each SAP NetWeaver PI component.

---

4 Exchange Profile is an XML document that is stored in an ABAP database table on the SAP NetWeaver PI system. It maintains the technical service users, connection data, and configuration data of an SAP NetWeaver PI landscape.

PI Component	Service User	Role
Enterprise Services Repository	PIREPUSER	SAP_XI_IR_SERV_USER_MAIN
Integration Directory	PIDIRUSER	SAP_XI_ID_SERV_USER_MAIN
System Landscape Directory	PILDUSER	SAP_BC_AI_LANDSCAPE_DB_RFC
Runtime Workbench	PIRWBUSER	SAP_XI_RWB_SERV_USER_MAIN
Sender applications	PIAPPLUSER	SAP_XI_APPL_SERV_USER
Advanced Adapter Engine	PIAFUSER	SAP_XI_AF_SERV_USER_MAIN
Change Mangement Server	PILSADMIN	SAP_XI_CMS_SERV_USER
Integration Server	PIISUSER	SAP_XI_IS_SERV_USER_MAIN
Principal Propagation	PIPPUSER	SAP_XI_APPL_SERV_USER

Table 10.1 Service Users Assigned to Each PI Component

In addition to internal communication between PI components, service users are also used for messaging communication between the Integration Server and SAP, non-SAP, or business partners. To send messages from the sender system to an Integration Server, a dedicated service user for each sender system with the role SAP_XI_APPL_SERV_USER is created on the Integration Server for allowing the sender systems to access the functionality on the Integration Engine. On the ABAP-based sender systems, an RFC destination of type ABAP connections (Transaction SM59) is created for this user and the Integration Server. To send messages to receiving systems, the Integration Server and the Adapter Engines need the appropriate authorizations to access the receiver systems. These users are defined in the Integration Builder as part of the communication channel definition.

10.4 Transport-Level Security

Transport-level security involves the security and encryption mechanisms used in transmitting the business data over the network (Internet or intranet). It involves authentication and encryption at the transport level and authorization at the end point. Using the network protocols such as HTTP and SMTP, the business-sensitive data is normally transmitted as plain text across the Internet, allowing intermediate parties to eavesdrop on the communication and tamper with the data. To safeguard the data from unauthorized access and to protect its integrity, transport-level security and encryption should be applied to both internal and external communication.

10.4.1 Transport-Level Security in SAP NetWeaver PI

As discussed earlier, all of the components of SAP NetWeaver PI communicate with each other for the purposes of administration, configuration, and monitoring and during the runtime. The internal communication between these components takes place via HTTP. This communication can be secured using Secure Socket Layer (SSL)/HTTPS. For external communication with SAP and non-SAP systems and with business partners in B2B communication, the encryption type depends on the type of adapter used for communication. Adapters based on HTTP communication can secure their communication layer by using SSL/HTTPS. The communication between RFC-based SAP applications and the Integration Server can be secured by using secure network communication (SNC).

Table 10.2 lists the adapters and the supported transport-level security mechanisms.

Adapter	Transport protocol	Transport security
XI protocol	HTTP	HTTPS (SSL)
WS protocol	HTTP	HTTPS (SSL)
IDoc adapter	RFC	SNC
RFC adapter	RFC	SNC
HTTP plain	HTTP	HTTPS (SSL)
File/FTP	FTP	FTPS (SSL/TLS)
SOAP adapter	HTTP	HTTPS (SSL)
Mail adapter	SMTP, IMAP4, POP3	HTTPS (SSL)
Marketplace	HTTP	HTTPS (SSL)
RNIF 2.0	HTTP	HTTPS (SSL)
RNIF 1.1	HTTP	HTTPS (SSL)
CIDX	HTTP	HTTPS (SSL)

Table 10.2 PI Adapters and Supported Transport Security Mechanisms

HTTP and SSL

The Secure Socket Layer (SSL) protocol provides secure transfer of business-sensitive information over the Internet. It allows client-server applications to communicate with each other while preventing others from eavesdropping and tampering with the confidential information. SSL requires all of the information exchanged between a client and server to be encrypted. It provides privacy through data encryption, server authentication, and data integrity. It also provides client authentication as an optional function. The SSL protocol supports a variety of cryptographic algorithms such as authenticating the server and client to each other, transmitting certificates, and establishing session keys.

An SSL session always starts with an exchange of messages called the SSL handshake. The handshake allows the server to authenticate itself to the client using asymmetric or public key encryption. It then allows the client and server to select the cryptographic algorithms they both support, use public key encryption techniques to generate shared secrets, and establish an encrypted SSL connection between them.

In SAP NetWeaver PI, SSL can be enabled on both the AS Java and AS ABAP stacks. To enable the SSL on these servers, the SAP cryptographic libraries must be installed on the both of the servers. In both cases, the certificates such as X.509 standard certificates must be issued by a trustworthy certification authority (CA). SSL can be configured either to server authentication, where the server authenticates itself to the client, or to client authentication, where the client authenticates itself to the server.

RFC and SNC

The secure network communications (SNC) protocol provides protection for the communication links between the distributed components of an SAP system that use remote function calls (RFC). In addition, SNC enables the use of cryptographic mechanisms to securely authenticate users. This is accomplished by integrating external security products with the SAP system. The interface used for the integration is the GSS-API V2 (Generic Security Services Application Programming Interface Version 2). The external product can provide authentication, data integrity, and data confidentiality services for the SAP system. SNC provides application-level end-to-end security for all of the SAP applications. SNC provides three levels of security protection: authentication only, integrity protection, and privacy protection. As a prerequisite for using SNC, SAP cryptographic libraries must be installed on the server.

FTP and FTPS

FTPS—also called FTP over SSL/TLS—is used for transferring the files over the SSL protocol. FTPS can be enabled by installing the appropriate cryptographic libraries and certificates as described in HTTP and SSL in the corresponding AS Java server. You can define the security settings in the communication channel of the FTP adapter in the Integration Directory. The use of FTPS in SAP NetWeaver PI is based on the specification RFC 4217.

10.4.2 Configuring SSL in AS Java

In this section, we discuss the steps to configure SSL in the AS Java server of SAP NetWeaver PI. You need to have administrator access and OS-level permission to perform the following steps.

1. **Deploy the Java cryptographic tool kit**
   The SAP cryptographic library can be downloaded from the SAP Service Marketplace (*http://service.sap.com*). You have to download and install it on the AS Java host.

2. **Maintain the ICM parameters for using SSL**
   To enable SSL, set the HTTPS port in the ICM parameter `icm/server_port_<xx>` of the instance profile (`<SID>_<instance>_<hostname>`) located in the file system of AS Java at `/usr/sap/<SID>/SYS/profile`. You also need to set the *ssl/ssl_lib* parameter with the location of the cryptographic library.

3. **Create the server's key pair to use for SSL**
   You need the public and private key pair on the AS Java server to enable SSL. This public key must be certified by a trustworthy CA such as Verisign, Thawte, or others.

   As of release 7.1 of SAP NetWeaver PI, the key storage functions are part of the SAP NetWeaver Administrator. You can access this key storage by following the menu path **Configuration Management • Certificates and Keys** on the SAP NetWeaver Administrator (see Figure 10.6). From the key store view Select the entry **ICM_SSL_<instance_id>**.

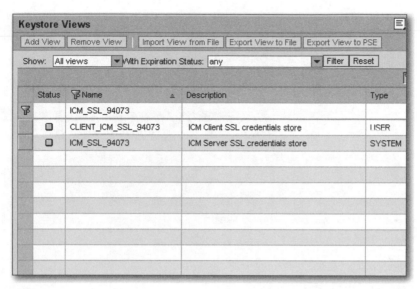

Figure 10.6 Key Storage View in the SAP NetWeaver Administrator

The AS Java server uses this view to store the key pair and the trusted client certificates to use for SSL (see Figure 10.7 and Figure 10.8). If no appropriate entry exists for the **ICM_SSL_<instance_id>** view, you have to perform tasks such as importing a saved key pair entry, importing trusted X.509 client certificates for SSL, creating a new key pair entry to use for SSL, and generating a certificate signing request. Configuring these tasks is not discussed in detail here, as it is beyond the scope of this book. For more-detailed information on how to perform these tasks, refer to SAP Help Portal (*http://help.sap.com*). You need to restart the SSL service of the AS Java to make the change of the SSL key pair effective.

4. **Create the client personal security environment (PSE)**
   The AS Java server uses the client PSE to authenticate itself on the other web servers. You can use the CLIENT_ICM_SSL_<instance ID> key store view to create the client PSE. The system associates this view with a PSE file called *SAPSSLC.pse* (see Figure 10.9).

5. **Test the connection**
   Using your web browser, access the AS Java start page via the URL *https://<AS Java hostname>:<SSL_port>*. If the SSL is configured correctly, AS Java should open with the start page.

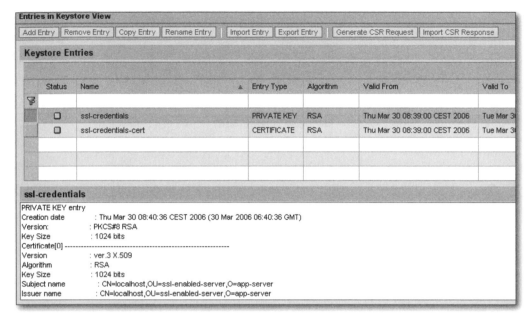

Figure 10.7 Private Key Entry for the Server

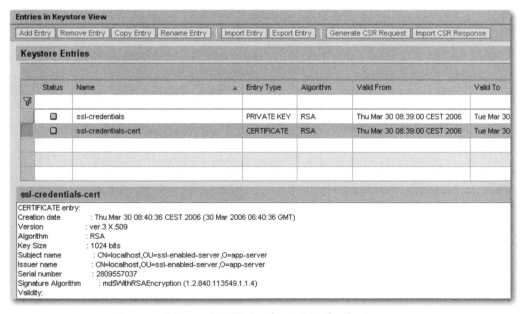

Figure 10.8 Trusted X.509 Certificate Entry for the Server

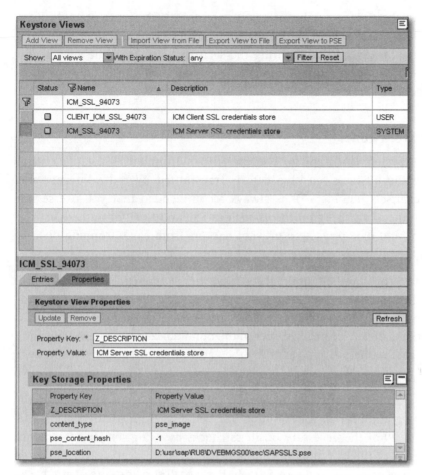

Figure 10.9 Client PSE Keystore Properties in the SAP NetWeaver Administrator

10.4.3 Transport-Level Security Settings in the Integration Directory

The security settings at the transport level depend on the type of adapter you use in the Integration Directory. You have to configure the appropriate communication channel in the Integration Directory for this purpose. For HTTP-based adapters the security levels are **HTTPS without client authentication** and **HTTPS with client authentication**. For FTPS adapters, you can set the connection security to either **Control Connection** or **Control and Data Connection**. With **Control Connection** only the connection is protected using TLS/SSL, whereas with **Control and Data Connection**, all communication with the FTP server is encrypted using TLS/SSL. If you have selected FTPS, you can also configure the adapter to authenticate itself to the FTP server by using the option **X.509 certificate for client authentication**. The corresponding key-certificate pair must be available in the key store view of AS Java. Configuring the security settings in the sender and receiver agreements for each of these adapters is discussed in detail in section 10.5 Message-Level Security.

10.4.4 Network Zones

Setting up the system landscape for a secure B2B environment is always a critical task because the business-sensitive data is transmitted over the Internet and beyond enterprise's boundary. It is always recommended that you use secure messaging connections using protocols such as SSL and SNC for authentication, data integrity, and data privacy to prevent hackers from eavesdropping or tampering with the business-sensitive data.

For additional protection and optimal security, the best practice is to establish a secure network infrastructure using network zones for the entire system landscape. The multiple firewalls reliably protect the network against external attacks. The application gateway or proxy server in the demilitarized zone (DMZ) ensures that the Internet requests are handled by the gateway or the proxy server's own cache.

Depending upon the security requirements, the best practice is to have a dedicated B2B integration server for handling B2B requests from partners. This B2B server handles all of the necessary business checks by using sender agreements and forwards all of the incoming messages to the A2A SAP NetWeaver PI server in the secure backend area. The A2A SAP NetWeaver PI server in the secure backend area does the actual routing and mapping. You can establish dedicated communication between B2B SAP NetWeaver PI system and the A2A business system by using the XI protocol. For external B2B communication with trading partners it is always recommended that you use the protocols that provide the security features for encryption and digital signing of messages such as RNIF, CIDX, SOAP, XI protocol, and so on. Figure 10.10 shows the recommended scenario for B2B messaging with external partners.

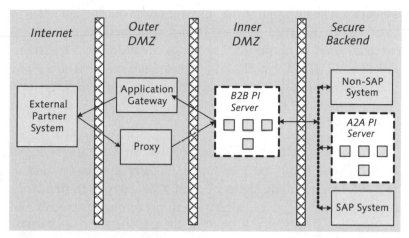

Figure 10.10 B2B Network Infrastructure

10.5 Message-Level Security

In B2B integration, message content needs to be confidential not only in communication lines but also in intermediate message stores. Message-level security improves transport-level security by adding security features that are particularly required for B2B communication. Therefore, message-level security is recommended and is sometimes a prerequisite for interenterprise communication. With the emergence of message security standards such as WS Security, message-level security is now possible for SOAP messages. Message-level security for SOAP messages is relatively new and offers more features than transport-level security. With message-level security, the complete message or parts of the message can be secured.

SOAP on its own does not provide any security mechanisms for message integrity, confidentiality, authentication, and nonrepudiation of origin or receipt. Until recently, best practice was to secure SOAP messages using SSL, but SSL provides only transport-level security and not application-level security. This is made possible by extending the SOAP message with the security features according to the WS Security specifications. WS Security describes enhancements to SOAP messages that provide message-level security through digital signatures, confidentiality through XML encryption, and identity propagation through security tokens.

There is always a question about when to use message-level security and when to use transport-level security for Web services. If the SOAP message exchange is between a client and server, with no intermediaries involved, then transport-level security with SSL and HTTPS is sufficient. If you are not sure that how many intermediaries the message hits in the message exchange, then message-level security should be utilized. In B2B communication, this depends on mutual agreements between the trading partners.

In SAP NetWeaver PI message-level security is enabled through the use of digital signatures and encryption. It is based on open industry standards such as S/MIME, PKCS#7, WS Security, XML signature, and XML encryption standards. SAP NetWeaver PI offers message-level security features through protocols and adapters such as XI protocol, WS, SOAP, Mail, RNIF 1.1, RNIF 2.0, and CIDX. Message-level security for each of these adapters is discussed in detail below.

▶ **XI Protocol**
The message-level security for XI protocol is based on the WS Security specifications and provides message-level security features such as digital signatures, encryption, nonrepudiation of origin, and nonrepudiation of receipt. Signed parts are the SAP main header, the SAP manifest, the payloads (SOAP attachments), and encrypted parts of the payloads (SOAP attachments). It supports the hash algorithm SHA-1 for signatures and the cryptographic algorithm AES256 with RSA15 key wrapping for encryption.

▶ **WS**
The message-level security for WS adapter is based on the WS Security specifications and provides message-level security through digital signatures and encryption. It supports the hash algorithm SHA-1 for signatures and the cryptographic algorithm AES256 with RSA15 key wrapping for encryption.

▶ **SOAP**
The message-level security for the SOAP adapter is based on the WS Security specifications or the S/MIME standard. It provides message-level security features through digital signatures, encryption, nonrepudiation of origin, and nonrepudiation of receipt. For WS Security policy only the SOAP body is signed.

  ▶ The SOAP adapter based on the WS Security specifications supports the hash algorithms SHA-1 and MD5 for signatures and the cryptographic algorithm AES256 with RSA15 key wrapping for encryption.

> ▹ The SOAP adapter based on the S/MIME standard supports the hash algorithm SHA-1 for signatures and the cryptographic algorithms 3DES, RC2-40, and RC2-128 for encryption.

▸ **Mail**

The message-level security for the Mail adapter is based on the S/MIME standard and provides message-level security features through digital signatures and encryption. It supports the hash algorithm SHA-1 for signatures and the cryptographic algorithms 3DES, RC2-40, and RC2-128 for encryption.

▸ **RNIF 2.0**

The message-level security for the RNIF 2.0 adapter is based on the S/MIME standard and provides message-level security features through digital signatures, encryption, nonrepudiation of origin, and nonrepudiation of receipt. It supports the hash algorithm SHA-1 for signatures and the cryptographic algorithms 3DES, RC2-40, and RC2-128 for encryption.

▸ **RNIF 1.1**

The message-level security for the RNIF 1.1 adapter is based on the PKCS#7 standard and supports message-level security features through digital signatures, nonrepudiation of origin, and nonrepudiation of receipt. It supports the hash algorithm SHA-1 for signatures. Encryption on the message level is not supported.

▸ **CIDX**

The message-level security for the CIDX adapter is based on the PKCS#7 standard and supports message-level security features through digital signatures, nonrepudiation of origin, and nonrepudiation of receipt. It supports the hash algorithm SHA-1 for signatures. Encryption on the message level is not supported.

In SAP NetWeaver PI, message-level security is done using the public and private X.509 certificates. The certificates and signed certificates from the certification authority (CA) are maintained in the certificate key store of the AS Java. The certificate maintained in the certificate key store is identified by its alias name and the key store view where it is stored.

10.5.1 Signing a Message

In message-level processing, the sender signs the message with its private key and attaches its certificate (with a public key) to the message. Upon the receipt of the message, the receiver verifies the digital signature of the message with the sender's certificate attached to the message. There are two different trust models[5] to be considered for the digital signatures to verify the authenticity of the sender's public certificate:

▸ **Direct trust model**
In the direct trust model, the public keys of the sender and receiver are exchanged offline beforehand. This model does not use a CA. All of the certificates of the business partners are stored in the certificate key store of the AS Java. The partner certificate is validated against the certificate saved in the local AS Java key store.

▸ **Hierarchical trust model**
In the hierarchical trust model, all of the certificates of the business partners are digitally signed by a certification authority. The relevant public certificates of the CAs must be stored in the key store of AS Java. In this model the sender and the receiver only need to agree upon the CA and the subject name that the sender has used in its certificate.

Table 10.3 shows the trust models supported by various adapters in SAP NetWeaver PI.

Adapter	Direct Trust Model	Hierarchical Trust Model (Single Level)	Hierarchical Trust Model (Multilevel)
RNIF	X	X	
CIDX	X	X	
XI Protocol		X	
SOAP (WS-Security)		X	
SOAP (S/MIME)			X
Mail			X
WS	X		X

Table 10.3 Trust Models Supported in SAP NetWeaver PI

---

5 Trust model refers to set of rules a system or application uses to decide whether a certificate is valid.

To enable digital certificate or message encryption in the sender or receiver agreement, the message security or security policy option in the appropriate communication channel (sender or receiver) must be set. Figure 10.11 shows example message security settings for the RNIF adapter in the Integration Directory.

Security Policy
- ☑ Sign Action Message
- ☑ Sign Signal Message
- ☑ Non-Repudiation of Origin and Content
- ☑ Non-Repudiation of Receipt Acknowledgement

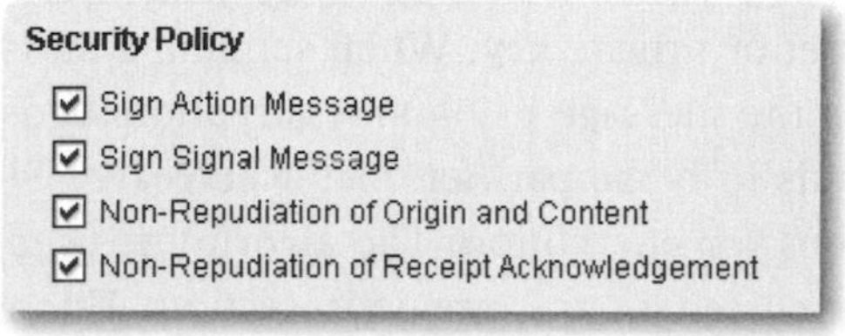

Figure 10.11 Message Security Settings in the Communication Channel

The sender and receiver agreements of the Integration Directory allow you to define the message security options, provided the security setting is set in the corresponding communication channel. The agreements will have options to specify the trust model, algorithm for signing, and references to the certificates in the key store of AS Java. For example, in the RNIF 2.0 protocol, the options for certificate signing include trust model either **Direct** or **Hierarchical**, the algorithm used for signing, and references to the current and partner certificates stored in the key store of AS Java. Figure 10.12 shows the sample settings for the certificate for signing in the receiver agreement using the RNIF protocol.

Adapter-Specific Attributes

Trust Model Direct

Current Certificate for Signing

Algorithm SHA-1

Keystore View *

Keystore Entry *

Partner Certificate for Signing

Keystore View *

Keystore Entry *

Figure 10.12 Certificate for Signing Settings in the Receiver Agreement

10.5.2 Encrypting a Message

The adapters RNIF 2.0, Mail, SOAP, WS, and XI protocols enable encryption at the message level. When exchanging business-sensitive data over the Internet, the sender and receiver require secure communication. Encryption is the process of scrambling the business-sensitive data such that it is only read by intended recipients, after decrypting it with a secret or private key. When sending a message to the partner, the sender encrypts the message using an encryption algorithm (the partner's public key) and sends it to the partner. SAP NetWeaver PI supports various cryptographic algorithms for encryption. The algorithms used for encryption for each adapter are discussed in the previous section. Upon receipt of the message, the receiving partner decrypts the message with its private key.

The sender and receiver agreements of the Integration Directory allow you to define the message security options if the security setting is set in the corresponding communication channel. The agreements will have options to specify the algorithm used for encryption, and references to the certificates in the key store of AS Java. For example, in the RNIF 2.0 protocol, the options for encryption include level of encryption (none, payload, or payload container), the algorithm used for encryption, and references to the current and partner encryption and decryption certificates stored in the key store of Java AS. Figure 10.13 shows the sample settings for message encryption in the receiver agreement using the RNIF protocol.

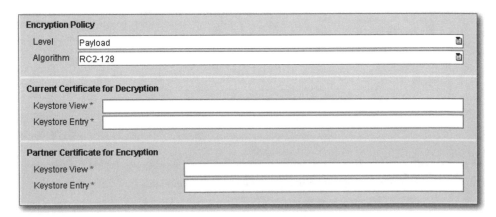

Figure 10.13 Message Encryption Settings in the Receiver Agreement

10.6 Summary

In this chapter, you have learned about security concepts and their importance in B2B integration. You have learned about the various security features such as authorization, authentication, user management, transport level, and message level security provided within SAP NetWeaver PI. You also have learned about the adapter-specific security configuration for B2B adapters such as the RNIF adapter.

All B2B scenarios require communication with an external party and therefore additional testing with this external party. In this chapter we discuss how to approach such tests by modularizing the complete scenario and using test tools for each of these modules.

11 Testing Considerations

Like any other implementation project, a B2B integration project requires a test of the implemented scenarios. However, for a B2B integration test you usually have special testing requirements due to the complexity of the scenario.

11.1 Overview

The following issues contribute to the complexity of a B2B integration test:

▶ **Alignment on message structure and message content**
In a B2B integration scenario you automate the communication process with your trading partner. This requires an initial agreement on the messages you want to exchange and their underlying message structures. Even though many different industry standards are available that define such message structures, each definition leaves room for some interpretation. Therefore, you also need to agree with your trading partner on the interpretation of the message structure you selected for your message exchange.

Whereas you usually exchange the information on the message structure and the interpretation of certain fields using documents such as spreadsheets, you use sample XML messages from your trading partner in an early stage for testing your mapping programs used for converting the messages provided by your trading partner into your internal message format.

▶ **Involvement of multiple systems**
A B2B integration scenario typically crosses multiple systems within your system landscape. As a minimum you have your backend application system and

the SAP NetWeaver PI system as your integration broker involved in the transmission of a message. Different system landscape options are discussed in Section 7.2 System Landscape.

▶ **Security setting requirements**
A B2B integration scenario not only crosses multiple systems, but it also crosses different security areas. Each message typically starts within a highly secured area at one end, and it ends in a highly secured area on the other end. In between, the message needs to cross a number of firewalls protecting these secured areas. In between, the message travels through unsecured areas such as the open Internet, which requires the message to be protected through other means such as encryption. For the B2B parties to be able to communicate, they need to exchange different types of information such as user certificates for authentication or public key certificates for encryption.

▶ **Involvement of multiple parties**
One characteristic of a B2B integration process is that multiple parties are involved. Therefore, you don't have control over the entire process, but you rely on your business partner to execute an integration test. To bypass this issue to some degree you can test your side of the scenario against tools simulating your trading partner.

Due to the complexity of a B2B integration process, we need to break the scenario into smaller units and first execute a unit test for each of these modules. Figure 11.1 shows the high-level message flow and a break down into different sections for testing. In particular, we take a closer look at the following areas:

❶ First, you need to test that messages send out from your backend system reach the SAP NetWeaver PI system that you use as your middleware layer and vice versa.

❷ Within the Integration Engine of SAP NetWeaver PI you can check if all pipeline steps can be executed appropriately. Here you check if the configuration in the Integration Directory is set up correctly and if the operation mapping you use returns valid results.

❸ Within SAP NetWeaver PI you can test if a message in the XI message format is processed correctly through the Integration Engine and further by the outbound adapter. You can test both outbound scenarios and inbound scenarios.

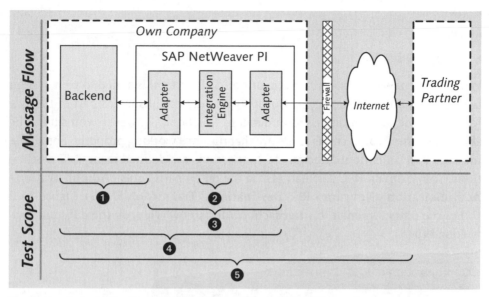

Figure 11.1 Areas for Testing Along the Message Flow of a B2B Message

❹ Within your system landscape you can test if a message that is created in your backend application system is processed correctly within your own system landscape and sent out in the correct format.

❺ Ultimately, you need to test if a message that you create in your backend application system is received and processed by your trading partner and vice versa.

In the next sections of this chapter we discuss each of these steps in detail and show the tools provided by SAP NetWeaver PI to support these modular tests.

11.2   Testing the Connections within your System Landscape

Any message you exchange with your trading partner is normally generated in the backend application system and then passed to the SAP NetWeaver PI system (as your integration server) for further processing. To exchange messages in such a scenario you first need to enable the connection between your backend application systems and your SAP NetWeaver PI system that serves as the integration server. The configuration of these connections can differ based on the type of message that is created in the backend application system, such as:

- ► IDocs

- ► RFCs

- ► Enterprise services

Whenever a new system (SAP system or non-SAP system) is added to your system landscape, these connections are normally already established as part of the system setup and are not discussed in detail in this book. However, you should be able to test these connections to ensure that they are working properly. For all the message types mentioned above, the connections are defined using RFC destinations. You maintain RFC destinations via the menu path **Tools • Administration • Administration • Network • RFC Destinations** (Transaction SM59). Figure 11.2 shows the entry screen of this transaction with an overview on the different connection types.

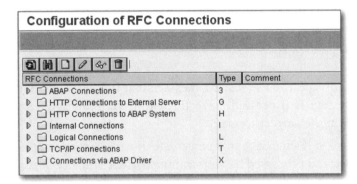

Figure 11.2 Configuration of RFC Destinations Using Transaction SM59

Depending on the type of message you use for communication, different types of connections need to be established. The following connection types are used to connect the different systems for message exchange:

- ► **ABAP connections**
  ABAP connections are used to connect to SAP application systems that are based on the SAP Web Application Server.

- ► **HTTP connections to ABAP system**
  This connection type enables you to conect to another SAP system using HTTP.

- ► **TCP/IP connections**
  TCP/IP connections are used for connections to external programs that communicate with the RFC library.

You can test the connection to the remote system using the same Transaction SM59. In the detailed view for a specific connection you can click the **Connection Test** button to test the connection (see Figure 11.3).

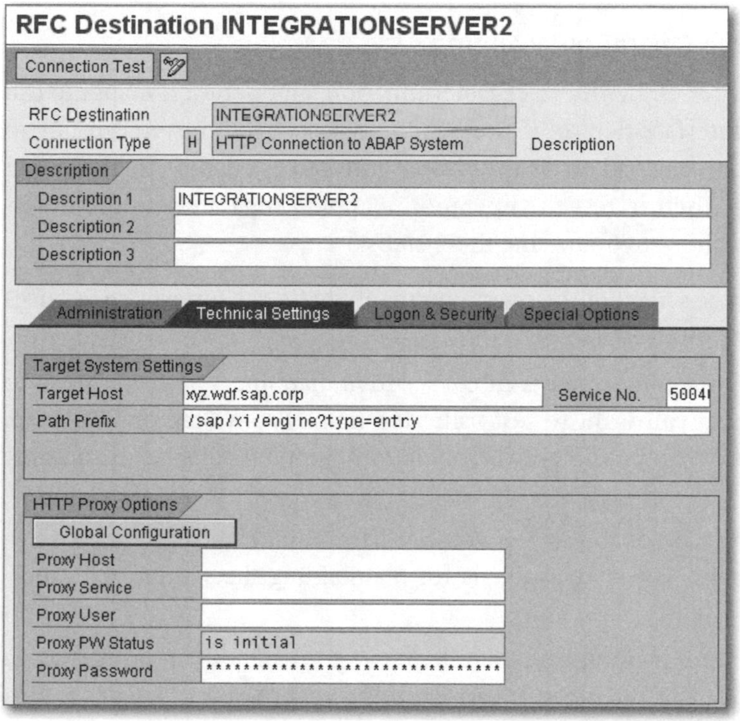

Figure 11.3 Detailed Screen for Configuration of RFC Destinations

11.3 Testing the Process in the Integration Engine

A number of test tools are available to test parts of the process that is executed in the Integration Engine. In particular, you can test the mappings (message mapping and operation mapping) and the configuration in the Integration Directory. In the next sections we discuss each of these test tools in detail.

11.3.1 Testing the Message Mapping

We already discussed the testing capabilities for message mappings in Section 8.4.4 Testing and Debugging Capabilities. You use this feature more during the development of a message mapping due to its debugging capabilities than for testing the finished scenario. For this reason we don't discuss this feature any further in this section.

11.3.2 Testing the Operation Mapping

As discussed in Section 9.3.2 Interface Determination, an operation mapping can be assigned to an interface determination where it is executed during runtime to convert the message payload from the source interface structure to the target interface structure. You can test the operation mapping separately in the Enterprise Services Repository by following these steps:

1. In the maintenance screen of the operation mapping (in the Enterprise Services Repository) select the **Test** tab.

2. If the operation mapping consists of consecutive mapping steps, you need to specify which step you want to test using the fields **From Step** and **To Step**. This information is only visible if the operation mapping consists of multiple steps.

3. In the right-hand side of the screen you need to provide a sample XML message. The following views are available for maintaining the sample XML message:

   ▶ You can view and maintain the sample message in a list form (as shown in Figure 11.4). This is the default view for this screen. You can always return to this view by clicking the **Tabular Tree View** icon (⊞).

   ▶ You can view and maintain the sample message in the form of an XML document. You can switch to this view by clicking the **Source Text View** icon (🔳).

   You can also import an XML message from your local file system by clicking the **Load Test Instance** icon (🔳). You can use this option to test the mapping with test XML messages provided by your trading partner.

4. If your mapping utilizes parameters, you can maintain sample values for these parameters on the **Parameters** tab.

5. You start the execution of the operation mapping by clicking the **Start the Transformation** icon (🔳). The result of the mapping is displayed in the left-hand side of the screen. If the mapping failed, you can find the trace with the information on the cause of the error in the bottom part of the screen.

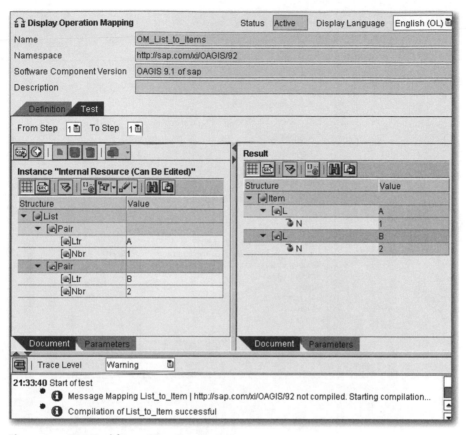

Figure 11.4 Test Tool for an Operation Mapping

11.3.3 Testing the Configuration

As just mentioned, the operation mapping we tested in the previous section is assigned to the configuration (setup in the Integration Directory) via the interface determination and executed during runtime. There is also a test tool for the configuration itself that is set up in the Integration Directory. This test tool uses as input a message in the XI message format and executes the configuration steps defined in the Integration Directory. The tool does not execute the steps handled by the inbound adapter or outbound adapter.

You can execute the test tool by following these steps:

1. In the Integration Directory follow the menu path **Tools • Test Configuration**. The configuration test screen is displayed as shown in Figure 11.5.

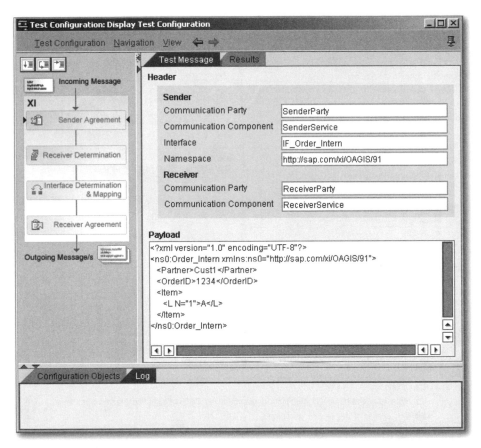

Figure 11.5 Configuration Test Screen

2. In the right-hand side of the screen maintain the following information for the message configuration you want to test:

   ▶ Maintain the header information and receiver information of the XI message you want to test in the section labeled **Header**. This information consists of the communication party and component for the sender and for the receiver, as well as the sender interface information.

   ▶ Enter the message payload of your test message in the form of an XML document in the section labeled **Payload**.

3. Execute the test of the configuration by choosing any of the following options:

   ▶ You can execute the complete configuration by clicking the **Run** icon (⬇≡). With this option all configuration steps are executed at once.

▶ You can execute each configuration step individually by clicking the **Step Over** icon (⬛). With this option only one configuration step is executed at a time.

After you execute the test you can view the result as shown in Figure 11.6. The following steps are executed as part of the test:

▶ Sender agreement

▶ Receiver determination

▶ Interface determination and mapping

▶ Receiver agreement

Figure 11.6 shows an example in which the sender agreement, receiver determination, and interface determination and mapping have been executed successfully, denoted by a green checkmark (✓),whereas the receiver agreement has failed, denoted by a red stop sign (⬤).

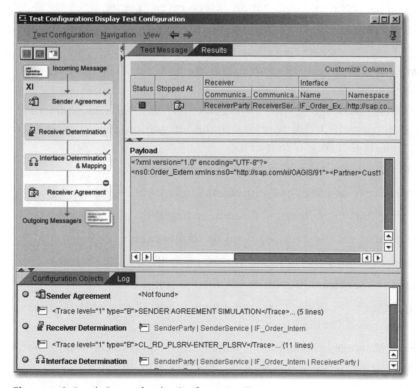

Figure 11.6 Result Screen for the Configuration Test

11.4   Testing the Process in SAP NetWeaver PI

You can trigger the execution of a message with a test tool available in the Runtime Workbench of your SAP NetWeaver PI system. Unlike the test tools discussed in the previous sections, this test tool not only simulates the execution of a message, but it actually triggers the execution of a message starting in the Integration Engine with the following consequences:

▶ In an inbound scenario triggered by the test tool, the relevant documents (for example, a sales order) can be created in the SAP backend application system, provided the required configuration is in place.

▶ In an outbound scenario triggered by the test tool, the message can be sent out to your business partner, provided the required configuration is in place.

You can trigger the execution of a message with this test tool by following these steps:

1. Start the Runtime Workbench in your SAP NetWeaver PI system.

2. In the Runtime Workbench select **Component Monitoring**. Display all components by clicking the **Display** button.

3. In the component list select **Integration Engine** under the list entry **Integration Server**.

4. Switch to the **Test Message** tab. Here you can enter your test data as shown in Figure 11.7. Because the test is triggered in the Integration Engine, a message using the XI message format is required.

5. In the section **Header Information** enter the following data:

   ▷ The **Sender Party** and **Sender Component** used by your test message

   ▷ The **Receiver Party** and **Receiver Component** used by your test message

   ▷ The **Interface** of your test message and its **Namespace**

   ▷ A **User** and **Password** that are used for the execution of the message

   ▷ The **Quality of Service** you want to use for the test message

6. Enter the message payload of your test message in form of an XML document in the section labeled **Payload**.

7. Click the **Send Message** button. The message is now triggered and can be monitored using the tools discussed in Chapter 5 Central Monitoring.

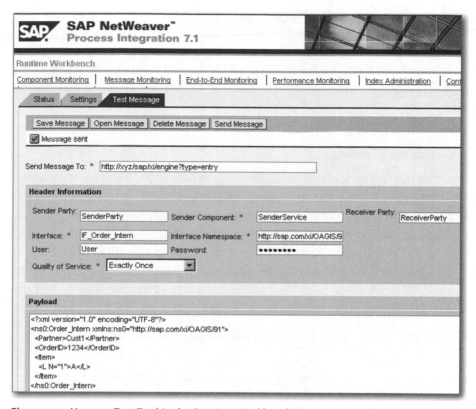

Figure 11.7 Message Test Tool in the Runtime Workbench

11.5 Testing the Process in your System Landscape

In Section 11.4 Testing the Process in SAP NetWeaver PI, we described a test tool that triggers the execution of an actual message. Whereas a message triggered by this test tool in an inbound scenario can also be processed in your backend application system, this is not true for an outbound scenario. Therefore, you need to perform some tests for your outbound scenarios not using a test tool, but starting the process in your backend system itself. Because the trigger of a message in the backend system depends on the scenario you want to execute, we cannot discuss such a configuration detail.

Typically, the B2B process is started with the creation of an IDoc or with the call of a B2B enterprise service. Some examples of how to set up such scenarios in the backend are provided in Chapter 12 Real-Life Test Scenarios.

11.6 Testing the Complete Scenario

Testing the complete scenario involves two types of testing. First, you can test the complete scenario by simulating your trading partner with an appropriate test tool (if available). Second, you need to perform the test with your actual trading partner.

11.6.1 Internal Testing

Several third-party test tools are available for each industry standard (for example, the RosettaNet self-test kit to perform an end-to-end scenario testing of Rosetta-Net scenarios) to test the complete end-to-end scenario. These test tools provide the tools and utilities with the capability to test the validity, interoperability, and compliance with the industry standard specifications. In the absence of any test tool for a given industry standard, the noncentral adapter engine or another instance of SAP NetWeaver PI can be used as a partner simulation tool to test the scenario. Several test scenarios can be developed to test the following test cases:

▶ Test the compliance with industry standard specifications for packaging, security, and transport.

▶ Perform transport and connectivity tests that include SSL, digital certificates, encryption, and use of multiple algorithms to support digital signatures and encryption.

▶ Test the choreography of business messages exchanged for each specific industry transaction implemented.

▶ Test the ability to handle exceptions and errors in the headers and message manifest of the B2B message and generate appropriate notification of failure (NOF) messages.

▶ Test the ability to retry messages and handle partner message retry.

11.6.2 Testing with the Trading Partner

The final step of your testing involves testing the scenario with your trading partner after the internal system and compliance testing has been completed. Effective testing of the scenario requires a collaborative effort between the trading partners and can be the most time-consuming process. It needs a dedicated time from the teams of both the trading partners to fully test and validate the scenario.

A typical B2B engagement with the trading partners involves the rollout and testing of the scenario at four different phases:

▸ **Trading partner engagement**
Prior to the testing, it is important to asses the readiness of the key trading partners with whom you want to exchange the business-to-business messages. This phase includes engaging the partner to test the scenario, choosing the processes, detailed integration, and achieving reliable results.

The process of working with the trading partner during the test phase can be achieved through the proper documentation outlining the test scenario, a sample business document with required elements, exact testing and production dates, discussion of retry and interpretation on timeouts, and the exchange of digital certificates. The trading partner agreement should clearly specify the interoperability and validity issues of the message exchange and set the overall expectations for the message processing.

▸ **Connectivity**
Connectivity testing ensures that your system is able to communicate with your trading partner's system outside the firewall and is able to send and receive messages. It ensures compliance with the industry standard specifications for the transport, routing, and packaging (TRP) of the message.

During this phase, it is important to outline the security requirements to your partner for encryption, authentication, and authorization at the network and at the message exchange level. This phase includes exchanging the HTTPS information with your trading partner such as URLs, digital certificates and digital signatures for test and production environment, D-U-N-S numbers, and so on. It also includes setting up firewalls, proxy servers, network routing, and role-based and controlled access to message content, performing transport and connectivity testing using HTTPS, SSL, and the use of digital certificates. This testing phase determines that a strongly encrypted trading session can be established between the trading partners.

▸ **Structure and syntax check**
This phase determines that the messages involed in the testing are well formed and valid. The testing includes checking the choreography of the message and adherence of the message to the message guidelines specified in the industry standard. This phase also includes testing the ability to handle exceptions and the ability to generate the appropriate notification of failures (NOF).

▶ **Data content validation**
During this phase, the data received from the trading partner is fed into the backend systems and checked for validity. This phase also includes testing the business alerts, testing the subsequent activities in case of failure, and checking the business process flows and exception flows.

11.7 Summary

After reading this chapter you should be familiar with the test tools available in SAP NetWeaver PI for testing message flow within your system landscape. In addition, you should have an understanding of the additional tests you are required to perform with your trading partner to set up a B2B integration scenario.

This chapter provides some sample test scenarios using various B2B indus-
try standards and protocols. For each scenario we provide step-by-step
instructions on how to design and configure these scenarios.

12   Real-Life Test Scenarios

In this chapter we cover a set of real-life business-to-business scenarios involving the design and configuration of SAP NetWeaver PI using various industry standards. As an example we use a purchase order that we receive from our trading partner and that we process in an SAP ERP backend system called XYZ using IDoc functionality. The SAP NetWeaver PI system used as the integration broker is a system called ABC.

This chapter is organized as follows:

▶ **Backend preparation**
In Section 12.1 we discuss some steps for the preparation of the backend. These steps are relevant for all industry standards we discuss in this chapter.

▶ **SAP NetWeaver PI preparation**
In Section 12.2 we discuss some generic steps to prepare the SAP NetWeaver PI system for B2B integration scenarios. These steps are relevant for all industry standards we discuss in this chapter as well.

▶ **B2B Integration using the CIDX standard**
In Section 12.3 we describe the implementation of the CIDX message Order Create (E41) using the business package available from SAP.

▶ **B2B Integration using the PIDX standard**
In Section 12.4 we describe the implementation of the PIDX message Order Create. For this scenario no predefined business package is available.

▶ **B2B integration using the RosettaNet standard**
In Section 12.5 we describe the implementation of the RosettaNet message PIP3A4 (Order Creation) along with the confirmation message using the business package available from SAP.

> ▶ **B2B integration using the EDI standard ANSI X12**
> In Section 12.6 we describe an implementation of an EDI scenario using the AS2 adapter provided by SEEBURGER.

12.1   Backend Preparation

This section describes the steps required for setting up the backend system for receiving and sending IDocs from your trading partners. Because the B2B system requires the purchasing and sales applications to be configured in order to receive the messages from your trading partners, the necessary configuration needs to be done in the SAP Material Management (MM), Sales and Distribution (SD), and Financials and Controlling (FI/CO) modules. However, this procedure is normally performed by the MM and SD configuration areas according to their requirements. Only the B2B-specific areas of MM and SD need to be set up for B2B purposes.

In the following examples we need to configure the Order Create inbound message to receive an inbound order IDoc for CIDX, PIDX, and EDI scenarios. For the RosettaNet scenario we need to configure the Order Create and Order Confirmation message used in a two-action process.

12.1.1   Inbound Processing

In the inbound process a purchase order request is sent from your trading partner and needs to be processed as a sales order in the SAP application system (XYZ) using IDoc functionality.

Definition of a Partner Profile

First, you need to maintain the partner profile for B2B communication to receive messages from your trading partner using the following steps:

1. In the SAP application system (XYZ) follow the menu path **Tools • Business Communication • IDoc Basis • IDoc • Partner Profile** or start Transaction WE20.

2. Maintain the inbound parameters for the sales order inbound message as listed in Table 12.1 (see Figure 12.1 for an example).

3. Save the partner profile.

Field	Value
Partner Number	Your customer, e.g., DEMO_CUST
Partner Type	KU (for customer)
Partner Role	SP (for sold-to party)
Message Type	ORDERS
Process Code	ORDE
Syntax Check	Checked
Trigger Immediately	Checked

Table 12.1 Inbound Parameters for a Partner Profile

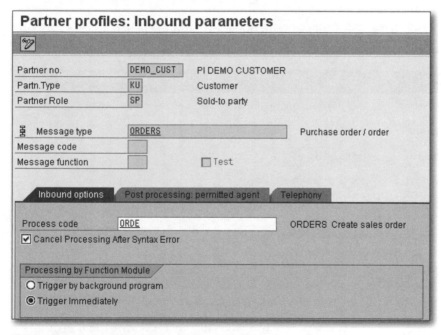

Figure 12.1 Example of an Inbound Partner Profile

12.1.2 Outbound Processing

In the outbound process a sales order confirmation is sent to your trading partner out of the SAP application system (XYZ) using IDoc functionality. A number of steps are required to set up the application system for this process.

Definition of an RFC Destination

You need to maintain an *RFC destination* (remote function call) in the SAP application system in order to communicate with SAP NetWeaver PI using the following steps:

1. In the SAP application system (XYZ) follow the menu path **Tools · Administration · Administration · Network · RFC Destination** or start Transaction SM59.

2. Create a new RFC destination of the type **R/3 Connections**. Maintain the name for the **RFC Destination** and the **Connection Type**. As the name use the value **XXXCLNT100,** where XXX stands for the system ID of your SAP NetWeaver PI system, and 100 is the client of your SAP NetWeaver PI system. Set the connection type to **3** (**R/3 Connection**).

3. On the **Technical Settings** tab maintain the information as listed in Table 12.2 (see Figure 12.2 for an example).

4. On the **Logon/Security** tab maintain the information as listed in Table 12.3 (see Figure 12.3 for an example).[1]

Field	Value
Target Host	\<PI system host name\>
System Number	\<PI system number\>
Balance Load	**Yes** or **No**
Gateway Host	\<PI system host name\>
Gateway Service	sapgw\<PI system number\>[1]

Table 12.2 Technical Settings of an RFC Destination

Field	Value
Trusted System	Select **Yes** if your SAP NetWeaver PI system is a trusted system
SNC	If you have an active SNC-supported security system, you can activate additional security
Language	Your language, for example, EN
Client	\<SAP NetWeaver PI system client number\>

Table 12.3 Logon/Security Settings of an RFC Destination

---

1 For information on the system number, use Transaction RZ03 on the SAP NetWeaver PI system.

Field	Value
User	<SAP NetWeaver PI user name>
Password	<SAP NetWeaver PI user password>

Table 12.3 Logon/Security Settings of an RFC Destination (cont.)

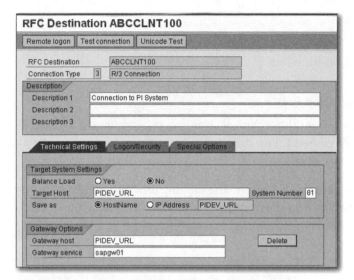

Figure 12.2 Technical Settings of an RFC Destination

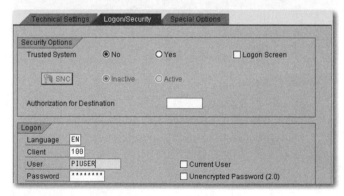

Figure 12.3 Logon/Security Settings of an RFC Destination

5. You can test the connection using the button **Test connection**. If the connection is successful, it will display the connection information as shown in Figure 12.4.

```
R F C - Connection Test

[icon]


                          Connection test ABCCLNT100

  Connection type:    R/3 connection

  Logon:                   1.712  msec
      0  KB:                  199  msec
     10  KB:                  186  msec
     20  KB:                  186  msec
     30  KB:                  186  msec
```

Figure 12.4 RFC Destination Connection Test

Definition of a Communication Port

The communication port defines the technical connection between the SAP back-end system and SAP NetWeaver PI. You define a communication port by following these steps:

1. In the SAP application system (XYZ) follow the menu path **Tools • ALE • ALE Administration • Runtime Settings • Port Maintenance** or start Transaction WE21.

2. Maintain a transactional RFC port with the values listed in Table 12.4 (see Figure 12.5 for an example).

3. Save the RFC port.

Field	Value
Port	PICLNT100
RFC destination	XYZCLNT100 (the RFC destination as defined in the previous step)

Table 12.4 Settings for a Transactional RFC Port

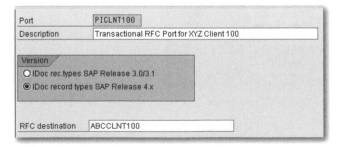

```
Port              PICLNT100
Description       Transactional RFC Port for XYZ Client 100

 Version
  O IDoc rec.types SAP Release 3.0/3.1
  ◉ IDoc record types SAP Release 4.x



RFC destination   ABCCLNT100
```

Figure 12.5 Communication Port Definition

Definition of an Outbound Partner Profile

You need to maintain the partner profile for B2B communication in order to send messages to your trading partner using the following steps:

1. In the SAP application system (XYZ) follow the menu path **Tools • Business Communication • IDoc Basis • IDoc • Partner Profile** or start Transaction WE20.

2. Maintain the header information of the outbound parameters for the sales order confirmation outbound message as listed in Table 12.5 (see Figure 12.6 for an example).

3. On the **Outbound Options** tab maintain the parameters as listed in Table 12.6 (see Figure 12.6 for an example).

4. On the **Message Control** tab maintain the parameters as listed in Table 12.7 (see Figure 12.7 for an example).

5. Save the partner profile.

Field	Value
Partner Number	Your customer, e.g., DEMO_CUST
Partner Type	KU (for customer)
Partner Role	SP (for sold-to party)
Message Type	ORDERS

Table 12.5 Header Settings for an Outbound Partner Profile

Field	Value
Receiver port	PICLNT100
Pack.size	1
Basic Type	ORDERS05
Syntax Check	Checked
Transfer IDoc Immediately	Checked

Table 12.6 Outbound Control Options for an Outbound Partner Profile

Field	Value
Application	V1
Message Type	BA00
Process Code	SD10

Table 12.7 Message Control Options for an Outbound Partner Profile

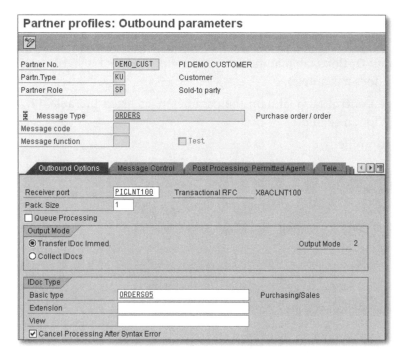

Figure 12.6 Outbound Options Tab of the Outbound Partner Profile

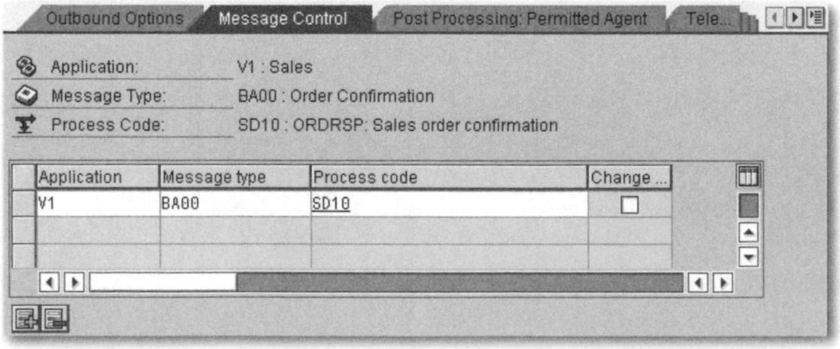

Figure 12.7 Message Control Tab of the Outbound Partner Profile

12.2 SAP NetWeaver PI Preparation

This section describes the steps required for setting up the SAP NetWeaver PI system for receiving and sending IDocs from your application system. This step is independent of the industry standard used for communication with your trading partner. Therefore, this section is relevant for all scenarios we discuss in the subsequent sections. In addition, we discuss some generic steps for the download and the installation of SAP NetWcaver PI content business packages.

12.2.1 System Landscape Directory

The appropriate software components for these industry standards are available in the System Landscape Directory (SLD) as part of the component repository content (CR content). This content is provided by SAP and is available in the SAP Service Marketplace (*http://service.sap.com*). Section 7.3.2 Implementation of Existing SAP NetWeaver PI Content Packages provides more information on how to download content from this marketplace. You need to ensure that the updated content is available for the respective industry standard in the SLD.[2]

12.2.2 Download and Installation of a Business Package

As discussed in Section 4.4 Predefined Integration Content (SOA Business Content), SAP delivers predefined integration content in the form of business packages for some industry standard verticals such as RosettaNet, CIDX, and so on. In addition, predefined content for EDI standards such as ANSI X12 and EDIFACT is delivered by the SAP partner SEEBURGER. These business packages contain the content for the most commonly used order-to-cash scenarios.

We use these business packages in implementing our test scenarios. They are available on the SAP Service Marketplace subject to the license agreement associated with each package. The industry content typically is composed of two software components, namely, the standard content and the integration content. Table 12.8 lists the software components that are available with each of the business packages.

---

2 For information on how to update the SAP component repository content (CR Content), see SAP Note 669669.

Standard	Standard Content	Integration Content
CIDX	CIDX	CIDX ERP
RosettaNet	RosettaNet	RosettaNet ERP
PIDX	PIDX	Not available
ANSI X12	▸ SEEBURGER_GENERIC_EDI ▸ SEEBURGER_EDI_ADAPTER	

Table 12.8 Software Components Containing Industry Standard — Specific Content

The business packages for the relevant industry standards are available in two archive files. These files have the extension of *.tpz*. You need to first download the content from the SAP Service Marketplace and then import it into the Enterprise Services Repository.[3] You can copy these imported archive files into the import directory of the SAP NetWeaver PI host machine via the path **<PI Host>** • **sapmnt** • **<PI System ID>** • **SYS** • **global** • **repository_server** • **import**.[4] Instructions to import these files into the Enterprise Services Repository will be discussed in detail in the scenario-specific section.

12.2.3 Definition of an RFC Destination

Just as in the SAP application system, you need to maintain an RFC destination in SAP NetWeaver PI to communicate with the SAP application system using the following steps:

1. In SAP NetWeaver PI (system ABC) start Transaction SM59.

2. You need to create a new RFC destination of the type **ABAP Connections**. Maintain the name for the **RFC Destination** and the **Connection Type**. As the name use the value XXXCLNT100, where XXX stands for the System ID of your SAP application system, and 100 is the client of your SAP application system. Set the connection type to **3 (ABAP Connection)**.

---

3 The installation guide for the relevant business package is available at the SAP Service Marketplace.

4 As of SAP NetWeaver PI 7.1, this content can be imported into the Enterprise Services Repository either from a server directory or from a directory of your local PC (client). SAP recommends that you import Enterprise Services Repository content from the server directory.

3. On the **Technical Settings** tab maintain the information as listed in Table 12.9 (see Figure 12.8 for an example).

Field	Value
Target Host	<SAP application system host name>
System Number	<SAP application system number>
Balance Load	**Yes** or **No**
Gateway Host	<SAP application system host name>
Gateway Service	sapgw<SAP application system number>[5]

Table 12.9 Technical Settings of an RFC Destination

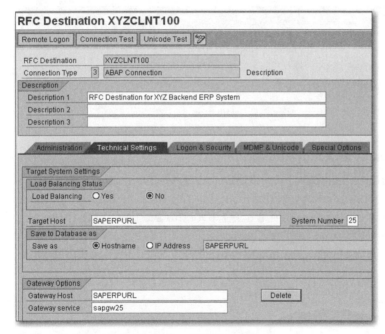

Figure 12.8 Technical Settings of an RFC Destination

4. On the **Logon & Security** tab maintain the information as listed in Table 12.10.

5. On the **MDMP & Unicode** tab maintain the information as listed in Table 12.11.

---

5 For information on the system number, use Transaction RZ03 on the SAP application system.

Field	Value
Trusted System	Select **Yes** if your SAP NetWeaver PI system is a trusted system
SNC	If you have an active SNC-supported security system, you can activate additional security
Language	Your language, for example, EN
Client	<SAP application system client number>
User	< SAP application user name>
Password	< SAP application user password>

Table 12.10 Logon & Security Settings of an RFC Destination

Field	Value
Unicode	Select **Unicode** if your SAP application system is a unicode system
MDMP Settings	Select **Active** if you have a multidisplay, multiprocessing (MDMP) code page system that uses more than one code page on the server

Table 12.11 MDMP & Unicode Settings of an RFC Destination

12.2.4 Definition of a Communication Port

You maintain the communication port in SAP NetWeaver PI to establish a connection to the SAP application system that contains the IDoc metadata. The IDoc adapter uses this metadata to convert the SAP IDocs to the IDoc XML format. In the SAP NetWeaver PI system (ABC) follow the menu path **Process Integration • Configuration • Port Maintenance in IDoc Adapter** or start Transaction IDX1 to load the IDoc metadata with the information as shown in Figure 12.9.

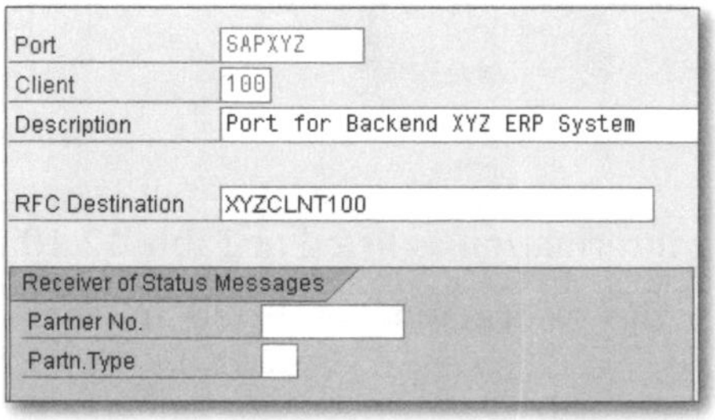

Figure 12.9 Definition of a Communication Port

12.2.5 Definition of a Communication Channel

We need to define a communication channel for the IDoc communication between the SAP application system and SAP NetWeaver PI. Because this channel is identical for all subsequent scenarios, we discuss the creation of a communication channel in this section. The creation of a communication channel is covered in Section 9.2.3 Communication Channel. We need to use the information listed in Table 12.12 and Table 12.13 (see also Figure 12.10 and Figure 12.11).

Field	Value
Transport Protocol	IDoc
Message Protocol	IDoc
Adapter Engine	Integration Server
RFC Destination	XYZCLNT100 (the RFC destination as defined in Section 12.2.3 Definition of an RFC Destination)
Interface Version	SAP Release 4.0 or higher
Port	SAPXYZ (the communication port as defined in Section 12.2.4 Definition of a Communication Port)
SAP Release	5.0 (the release of your SAP application system)
Apply Control Record Values from Payload	Checked

Table 12.12 Parameter Settings of the Communication Channel

Field	Value
Sender Agency	<Business system as defined in the SLD>
Sender Schema	ALE#LI#LF
Receiver Agency	<Business system as defined in the SLD>
Receiver Schema	ALE#LS

Table 12.13 Identifiers Used in the Communication Channel

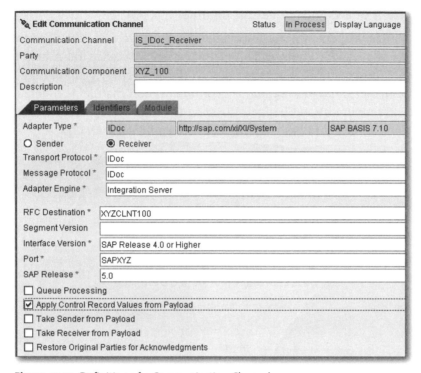

Figure 12.10 Definition of a Communication Channel

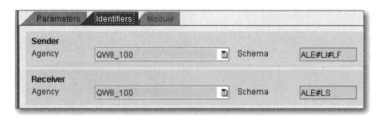

Figure 12.11 Identifiers Used in the Communication Channel

12.3 B2B Integration Using the CIDX Standard

In this scenario we implement an asynchronous single-action Order Create scenario. The Order Create process is initiated when a buyer commits to buy a product from the seller. The buyer sends an Order Create message (E41) to the seller. Upon receipt of the message the seller sends a technical receipt acknowledgement to the buyer. Figure 12.12 shows the scenario we implement in this section.

Seller   Buyer

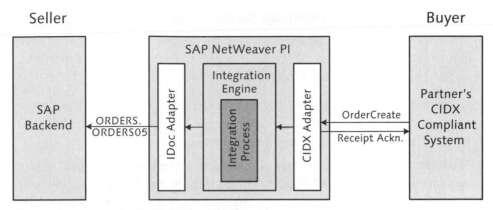

Figure 12.12 CIDX Order Create Single-Action Asynchronous Scenario

12.3.1 Activities in the System Landscape Directory

First, you need to check in the System Landscape Directory (SLD) to see if the software components containing the CIDX-specific content exist. You can do that by following these steps:

1. In the Enterprise Services Builder home page, select **System Landscape Directory**. This will launch the SLD in a separate window.

2. In the next screen, select **Software Components** from the software catalog panel.

3. The CIDX software components are part of the component repository content (CR content) in the SLD delivered by SAP. In the software components page, enter a filter CIDX* to restrict the number of software components displayed. The search results should display two software components, as shown in Figure 12.13. If the search results in a blank screen, you must update the CR content in the SLD.[6]

▲ Software Component	▲ Version	Vendor
CIDX	CIDX 1.0	sap.com
CIDX AP	CIDX AP 1.0	sap.com
CIDX ERP	CIDX ERP 1.0	sap.com

Figure 12.13 Software Components in the SLD Related to CIDX

---

6 For more details on updating the CR content, refer to SAP Note 669669.

12.3.2 Activities in the Enterprise Services Repository

In the Enterprise Services Repository you need to check to see if the software components containing the CIDX-specific content are imported into the Enterprise Services Repository. You can do that by following these steps:

1. In the Enterprise Services Builder check to see whether the software components **CIDX** and **CIDX ERP** are available in the list structure on the left-hand frame. You can skip step 2 if they are available.

2. From the main menu, select **Tools • Import Design Objects**. In the next pop-up window, select **Server** and import the *.tpz* files for the software components CIDX and CIDX ERP from the import directory of the PI Host System. The sequence in which you import these files is not important. The newly imported software components should appear in the left-hand frame of the Enterprise Services Builder.

3. The CIDX software component consists of ChemeStandard content such as process integration scenarios, actions, service interfaces, communication channel templates, and the ChemeStandard interfaces in the form external definitions. Figure 12.14 shows an example of the CIDX software component in the Enterprise Services Repository. You need to ensure that the necessary objects for your scenario are available in this software component.

4. The CIDX ERP software component consists of integration content such as process integration scenarios, actions, operations mappings, and message mappings. Figure 12.15 shows an example of the CIDX ERP software component in the Enterprise Services Repository. You need to ensure that the necessary objects for your scenario are available in this software component.

5. The mapping objects in the software component CIDX ERP assume that the SAP IDoc interfaces that are used in the mapping are available in the SAP APPL software component. You must ensure that all relevant SAP interfaces for your scenario are imported and available under this software component. For our scenarios we need the IDoc ORDERS.ORDERS05.

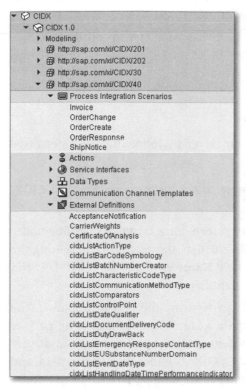

Figure 12.14 CIDX Software Component in the Enterprise Services Repository

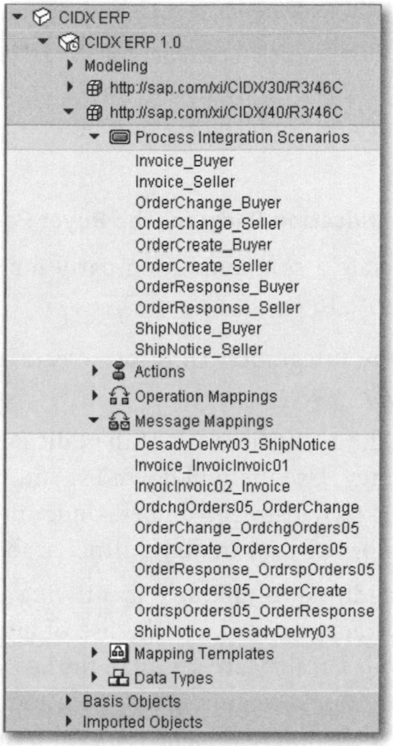

Figure 12.15 CIDX ERP Software Component in the Enterprise Services Repository

12.3.3 Creation of Collaboration Profiles

We use the Model Configurator for the creation of the configuration in the Integration Directory. Before you can use the configurator you need to set up the collaboration profile for the buyer party and the sender party. Overall you need to create the following objects:

- A *buyer party* in the form of a communication party representing your trading partner. We assume that the buyer party is called CIDXBuyer.
- A *business component* assigned to the buyer party.
- A *communication channel* assigned to the business component underneath the buyer party.
- A *seller party* in form of a communication party representing your own company. We assume that the seller party is called SAPSeller.

▸ A *business component* assigned to the seller party.

▸ A *communication channel* for the seller party has been created centrally in Section 12.3.2 Activities in the Enterprise Services Repository. Therefore, we don't need to take care of it here.

Communication Party for the Buyer Party

You create a communication party for your buyer by following these steps (see Figure 12.16 for an example):

1. In the Integration Directory create a new communication party called CIDX-Buyer.

2. On the **Identifiers** tab of the **Edit Party** screen, click on the empty line under **Agency**. Use the pull-down list and select **016** as the agency, representing the DUN & Bradstreet Number. Under the field **Name** enter the nine-digit D-U-N-S number of your trading partner as the identifier.

3. In addition to uniquely identifying the party using the D-U-N-S number, the IDoc adapter requires the use of alternative identifiers to link to the partner profiles as they are set up in the SAP systems. Use the pull-down list and enter XYZ_100 under the **Agency** field and ALE#KU#AG under the **Scheme** field, and enter the internal name for your customer (for example, DEMO_CUST) under the **Name** field. This field is used to uniquely identify the party in the SAP back-end application system.

4. Save and activate the communication party.

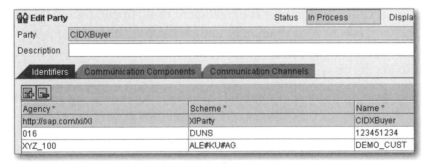

Figure 12.16 Definition of the Buyer Party

Communication Component for the Buyer Party

The communication components must follow specific naming conventions to work with the CIDX adapter. The name must be of the form `CIDX<Transaction Code>_Version_<Partner Role>`, for example, `CIDXE41_201_Buyer`. `E41` is the ChemeStandard transaction code, `2.0.1` is the version, and `Buyer` is the partner role. You create a communication component underneath the communication party for your buyer by following these steps:

1. In the Integration Directory create a new communication component called CIDXE41_201_Buyer as a business component under the party CIDXBuyer.

2. On the **Sender** tab add the ChemeStandard interface OrderCreate (see Figure 12.17 for an example).

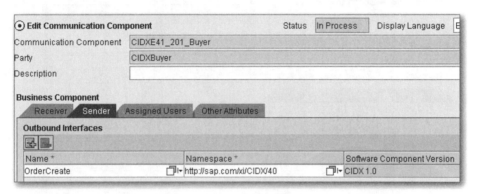

Figure 12.17 Definition of the Communication Component for the Buyer Party

3. Save and activate the communication component.

Communication Channel for the Buyer Party

In this scenario the buyer party communicates via the CIDX standard. Therefore, the communication channel must be based on the CIDX adapter. You create the communication channel by following these steps:

1. In the Integration Directory create a new communication channel under the party CIDXBuyer called Buyer_Send_OrderCreate.

2. Because we use an existing business package for the creation of the configuration, we can utilize a communication channel template for the creation of a communication channel. Select **Communication Channel • Apply Template** to

import the message-specific channel template Buyer_Send_OrderCreate from the Enterprise Services Repository. Most of the fields in the communication channel will be populated with this template. You still need to add some partner-specific information about the transport protocol and security information (see Figure 12.18).

3. Save and activate the communication channel.

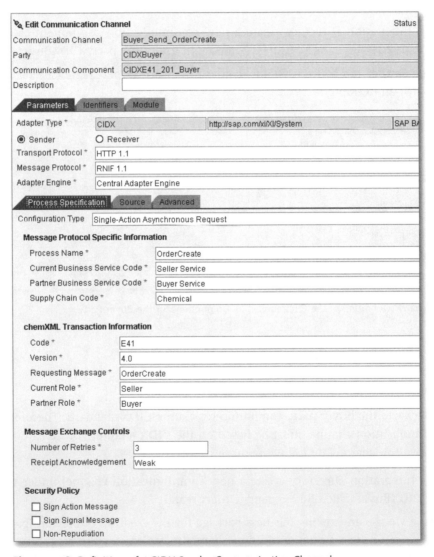

Figure 12.18 Definition of a CIDX Sender Communication Channel

Communication Party for the Seller Party

You create a communication party for your seller by following these steps:

1. In the Integration Directory create a new communication party called SAPSeller.

2. On the **Identifiers** tab of the **Edit Party** screen, click on the empty line under **Agency**. Use the pull-down list and select **016** as the agency, representing the DUN & Bradstreet Number. Under the field **Name** enter the nine-digit D-U-N-S number of your company as the identifier (see Figure 12.19 for an example).

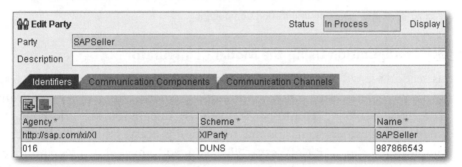

Figure 12.19 Definition of the Seller Party

3. Save and activate the communication party.

Communication Component for the Seller Party

The communication components must follow specific naming conventions to work with the CIDX adapter. The name must be of the form `CIDX<Transaction Code>_Version_<Partner Role>`, for example, `CIDXE41_201_Seller`. E41 is the ChemeStandard transaction code, `2.0.1` is the version, and `Buyer` is the partner role. You create a communication component underneath the communication party for your buyer by following these steps:

1. In the Integration Directory create a new communication component called CIDXE41_201_Seller as a business component under the party SAPSeller.

2. On the **Receiver** tab add the ChemeStandard interface OrderCreate (see Figure 12.20 for an example).

3. Save and activate the communication component.

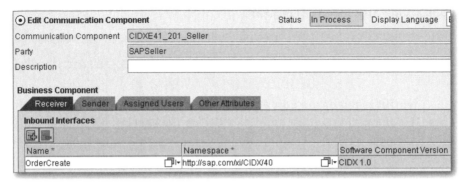

Figure 12.20 Definition of a Communication Component

12.3.4 Configuration Using the Model Configurator

In this section we will use the *Model Configurator* wizard to create the necessary configuration objects using a *process integration scenario* template selected from the Enterprise Services Repository. The process integration scenario contains information for business scenarios and integration processes that are relevant for communication using SAP NetWeaver PI. You need to have this integration scenario available in the Enterprise Services Repository in order to use the Model Configurator, which we discussed in detail in Section 9.6.1 Execution of the Model Configurator. In the first phase of the Model Configurator we need to provide the following information:

1. Enter the process integration scenario "OrderCreate_Seller" from software component CIDX ERP as your reference model (see Figure 12.21).

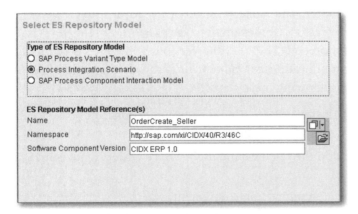

Figure 12.21 Transfer the Scenario from the ES Repository

2. Define a name for your configuration scenario. We use the name CIDXE41_
   CIDXBuyer_201_Buyer based on the naming convention `CIDX <Transaction`
   `Code>_<Partner>_<Version>_<Role>`.

In the second phase of the Model Configurator we need to provide the following
information:

1. You can skip the step **Select Model** because the process integration scenario
   contains only one model.

2. In the **Assign Components** step we need to provide assignments for two application components:

   ▶ For the component representing your company, use the business system
   component XYZ_100 (without a party), and for the external communication, use the party representing your company (for example, SAPSeller)
   and the service CIDXE41_201_Seller (see Figure 12.22).

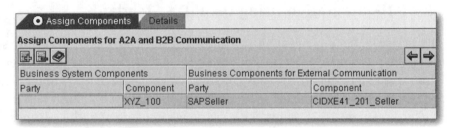

Figure 12.22 Component Assignment for the Seller Role

   ▶ For the component representing your business partner, use the name of
   your trading partner as the party (for example, CIDXBuyer) and the communication component CIDXE41_201_Buyer (see Figure 12.23).

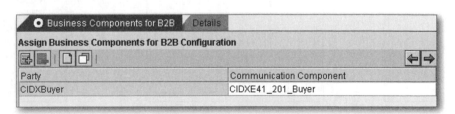

Figure 12.23 Component Assignment for the Buyer Role

3. In the **Configure Connections** step we need to assign the communication channels that should be used in our scenario:

▶ Enter "Buyer_Send_OrderCreate" as the sender communication channel.

▶ Enter "IS_IDoc_Receiver" as the receiver communication channel (see Figure 12.24).

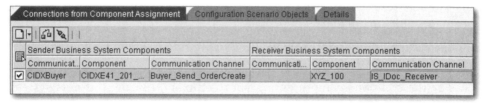

Figure 12.24 Configuration of Connections

12.4 B2B Integration Using the PIDX Standard

In this scenario we implement an asynchronous single-action Order Create scenario. The Order Create process is initiated when a buyer commits to buy a product from the seller. The buyer sends an Order Create message (P31) to the seller. Upon receipt of the message the seller sends a technical receipt acknowledgement to the buyer. Figure 12.25 shows the scenario we implement in this section.

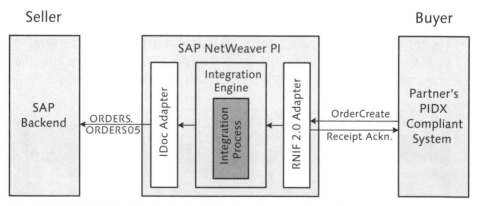

Figure 12.25 PIDX Order Create Single-Action Asynchronous Scenario

12.4.1 Activities in the System Landscape Directory

First, you need to check in the System Landscape Directory (SLD) to see if the software components containing the PIDX-specific content exist.

You can do that by following these steps:

1. In the Enterprise Services Builder home page, select **System Landscape Directory**. This will launch the SLD in a separate window.

2. In the next screen, select **Software Components** from the software catalog panel.

3. The PIDX software component is part of the component repository content (CR content) in the SLD delivered by SAP. On the software components page, enter a filter PIDX* to restrict the number of software components displayed. The search results should display two software components, as shown in Figure 12.26. If the search results in a blank screen, you must update the CR content in the SLD.[7]

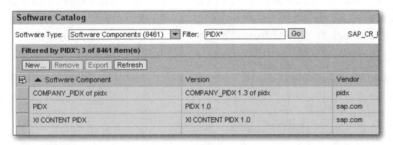

Figure 12.26 Software Components in the SLD Related to PIDX

4. Because the PIDX software component consists of only the standard content, you have to build your own software component with dependencies to the PIDX software component to house all of the integration objects such as process integration scenarios, mappings, communication channel templates, and so on. We named the newly created software component `<Company>_PIDX` (where `Company` is your own company).

---

7 For more details on updating the CR content, refer to SAP Note 669669.

12.4.2 Activities in the Enterprise Services Repository

In the Enterprise Services Repository you need to check if the software components containing the PIDX-specific content are imported into the Enterprise Services Repository.

You can do that by following these steps:

1. In the ES Builder check whether the software component PIDX is available in the list structure on the left-hand frame. You can skip step 2 if they are available.

2. From the main menu, select **Tools • Import Design Objects**. In the next pop-up window, select **Server** and import the *.tpz* files for the software component PIDX from the import directory of the SAP NetWeaver PI host system. The newly imported software component should appear in the left-hand frame of the ES Builder.

3. The PIDX software component consists of PIDX standard content such as service interfaces and the PIDX standard interfaces in the form of external definitions. Figure 12.27 shows as an example of the PIDX software component in the Enterprise Services Repository. You need to ensure that the necessary objects for your scenario are available in this software component.

4. Unlike the business package for CIDX, the package for PIDX does not contain any mappings between the PIDX standard interfaces and the SAP IDocs. Therefore, you need to create a new software component (for example, <Company>_PIDX) with a reference to software component PIDX. In this software component create the namespace http://sap.com/xi/RosettaNet/ <PIP version identifier>. As <PIP version identifier> use the version of the PIDX standard you want to support (for example, 10). This naming convention is required by the RNIF adapter that is used for the transport of PIDX messages.

5. In the namespace defined in the previous steps, create the following objects as listed in Table 12.14. Figure 12.28 shows an example of the created objects.

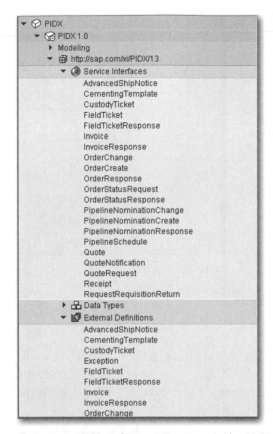

Figure 12.27 PIDX Software Component in the ES Repository

Object	Description
Message Mapping	Create a message mapping from the PIDX message P31 (Order Create) to the SAP IDoc ORDERS.ORDERS05.
Operation Mapping	Assign the message mapping to an operation mapping.
Process Integration Scenario	Create a process integration scenario for the order creation process using a PIDX message. We assume that the scenario is called OrderCreate_Seller.
Communication Channel Template	You can create a communication channel template that will be used in the creation of the sender communication channel (called Buyer_Send_OrderCreate).

Table 12.14 Objects To Be Created in Software Component <Company>_PIDX

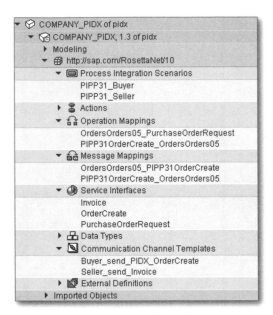

Figure 12.28 Objects Created in Software Component <Company>_PIDX

6. We assume that the SAP IDoc interfaces that are used in the mapping are available in the SAP APPL software component. You must ensure that all relevant SAP interfaces for your scenario are imported and available in this software component. For our scenarios we need the IDoc `ORDERS.ORDERS05`.

12.4.3 Creation of Collaboration Profiles

We use the Model Configurator for the creation of the configuration in the Integration Directory. Before you can use the configurator you need to set up the collaboration profile for the buyer party and for the sender party. Overall you need to create the following objects:

▶ A *buyer party* in the form of a communication party representing your trading partner. We assume that the buyer party is called PIDXBuyer.

▶ A *business component* assigned to the buyer party.

▶ A *communication channel* assigned to the business component underneath the buyer party.

▶ A *seller party* in the form of a communication party representing your own company. We assume that the seller party is called PIDXSeller.

▶ A *business component* assigned to the seller party.

▶ A *communication channel* for the seller party was created centrally in Section 12.3.2 Activities in the Enterprise Services Repository. Therefore, we don't need to take care of it here.

Communication Party for the Buyer Party

You create a communication party for your buyer by following these steps:

1. In the Integration Directory create a new communication party called PIDX-Buyer (see Figure 12.29).

2. On the **Identifiers** tab of the **Edit Party** screen, click on the empty line under **Agency**. Use the pull-down list and select **016** as the agency, representing the DUN & Bradstreet Number. Under the field **Name** enter the nine-digit D-U-N-S number of your trading partner as the identifier.

3. In addition to uniquely identifying the party using the D-U-N-S number, the IDoc adapter requires the use of alternative identifiers to link to the partner profiles as they are setup in the SAP systems. Use the pull-down list and enter "XYZ_100" under the **Agency** field, enter "ALE#KU#AG" under the **Scheme** field, and enter the internal name for your customer (for example, DEMO_CUST) under the **Name** field. This field is used to uniquely identify the party in the SAP backend application system.

4. Save and activate the communication party.

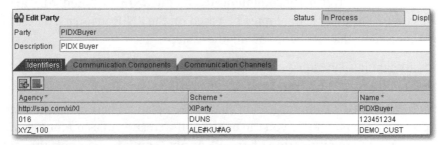

Figure 12.29 Definition of the Buyer Party

Communication Component for the Buyer Party

The communication components must follow specific naming conventions to work with the RNIF adapter. The name must be of the form PIP<Transaction

Code>_<Version>_<Partner Role>, for example, `PIPP31_10_Buyer`. Here `P31` is the PIDX standard interface, `1.0` is the version, and `Buyer` is the partner role. You create a communication component underneath the communication party for your buyer by following these steps:

1. In the Integration Directory create a new communication component called PIPP31_10_Buyer as a business component under the party PIDXBuyer.

2. On the **Sender** tab add the PIDX standard interface OrderCreate (see Figure 12.30 for an example).

3. Save and activate the communication component.

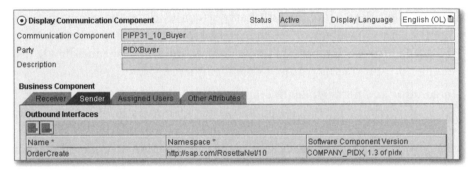

Figure 12.30 Definition of the Communication Component for the Buyer Party

Communication Channel for the Buyer Party

In this scenario the buyer party communicates via the RNIF 2.0 standard. Therefore, the communication channel must be based on the RNIF adapter. You create the communication channel by following these steps:

1. In the Integration Directory create a new communication channel under the party PIDXBuyer called Buyer_Send_OrderCreate.

2. If you have created a communication channel template as part of the software component <Company>_PIDX, you can use it for the creation of a communication channel. Select **Communication Channel • Apply Template** to import the message-specific communication channel template from the Enterprise Services Repository. Most of the fields in the communication channel will be populated with this template. You still need to add some partner-specific information about the transport protocol and security information (see Figure 12.31).

3. Save and activate the communication channel.

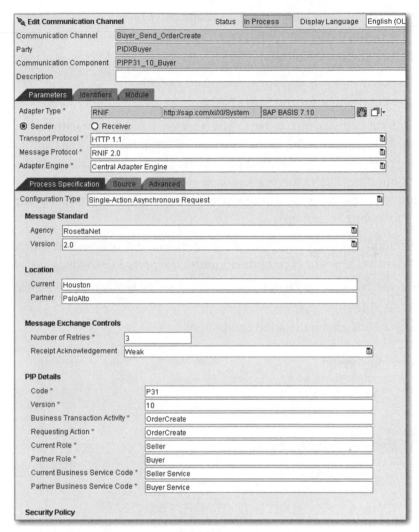

Edit Communication Channel		Status	In Process	Display Language	English (OL

Communication Channel Buyer_Send_OrderCreate

Party PIDXBuyer

Communication Component PIPP31_10_Buyer

Description

Parameters / Identifiers / Module

Adapter Type * RNIF http://sap.com/xi/XI/System SAP BASIS 7.10

◉ Sender ○ Receiver

Transport Protocol * HTTP 1.1

Message Protocol * RNIF 2.0

Adapter Engine * Central Adapter Engine

Process Specification / Source / Advanced

Configuration Type Single-Action Asynchronous Request

Message Standard

Agency RosettaNet

Version 2.0

Location

Current Houston

Partner PaloAlto

Message Exchange Controls

Number of Retries * 3

Receipt Acknowledgement Weak

PIP Details

Code * P31

Version * 10

Business Transaction Activity * OrderCreate

Requesting Action * OrderCreate

Current Role * Seller

Partner Role * Buyer

Current Business Service Code * Seller Service

Partner Business Service Code * Buyer Service

Security Policy

Figure 12.31 Definition of a PIDX Sender Communication Channel

Communication Party for the Seller Party

You create a communication party for your buyer by following these steps:

1. In the Integration Directory create a new communication party called PIDX-Seller.

2. On the **Identifiers** tab of the **Edit Party** screen, click on the empty line under **Agency**. Use the pull-down list and select **016** as the agency, representing the

DUN & Bradstreet Number. Under the field **Name** enter the nine-digit D-U-N-S number of your company as the identifier.

3. Save and activate the communication party.

Communication Component for the Seller Party

The communication components must follow specific naming conventions to work with the RNIF adapter. The name must be of the form `PIP<Transaction Code>_Version_<Partner Role>`, for example, `PIPP31_10_Seller`. Here `P31` is the PIDX standard interface, `1.0` is the version, and `Seller` is the partner role. You create a communication component underneath the communication party for your buyer by following these steps:

1. In the Integration Directory create a new communication component called PIPP31_10_Seller as a business component under the party PIDXSeller.

2. On the **Receiver** tab add the PIDX standard interface OrderCreate (see Figure 12.32 for an example).

3. Save and activate the communication component.

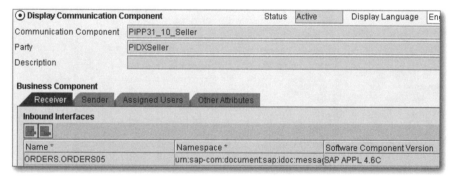

Figure 12.32 Business Component Assigned to the Seller Party

12.4.4 Configuration Using the Model Configurator

In this section we will use the Model Configurator wizard to create the necessary configuration objects using the *process integration scenario* template that you created as described in Section 12.4.2 Activities in the Enterprise Services Repository. In the first phase of the Model Configurator we need to provide the following information:

1. Select the process integration scenario OrderCreate_Seller from the software component `<Company>_PIDX` as your reference model.

2. Name your configuration scenario. We use the name PIPP31_PIDXBuyer_ 10_Buyer, based on the naming convention `PIP<Transaction Code>_<Partner>_<Version>_<Role>`.

In the second phase of the Model Configurator we need to provide the following information:

1. We can skip the **Select Model** step because the process integration scenario contains only one model.

2. In the **Assign Components** step we need to provide assignments for two application components:

   ▶ For the component representing your company, use the business system component XYZ_100 (without a party), and for the external communication, use the party representing your company (for example, PIDXSeller) and the service PIPP31_10_Seller (see Figure 12.33).

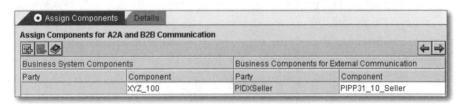

Figure 12.33 Component Assignment for the Seller Role

   ▶ For the component representing your business partner, use the name of your trading partner as the party (for example, PIDXBuyer) and use the communication component PIPP31_10_Buyer (see Figure 12.34).

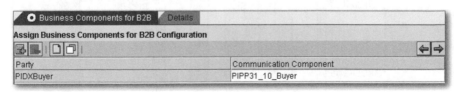

Figure 12.34 Component Assignment for the Buyer Role

3. In the **Configure Connections** step we need to assign the communication channels that should be used in our scenario (see Figure 12.35):

▸ Select Buyer_Send_OrderCreate as the sender communication channel.

▸ Select IS_IDoc_Receiver as the receiver communication channel.

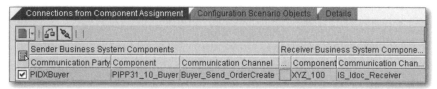

Figure 12.35 Configuration of Connections

12.5 B2B Integration Using the RosettaNet Standard

In this scenario we implement an asynchronous two-action Order Create scenario. The Order Create process is initiated when a buyer commits to buy a product from the seller. The buyer sends an Order Create message (PIP3A4 Request) to the seller. Upon receipt of the message, the seller sends a technical receipt acknowledgement to the buyer. The seller also sends an order confirmation message (PIP3A4 Confirmation) back to the buyer. Upon receipt of the message, the buyer sends a technical receipt acknowledgement to the seller. Figure 12.36 shows the scenario we implement in this section.

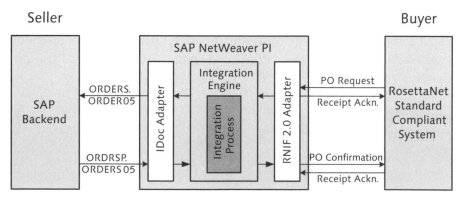

Figure 12.36 Order Create Scenario Including Order Confirmation

12.5.1 Activities in the System Landscape Directory

First, you need to check in the System Landscape Directory (SLD) if the software components containing the RosettaNet-specific content exist. You can do that by following these steps:

1. In the Enterprise Services Builder home page, select **System Landscape Directory**. This will launch the SLD in a separate window.

2. In the next screen, select **Software Components** from the Software catalog panel.

3. The RosettaNet software components are part of the component repository content (CR content) in the SLD delivered by SAP. In the software components page, enter a filter RosettaNet* to restrict the number of software components displayed. The search results should display the software components as shown in Figure 12.37. If the search results in a blank screen, you must update the CR content in the SLD.[8]

Figure 12.37 Software Components in the SLD Related to RosettaNet

12.5.2 Activities in the Enterprise Services Repository

In the Enterprise Services Repository you need to check if the software components containing the RosettaNet-specific content are imported into the Enterprise Services Repository. You can do that by following these steps:

1. In the ES Builder check whether the software components ROSETTANET and ROSETTANET ERP are available in the list structure on the left-hand frame. You can skip step 2 if they are available.

---

8 For more details on updating the CR content, refer to SAP Note 669669.

2. From the main menu, select **Tools • Import Design Objects**. In the next pop-up window, select **Server** and import the *.tpz* files for the software components ROSETTANET and ROSETTANET ERP from the import directory of the SAP NetWeaver PI host system. The sequence in which you import these files is not important. The newly imported software components should appear in the left-hand frame of the ES Builder.

3. The ROSETTANET software component consists of the RosettaNet content such as process integration scenarios, actions, service interfaces, communication channel templates, and the RosettaNet interfaces (PIPs) in the form of external definitions. Figure 12.38 shows an example of the ROSETTANET software component in the Enterprise Services Repository. You need to ensure that the necessary objects for your scenario are available in this software component.

4. The ROSETTANET ERP software component consists of integration content such as process integration scenarios, actions, operation mappings, and message mappings. Figure 12.39 shows an example of the ROSETTANET ERP software component in Enterprise Services Repository. You need to ensure that the necessary objects for your scenario are available in this software component.

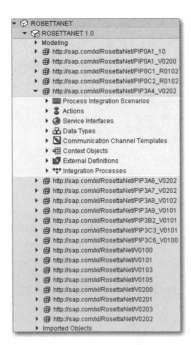

Figure 12.38 Content of the Software Component ROSETTANET

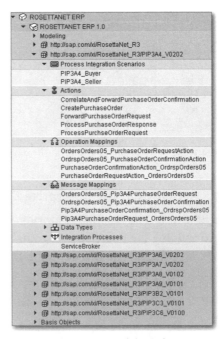

Figure 12.39 Content of the Software Component ROSETTANET ERP

5. The mapping objects in the software component ROSETTANET ERP assume that the SAP IDoc interfaces that are used in the mapping are available in the SAP APPL software component. You must ensure that all relevant SAP interfaces for your scenario are imported and available in this software component. For our scenarios we need the IDocs `ORDERS.ORDERS05` and `ORDRSP.ORDERS05`.

12.5.3 Creation of Collaboration Profiles

We use the Model Configurator for the creation of the configuration in the Integration Directory. Before you can use the configurator you need to set up the collaboration profile for the buyer party and for the sender party. Overall you need to create the following objects:

▶ A *buyer party* in the form of a communication party representing your trading partner. We assume that the buyer party is called RNetBuyer.

▶ A *business component* assigned to the buyer party.

▶ A sender *communication channel* assigned to the business component underneath the buyer party used by the request message.

▶ A receiver *communication channel* assigned to the business component underneath the buyer party used by the confirmation message.

▶ A *seller party* in the form of a communication party representing your own company. We assume that the seller party is called SAPSeller.

▶ A *business component* assigned to the seller party.

▶ A *communication channel* for the seller party was created centrally in Section 12.3.2 Activities in the Enterprise Services Repository. Therefore, we don't need to take care of it here.

▶ A *communication component* representing the integration process which is required to manage the two-action process.

Communication Party for the Buyer Party

You create a communication party for your buyer by following these steps:

1. In the Integration Directory create a new communication party called RNetBuyer (see Figure 12.40).

2. On the **Identifiers** tab of the **Edit Party** screen, click on the empty line under **Agency**. Use the pull-down list and select **016** as the agency, representing the

DUN & Bradstreet Number. Under the field **Name** enter the nine-digit D-U-N-S number of your trading partner as the identifier.

3. In addition to uniquely identifying the party using the D-U-N-S number, the IDoc adapter requires the use of alternative identifiers to link to the partner profiles as they are set up in the SAP systems. Use the pull-down list and enter "XYZ_100" under the **Agency** field, enter "ALE#KU#AG" under the **Scheme** field, and enter the internal name for your customer (for example, DEMO_CUST) under the **Name** field. This field is used to uniquely identify the party in the SAP backend application system.

4. Save and activate the communication party.

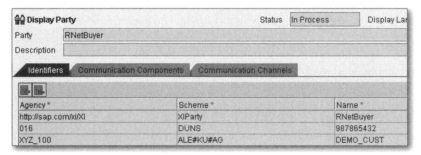

Figure 12.40 Definition of the Buyer Party

Communication Component for the Buyer Party

The communication components must follow specific naming conventions to work with the RNIF adapter. The name must be of the form PIP<Transaction Code>_<Version>_<Partner Role>, for example, PIP3A4_V0202_Buyer. Here 3A4 is the RosettaNet standard interface, V02.02 is the version, and Buyer is the partner role. You create a communication component underneath the communication party for your buyer by following these steps:

1. In the Integration Directory create a new communication component called PIP3A4_V0202_Buyer as a business component under the party RNetBuyer.

2. On the **Sender** tab add the RosettaNet message PIP3A4 called PurchaseOrder-RequestAction (see Figure 12.41 for an example). In addition, you need to add the corresponding confirmation message called PurchaseOrderConfirmation-Action on the **Receiver** tab.

3. Save and activate the communication component.

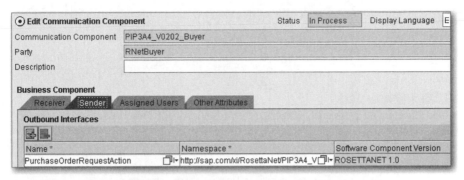

Figure 12.41 Definition of the Communication Component for the Buyer Party

Sender Communication Channel for the Buyer Party

In this scenario the buyer party communicates via the RNIF 2.0 standard. Therefore, the communication channel must be based on the RNIF adapter. You create the communication channel by following these steps:

1. In the Integration Directory create a new communication channel called Buyer_Send_PurchaseOrderRequestAction under the party RNetBuyer.

2. Because we use an existing business package for the creation of the configuration, we can utilize a channel template for the creation of a communication channel. Select **Communication Channel** · **Apply Template** to import the message-specific channel template from the Enterprise Services Repository. Most of the fields in the communication channel will be populated with this template. You still need to add some partner-specific information about the transport protocol and security information (see Figure 12.42).

3. Save and activate the communication channel.

Receiver Communication Channel for the Buyer Party

In this scenario the buyer also sends out an order confirmation message using the RNIF 2.0 standard. Therefore, the communication channel must be based on the RNIF adapter. You create the communication channel by following these steps:

1. In the Integration Directory create a new communication channel called Buyer_Send_PurchaseOrderConfirmationAction under the party RNetBuyer.

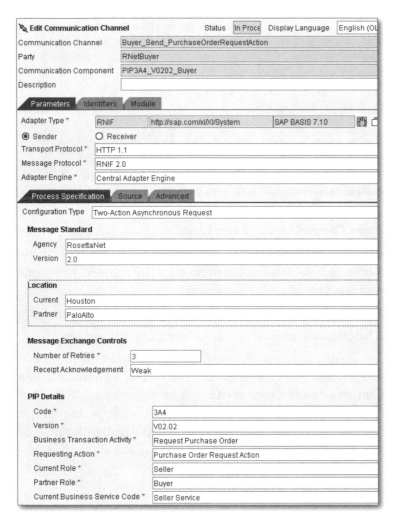

Figure 12.42 Sender Communication Channel for RNIF Communication

2. Because we use an existing business package for the creation of the configuration, we can utilize a channel template for the creation of a communication channel. Select **Communication Channel • Apply Template** to import the message-specific channel template from the Enterprise Services Repository. Most of the fields in the communication channel will be populated with this template. You still need to add some partner-specific information about the transport protocol and security information.

3. Save and activate the communication channel.

Communication Party for the Seller Party

You create a communication party for your seller by following these steps:

1. In the Integration Directory create a new communication party called SAPSeller.

2. On the **Identifiers** tab of the **Edit Party** screen, click on the empty line under **Agency**. Use the pull-down list and select **016** as the agency, representing the DUN & Bradstreet Number. Under the field **Name** enter the nine-digit D-U-N-S number of your company as the identifier.

3. Save and activate the communication party.

Communication Component for the Seller Party

The communication components must follow specific naming conventions to work with the RNIF adapter. The name must be of the form `PIP<Transaction Code>_Version_<Partner Role>`, for example, `PIP3A4_V0202_Seller`. Here 3A4 is the RosettaNet PIP interface, `V02.02` is the version, and `Seller` is the partner role. You create a communication component underneath the communication party for your buyer by following these steps:

1. In the Integration Directory create a new communication component called PIP3A4_V0202_Seller as a business component under the party SAPSeller.

2. On the **Receiver** tab add the RosettaNet message PIP3A4 called PurchaseOrder-RequestAction. In addition, you need to add the corresponding confirmation message called PurchaseOrderConfirmationAction under the **Sender** tab.

3. Save and activate the communication component.

Communication Component for the Integration Process

In the two-action scenario, you must define an integration process component in the Integration Directory. This integration process can be treated like a business system at configuration time and can be used as service broker to correlate the incoming purchase order request with the purchase order confirmation message. The integration process must be defined under the party SAPSeller as shown in Figure 12.43. You do not have to assign a communication channel to the integration process.

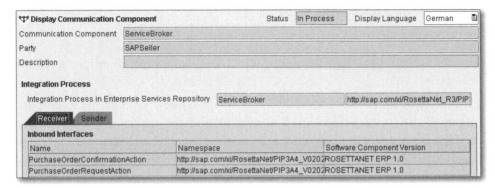

Figure 12.43 Service Broker Integration Process

12.5.4 Configuration Using the Model Configurator

In this section we will use the Model Configurator wizard to create the necessary configuration objects using a process integration scenario template selected from the Enterprise Services Repository. The process integration scenario contains information for business scenarios and integration processes that are relevant for communication using SAP NetWeaver PI. You need to have this integration scenario available in the Enterprise Services Repository to use the Model Configurator, which we discussed in detail in Section 9.6.1 Execution of the Model Configurator. In the first phase of the Model Configurator we need to provide the following information:

1. Select the process integration scenario PIP3A4_Seller from the software component ROSETTANET ERP as your reference model (see Figure 12.44 for an overview on the process integration scenario).

2. Define a name for your configuration scenario. We use the name RNIF_RNetBuyer_PIP3A4_V0202_Buyer.

In the second phase of the Model Configurator we need to provide the following information:

1. Because the process integration scenario contains multiple models, we need to select the appropriate model in the **Select Model** step.

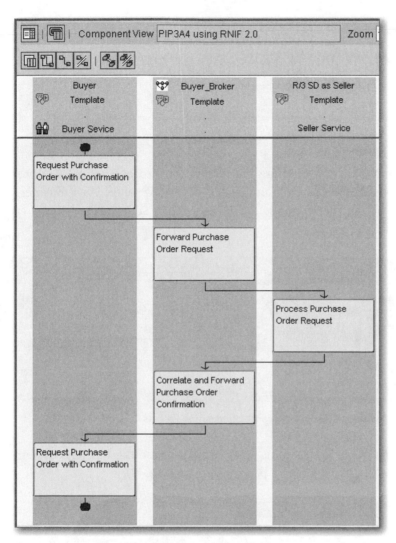

Figure 12.44 Process Integration Scenario for Order Request as a Seller

2. In the **Assign Components** step we need to provide assignments for three application components:

   ▶ For the component representing your business partner, use the name of your trading partner as the party (for example, RNetBuyer) and the communication component PIP3A4_V0202_Buyer (see Figure 12.45).

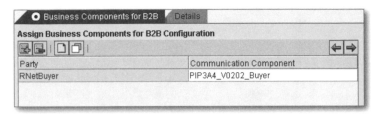

Figure 12.45 Component Assignment for the Buyer Role

▷ For the component representing the integration process, assign the integration process ServiceBroker under the party SAPSeller. As a business component assign the component PIP3A4_V0202_Seller under the party SAPSeller (see Figure 12.46).

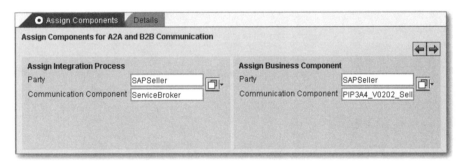

Figure 12.46 Component Assignment for the Integration Process

▷ For the component representing your company, use the business system component XYZ_100 without a party (see Figure 12.47).

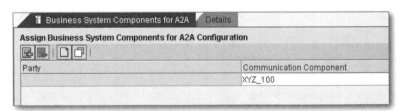

Figure 12.47 Component Assignment for the Seller Role

3. In the **Configure Connections** step we need to maintain the following connections:

▶ For the connection between the buyer and the service broker (for the request message) select Buyer_Send_PurchaseOrderRequestAction as the sender communication channel. No receiver communication channel is required (see Figure 12.48).

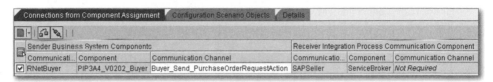

Figure 12.48 Connection Between Buyer and Service Broker

▶ For the connection between the service broker and the seller (for the request message) select IS_IDoc_Receiver as the receiver communication channel. No sender communication channel is required (see Figure 12.49).

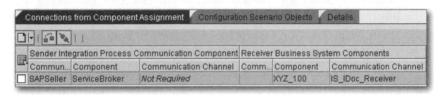

Figure 12.49 Connection Between Service Broker and Seller

▶ For the connection between the seller and the service broker (for the confirmation message) no communication channels are required (see Figure 12.50).

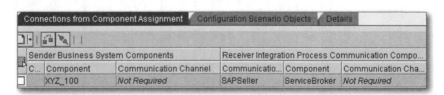

Figure 12.50 Connection Between Seller and Service Broker

▶ For the connection between the service broker and the buyer (for the confirmation message) select Buyer_Receive_PurchaseOrderConfirmation-Action as the receiver communication channel. No sender communication channel is required (see Figure 12.51).

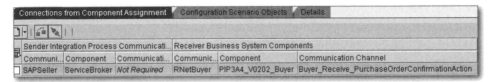

Figure 12.51 Connection Between Service Broker and Buyer

12.6 B2B Integration Using the EDI Standard ANSI X12

This scenario is a simple demo example of how an EDI scenario can be implemented using SAP NetWeaver PI and SEEBURGER's AS2 adapter. The Order Create transaction takes place between the buyer and the seller. It enables new purchase orders to be communicated to the seller. When the purchase order is initiated at the buyer, an ANSI X12 850 Order Create message is generated and sent to the EDI seller (trading partner). Once the Order Create message is received from the buyer system, the prebuilt mapping in the Enterprise Services Repository converts the IDoc ORDERS05 to the EDI 850 ANSI X12 standard XML message. This EDI-XML message is then forwarded to the SEEBURGER Business Integration Converter (BIC) module, which converts it into the native EDI 850 ANSI X12 standard format. The converted message is then forwarded to the seller's AS2 server using the SEEBURGER AS2 adapter (see Figure 12.52).

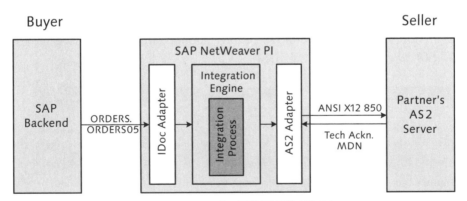

Figure 12.52 Order Create Scenario Using the SEEBURGER AS2 Adapter

12.6.1 Preconditions

This scenario assumes that the following preconditions are met:

▸ SEEBURGER's XI content of the business package Generic EDI and the adapter metadata are installed and available on the SAP NetWeaver PI system. SEEBURGER's XI content and metadata can be downloaded from the SAP Service Marketplace subject to license agreement associated with the package.

▸ SEEBURGER's AS2 adapter is installed and available in SAP NetWeaver PI. SEEBURGER adapters can be downloaded from the SAP Service Marketplace subject to license agreement associated with the adapter. For information on installing the AS2 adapter, refer to SEEBURGER's setup and configuration guide on the AS2 adapter, which you can find in the download section of the software distribution center in the SAP Service Marketplace. Select the application group **Adapters from SEEBURGER** there.

▸ SEEBURGER's Business Integration Converter (BIC) module is installed and available on the SAP NetWeaver PI system. The BIC module is used to translate native EDI and legacy data formats into XML and vice versa. For more information on installing the BIC module, refer to SEEBURGER's documentation on installing and setting up the BIC module.

▸ Configuration of the Material Management (MM) module for outbound orders is in place in the SAP ERP backend system.

▸ Configuration of the port and the partner profile is in place in the SAP backend system.

▸ Configuration of the IDoc adapter is in place in SAP NetWeaver PI.

12.6.2 AS2 Basics

EDI over the Internet (EDIINT) is a working group of the Internet Engineering Task Force (IETF), enabling secure transport of EDI and XML data over the Internet. It is an alternative data transport to data communications between EDI trading partners based on value added network (VAN). AS2 (Applicability Statement 2) is one of the standard protocols used by the EDIINT. AS2 provides S/MIME encryption over HTTP/S. It essentially creates a wrapper around the EDI message and sends it securely over the Internet. Any type of data can be exchanged using the AS2 protocol, including EDI messages, XML, flat files, and spreadsheets.

AS2 uses two different message types, the actual payload message and technical acknowledgement or Message Disposition Notification (MDN). AS2 uses MDNs for message receipt, which can be sent synchronously or asynchronously upon successful receipt of the AS2 message. The SEEBURGER AS2 adapter is used for transmitting the EDI and other files according to the AS2 protocol.

12.6.3 Activities in the System Landscape Directory

The SEEBURGER software components are part of the component repository content (CR content) in the SLD delivered by SAP. SEEBURGER solutions contain many software components that are used for implementing several industry standards. For this scenario we will only search for SEEBURGER_EDI_ADAPTER of SEEBURGER and SEEBURGER_GENERIC_EDI of SEEBURGER Software Components.

On the Software Components page, enter a filter "SEEBURGER*" to restrict the number of software components displayed. The search results should display the software components as shown in Figure 12.53. If the search results in a blank screen, you must update the CR content in the SLD.[9]

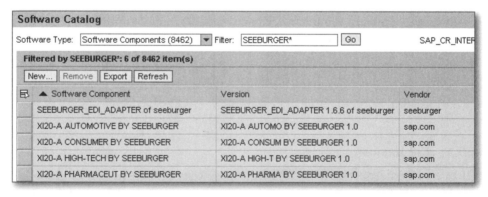

Figure 12.53 SEEBURGER Software Components in the SLD

12.6.4 Activities in the Enterprise Services Repository

In the Enterprise Services Repository you need to check if the software components containing the ANSI X12- and AS2-specific content are imported into the Enterprise Services Repository. You can do that by following these steps:

---

9 For more details on updating the CR content, refer to SAP Note 669669.

1. In the ES Builder check whether the software components SEEBURGER_EDI_ ADAPTER and SEEBURGER_GENERIC_EDI are available in the list structure on the left-hand frame. You can skip step 2 if they are available.

2. From the main menu, select **Tools • Import Design Objects**. In the next pop-up window, select **Server** and import the *.tpz* files for the software components SEEBURGER_EDI_ADAPTER and SEEBURGER_GENERIC_EDI from the import directory of the SAP NetWeaver PI host system. The sequence in which you import these files is not important. The newly imported software components should appear in the left-hand frame of the Enterprise Services Builder.

3. In the software component SEEBURGER_EDI_ADAPTER create a new adapter metadata object called "AS2" and import the corresponding XML description.

4. The integration scenarios, actions, EDI, and SAP interfaces in the form of external definitions, mappings, integration processes, and so on can be found in the software component version SEEBURGER_GENERIC_EDI in the Enterprise Services Repository. The mappings include mappings between SAP IDocs and EDI standard (both ANSI X12 and EDIFACT) interfaces.[10]

5. You can enhance the mappings provided by SEEBURGER to meet your specific mapping requirements. To enhance the mappings, you need to create your own software component in the SLD with a dependency to the SEEBURGER_GENERIC_EDI software component such that all of the original mappings and any subsequent changes or modifications are visible in the new software component.

12.6.5 Creation of Collaboration Profiles

We use the Model Configurator for the creation of the configuration in the Integration Directory. Before you can use the configurator you need to set up the collaboration profile for the buyer party and for the sender party. Overall you need to create the following objects:

▶ A *buyer party* in the form of a communication party representing your own company. We assume that the buyer party is called EDI_Buyer.

▶ A *business component* assigned to the buyer party.

▶ A *seller party* in the form of a communication party representing your trading partner. We assume that the seller party is called EDI_Seller.

---

10 For more information on SEEBURGER's EDI content, refer to SEEBURGER's documentation.

- A *business component* assigned to the seller party.

- A *communication channel* assigned to the business component underneath the seller party used by the request message.

- A *communication channel* assigned to the business component underneath the seller party for sending MDN reports.

- A *business component* for receiving the MDN reports that are sent out by the seller party. We assume that this business system is called MDN_Receiver.

- A *communication channel* assigned to the business system that was set up for MDN reports for receiving these reports.

Communication Party for the Buyer Party

You create a communication party for your buyer by following these steps:

1. In the Integration Directory create a new communication party called EDI_Buyer (see Figure 12.54).

2. On the **Identifiers** tab of the **Edit Party** screen, click on the empty line under **Agency**. Define an entry with the agency "Seeburger" and the scheme "AS2ID." Under the field **Name** enter the AS2 ID of your company as the identifier.

3. Save and activate the communication party.

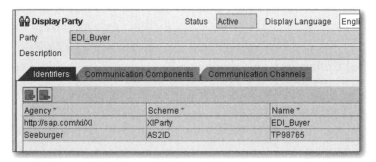

Figure 12.54 Definition of the Buyer Party

Communication Party for the Seller Party

You create a communication party for your seller by following these steps:

1. In the Integration Directory create a new communication party called EDI_Seller.

2. In the **Identifiers** tab of the **Edit Party** screen, click on the empty line under **Agency**. Define an entry with the agency "Seeburger" and the scheme "AS2ID." Under the field **Name** enter the AS2 ID of your trading partner as the identifier (see Figure 12.55).

3. Save and activate the communication party.

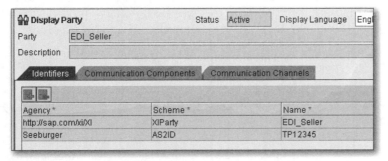

Figure 12.55 Definition of the Seller Party

Communication Component for the Seller Party

You need to create a communication component for your seller by following these steps:

1. In the Integration Directory create a new communication component called ANSI_X12_850_V4010_Seller as a business component under the party EDI_Seller.

2. On the **Receiver** tab add the EDI ANSI X12 standard interface EDI_850_A_4010.

3. Save and activate the communication component.

Communication Channel for the Seller Party

In this scenario the seller party communicates via the ANSI X12 standard using the AS2 protocol. Therefore, the communication channel must be based on the AS2 adapter. You create the communication channel by following these steps:

1. In the Integration Directory create a new communication channel called Seeburger_AS2_Receiver under the party EDI_Seller.

2. Select the receiver adapter type AS2 from the drop-down list of adapters.

3. On the **Parameters** tab, maintain AS2-specific parameters. The AS2-specific parameters are listed in Table 12.15 (see also Figure 12.56).

Parameter	Value
Compress	Not selected
Sign	Not selected
Encrypt	Not selected
MDN Mode	**Synchron** or **Async** or **No MDN**
Sign MDN	Not selected
Handle received MDN	**Refer MDN to XI System**
Message Subject	**AS2** (this text is sent to the AS2 server)
Content Type	**application/edi-X12** for ANSI X12 files. Other formats include **application/EDIFACT** for EDIFACT files **application/XML** for XML files **application/octet-stream** for binary files
Deliver transmission report	Not selected

Table 12.15 AS2-Specific Parameters

4. On the **Module** tab you need to add the module `localejbs/CallBicXIRaBean` as the first entry under the section **Processing Sequence**. This module is the realization of SEEBURGER's *Business Integration Converter* (BIC) virtual adapter, which converts the XML messages to native EDI formats and vice versa.

5. In the **Module Configuration** section you need to assign the attributes required by the BIC module. Here we only list in Table 12.16 the parameters that were used in this scenario. The BIC module has many parameters that can be used in the conversion of the mapping from XML to native EDI format.[11] See Figure 12.57 for an example of the settings for the BIC adapter.

6. Save and activate the communication channel.

---

11 For more information on the BIC module and the parameters that can be used, refer to SEEBURGER's documentation on the BIC Adapter.

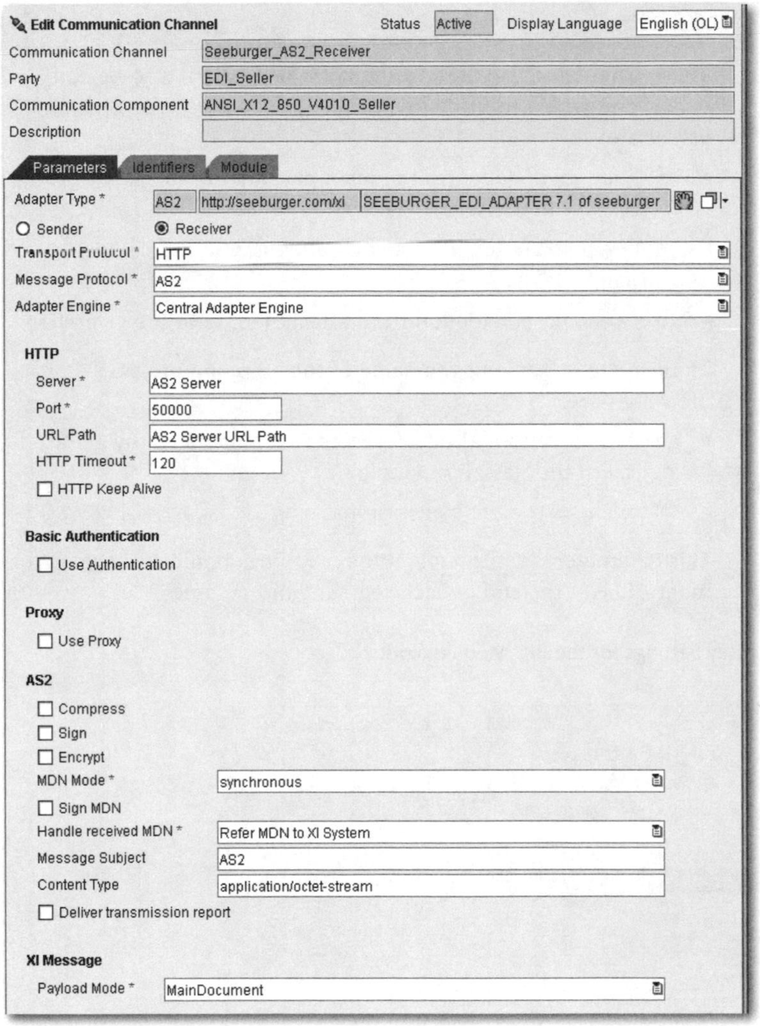

Figure 12.56 Sender Communication Channel for AS2 Communication

Parameter	Value
destDelimiter	This parameter sets the destination delimiter. It must use a string of six characters that denote the delimiters for the following entries: subfield, field, decimal, quoting, fieldgroup, segment

Table 12.16 Module Key Settings for the BIC Module

Parameter	Value
destSourceMsg destTargetMsg	These parameters are used to specify which data has to be converted and where to place the resulting document. The possible values are: ▶ MainDocument (denotes the main payload of the SAP NetWeaver PI message) ▶ SeeburgerMain (denotes an attachment with the name SeeburgerMain) ▶ <AttachmentID> (denotes the attachment with the given ID
mappingName	The parameter contains the name of the mapping program. Possible values are: ▶ AUTO for an automatically detected mapping name (by a preceding call of the classifier module) ▶ <Mapping name> to specify a mapping
newLine	This parameter is set to true if the mapping should add an element CRLF at the end of each segment and record.

Table 12.16 Module Key Settings for the BIC Module (cont.)

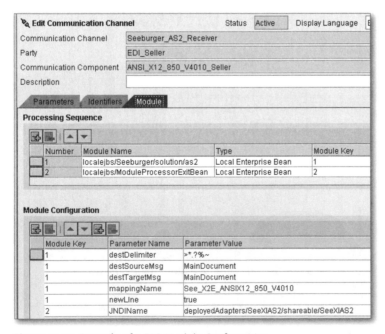

Figure 12.57 Example of a BIC Module Configuration

Communication Channel for Sending MDN Reports

The seller party responds to the AS2 message with an acknowledgement message (MDN). To receive this message you need to create a communication channel based on the AS2 adapter. You create the communication channel by following these steps:

1. In the Integration Directory create a new communication channel called MDN_Reports under the party EDI_Seller.

2. Select the adapter type AS2 and maintain the attributes as shown in Figure 12.58.

3. Save and activate the communication channel.

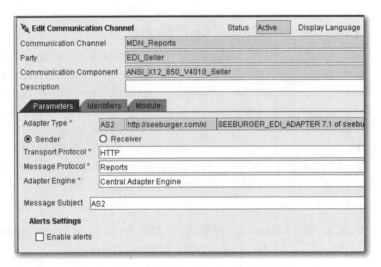

Figure 12.58 Sender Communication Channel for MDN Reports

Communication Component for Receiving MDN Reports

You need to create a communication component for receiving MDN reports by following these steps:

1. In the Integration Directory create a new communication component called MDN_Receiver (without a party).

2. On the **Receiver** tab add the MDN_Reports interface.

3. Save and activate the communication component.

Communication Channel for Receiving MDN Reports

In this scenario the seller party sends MDN reports to a file system of your company. Therefore, a communication channel based on the file adapter must be created in order to receive these reports. You create the communication channel by following these steps:

1. In the Integration Directory create a new communication channel called MDN_Receiver under the service MDN_Receiver (without a party).

2. Select the adapter type File as a receiver and enter the values for the **File Name** and the **Target Directory**.

3. Save and activate the communication channel.

12.6.6 Configuration Using the Model Configurator

In this section we will use the Model Configurator wizard to create the necessary configuration objects using a process integration scenario template selected from the Enterprise Services Repository. The process integration scenario contains information for business scenarios and integration processes that are relevant for communication using SAP NetWeaver PI. You need to have this integration scenario available in the Enterprise Services Repository to use the Model Configurator, which we discussed in detail in Section 9.6.1 Execution of the Model Configurator. In the first phase of the Model Configurator we need to provide the following information:

1. Select the process integration scenario ANSI_X12_850_4010 from the software component SEEBURGER_GENERIC_EDI as your reference model.

2. Define a name for your configuration scenario. We use the name EDI_Seller_ANSI_X12_850_4010.

In the second phase of the Model Configurator (see Figure 12.59) we need to provide the following information:

1. We can skip the **Select Model** step because the process integration scenario contains only one model.

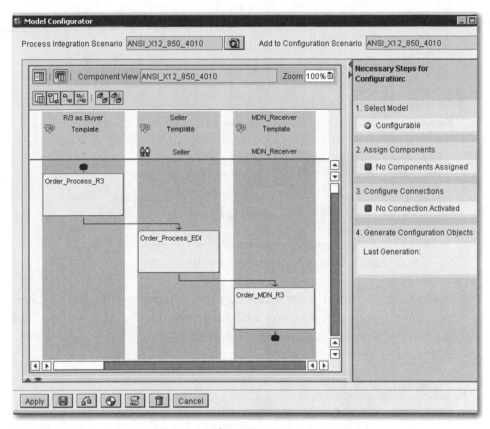

Figure 12.59 Process Integration Scenario for ANSI X12 Communication

2. In the **Assign Components** step we need to provide assignments for two application components:

  ▶ For the component representing your company, use the business system component XYZ_100 without a party for the A2A portion, and the party EDI_Buyer and the service ANSI_X12_850_V4010_Buyer for the B2B portion (see Figure 12.60).

  ▶ For the component representing your trading partner, use the name of your trading partner as the party (for example, EDI_Seller) and the communication component ANSI_X12_850_V4010_Seller (see Figure 12.61).

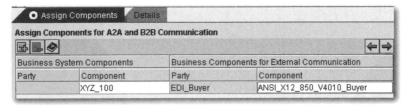

Figure 12.60 Business System and Business Component Assignment for the Buyer

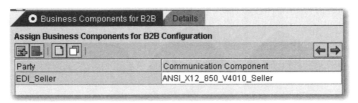

Figure 12.61 Business Service Assignment for the Seller

▶ For the component used for receiving MDN reports, use the business service component MDN_Receiver without a party for the A2A portion, and the party EDI_Buyer and the service ANSI_X12_850_V4010_Buyer for the B2B portion (see Figure 12.62).

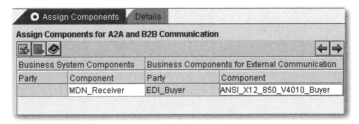

Figure 12.62 Business System and Business Component Assignment for MDN Receiver

3. In the **Configure Connections** step we need to maintain the following connections:

▶ For the connection between the buyer and the seller select **Seeburger_ AS2_Receiver** as the receiver communication channel. No sender communication channel is required (see Figure 12.63).

▶ For the connection between the seller and the receiver of MDN reports select **MDN_Reports** as the sender communication channel and **MDN_ Receiver** as the receiver communication channel (see Figure 12.64).

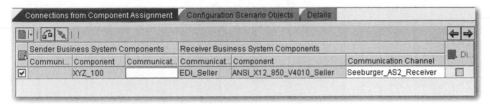

Figure 12.63 Communication Channel Assigned to the Seller

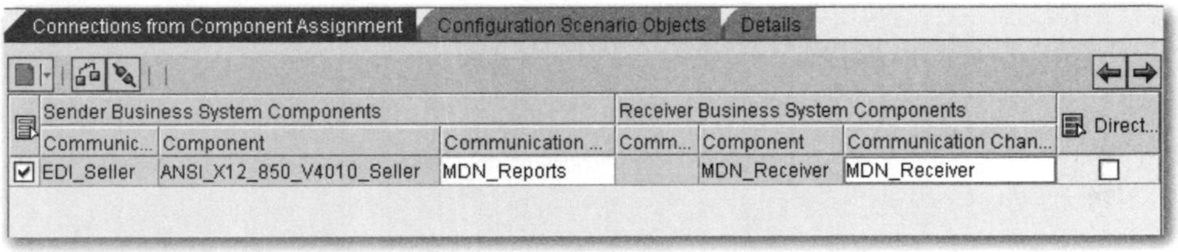

Figure 12.64 Communication Channel Assignments for MDN Reports

12.7 Summary

After reading this chapter you should have a better understanding of how the individual Enterprise Services Repository objects and configuration steps in the Integration Directory work together to set up a complete B2B integration scenario.

In addition, you should have a better understanding on how you can utilize partner products within the SAP NetWeaver PI platform to support additional scenarios such as the support of the ANSI X12 EDI standard.

APPENDIX

A   Message Mapping Examples

The best way to understand the different features of the graphical message mapping tool provided in the Enterprise Services Builder is by going through a number of examples. We discussed the main concepts of the tool in Section 8.4 Mapping Techniques, and we now explain some examples that we found to be useful in real-life scenarios.

A.1   Simple Looping

When we need to provide message mappings between IDocs and standard message formats, the respective message structures often don't fit together well. The handling of different partner types (sold-to party, ship-to party, bill-to party, and so on) is an example where such an issue can occur, due to the following difference in the message structures:

▶ An IDoc message only uses one segment, E1EDKA1, where all partners are listed. An identifier (in field PARVW) in this list is used to distinguish between the different partner types.

▶ Many industry standards provide different segments for each partner type, for example, one dedicated node for the sold-to party, one dedicated node for the ship-to party, and so on.

In this use case we show how the message mapping must be built in order to map the partner types correctly to the target message structure. We show the message mappings in both directions.

A.1.1   Sample Problem

To keep the example small and easy to reproduce we don't use the complete IDoc message or a complete standard message; instead we use small message types that replicate the key elements but leave out all elements that are not relevant for this particular example.

▶ Figure A.1 shows the structure we use to mimic the IDoc segment E1EDKA1 containing partner-related information. As you can see, we only use the fields PARVW and PARTN out of this segment, which is sufficient for our purposes.

▶ Figure A.2 shows the structure we use to mimic an industry standard definition. Again, we only focus on elements that are relevant for this example.

Name	Category	Type	Occurrence
▼ IDOC	Element	IDOC	
▼ E1EDKA1	Element	E1EDKA1	1..unbounded
PARVW	Element	xsd:string	1
PARTN	Element	xsd:string	1

Figure A.1 Message Structure Based on IDoc Segment E1EDKA1

Name	Category	Type	Occurrence
▼ Partner	Element	Partner	
▼ SellTo	Element	SellTo	1
Name	Element	xsd:string	1
▼ ShipTo	Element	ShipTo	0..1
Name	Element	xsd:string	1
▼ BillTo	Element	BillTo	0..1
Name	Element	xsd:string	1

Figure A.2 Message Structure Based on Different Industry Standards

Whereas the message definition mimicking an industry standard has a predefined set of available partner types (sold-to party, ship-to party, bill-to party), the message representing the IDoc only has one segment that can be repeated to hold multiple partner types. The field PARVW is used as an identifier that specifies the partner type of the specific instance of the element E1EDKA1. Table A.1 lists the relevant values for our example.

Value of PARVW	Partner Type
AG	Sold-to party
WE	Ship-to party
RE	Bill-to party

Table A.1 Partner Type Identifiers in IDocs

Figure A.3 shows two sample messages that we use to test our message mappings. Note that the order in which the partner types appear in segment E1EDKA1 of the IDoc message is arbitrary.

```
<IDOC>                              <Partner>
  <E1EDKA1>                           <SellTo>
    <PARVW>RE</PARVW>                    <Name>Name_AG</Name>
    <PARTN>Name_RE</PARTN>            </SellTo>
  </E1EDKA1>                          <ShipTo>
  <E1EDKA1>                             <Name>Name_WE</Name>
    <PARVW>WE</PARVW>                 </ShipTo>
    <PARTN>Name_WE</PARTN>            <BillTo>
  </E1EDKA1>                            <Name>Name_RE</Name>
  <E1EDKA1>                           </BillTo>
    <PARVW>AG</PARVW>               </Partner>
    <PARTN>Name_AG</PARTN>
  </E1EDKA1>
</IDOC>
```

Figure A.3 Sample Messages of Type IDOC and Type Partner

A.1.2 Mapping from Standard Message to IDoc

We can map the node SellTo and its subsequent field SellTo/Name of message Partner easily to the segment E1EDKA1 and its subsequent nodes of the message IDOC as shown in Figure A.4. Before we can map the additional nodes ShipTo and BillTo to the message IDOC, we need to duplicate the node E1EDKA1 twice in the graphical display of the structure overview of the message IDOC. This can be done as described in Section 8.4.2 Message Mapping.

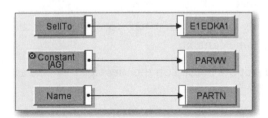

Figure A.4 Mapping of the Node SellTo and Its Subsequent Fields

Once the node E1EDKA1 is available for additional mappings, we can maintain it with ShipTo and BillTo as the source node analogue to the mapping shown in Figure A.4.

A.1.3 Mapping from IDoc to Standard Message

Because the partner types in the node E1EDKA1 of the message IDOC can appear in any arbitrary order, we need to loop for each partner type through the complete data queue of the node E1EDKA1 to ensure that we find the corresponding entry in the node E1EDKA1.

Mapping for Sold-To Party

The message structure Partner contains two fields that are relevant for the sold-to party:

▶ The structure node SellTo. Because the cardinality of this node is exactly one, the graphical mapping tool creates this node automatically (see also Section 8.4.2 Message Mapping). Therefore, no field mapping is required for this node.

▶ The leaf node Name underneath the node SellTo. For this node we need to map the name information (in the field PARVW) from the correct line of the message IDOC.

The mapping for the node Name is shown in Figure A.5. The following properties need to be set in the involved functions:

▶ The **Context** of the field PARVW needs to be set to **IDOC** to ensure that all instances of this field are within the same context.

▶ The **Value** of the function Constant needs to be set to **AG**.

▶ The **Context** of the field PARTN needs to be set to **IDOC** to ensure that all instances of this field are within the same context.

Figure A.5 also shows the result of the mapping based on the message instance as shown in Figure A.3.

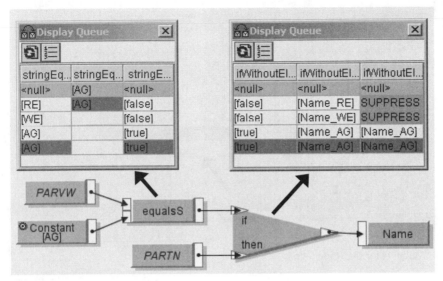

Figure A.5 Mapping for the Node Name Underneath SellTo

Mapping for Ship-To Party

The message structure `Partner` contains two fields that are relevant for the ship-to party:

▸ The structure node `ShipTo`. Because the cardinality of this node is zero to one, a field mapping is required to ensure that the node is created if necessary (see also Section 8.4.2 Message Mapping).

▸ The leaf node `Name` underneath the node `ShipTo`. For this node we need to map the name information (in the field `PARVW`) from the correct line of the message `IDOC`.

The mapping for the node `ShipTo` is shown in Figure A.6. The following properties need to be set in the involved functions:

▸ The **Context** of the field `PARVW` needs to be set to **IDOC** to ensure that all instances of this field are within the same context.

▸ The **Value** of the function `Constant` needs to be set to **WE**.

Figure A.6 also shows the result of the mapping based on the message instance as shown in Figure A.3.

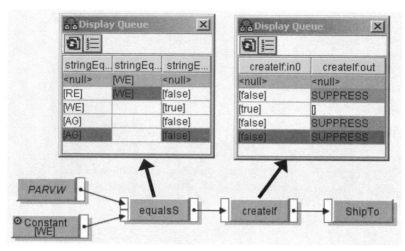

Figure A.6 Mapping for the Node ShipTo

The mapping for the node Name is shown in Figure A.7. The **Context** of the field PARTN needs to be set to **E1EDKA1** (this is the default setting) to ensure that there is a context change after each instance. Figure A.7 also shows the result of the mapping based on the message instance as shown in Figure A.3.

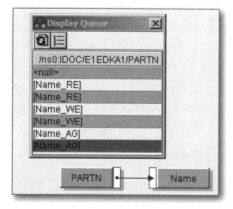

Figure A.7 Mapping for the Node Name Underneath ShipTo

Mapping for Bill-To Party

The mapping structure for the bill-to party is identical to the mapping for the ship-to party.

A.2   Message Splitting

You often are required to split one large message into multiple parts based on predefined rules. We use a simple example to illustrate how to realize a message split that can also be used in a more complex environment.

A.2.1   Sample Problem

In our example we receive a source message containing purchase orders in a flat format. This message can contain multiple purchase orders with an unlimited number of line items. The structure of the source message is shown in Figure A.8, and the sample message we will use in this example is given in Figure A.9.

	Name	Category	Type	Occurrence	Defa
	▼ Source	Element	Source		
	▼ Line	Element	Line	1..unbounded	
	PONumber	Element	xsd:string	1	
	Item	Element	xsd:string	1	
	Material	Element	xsd:string	1	

Figure A.8 Message Structure of the Source Message

We need to map the source message to a new target structure, which is shown in Figure A.10. As we can see, the target structure has a number of limitations in regard to the message size. In particular, we have the following two restrictions:

▶ The target structure is limited to one purchase order number per message, forcing a message split with each new purchase order number.

▶ The maximum number of line items per message is limited to three, forcing a message split after three lines, independent of the purchase order number.

Let's now convert the sample message shown in Figure A.9 to the new structure given by Figure A.10. The sample message contains two purchase order numbers. Therefore, we need to create (at least) two messages—one per purchase order number. The new target message for the first purchase order number looks as shown in Figure A.11.

```
<Source>
  <Line>
    <PONumber>490000</PONumber>
    <Item>010</Item>
    <Material>Bread</Material>
  </Line>
  <Line>
    <PONumber>490000</PONumber>
    <Item>020</Item>
    <Material>Cheese</Material>
  </Line>
  <Line>
    <PONumber>490001</PONumber>
    <Item>011</Item>
    <Material>Water</Material>
  </Line>
  <Line>
    <PONumber>490001</PONumber>
    <Item>021</Item>
    <Material>Beer</Material>
  </Line>
  <Line>
    <PONumber>490001</PONumber>
    <Item>031</Item>
    <Material>Wine</Material>
  </Line>
  <Line>
    <PONumber>490001</PONumber>
    <Item>041</Item>
    <Material>Juice</Material>
  </Line>
</Source>
```

Figure A.9 Example of a Source Message Instance

	Name	Category	Type	Occurrence
	▼ PurchaseOrder	Element	PurchaseOrder	
	PurchaseOrderNumber	Element	xsd:string	1
	▼ LineItem	Element	LineItem	1..3
	ItemNumber	Element	xsd:string	1
	Material	Element	xsd:string	1

Figure A.10 Message Structure of the Target Message

The second purchase order contains a total of four line items. Because the target message has a limit of three line items per message, the target message containing the second purchase order number needs to be split into two messages, as shown in Figure A.12.

```
<PurchaseOrder>
  <PurchaseOrderNumber >490000</PurchaseOrderNumber >
  <LineItem>
    <ItemNumber >010</ItemNumber >
    <Material>Bread</Material>
  </LineItem>
  <LineItem>
    <ItemNumber >020</ItemNumber >
    <Material>Cheese </Material>
  </LineItem>
</PurchaseOrder >
```

Figure A.11 Target Message for the First Purchase Order Number

```
<PurchaseOrder>
  <PurchaseOrderNumber >490001</PurchaseOrderNumber >
  <LineItem>
    <ItemNumber >011</ItemNumber >
    <Material>Water</Material>
  </LineItem>
  <LineItem>
    <ItemNumber >021</ItemNumber >
    <Material>Beer</Material>
  </LineItem>
  <LineItem>
    <ItemNumber >031</ItemNumber >
    <Material>Wine</Material>
  </LineItem>
</PurchaseOrder >
```

```
<PurchaseOrder>
  <PurchaseOrderNumber >490001</PurchaseOrderNumber >
  <LineItem>
    <ItemNumber >041</ItemNumber >
    <Material>Juice</Material>
  </LineItem>
</PurchaseOrder >
```

Figure A.12 Target Messages for the Second Purchase Order Number

A.2.2 Mapping

Because one source message can result in multiple target messages, we need to create a multi-mapping for this use case. As discussed in Section 8.4.6 Multi-Mappings, you can use this mapping directly in your scenario as long as the adapter that picks up the message is part of the Adapter Engine. For other adapters (e.g., the IDoc adapter) you need to add this mapping to an integration process.

Creation of the Multi-Mapping

Before we can start with the field mapping, we need to set up the mapping as a multi-mapping. As described in Section 8.4.6 Multi-Mappings, we need to change the occurrence of the target message to **0..unbounded**. This results in a message structure as shown in Figure A.13.

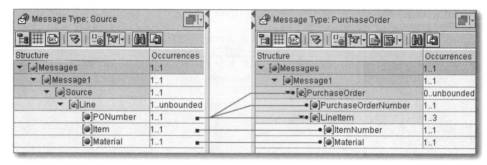

Figure A.13 Message Structure after Set Up for Multi-Mapping

Creation of a User-Defined Function

The target message only allows a maximum of three line items per message. Therefore, we need as part of the message mapping a function that can count the number of line items and enforce a context change once the maximum number of line items is reached. For this purpose we define a user-defined function, limit-LineNumber, with the settings shown in Figure A.14.

The source code for the user-defined function limitLineNumber is shown in Listing A.1. In this function we count the number of entries in the input queue a using the field cnt. Once the number of entries exceeds the maximum allowed count (given by the input field b[0]), a context change is enforced and the counters are reset.

```
int cnt = 0;
int max_cnt;
max_cnt = Integer.parseInt(b[0]);
for (int i = 0; i < a.length; i++) {
```

```
  cnt++;
  if (cnt > max_cnt) {
    result.addContextChange();
    cnt = 1;
  }
  result.addValue(a[i]);
}
```

Listing A.1 Coding for User-Defined Function limitLineNumber

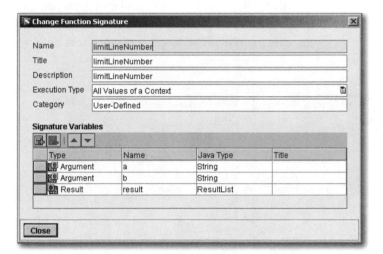

Figure A.14 Variable of the User-Defined Function limitLineNumber

At the end of this use case we will see that we can achieve the same functionality as with the user-defined function `limitLineNumber`, also with the use of standard functions only.

Mapping for the Field PurchaseOrder

Because the node `PurchaseOrder` is of the cardinality **0..unbounded**, we need to provide a field mapping for this node. In this mapping we need to identify how often the source message needs to be split based on the given restrictions. The mapping for this node is shown in Figure A.15, which consists of the following steps:

❶ The values of the field `PONumber` are retrieved. As a starting point we need all instances of this field within the same context. Therefore, the **Context** of the field needs to be set to **Source**.

❷ Next we use the function `SplitByValue` to create a context change for each new PO number. For this function the property **Event After Which Content Should Change** of the function `SplitByValue` needs to be set to **Value Change**.

❸ We use the user-defined function `limitLineNumber` to create additional context changes each time the maximum number of lines per message is reached. The maximum number of lines per message is given by the function `Constant` (the property **Value** needs to be set to **3**).

❹ In the final step we use the function `collapseContext` to collapse each context down to one value. In addition, the context changes are removed. This leaves us with only one context with as many entries as target messages that need to be created.

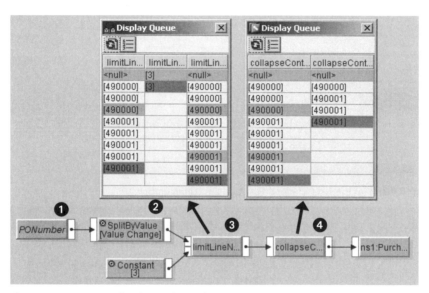

Figure A.15 Mapping for the Node PurchaseOrder

Mapping for the Field PurchaseOrderNumber

The field `PurchaseOrderNumber` appears exactly once for each message instance. Because we can have multiple target messages, we need as many occurrences of this field as we have target messages, each occurrence separated by a context change. The mapping for the node `PurchaseOrderNumber` is shown in Figure A.16, which consists of the following steps:

1. The mapping up to point ❶ is identical to the mapping of the node Purchase-Order. As a result, we already have the correct values in the queue, missing only the context changes.

2. In the last step ❷ we use the function `SplitByValue` to add a context change to the queue between each value item. In this step the property **Event After Which Content Should Change** needs to be set to **Value Change**.

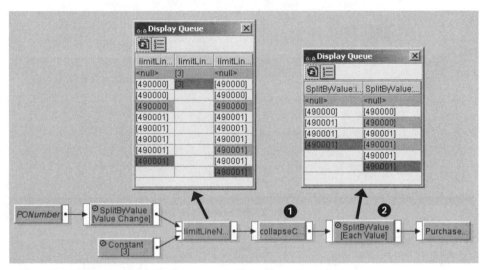

Figure A.16 Mapping for the Field PurchaseOrderNumber

Mapping for the Field LineItem

For each target message we need to provide the correct number of line items. Because we used the line item count to derive the total number of target messages, we already have the information available with the mapping we used for the previous nodes up to point ❶, as shown in Figure A.17. We don't need to adjust this information any further, since it contains exactly the required structure. As discussed in Section 8.4.2 Message Mapping, because only the queue structure is relevant, the actual values in the queue are ignored.

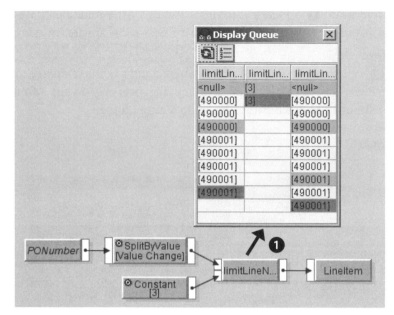

Figure A.17 Mapping for the Node LineItem

Mapping for the Fields ItemNumber and Material

Figure A.18 shows the mapping for the fields `ItemNumber` and `Material`. The mapping for both fields is a pass-through of the corresponding information provided in the source message.

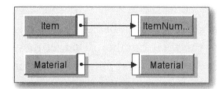

Figure A.18 Mapping for the Fields ItemNumber and Material

Mapping without Use of a User-Defined Function

In the mapping for most of the fields above we used the user-defined function `limitLineNumber`. It is also possible to achieve the same result using the standard delivered functions only. The solution is shown in Figure A.19 and consists of the following steps:

❶ The function `index` counts the number of occurrences of each purchase order number. The properties of this function need to be set to the following values:

▶ The **Initial Value** needs to be set to **0**.

▶ The **Increment** needs to be set to **1**.

▶ The **Reset Index** needs to be set to **Reset Index to Initial Value with Each New Context**.

This function expects as input the list of purchase order numbers with a context change between different purchase order numbers. This is the same input as the first input parameter of the user-defined function `limitLineNumber`.

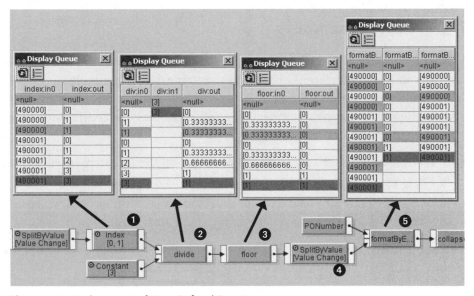

Figure A.19 Replacement of User-Defined Function

❷ With the function `divide` we divide the actual counter by the maximum number of allowed line items, with the result that each time the maximum number of line items is exceeded, the calculated number jumps to the next full integer. This function expects as the second input parameter a constant containing the maximum number of line items allowed in the target message. This is the same input as the second input parameter of the user-defined function `limitLine-Number`.

❸ With the function `floor` we eliminate the fraction of each calculated number. This way we prepare the output for the correct creation of context changes.

❹ With the function `SplitByValue` we create a context change each time the number in the output changes (i.e., each time the maximum number of line items is reached). For this function the property **Event After Which Content Should Change** needs to be set to **Value Change**.

❺ The function `formatByExample` takes the list of purchase order numbers and creates a context change based on the second input list, which contains the correct context changes.

Because this mapping uses the function `divide` as part of the calculation process, the accuracy for large numbers may not be sufficient to guarantee exact results.

A.3   Duplicating Nodes

When the message structures between the source message and the target message are different, you often face the challenge that some data are provided at different levels within the message structure. Many objects contain header information and line item information underneath. For different messages representing these objects we then can have the following issues:

▶ In the source message some data are provided on the line item level, whereas in the target message they are required on the header level.

▶ In the source message some data are provided on the header level, whereas in the target message they are required on the line item level.

Whereas the first case is easy to realize, the second is more challenging and may require a different solution based on the detailed requirements.

A.3.1   Sample Problem

In this example the source message is built based on the SAP IDoc for order processing. It contains a segment `E1EDP01` for each order line item with segments `E1EDP20` for the delivery schedule underneath. If a line item is delivered completely, no segment `E1EDP20` is required. The subset of these segments that we use for our example is shown in Figure A.20, and two sample messages are listed in Figure A.21. The second sample message contains one segment (highlighted in bold) that does not have a segment `E1EDP20` included.

Name	Category	Type	Occurrence	Default
▼ IDOC2	Element	IDOC2		
▼ E1EDP01	Element	E1EDP01	1..unbounded	
POSEX	Element	xsd:string	1	
MENGE	Element	xsd:string	0..1	
▼ E1EDP20	Element	E1EDP20	0..unbounded	
WMENG	Element	xsd:string	1	

Figure A.20 Message Structure of the Source Message

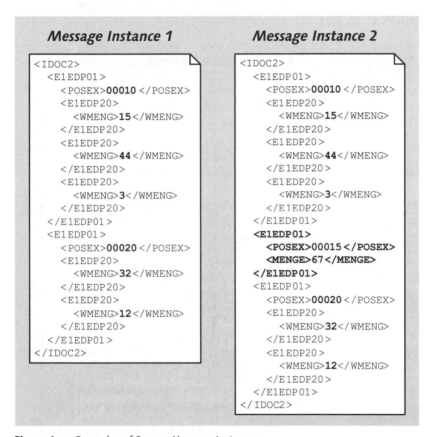

Figure A.21 Examples of Source Message Instances

We need to map the source messages to a new target structure, which is shown in Figure A.22. Because the target structure does not have a separate level for delivery schedule items, all information needs to be entered under the flat structure OrderItem.

Name	Category	Type	Occurrence	Default
▼ Order	Element	Order		
▼ OrderItem	Element	OrderItem	1..unbounded	
Item	Element	xsd:string	1	
Quantity	Element	xsd:string	0..1	

Figure A.22 Message Structure of the Target Message

Figure A.23 shows the result of the mapping for the two source message instances listed in Figure A.21.

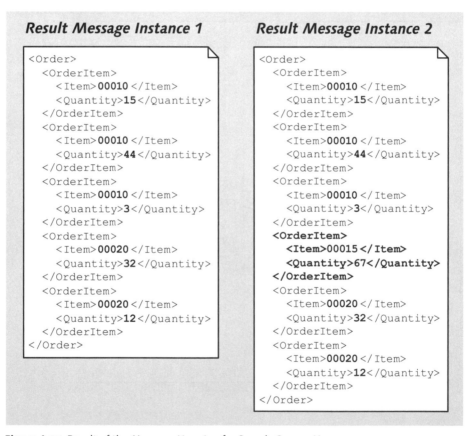

Result Message Instance 1

```
<Order>
  <OrderItem>
    <Item>00010</Item>
    <Quantity>15</Quantity>
  </OrderItem>
  <OrderItem>
    <Item>00010</Item>
    <Quantity>44</Quantity>
  </OrderItem>
  <OrderItem>
    <Item>00010</Item>
    <Quantity>3</Quantity>
  </OrderItem>
  <OrderItem>
    <Item>00020</Item>
    <Quantity>32</Quantity>
  </OrderItem>
  <OrderItem>
    <Item>00020</Item>
    <Quantity>12</Quantity>
  </OrderItem>
</Order>
```

Result Message Instance 2

```
<Order>
  <OrderItem>
    <Item>00010</Item>
    <Quantity>15</Quantity>
  </OrderItem>
  <OrderItem>
    <Item>00010</Item>
    <Quantity>44</Quantity>
  </OrderItem>
  <OrderItem>
    <Item>00010</Item>
    <Quantity>3</Quantity>
  </OrderItem>
  <OrderItem>
    <Item>00015</Item>
    <Quantity>67</Quantity>
  </OrderItem>
  <OrderItem>
    <Item>00020</Item>
    <Quantity>32</Quantity>
  </OrderItem>
  <OrderItem>
    <Item>00020</Item>
    <Quantity>12</Quantity>
  </OrderItem>
</Order>
```

Figure A.23 Result of the Message Mapping for Sample Source Messages

A.3.2 Mapping Solution 1

The first solution is based on the assumption that in the source message each segment E1EDP01 contains at least one segment E1EDP20. Luckily, this assumption holds true for IDocs created via the purchase order creation process in SAP ERP.

Mapping for the Nodes OrderItem and Quantity

The mapping for the nodes OrderItem and Quantity is very simple, as shown in Figure A.24. You need to change the context for the node E1EDP20 to IDOC2 to ensure that all occurrences of this node are within the same context.

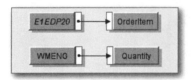

Figure A.24 Mapping for the Nodes OrderItem and Quantity

Mapping for the Field Item

For the field Item we need to duplicate the values provided by the field POSEX as often as required. For the mapping of this field we can use the function useOneAs-Many (❶) with the following input parameters:

▶ The first input parameter is the field POSEX. This field contains the data that needs to be duplicated as a result of this function. Between each occurrence of this field we have a context change.

▶ The second input parameter is the field WMENG. For this field we need to set the context to E1EDP01 to ensure that we have exactly as many context changes as the first input parameter provides. Within each context the values provided by the first input parameter need to be duplicated.

▶ The third input parameter is used as a template for the use of context changes for the values listed in the queue for the field POSEX.

The mapping as described in Figure A.25 works fine as long as there is always at least one segment E1EDP20 within each occurrence of segment E1EDP01. Therefore, the mapping works fine for the first message instance listed in Figure A.21, but it fails with an error for the second message instance. To support such scenarios we need to adjust the mapping accordingly.

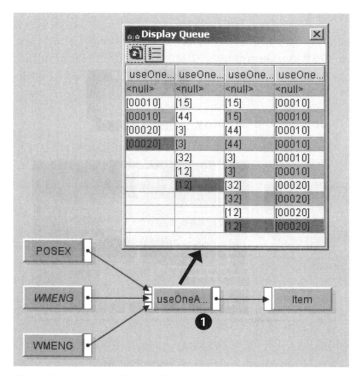

Figure A.25 Mapping for the Node Item

A.3.3 Mapping Solution 2

In this solution we assume that a node Item should be created based on the appearance of the node E1EDP20. Any nodes E1EDP01 without a subsequent node E1DEDP20 should be ignored. For example, the second message instance listed in Figure A.21 would result in the first result message instance listed in Figure A.23.

In this scenario the mapping for the nodes OrderItem and Quantity are identical to the previous mapping (see Figure A.24). The mapping for the node Item is shown in Figure A.26.

❶ First, we need to use the function exists to check for under which nodes E1EDP01 a segment E1EDP20 exists.

❷ Only if a segment E1EDP20 exists must we use the corresponding value of the field POSEX as the value for the field Item. With the function ifWithoutElse we take care of the following:

▶ If the segment E1EDP20 is missing in a segment E1EDP01, the corresponding field POSEX is suppressed.

▶ The value of the field POSEX is duplicated based on the occurrence of the segment E1EDP20 (compare with Figure 8.47).

❸ Because we cannot be sure where the context changes take place, we first use the function removeContext to remove all context changes.

❹ In the next step we use the function SplitByValue to introduce a context change after each value. Here the property **Event After Which Content Should Change** needs to be set to **Each Value**.

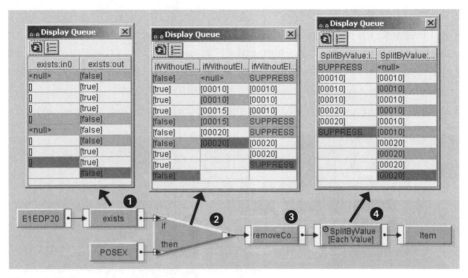

Figure A.26 Mapping for the Node Item

A.3.4 Mapping Solution 3

In this solution we assume that we have to create the node Item at least once per segment E1EDP01. In detail, we have the following rules:

▶ If a segment E1EDP20 exists underneath the segment E1EDP01, the node Item must be created once per occurrence of the segment E1EDP20, and the value of the field Quantity is derived from the field WMENG.

▶ If no segment E1EDP20 exists underneath the segment E1EDP01, the node Item must be created once, and the value of the field Quantity is derived from the field MENGE.

For example, the second message instance listed in Figure A.21 would result in the second result message instance listed in Figure A.23. In this scenario we need to adjust the mapping for all three nodes of the target message.

Mapping for the Node OrderItem

For the node OrderItem we need to implement the logic as described above. This logic can be realized in a field mapping as shown in Figure A.27 using the following steps:

❶ First, we need to use the function exists to check for under which nodes E1EDP01 a segment E1EDP20 exists .

❷ If a segment E1EDP20 exists, we create an item using the constant P20 as often as the segment exists. If no segment E1EDP20 exists, we create one item using the constant P01. The value used in the function Constant is of no relevance; we use the values P01 and P20 for better readability only.

❸ We need to remove all context changes using the function removeContext.

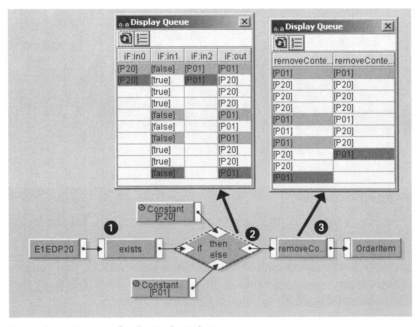

Figure A.27 Mapping for the Node OrderItem

Mapping for the Field Item

The mapping for the field Item can be realized as shown in Figure A.28:

❶ First, we need to use the function exists to check for under which nodes E1EDP01 a segment E1EDP20 exists.

❷ We always need to use the value of the field POSEX as the input for the field Item. Using the function if, we can distinguish between the case where a corresponding segment E1EDP20 exists (and we need to duplicate the value based on the number of occurrences of the segment E1EDP20) and the case where no segment E1EDP20 exists (and we need to use one occurrence of the field POSEX).

❸ Because we cannot be sure where the context changes take place, we first remove all context changes using the function removeContext.

❹ Next, we use the function SplitByValue to introduce a context change after each value. Here the property **Event After Which Content Should Change** needs to be set to **Each Value**.

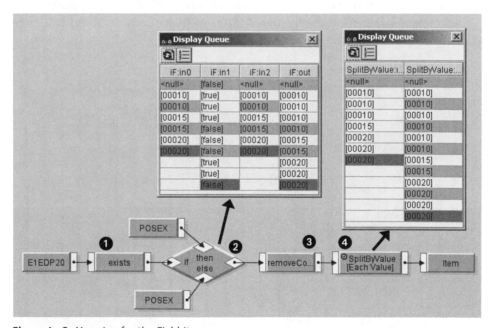

Figure A.28 Mapping for the Field Item

559

Mapping for Field Quantity

The field `Quantity` needs to be filled either from the field `WMENG` or from the field `MENGE`, depending on the existence of the segment `E1EDP20`. The mapping for the field is shown in Figure A.29:

❶ First, we need to use the function `exists` to check for under which nodes `E1EDP01` a segment `E1EDP20` exists.

❷ Depending on the existence of the segment `E1EDP20`, we need to use different input values for the field `Quantity`. Using the function `if`, we can distinguish between the case where a corresponding segment `E1EDP20` exists (and we need to use the field `WMENG` as input) and the case where no segment `E1EDP20` exists (and we need to use the field `MENGE` as input). The context of the field `WMENG` must be changed to `E1EDP01`.

❸ Because we cannot be sure where the context changes take place, we first use the function `removeContext` to remove all context changes.

❹ Next, we use the function `SplitByValue` to introduce a context change after each value. Here the property **Event After Which Content Should Change** needs to be set to **Each Value**.

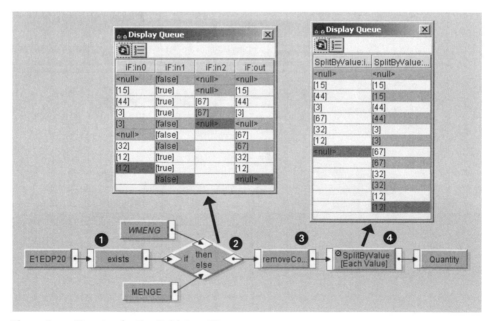

Figure A.29 Mapping for the Field Quantity

A.4   Java Mapping Example

In Figure 8.59 of Section 8.4.8 Other Mapping Options we showed an extract of
a Java mapping program that transforms a message between the two message
interfaces shown in Figure 8.41. The complete Java code is shown in Listing A.2:

```
package com.sap.xi.mappings;

import java.io.InputStream;
import java.io.OutputStream;
import java.util.Map;
import javax.xml.parsers.DocumentBuilder;
import javax.xml.parsers.DocumentBuilderFactory;
import javax.xml.transform.Result;
import javax.xml.transform.Source;
import javax.xml.transform.Transformer;
import javax.xml.transform.TransformerFactory;
import javax.xml.transform.dom.DOMSource;
import javax.xml.transform.stream.StreamResult;
import org.w3c.dom.Attr;
import org.w3c.dom.Document;
import org.w3c.dom.Element;
import org.w3c.dom.NodeList;
import org.w3c.dom.Text;
import com.sap.aii.mapping.api.StreamTransformation;
import
 com.sap.aii.mapping.api.StreamTransformationException;

public class List2ItemJava implements StreamTransformation {

 public void setParameter(Map param) {
 }

 public void execute(InputStream in, OutputStream out)
  throws StreamTransformationException {
  try {
   //Process the incoming source XML document
   DocumentBuilderFactory documentBuilderFactory =
    DocumentBuilderFactory.newInstance();
   DocumentBuilder documentBuilder;
   documentBuilder =
    documentBuilderFactory.newDocumentBuilder();
```

```
Document inDoc = documentBuilder.parse(in);

//Construct output XML document
Document outDoc = documentBuilder.newDocument();
Element item = outDoc.createElement("Item");

Element list = inDoc.getDocumentElement();
NodeList pairs = inDoc.getElementsByTagName("Pair");

//Process src "Pair" Nodes and construct trgt "L" Nodes
for (int i = 0; i < pairs.getLength(); i++) {

 Element e = (Element) pairs.item(i);
 Element ltrElement =
  (Element) e.getElementsByTagName("Ltr").item(0);

 //Proceed only if El "Ltr" exists in curr "Pair" Sgmt
 if (ltrElement != null) {
  String ltr =
   (ltrElement.getChildNodes().getLength() > 0)
    ? ltrElement.getChildNodes().item(0).getNodeValue()
    : "";
  Element nbrElement =
   (Element) e.getElementsByTagName("Nbr").item(0);
  String nbr =
   (nbrElement.getChildNodes().getLength() > 0)
    ? nbrElement.getChildNodes().item(0).getNodeValue()
    : "";

  //Mapping from source to target
  String valueL = ltr;
  String valueN = nbr;
  Attr attrN = outDoc.createAttribute("N");
  attrN.setValue(valueN);
  Element nodeL = outDoc.createElement("L");
  Text textL = outDoc.createTextNode(valueL);
  nodeL.appendChild(textL);
  nodeL.setAttributeNode(attrN);
  item.appendChild(nodeL);
 }
}
```

```
    outDoc.appendChild(item);

    // write output XML
    TransformerFactory transformerFactory =
     TransformerFactory.newInstance();
    Transformer transformer =
     transformerFactory.newTransformer();
    Result result = new StreamResult(out);
    Source domSource = new DOMSource(outDoc);
    transformer.transform(domSource, result);

   } catch (Exception e) {
    e.printStackTrace();
   }
  }
}
```

Listing A.2 Example of a Java Mapping

B   Integration Process Examples

The best way to understand the features available in integration processes is by going through a number of examples. We discussed the main concepts of this tool in Chapter 6 Business Process Management Capabilities, and we now explain some examples that we have found to be useful in real life scenarios.

B.1   Establishing a Correlation between Messages

One of the most common reasons for the use of an integration process is the need to correlate messages in an asynchronous message exchange, for example, a response message that needs to correlate to the corresponding request message. Figure B.1 shows an example of a RosettaNet message for an order request and the corresponding response (confirmation) message.

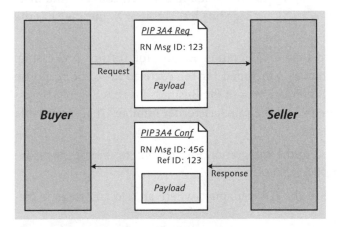

Figure B.1 Process Flow of a Two-Action PIP

The RNIF protocol used for RosettaNet messages specifies that the confirmation message must contain a reference to the message ID of the request message in the message envelope itself. In RosettaNet, such a pattern is called a two-action pattern. Let's take a look at this pattern from the viewpoint of each party.

▶ The buyer initiates the process by sending out a request message. This request message is identified by a message ID that is not correlated to any previous message and therefore does not require any special handling. The buyer receives the response message where the message ID and the reference ID must already be filled. Therefore, no special handling is required for the response message.

▶ The seller receives the request message with a message ID that is not correlated to any other message. When the seller sends out the response message, this message must contain the message ID of the request message as a reference in the message header. To retrieve this reference message ID, a correlation between the request message and the response message must be established using an integration process.

Figure B.2 shows a more detailed picture of the process flow of the order request message and the corresponding response message from the seller's point of view using SAP NetWeaver PI.

1. The seller receives an order request message as a RosettaNet PIP3A4 message with the message ID 123.

2. This message is first picked up by the RNIF adapter, which converts the message to a new message using an XI message header. This new XI message has the message ID ABC.

3. The XI message is passed to the Integration Engine for further processing. Because an integration process is included for the correlation to the response message, the XI message is handed over to the Business Process Engine. Here a new correlation is activated using the purchase order number[1] that is available in the payload of the message.

4. The XI message is returned to the Integration Engine, where the message payload is transformed to an IDoc-based message.

5. The XI message is passed to the IDoc adapter, where an IDoc message is created.

6. The IDoc is passed to the SAP backend system, where the IDoc is processed and a sales order with the number 4711 is generated.

7. The sales order is confirmed in the SAP backend system, triggering the creation of an IDoc for the confirmation message.

---

1 Instead of the purchase order number, other fields or a group of fields can be utilized as well.

8. The IDoc is passed to the IDoc adapter, where the IDoc message is converted into an XI message with the number XYZ.

9. The XI message is passed to the Integration Engine, where the message payload is transformed to a RosettaNet message (PIP3A4 confirmation).

10. Because an integration process is included in this scenario, the message is handed over to the Business Process Engine. Here the correlation is used to find the corresponding request message, and the information is added to the message header as a reference ID with the value ABC.

11. The XI message is passed to the RNIF adapter, which converts the message to a new message with a RosettaNet header format. Because the RNIF adapter captured the link between the RosettaNet request message 123 and the corresponding XI message ABC, the adapter is able to provide the reference ID 123 in the response message.

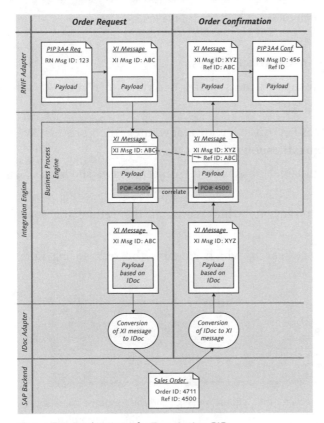

Figure B.2 Realization of a Two-Action PIP

B.1.1 Prerequisites

For this example we don't use a complete RosettaNet message (PIP3A4), but only a simplified request and response message with a structure as shown in Figure B.3. These message structures are used in the service interface IF_Msg by the following operations:

▶ The operation Req is assigned to the message type MsgReq.

▶ The operation Resp is assigned to the message type MsgResp.

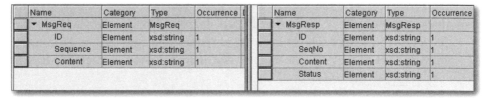

Figure B.3 Message Structure of the Request Message and the Response Message

B.1.2 Creation of the Integration Process

The integration process to support the scenario described in Figure B.1 can be created by following these steps:

1. In the Enterprise Services Repository create a new integration process. We use the name **CorrelateRequestResponse** for this process.

2. Define the following container objects in the object area as shown in Figure B.4:

▶ The container object Request, which contains the requesting interface operation

▶ The container object Response, which contains the responding interface operation

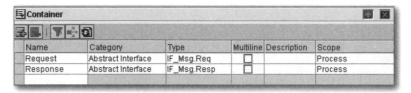

Figure B.4 Container Objects for the Request Message and the Response Message

3. In the object area switch to the **Correlation List** view and define the correlation RequestResponse as shown in Figure B.5.

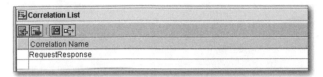

Figure B.5 Definition of the Correlation Object

4. Switch to the **Correlation Editor** and maintain the correlation containers Correlation1 and Correlation2 as shown in Figure B.6.

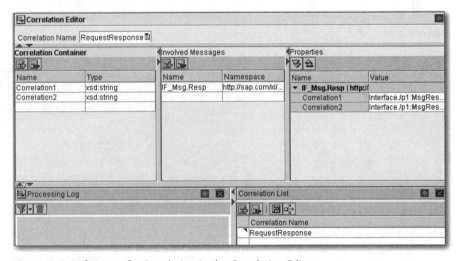

Figure B.6 Definition of a Correlation in the Correlation Editor

The property values are defined in the **Expression Editor** as shown in Figure B.7.

5. Add a **Receive** step to the process flow with the properties shown in Figure B.8. In this step we receive the request message that later needs to be correlated with the response message.

6. Add a **Block** step after the receive step. Right-click on the block step and select **Insert • Exception Branch** from the list. Maintain the properties of the block step as shown in Figure B.9.

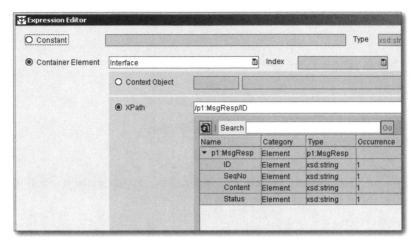

Figure B.7 Definition of an XPath Expression

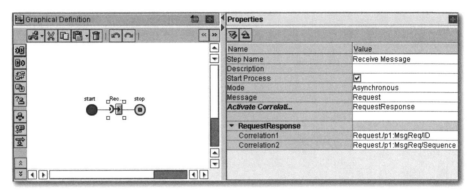

Figure B.8 Properties of the Receive Step for Receiving the Request Message

7. Click on the block shown in the upper branch of the block labeled **Process Correlation** and maintain the properties of the exception branch as shown in Figure B.10.

8. Add a **Send** step into the exception branch for sending a negative acknowledgement in case of failure as shown in Figure B.11.

9. Add a **Control** step after the negative acknowledgement message to throw an alert as shown in Figure B.12.

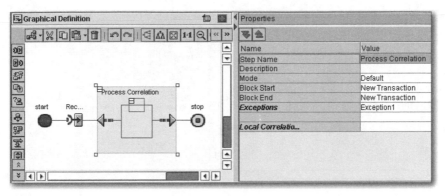

Figure B.9 Properties of the Block Step

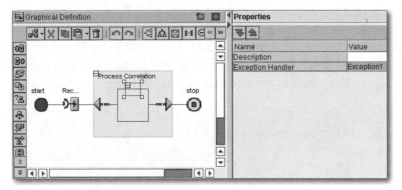

Figure B.10 Properties of the Exception Branch of the Block

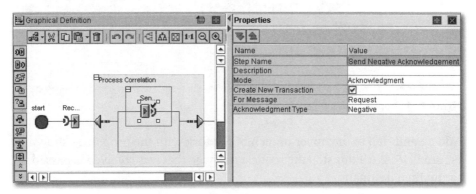

Figure B.11 Properties of the Send Step for Sending a Negative Acknowledgement

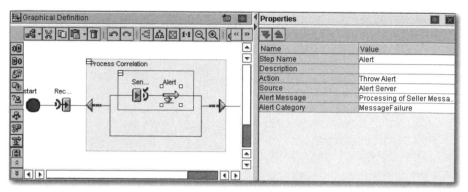

Figure B.12 Properties of the Control Step for Throwing an Alert

10. Add a **Fork** step to the lower branch of the block labeled **Process Correlation** with the properties shown in Figure B.13. You maintain the **End Condition** using the Condition Editor as shown in Figure B.14. In the Condition Editor you need to drag and drop the required objects into the maintenance screen for the conditions. You cannot type any text directly in there.

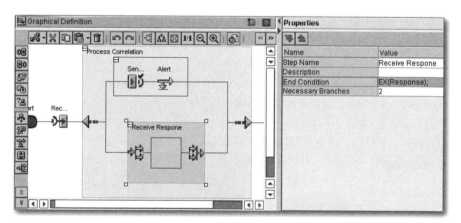

Figure B.13 Properties of the Fork Step

11. Add a **Send** step to the upper branch of the fork with the properties shown in Figure B.15. With this step the request message that was received is passed on to the final destination.

12. Add a **Receive** step to the lower branch of the fork with the properties shown in Figure B.16. Here we receive the response message that needs to be correlated to the original request message.

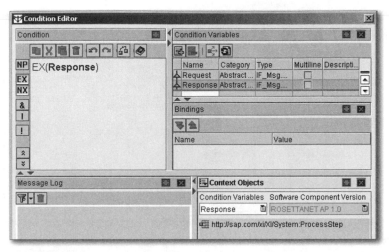

Figure B.14 Definition of a Condition in the Condition Editor

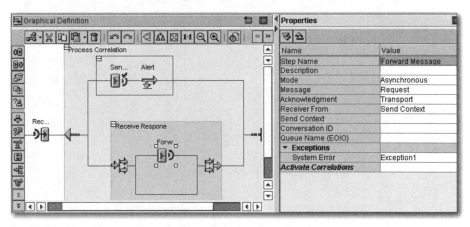

Figure B.15 Properties of the Send Step to Forward the Request Message

13. Add a **Send** step to the upper branch of the fork to send out a positive acknowledgement following the request message, with the properties shown in Figure B.17.

14. Add a **Send** step to the lower branch of the fork to send out a positive acknowledgement following the receipt of the response message, with the properties shown in Figure B.18.

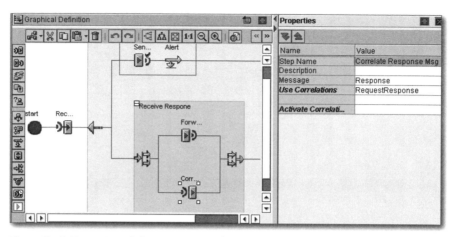

Figure B.16 Properties of the Receive Step for the Response Message

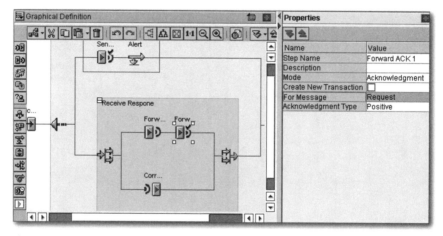

Figure B.17 Properties of the Send Step for the Acknowledgement of the Request Message

15. Add a **Send** step to the lower branch of the fork with the properties shown in Figure B.19. Here we send the response message that corresponds to the request message back to our trading partner.

The integration scenario we just created performs the steps described in Figure B.2. For this scenario to run properly you need to create the configuration in the Integration Directory for processing the purchase order request message and for processing the purchase order response message.

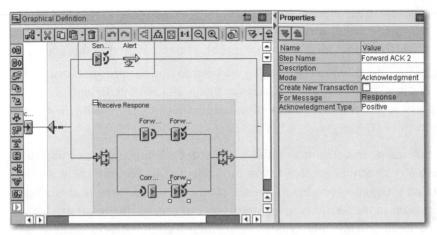

Figure B.18 Properties of the Send Step for the Acknowledgement of the Response Message

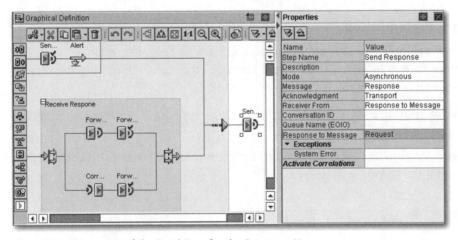

Figure B.19 Properties of the Send Step for the Response Message

B.2 Collect Data

In this example we want to know for one specific material the processing times of each plant to which this material is assigned. This request can be broken down into the following steps:

1. For the given material we need to find all plants to which this material is assigned. This can be done using the remote function call `MATERIAL_READ_PLANTS`, which returns for a given material all plants assigned to this material.

2. For all plants identified in the first step we need to find the processing times for the given material. This information is available in the table field `MARC-BEARZ`. For a given material and plant this information can be derived using the remote function call `MATERIAL_READ_ALL_SINGLE`.

If you create a new remote function call in the SAP backend application that combines both RFCs mentioned above, you can execute this request easily without the use of an integration process. However, if you are not allowed to create additional functions in the SAP backend system, you can execute the request using the existing backend functionality by introducing an integration process as described below.

B.2.1 Prerequisites

For this example we use a request message and a response message with the structure shown in Figure B.20. These message structures are used in the service interface `Material` by the following operations:

▶ The operation `ID` is assigned to the message type `Material` representing the request message.

▶ The operation `Detail` is assigned to the message type `Material_Detail` representing the response message.

Name	Category	Type	Occurrence		Name	Category	Type	Occurrence
▼ Material	Element	Material			▼ Material_Detail	Element	Material_Plants	
MatID	Element	xsd:string	1		▼ MatItem	Element	MatItem	0..unbounded
					MatID	Element	xsd:string	1
					Plant	Element	xsd:string	1
					ProcessTime	Element	xsd:string	0..1

Figure B.20 Message Structure of the Request Message and the Response Message

B.2.2 Creation of the Integration Process

The integration process to support the scenario described above can be created by following these steps:

1. In the Enterprise Services Repository create a new integration process. We use the name **DataCollection** for this process.

2. Define the following container objects in the object area as shown in Figure B.21:

   ▶ The container object `MaterialID` is an abstract interface that represents the incoming request message represented by the service operation `Material.ID`. It only contains the material ID as input.

   ▶ The container object `MaterialDetail` is an abstract interface that represents the message that is returned as the response message represented by the service operation `Material.Detail`.

   ▶ The container object `MaterialPlant` is an abstract interface that is used internally in the integration process to carry the information on all plants available. The result of the remote function call `MATERIAL_READ_PLANTS` is captured in this object.

   ▶ The container object `MaterialPlant_Single` contains a single plant and material combination. This container is set up as a multiline object because multiple plant and material combinations are possible and need to be captured.

   ▶ The container object `MaterialPlant_Row` is used to represent one occurrence of the message `MaterialPlant_Single`. This container object is only visible within the block step of the integration process.

   ▶ The container object `MATERIAL_READ_ALL_SINGLE` contains the input interface of the remote function call `MATERIAL_READ_ALL_SINGLE`. This container object is only visible within the block step of the integration process.

   ▶ The container object `MATERIAL_READ_ALL_SINGLE_Resp` contains the response interface of the remote function call `MATERIAL_READ_ALL_SINGLE`. This container object is only visible within the block step of the integration process.

   ▶ The container object `MATERIAL_READ_ALL_SINGLE_COLLECT` contains the response interface of the remote function call `MATERIAL_READ_ALL_SINGLE` in the form of a multiline object.

Note that the container objects that are only visible within the block step of the integration process cannot be created before the block step has been added to the process.

Name	Category	Type	Multiline	...	Scope
MaterialDetail	Abstract Interface	Material.Detail	☐		Process
MaterialID	Abstract Interface	Material.ID	☐		Process
MaterialPlant	Abstract Interface	Material_Plant_Multi	☐		Process
MaterialPlant_S...	Abstract Interface	Material_Plant_Single	☑		Process
MATERIAL_REA...	Abstract Interface	MATERIAL_READ_ALL_SINGLE_Resp_Abstract	☑		Process
MaterialPlant_R...	Abstract Interface	Material_Plant_Single	☐		For Each Plant
MATERIAL_REA...	Abstract Interface	MATERIAL_READ_ALL_SINGLE_Abstract	☐		For Each Plant
MATERIAL_REA...	Abstract Interface	MATERIAL_READ_ALL_SINGLE_Resp_Abstract	☐		For Each Plant

Figure B.21 Container Objects Used for Collecting Data

3. Add a **Receive** step to the process flow with the properties shown in Figure B.22. In this step we receive the request message with the material ID for which the corresponding purchasing organizations need to be returned.

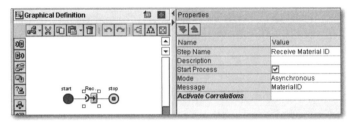

Figure B.22 Properties of the Receive Step for Receiving the Request Message

4. Add a **Send** step to the process flow with the properties shown in Figure B.23. In this step the function MATERIAL_READ_PLANTS is called synchronously, and the result is returned to the integration process. To call the function, the configuration in the Integration Directory must be available including a mapping from the abstract interfaces used in the integration process to the request and response interface of the function.

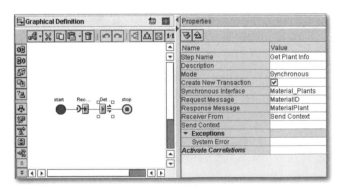

Figure B.23 Properties of the Send Step for the Call of the RFC MATERIAL_READ_PLANTS

5. Add a **Switch** step to the process flow with the properties shown in Figure B.24 to allow a different handling in case no plants are assigned to the material. The property **Condition** determines when the first branch of the switch is executed. The condition is defined using the Condition Editor as shown in Figure B.25. You need to define a new condition variable Plant that is assigned in the binding process to an XPath expression representing the plant in the message structure of the response message of the RFC MATERIAL_READ_PLANTS. This XPath expression is created using the Expression Editor as shown in Figure B.26.

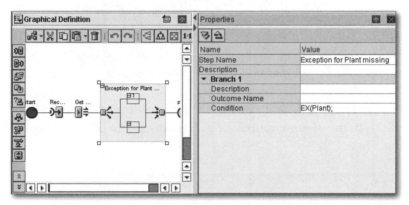

Figure B.24 Properties of the Switch Step

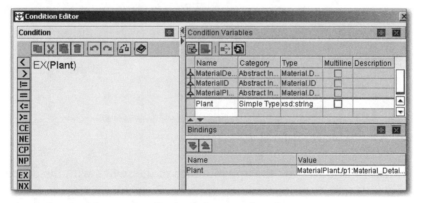

Figure B.25 Condition Editor for the Definition of Conditions

579

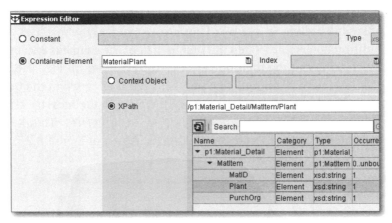

Figure B.26 Expression Editor for the Definition of an XPath Expression

6. Add a **Control** step to the lower branch of the switch with the properties shown in Figure B.27. In this step we cancel the process in case no plant is assigned to the material.

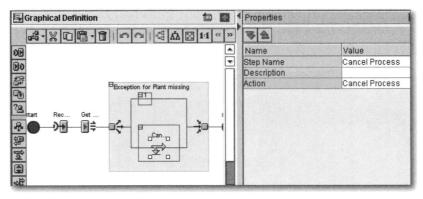

Figure B.27 Properties of the Control Step

7. Add a **Transformation** step to the upper branch of the switch with the properties shown in Figure B.28. In this step we transform the message Material-Plant, which contains all plants that are assigned to the material into n messages MaterialPlant_Single containing one plant per message using a 1:n mapping.

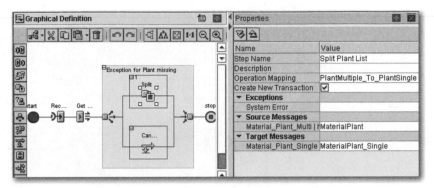

Figure B.28 Properties of the Transformation Step

8. Add a **Block** step to the upper branch of the switch after the transformation step, with the properties shown in Figure B.29. This block is executed once for each occurrence of the message MaterialPlant_Single (specified by the **Mode** property). Within the block the abstract interface MaterialPlant_Row carries the message executed by the current loop through the block step.

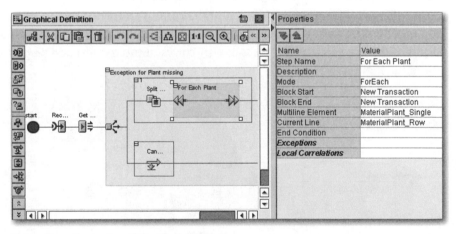

Figure B.29 Properties of the Block Step

9. Add a **Transformation** step within the block, with the properties shown in Figure B.30. In this step we transform the message MaterialPlant_Row to match the input structure of the remote function call MATERIAL_READ_ALL_SINGLE (represented by the container object MATERIAL_READ_ALL_SINGLE).

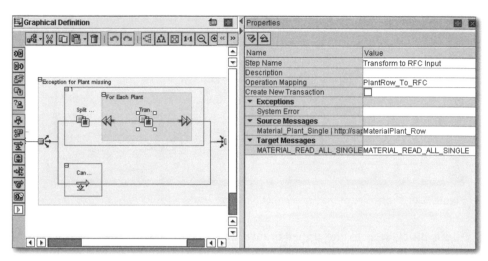

Figure B.30 Properties of the Transformation Step

10. Add a **Send** step to the process flow after the transformation step, with the properties shown in Figure B.31. In this step the function MATERIAL_READ_ALL_SINGLE is called synchronously, and the result is returned to the integration process. The abstract interfaces used for the request message and for the response message contain the message structures of the request and response of the function.

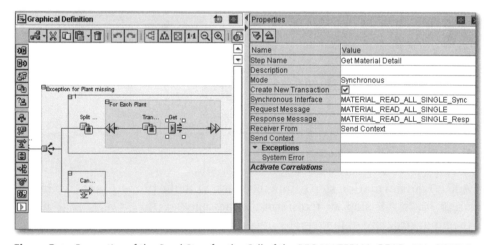

Figure B.31 Properties of the Send Step for the Call of the RFC MATERIAL_READ_ALL_SINGLE

11. Add a **Container Operation** after the send step to collect the results of the function calls of the previous step, with the properties shown in Figure B.32. The result of each function call (specified through the **Expression** property) is appended to the abstract interface MATERIAL_READ_ALL_SINGLE_COLLECT. The **Expression** property is defined using the Expression Editor as shown in Figure B.33.

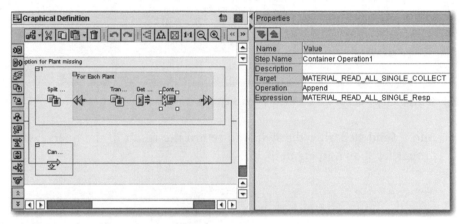

Figure B.32 Properties of the Container Operation

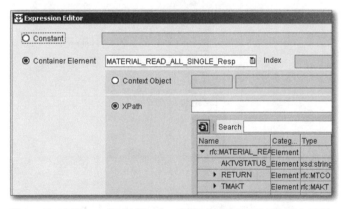

Figure B.33 Expression Editor for the Definition of a Container Element

12. Add a **Transformation** step after the container operation, with the properties shown in Figure B.34. In this step we transform the message MATERIAL_READ_ALL_SINGLE_COLLECT to match the message structure of the response message.

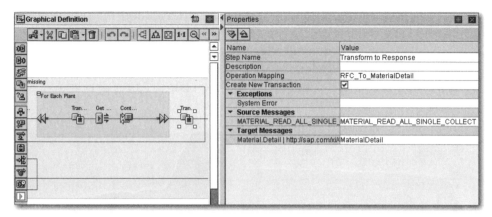

Figure B.34 Properties of the Transformation Step

13. Add a **Send** step after the switch to return the result of the query, with the properties shown in Figure B.35.

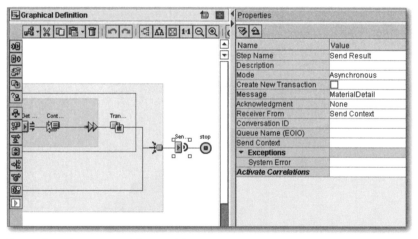

Figure B.35 Properties of the Send Step

The integration scenario we just created retrieves the required information about the material by first calling an RFC synchronously to retrieve all plants assigned to the material and then by calling a second RFC per plant to retrieve the required information about the material. Therefore we need to create the configuration in the Integration Directory for both RFC calls in addition to the configuration for processing the request message and the response message.

C   Enterprise Service Enhancements

In Section 7.5 Backend Adoption we discussed enhancements of the SAP backend functionality for different types of interfaces. At that point we deferred the discussion of how to enhance an enterprise service interface to the Appendix, because these interfaces are defined in the Enterprise Services Repository and thus utilize Enterprise Services Repository features for enhancements. Therefore, we first had to talk about the Enterprise Services Repository capabilities in detail.

Because we covered all the required steps for the enhancement of an enterprise service interface in Chapter 8 Development, we only need to put the steps together as listed in Table C.1. The information in the Reference column points to the section of the book where this particular step is discussed in detail.

Step	Description	Reference
1	In the System Landscape Directory create a software component version SWCV2, where the enhanced enterprise service will be located.	Section 8.2.2 Software Catalog
2	In the System Landscape Directory create a dependency to the software component version SWCV1, where the original enterprise service resides.	Section 8.2.2 Software Catalog
3	In the Enterprise Services Repository import the software component version SWCV2 from the System Landscape Directory.	Section 8.2.2 Software Catalog
4	In the Enterprise Services Repository create a new namespace, ns2, under the software component version SWCV2.	Section 8.2.2 Software Catalog
5	In the Enterprise Services Repository create additional data types under the namespace ns2, which can be added to the data types representing the enterprise service (only if necessary).	Section 8.3.7 Message Types and Data Types

Table C.1 Enhancement of an Enterprise Service Interface

Step	Description	Reference
6	In the Enterprise Services Repository create enhancements to the required data types under the namespace ns2 of software component version SWCV2. You can utilize the data types you created in step 4, as well as existing data types available under the software component version SWCV2.	Section 8.3.7 Message Types and Data Types
7	In the SAP application system you need to create a proxy for the data type enhancement you created in step 6 by using transaction SPROXY.	Section 7.5.7 Proxy Development

Table C.1 Enhancement of an Enterprise Service Interface (cont.)

After completing the steps listed in Table C.1, you have enhanced the enterprise service interface, but the implementation is still unchanged. You can enhance the programming logic of the enterprise service by utilizing a number of BAdIs, as discussed in Section 7.5.5 Enterprise Service Enhancements.

D   Process Component Architecture Models

As of release 7.1 of SAP NetWeaver PI, the process component architecture models (also known as ARIS models) are part of the Enterprise Services Repository. These models describe a certain part of your process by describing the relationships between some of the following objects for a set of particular processes:[1]

▶ The deployment unit, which represents a software unit that can be deployed separately in your system landscape.

▶ The process component, which is a central modeling object that represents a part of a value chain that is normally performed within a company's department (see also Section 2.3.2 Message Interface Objects). Each process component is assigned to exactly one deployment unit.

▶ The business object, which is a logical object such as a purchase order that is significant to the business.

▶ The service interface, which groups together a set of operations that are performed on a business object. Service interfaces and operations are discussed in detail in Section 2.3.2 Message Interface Objects.

Many views (models) are available for modeling different aspects of your scenario. Here we only list the most frequently used models:

▶ **Process component model**
The process component model describes the processes within one component, where a component usually represents one department within your company. This model contains information on the business objects utilized by these processes and the related service interfaces with its operations.

▶ **Integration scenario model**
The integration scenario model describes a complete scenario across different deployment units and process components. It also describes which process components interact with each other using service calls without specifying the

---

1 Depending on the type of model, additional objects such as a message type can be part of the model as well.

service interfaces and operations in detail. An example of an integration scenario model is shown in Figure D.1.

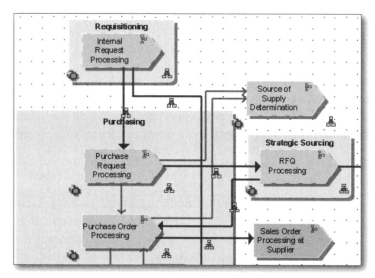

Figure D.1 Example of an Integration Scenario Model

▶ **Process component interaction model**
The process component interaction model describes in detail how different process components interact with each other. Because these models can be used in the model configurator to create the configuration in the Integration Directory (see also Section 2.4.1 Integration Builder), we discuss these models in more detail in the next section.

The process component interaction model describes the interaction between two (or more) process components via enterprise services. You cannot create a process component interaction model when other means of communication are used, such as IDocs or BAPIs. In this model you define which service interfaces and operations are used for the communication along with the underlying message types.

Figure D.2 shows an example of a process component interaction model for a purchase order process from a buyer's point of view. The following objects are involved in this model:

❶ Process components

This model shows the interaction between the process components **Purchase Order Processing** and **Sales Order Processing at Supplier**. In this scenario the second process component represents an external party with which you communicate.

❷ Business objects

The process component **Purchase Order Processing** contains the business objects **Purchase Order** and **Purchase Order Confirmation**. In this model the confirmation has been defined as a business object separate from the purchase order object itself.

❸ Service interfaces

The business object **Purchase Order** is linked to the service interface **Ordering Out**, whereas the business object **Purchase Order Confirmation** is linked to the service interface **Ordering In**. From the direction of the arrows, you can see that the first service interface is an outbound interface, and the second one is an inbound interface.

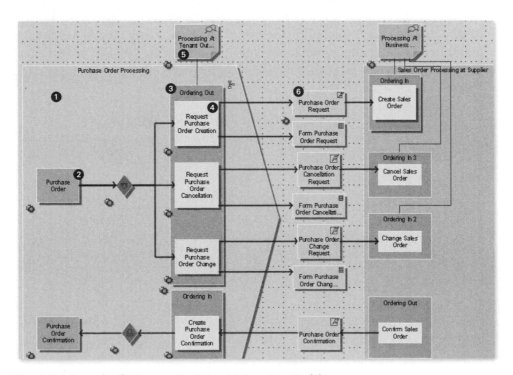

Figure D.2 Example of a Process Component Interaction Model

❹ **Operations**
The service interface **Ordering Out** contains multiple operations, one each for the creation, change, and cancellation of a purchase order. The service interface **Ordering In** is modeled in such a way that it contains only one operation for the confirmation of a purchase order (independent if the confirmation is for a create request, a change request, or a cancellation request).

❺ **Communication channel templates**
Each service interface can have a communication channel template assigned to it. We discussed communication channel templates in Section 9.2.4 Communication Channel Template. They are used as templates for the definition of a communication channel in the Integration Directory.

❻ **Message types**
Each operation has one or more message types assigned to it. The process component interaction model allows you to specify multiple message types as alternatives for one operation.

As you can see, all objects that you specify in a process integration scenario are also specified in a process component interaction model (see Section 8.5 Process Integration Scenarios). Therefore, these models can be used by the Model Configurator to create a configuration in the Integration Directory analogous to the creation of a configuration with the Model Configurator via a process integration scenario.

E   XML Schema Validation

XML schema validation allows you to validate incoming XML messages against a set of stored XML schemas. Many XML-based industry standards contain detailed validation rules for messages exchanged between trading partners in B2B integration. These standards explicitly specify the requirement for validating the messages at various stages of message processing. XML schema validation eliminates errors caused by interpretation and ensures conformance to the standard agreed upon by the partners.

SAP NetWeaver PI provides support for validating XML messages against their schemas stored in the file system for both B2B and A2A application integration. The XML validation for the incoming messages is done at the adapter level either in the advanced Adapter Engine (central or noncentral) or at the Integration Engine. The XML validation for outgoing messages is done only at the Integration Engine. As of SAP NetWeaver PI 7.1, the schemas used for validating the incoming and outgoing messages are stored in the directory structure of the system where SAP NetWeaver PI is installed. In upcoming releases, this feature might be enhanced to allow automated schema transports to caches instead of using the file system.

As a prerequisite for XML validation, you need to create an RFC destination AI_VALIDATION_JCOSERVER on AS ABAP and AS Java servers for validating the messages against their schemas. The schemas used for validation must reside in the Enterprise Services Repository and must be exported and saved in the directory */validation/schema/<GUID of the software component>/<Repository Namespace of Service Interface>* of the system where SAP NetWeaver PI is installed. For validation on the Integration Engine, this directory structure must be created in the directory *<sysdir>/xi/runtime_server*, and for validation on the Adapter Engine this directory structure must be created in the directory *<SAP installation directory>/<system ID>/<instance number>/j2ee/cluster/server0* of the SAP NetWeaver PI system. For a clustered installation of AS Java the above directory structure must be created in the respective server node directories.

The configuration of the schema validation can be set in the respective collaboration agreements. The schemas used for validation can be uniquely identified by the combination of interface, interface namespace, and the software component version. In the sender agreement, the validation can be set to **No Validation**, **Validation by Adapter**, or **Validation by Integration Engine** (see Figure E.1). The validation on the Adapter Engine can be set for all of the adapters including third-party adapters. If an error occurs, an exception is raised that informs the sender via a synchronous response about the cause of the error. With industry-standard adapters such as RNIF and CIDX, the sender is informed asynchronously.

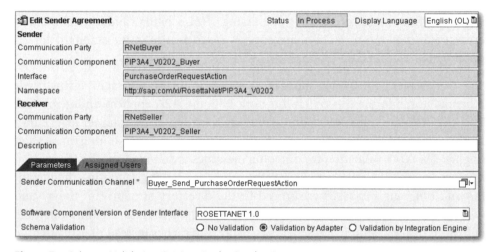

Figure E.1 Schema Validation Settings in the Sender Agreement

Validation at the Integration Engine takes place as a separate pipeline step in the Integration Engine. If an error occurs, the message is set to error status and can be processed further by the administrator in the Runtime Workbench or in the ABAP monitor using Transaction code SXMB_MONI. Based on the type of error, the administrator can either reject the message or resend the message by skipping the validation step in the sender agreement.

For outgoing messages, the validation can be set in the receiver agreement and can only be set for the Integration Engine (see Figure E.2). As in the case of incoming messages, the validation for outgoing messages takes place as a separate pipeline step in the Integration Engine. If an error occurs, the message is set to error status, and the administrator can process the message further based on the type of error.

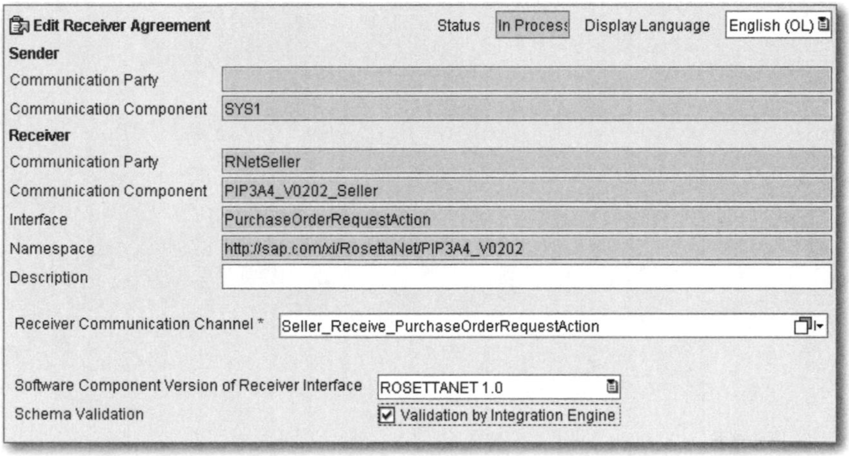

Figure E.2 Schema Validation Setting in the Receiver Agreement

F   The Authors

Sam Raju is a Platinum Expert at the SAP NetWeaver Regional Implementation Group (RIG) at SAP Labs. His primary focus is SAP NetWeaver Process Integration, and he partially works with master data management and global data synchronization. Sam has over 20 years of IT experience including in the areas of SAP R/3, EDI, B2B (business-to-business), data warehousing, and enterprise application integration. As a B2B expert, Sam has successfully led several national and international SAP NetWeaver PI and B2B implementation projects for customers from multiple industries including high tech, chemical, consumer products, petroleum, banking, and pharmaceuticals. He also works with internal development teams that build the SOA content for industry standards such as RosettaNet, CIDX, and PIDX. Prior to joining SAP Labs in 2003, Sam worked for British Petroleum/Amoco in Houston as a senior exploration systems analyst and as an SAP and B2B consultant at National Oilwell, Solvay Chemicals, Hewlett Packard, and several marketplaces in Houston. Sam holds a master's degree in computer science and a postgraduate diploma in business administration. Sam Raju is married with two children and resides in Houston, Texas.

Dr. Claus Wallacher has worked at SAP for over 15 years in different roles in development and product management. He designed and developed a number of industry-specific solutions, which are available as part of the SAP Business Suite, including for the petroleum industry, utilities, and the construction industry. For the past four years Claus has headed a development team focusing on collaboration topics such as out-of-the-box support of different industry standards, global data synchronization, and the support of B2B scenarios via enterprise services. Prior to joining SAP, Claus studied mathematics and physics at the Technical University of Braunschweig, Germany, where he received his doctorate in the area of mathematical optimization. Claus lives with his family in the Bay Area in California.

Index

S

W

X